Electricity Economics

Electricity Economics
Essays and Case Studies

Ralph Turvey and Dennis Anderson

PUBLISHED FOR THE WORLD BANK
THE JOHNS HOPKINS UNIVERSITY PRESS
BALTIMORE AND LONDON

Chapter 13 appeared previously with minor alterations as "Models for Determining
Least-cost Investments in Electricity Supply," copyright © 1972, The American
Telephone and Telegraph Company, 195 Broadway, New York, New York 10007
U.S.A. Reprinted with permission from *The Bell Journal of Economics and Management Science.*

Library of Congress Cataloging in Publication Data
Turvey, Ralph.
    Electricity economics.

    Includes index.
       1. Electric utilities—Rates. 2. Electric
utilities—Costs. I. Anderson, Dennis, 1937–
joint author. II. International Bank for Recon-
struction and Development. III. Title.
HD9685.A2T85   338.4′3   76-9031
ISBN 0-8018-1866-4
ISBN 0-8018-1867-2 paperback

Table of Contents

Tables

Figures and Maps

Figures

Maps

Preface

The studies brought together in this book deal with the economic theory and practice of pricing and investment in electricity supply. Most of the studies were written for a broad audience in an attempt to explain and demonstrate a fresh point of view toward pricing policy, investment planning, and project selection. Others are recognizably written for engineers and economists, and are concerned with theory and technique. Taken together, the studies provide a full statement of our approach.

There are seven chapters on applications, five on principles, and four—the last four—to clear up some deficiencies in existing theory. There is occasional duplication among the chapters but we have not removed it, since it makes each chapter independent, enabling the reader to pick out the chapters that interest him. Only Chapter 13, on investment planning models, has been published before; it is reprinted here with minor editing and additional references to make the book self-contained and more complete.

One of us has already published a book on public enterprises [Turvey, *Economic Analysis and Public Enterprises*, 1971], and a book on electricity supply [Turvey, *Optimal Pricing and Investment in Electricity Supply*, 1968]. This book can be seen as a continuation of these two, since it applies and extends the analysis further. It can be read by itself, however, and only occasional reference is made to the other two titles.

Ten of the seventeen chapters were written jointly, including the case studies in Thailand, Tunisia, and Sudan; four were written by Ralph Turvey (Chapters 6, 9, 12, and 16), and three by Dennis Anderson (Chapters 7, 8, and 13).

All but Chapter 6 have been prepared during the past four years under the aegis of the World Bank and sponsored by its Research Committee as part of the Bank's research program in public utility economics. This program has the general aim of investigating those pricing and investment policies in the developing countries which would promote economic efficiency in developing the sector and in providing service to low-income groups in rural and urban areas. The Bank has provided us with the opportunity to visit many countries while developing our ideas and to be exposed to a wide range of viewpoints and of institutional and economic situations. This has been a most rewarding and stimulating experience, and we are naturally grateful to have had the opportunity to do the work and to have permission to publish.

The case studies were prepared at intervals over a three-year period. The case study in Tunisia was written during a short trip to Tunis in October 1972; in Sudan, during a visit to Khartoum in May 1973; and in Thailand, during a visit to Bangkok in October 1973. The case study in Turkey was completed during 1972, with supplementary work in the spring and summer of 1973, before the major rise in oil prices.

We are, of course, enormously grateful for the cooperation and hospitality we received when visiting these countries. In Thailand we should like to thank the general managers of the three electricity authorities, Kasame Chatikaranij of the Electricity Generating Authority of Thailand, Lek Savanayana of the Metropolitan Electricity Authority, and Vira Pitrachart of the Provincial Electricity Authority; we also wish to thank Manfred Blobel, then with the Bank's Resident Mission in Bangkok, for arranging for the study, and many of the staff of the authorities, particularly Chinda Vathananai, director of System Operations, and Somboonkiat Kasemsuwan of the Electricity Generating Authority Thailand. In Tunisia, we are indebted to the general manager of Société Tunisienne de l'Electricité et du Gaz, M. Bahroun, and to M. Rekik and M. Turki, for exceptionally frank discussions; in Sudan, to the general manager of the Central Electricity and Water Corporation, Sayed Zein, and to Hassan Bashir; and in Turkey to the management of the Turkish Electricity Authority, in particular to Mrs. Baykal for arranging for the study and to Orhan Tarhan, who did much of the computer analysis and was coauthor of the original report. Ernst Bolte worked with us in Sudan, and was a great help; Narong Thananart provided invaluable help by writing the computer program for the matrix generator and report writer for the study in Turkey.

The chapter on rural electrification owes much to Marcelo Selowsky of the World Bank and to many people in El Salvador who worked with the Bank in a study of the costs and benefits of rural electrification. Particular thanks are offered to Benjamín Valiente and his colleagues at Comisión Ejecutiva Hydroeléctrica del Rio Lempa; and to Luís Achaerandio and his staff at Universidad Centroamericana José Simeon Cañas, San Salvador. John Gunning of the World Bank was also most helpful at a critical stage of the study. Reference is frequently made to their work in Chapter 7.

There are also many people who at various times have encouraged and commented helpfully on the studies, and whom we should like to thank: Yves Rovani, Mervyn Weiner, Herman van der Tak, Jeremy Warford, Gavin Wyatt, Charles Morse, Fred Howell, Richard Sheehan, Anthony Churchill, Christopher Willoughby, James Fish, Bernard Russell, A. A. Raizen, Efrain Friedmann, Thomas Berrie, James Jennings, Bernard Montfort, John Sneddon, David Knox, Anandarup Ray, and Alan Manne. We should also like to thank Maria del Solar for typing the early reports, Phyllis Peter for looking after budgeting matters, Celeste Boland and Brian J. Svikhart for editing various drafts of the book, and Donald J. Pryor for preparing the index. Thanks are also due to Scientific Control Systems, Ltd., for which Ralph Turvey worked when the book was being prepared.

The institutions mentioned above and the World Bank have agreed to publication on the understanding, of course, that they do not necessarily concur with the authors' views, and that the views expressed are the sole responsibility of the authors. It should be added that we would not wish to attribute any errors in the text to the individuals whom we have thanked for helping and encouraging us.

RALPH TURVEY
International Labour Office
Geneva

DENNIS ANDERSON
World Bank
Washington, D.C.

PART ONE

Descriptive and Case Studies

CHAPTER 1

Introduction

Although for many years economists have discussed the merits of relating prices to the marginal or incremental costs of supply in electric utilities, the concept has been slow to win acceptance, except in France and Britain. One reason for this is that other concerns have been felt to be more important. The need to meet revenue requirements is one such concern; another concern is the problem of planning for and financing very high rates of system expansion, generated by demands that have typically doubled every five to ten years. Another reason, however, is that marginal cost pricing has yet to win the confidence of people responsible for running and regulating the industry. Most of the industry's engineers, accountants, financial analysts, and administrators do not understand marginal cost pricing and most have concepts about the aims and equity of tariffs that are quite different from those of economists.

The first five studies in this book (Chapters 2 through 6) are addressed to difficulties regarding the acceptability of the economist's approach to pricing. Chapter 2 presents a general discussion on economics, equity, and finance in formulating pricing policy (often referred to as tariff or rate policy). Four case studies follow to illustrate practical applications of the approach in Thailand, Tunisia, Sudan, and an American utility.

The approach we follow generally comprises three steps. We always begin with an analysis of daily and seasonal fluctuations of demand on the system, of demand growth, and of system operation and expansion plans. This enables us to estimate marginal costs of supply at various points in time. The next step is to decide what kind of tariff and metering system would best reflect these marginal costs to various consumer groups, allowing for the costs and practicalities of metering. This step gives us an "ideal tariff," so to speak, from an economic point of view. The third step is to adjust such elements in

3

this "ideal tariff" structure as proves necessary for reasons of finance, fairness, or acceptability. The criterion for these adjustments is the general one that they should do least damage to the economic aims of the tariffs.

This approach in no way conflicts with sound principles of finance. What we suggest is that the analysis of tariffs should begin with economic analysis, to get the resource allocation aspect of the tariffs right, and be followed by appropriate questions of finance, fairness, and acceptability. In practice, the approach leads to nothing more than, for example, (a) time of day and sometimes seasonal variations in tariffs for large consumers, for whom metering cost is a negligible fraction of supply cost; and (b) fairly simple flat-rate tariffs, perhaps seasonally varying, for smaller consumers, for whom the cost of more elaborate metering makes anything more complicated undesirable. The result, of course, varies with the case. But it is interesting that the tariffs that emerge from the economic analysis are almost invariably much simpler than the existing tariffs, which are usually based on accounting analysis and which have evolved over a period of time.

We have often found an enormous difference between the structure of existing tariffs and the structure that would reflect marginal cost, even though their average levels are often comparable. (For an explanation of why this is the case, see Chapter 2.) Apart from the implication, therefore, that big gains in economic efficiency may be obtained from a transition to tariffs based on marginal cost, there is also the implication that the transition will be difficult, and it is this that causes utilities and regulators most concern. There is no simple solution; the best procedure is first to establish what tariffs are right and should be aimed at ultimately, and then to effect a gradual transition, perhaps giving consumers an initial chance to opt for old or new tariffs.

The other two case studies in Part I need less introductory comment; one deals with rural electrification in developing countries and the other with least-cost investment planning. Rural electrification is becoming a major area of investment in developing countries, and is often an important component of rural development programs. Rural electrification investments are lumpy, with large initial costs and large economies of scale; demand, revenues, and financial returns tend to be low in the early years; and information about consumer response is relatively scarce, making forecasting difficult. Chapter 7 discusses these problems, reviews what is being done by various countries, and suggests an approach toward pricing and investment in rural electrification.

The case study of least-cost investment planning, which exam-

4

ines the experience and future options of Turkey, illustrates that, with the very rapid rate of growth of demand and system size, the comparison among fossil, hydro, and nuclear resources for electricity generation should not be made in terms of simple arithmetic comparisons of the present worth of a few alternatives. A complete, systems analysis is required to examine the interdependence of cost components and the development of power systems over time. A short section on risk concludes this case study; this section pays particular attention to price uncertainties, the importance of which hardly needs underlining at the present time.

The studies of principles begin in Chapter 9 with a discussion of questions that need to be addressed in tariffmaking. This discussion serves as a kind of practical epilogue or debriefing to the case studies on tariffs. Although it was written for noneconomists, we hope that there is practical material in it that will be helpful to economists, too. There follow three essays that seek to answer three questions often raised by engineers and administrators. These questions concern interactions between pricing and investment decisions (for example: Would a price increase or a change of structure mean cutting back on planned projects? What if we are ignorant about short- and long-run price elasticities?); income distribution and the validity of basing investment plans and pricing policy on consumers' willingness to pay for service; and distortions in the pricing system of the economy.

Five theoretical studies conclude the book. The first of these reviews the kinds of simulation and global system planning models commonly used by the electricity industry, and presents some developments of the linear programming models. The last four chapters all deal with problems in applying the simple theory of marginal cost pricing—uncertainty, (hydro) storage and seasonality, constraints presented by metering costs, and indivisibilities (or lumpiness) in investments.

The papers thus cover quite a variety of topics. But there is one underlying notion to be found in all of them. This is that the aim of an optimal pricing and investment policy is to maximize the net economic benefits to the economy, subject to all relevant constraints; that is, to achieve economic efficiency. The constraints generally reflect revenue requirements, what is practicable, and what is socially acceptable.

CHAPTER 2

Economics, Finance, and Equity in Tariff Policy

Pricing and investment decisions in the electricity industry, as in other industries, have to be made in the context of uncertainty; limited or no information on some matters; distortions in the pricing system; technical feasibility; imperfect institutions; a need, with regard to prices, for simplicity and clarity; and generally a number of restrictions stemming from political, financial, and equity objectives.[1] The economist, in deciding which prices and investments are efficient, no less than the engineers and financial analysts in their work, has to consider these factors if his recommendations are to be useful.

Most of the studies in this book deal with some of these factors specifically or, as in the case studies, with several of them in a particular context. In this chapter we discuss the factors collectively so as to outline our general approach to pricing.

Since economic analysis in public enterprises has still to gain a foothold in many countries, it might be worthwhile to begin by showing why such analysis is needed. This we do by considering the shortcomings of the very widely held view that electricity tariffs should be determined purely by accounting criteria. These criteria—if only because they are accepted by financiers—have often served the important function of enabling enterprises, in low income as well as in high income countries, to mobilize resources to finance much needed expansion. Our arguments, therefore, are mostly about improvements. The high costs of generating electrical energy,

---

1. It may be well to note at this point that, throughout this book, we use the terms *financial targets* and *financial objectives* interchangeably with what is perhaps a more appropriate term, *revenue requirements*. Revenue requirements are normally defined as revenues sufficient to cover operating expenses, to service debt, and to provide a reasonable contribution toward funds for expansion.

and the very large expansion programs in all countries, undoubtedly make striving for improvements worthwhile. (The demand for capacity, on average, triples every decade in low income countries, at a cost that generally ranges (in 1973 prices) from $500 to $700 per kilowatt supplied, but is sometimes higher.)

Traditional Approach to Pricing

Britain, France, and Sweden are three countries where a modern, economist's approach to tariffmaking has been applied in recent years. Economists are aware at least of some of the earlier postwar French theoretical contributions, but these developments generally are not well documented. Many engineering consultants, financial consultants, and administrators are unaware of them. This is particularly understandable in the United States, where the system of regulation of public utilities positively requires an approach to tariffs that has nothing to do with efficient resource allocation. Unfortunately, a narrow concentration on accounting data—which are relevant to resource allocation only as a poor substitute for unobtainable engineering cost estimates—still typifies some of the tariff advice given to countries that are sufficiently poor to worry about efficient resource allocation. It may be useful, therefore, to describe the typical traditional accounting approach and highlight its shortcomings.

This traditional approach usually begins with a comprehensive stocktaking and evaluation of all assets, old and new, from which, by the application of certain depreciation rules, the annual "capacity-related" or "kilowatt-related" costs are derived. Then there is an evaluation of various running, fuel, and other "energy-related" or "kilowatt-hour–related" costs. Some costs, such as those for maintenance, have fixed and variable components and are allocated accordingly to capacity- and energy-related costs, respectively. Finally, there are some costs, such as those for metering and billing, that are "customer-related" and not correlated with either capacity or energy demands. The procedure then is to allocate these costs as "equitably" as possible among consumers through the tariff structure—where the notion of equity is that consumers are responsible for covering those accounting costs that they are considered to have imposed on the enterprise. With research into consumer demand patterns (load research), the more advanced enterprises are able to find out how much each consumer class is contributing to the peak and, thus, to the capacity-related accounting costs. Then energy- and customer-related costs are added in and a "cost-based" tariff is formulated for each consumer class. Typi-

7

cally, a consumer may have one, two, or some combination of three elements in his bill: a fixed or minimum charge (to recover customer cost); a kilowatt charge related to his contribution to capacity cost; and a kilowatt-hour charge. Simplifications are often sought, some resting on complicated analysis which nevertheless leads to a simpler tariff and which meets the general aims of the traditional approach. For example, frequently it is found that consumers who take more kilowatt-hours take relatively less kilowatts at the time of peak demand. When peak kilowatt and kilowatt-hour consumption are empirically related in this way it is possible to simplify the tariffs, eliminating the kilowatt charges by incorporating them in the kilowatt-hour charges. Consumers (even very large consumers) are then given declining-block kilowatt-hour tariffs, because their total capacity requirements for each kilowatt-hour consumed decrease with the number of the kilowatt-hours consumed. In addition, the fixed or minimum charge may be added onto the first block, leading to a very simple tariff related only to kilowatt-hour consumption. Provided the empirical relationships used to derive this simplified tariff hold, the simplified tariff will certainly meet the equity principle that customers should pay for the accounting costs allocated to them.

This is, albeit in simplified form, the basis of an ideal accounting approach. An enormous amount of information is collected and manipulated in the process, and enterprises paying consultants to do this sort of thing find it a very expensive and time-consuming exercise. Divergences from these ideal tariffs—sometimes very substantial divergences—often creep in, but for now consider the ideal accounting tariff in general terms.

The first limitation of this approach is that, except by chance, prorated accounting costs are quite different from the costs relevant to resource allocation. One reason for this is that the accountant is concerned with recovering sunk costs whereas, for efficient resource allocation, it is the actual resources used or saved by consumer decisions that are important. Prices are the amounts paid for extra consumption, and need to be related to the incremental costs in meeting extra consumption. If new consumers are connected to the system, or if existing consumers increase their consumption (for example, during the system's peak), additions to generating and network capacity may be required. It is important, therefore, that prices should signal to consumers the costs of such consumption changes. The argument works the other way, too. If consumers reduce consumption (for example, during the system's peak), such costs are avoided, and if prices reflect these costs, the savings on their bills will equal the resource savings. Hence, prices should be related to the value of resources used or saved, and the valuation of these resources—the estimation of costs—requires a forward-looking estimate. The backward-looking estimate of the traditional approach creates the illusion that resources which can be used or saved are as cheap or as expensive as in the past; that is, that resources are as abundant or as restricted as in the past. On the one hand this may cause overinvestment and waste; on the other, it may lead to underinvestment and unnecessary scarcity. In addition, if the past holds a number of poor projects, the sunk costs of mistakes, if reflected in prices, will overstate the costs to the consumer of extra consumption, which is not efficient.

Another reason why prorated accounting costs differ from those relevant to resource allocation is that the tariff schedules and the various simplifications thereof are derived by spreading total accounting costs among consumers. Broadly speaking, this generates tariffs which relate to average rather than to marginal costs. But for efficient resource allocation, prices should be related to the resource costs of *changes* in consumption; that is, what is needed is pricing according to marginal, not average, cost. The addition of a new consumer or an increase in the consumption of an existing consumer will impose additional costs on the enterprise, while a reduction in consumption will save costs. These alterations in costs are the ones that need to be reflected in tariffs. The change in the cost to a consumer of altering his electrical behavior will then mirror the change in the cost to the enterprise.

This brings us to the second limitation of the accounting approach. Fairness or equity in the approach is couched in rather narrow terms: consumers should pay for their allocated share of accounting costs. These allocated costs, as previously explained, may very well differ from the costs that consumers are causing the enterprise to incur. Apart from this fact, it is evident that such allocation of costs involves judgments that may be arbitrary. Fairness is surely an attribute of tariffs considered in relation to consumers, not of costs considered in isolation. As such, it depends on, for example, whether a consumer is rich or poor, and whether he deserves special concessions. As we shall make clear later in this chapter, we fully accept the notion that questions of equity are relevant in tariff-making. Because of the huge capital requirements of the power sector, we also accept the point that electricity tariffs should often yield revenues sufficient to cover accounting costs and, in addition, should make a substantial contribution to the self-financing of future system growth. Electrification projects in backward areas are pos-

9

sible exceptions. But fairness, revenue requirements, and cost analysis require separate analyses in tariffmaking. First we must analyze costs, then consider revenue requirements and bring in views of what is fair. Compromise may be necessary, but it is absolutely necessary to start off with a purely objective analysis of costs.

The third limitation of the accounting approach stems from its neglect of the incentive effects of tariffs. Even if the allocated accounting costs were equal to the marginal costs of resources, and equity issues were unimportant, this still would be a serious defect. Tariffs often, if not always, have to be simpler than the cost structure they represent. Generally, billing can be done only monthly at most; there are restrictions on how much prices can be varied in response to random changes in demand and supply conditions; and elaborate metering both is too costly for all but the largest consumers and, because it bewilders many consumers, can be counterproductive. Simplification is a central part of the formulation of policy on tariff and metering. But how do we simplify without nullifying the aims of the tariffs? We have found that the answer, perhaps not surprisingly, depends on the aims of the tariffs—simplified tariffs designed with only accounting aims in mind may differ enormously from those suggested by economic analysis. It is easier to show this through a concrete example.

Consider, for example, the problem of charging a consumer for capacity costs induced by his demand at the time of the system's peak. The traditional approach may use any one of several devices to make sure that the consumer pays for the costs incurred. There may be a fixed charge related to the consumer's demand at the time of the system's peak demand, or, as discussed above, capacity charges may be incorporated into the energy charges, based on an empirical (but not a causal) relation between consumers' energy consumptions and demands for capacity; or there may be an empirical relation between the size of a consumer's house (measured in terms of floor area) and his demands for capacity, so that capacity charges may be related to floor area. These are only three examples. Very simple single or two-part tariffs, with the "variable" part having a declining-block pattern, can be developed on such bases. It is evident that, while such devices may satisfy the accountant's equity principles, only a charge related to consumption during peak is likely to provide the consumer with the incentive to economize—and this is, of course, on the proviso that he knows what he is being charged for and that he knows approximately when the peak is occurring.

From an economic viewpoint, tariff simplifications should be designed to retain the incentive effects as far as possible. The entire design of the tariff and metering policy turns on this aim (case studies in subsequent chapters demonstrate this point). As far as is possible, consumers should know when consumption is expensive and when it is cheap. Declining-block tariffs, however ingeniously concocted, do not tell consumers that peak-hour consumption is expensive, nor do kilowatt charges that are related to, for example, the floor area of the consumer's house. Time-of-day metering will; so will peak-load limiters if they are properly adjusted; so, under certain circumstances, will kilowatt charges related to a consumer's demand during peak. The essential condition which declining-block and floor area tariffs fail to meet is that of making peak-period consumption more expensive than off-peak consumption.

An entirely different tariff and metering policy may follow when incentive effects of tariffs on consumers' demands are considered. We have found that, in most countries, financial questions and accounting rules dominate the level, structure, and types of tariffs. Incentive effects are sometimes considered, but generally only as an afterthought or out of the necessity of holding back a very rapidly growing peak demand (often 20 percent a year or more in developing countries). What is needed, in our view, is the opposite philosophy. Incentive effects should be considered first when choosing tariff types and meters. Financial targets can still be set and deserving consumers can be given concessions, but this should be done in a way that has the least damaging effect on incentives.

We can now state our approach in general terms. We accept the importance of financial targets and we accept the importance of equity—although we disagree with the traditional accounting approach to the meaning of equity. We also stress the importance of resource allocation. We begin with resource allocation by analyzing cost structure and the incentive effects of the various simplified tariff and metering policies open to the enterprise. Next, if required, come questions of equity to allow, for example, for the problems of low income groups. Finally, financial targets enter into the picture as we confine any necessary increases to certain elements of the tariffs so that the least possible damage is done to equity and resource allocation.

From what we have just said, it is natural that we proceed in sequence to consider costs for pricing, tariff simplification and incentives, approaches to cost distortions (shadow prices, second-best), and equity and finance. There is, however, one technical matter to clear up first, and this is the interaction of pricing and investment.

11

Interaction of Pricing and Investment

The approach to investment planning usually begins with a forecast of demand, and this is followed by a search for a least-cost policy for investment using one or another of the various cost-minimizing techniques outlined in Chapter 13. Once the least-cost policy for investment has been determined, the cost structure relevant for pricing can be derived (sometimes directly from the output of the cost-minimizing technique). At this stage it might be argued that new prices set on the basis of these costs would alter the demand forecasts so that the investment program should be revised accordingly, giving a new cost structure. But this iterative procedure may be an unnecessary refinement. In practice, prices can only be adjusted slowly, often with a considerable time lag for debate and approval. Prices also take a long time to act, since the demand for electricity is linked largely to the stock of electrical appliances and machines. Anyway, by the time that price revisions have been made and have begun to have their effects, the time will have arrived for revised forecasts and programs. The effects of prices on demand should be evident in the trends in the revised forecasts. Thus, while the feedback of prices on forecasts and the investment program is important, feedback is best dealt with iteratively (as in automatic control systems) by waiting for prices to begin to have their effects on forecast demand levels, and changing investment plans accordingly.

This process of gradual adjustment and of slow response to prices is fortunate in that we need not bother with the value of price elasticities, which are notoriously difficult to estimate reliably. On the other hand, the process is unfortunate if prices are badly out of line with costs, for then it may take a long time to put things right. This raises a dilemma for project justification, which is discussed in Chapter 10. A project may show poor economic returns on current prices because the prices are too low when the project is operating. But if price adjustments have to be gradual and price response is slow, we still may have to accept the project rather than make matters worse and accept physical rationing. Until price reforms have had their effect, decisionmakers may have to accept projects with apparently poor economic rates of return, however unwelcome they may find such a situation.

Costs for Pricing

We begin with a theoretical issue—pricing according to short-run versus long-run marginal costs. It is now many years since their equivalence under conditions of certainty was demonstrated by Boiteux and other French authors.[2] In Chapter 14 we extend this theory to the analysis of pricing with uncertain (stochastic) demand and plant availability. The important point is that there are definite limitations on the possibilities of using prices to ration available capacity when demand and supply conditions turn out to be different from those expected when prices were set. Thursday's prices cannot be raised because some turbines do not start on that morning, and January's prices cannot be raised if it becomes apparent that the month is colder than usual—if only because meters are read just once a month or because consumers get irritated with sudden price increases. Consequently, physical rationing (load shedding) is unavoidable at times. In the cost function we include a term representing the expected social costs of load shedding, including losses of industrial output, and the nuisance and cost to consumers of having to substitute candles, batteries, or oil heaters, or of having to do without. Thus an increase in the level of (the probability distribution of) demand in the short run—that is to say, when capacity adjustments are not possible—will increase both the expected demand that is met and the expected demand that is not met. The expected costs of outages and expected fuel and other variable costs also rise. Thus the relevant cost for short-run pricing is a probability-weighted average of the marginal costs of not meeting demand and the marginal variable costs of meeting it. (Capacity costs do not change in the short run.)

In the long run, capacity adjustments can be made to keep the probability of interruptions down to an acceptable level. The long-run marginal cost of supply is the marginal cost of extra capacity plus the expected costs of extra output. (There is also a rule to define the optimal level of extra capacity: the marginal costs of extra capacity should equal the expected social savings from marginal reductions of supply interruptions.)

Chapter 14 notes, however, that once short-run conditions become different from those anticipated when long-run capacity decisions were made, one might as well optimize for the short run. This point derives its force from the length of time it takes to plan and install new generating plants—six years is typical. If demand has grown faster than anticipated, it will take a long time before the rate of growth of capacity can be accelerated. Meanwhile, it may be preferable to raise the price of electricity during periods of peak demand rather than to accept an increased probability of power cuts.

2. See Appendix B to Chapter 13.

Accepting this point in principle, we have found that there are situations where it is not very helpful. The argument assumes that the tariff structure is such that there are appropriate peak kilowatt-hour prices or kilowatt charges that can be raised. But this is not always the case. The tariff structure may contain no such elements. The problem is then to suggest a new structure, not to alter some elements of existing tariffs. In addition, information generally is not available on the expected costs of load shedding, and this, too, adds to the difficulties of applying the short-run rule.

This is more or less the problem faced in the case studies appearing in this book. Here we analyzed the cost structure and tentatively suggested some new tariffs for consideration. In short-run terms, it was too difficult to calculate or even to guess the level of peak charges that would bring peak demand in relation to capacity down to a level where the risk of supply failure would be acceptably low. (Even in countries that carry out a great deal of market research on electricity, very little is known about price elasticities and time lags in demand.) We had to rely on cost analysis to suggest both the structure of possible tariffs and the approximate levels of their various elements. Pricing according to long-run marginal costs simply has to be used in such circumstances; there is no practical alternative.

This lack of information about consumer response is a great drawback. For this reason, we admire the idea of obtaining information by tariff experiments on the lines pioneered by The Electricity Council in Britain.[3]

Simplifications and Incentives

The long-run marginal costs of supply can be stated very simply for most systems, though in practice a lot of work is needed to estimate them for the various voltage levels of service. Most writers derive rules about marginal cost for public enterprises having nonstorable inputs (or where storage is without cost), so these rules apply only to predominantly thermal systems. They have two elements: marginal energy (fuel) and running costs; plus (during peak times) marginal capacity costs. We have adjusted these rules to allow for indivisibilities in capacity expansion in Chapter 17, where we show that it is best to consider the marginal capacity costs as

3. See especially The Electricity Council, *Domestic Tariff Experiment*, Load and Market Research Report no. 121 (London, 1974).

being the present worth of the costs of bringing forward capacity expansion by T years, averaged over T, where T is the interval between investments. In many cases, this is approximately the average of incremental costs of expansion. Additionally we have derived the rules for mixed hydro-thermal systems, that is, where storage is important. In the simpler cases, marginal energy cost is zero in the wet or filling-up seasons. In the dry or discharge seasons, however, marginal energy cost rises to: the cost of adding to storage capacity (long-run rule); or the rationing price needed to keep the dry season energy demand down to the point where the probability of interruptions is at an acceptable level (short-run rule); or the fuel cost of thermal plant, if this is used to provide for extra output, less net capacity savings (over hydro) if extra thermal plant is needed (again, this is a long-run rule). There are more complicated rules than this for some systems, particularly, as is evident from our study in Sudan (Chapter 5), where constraints on when to store and discharge result from silting or irrigation and flood control. But this is roughly the form that marginal costs may take.

If marginal cost can be described so briefly, why is it so difficult, technically speaking, to reflect accurately in tariffs? We have touched on the answers earlier: high variability and unpredictability in demand, and cost and bother in metering. For many large industrial, agricultural, and commercial consumers, even quite sophisticated metering may cost less than 0.1 percent of their bills, so only the first of these problems is important. Meter reading can be done monthly, so seasonal variations in prices are possible. The main problem lies in determining first the times of day when demand is pressing on available capacity and then a means to meter and charge for it. There is a fair range of choice. Supplies that are subject to interruption can be offered at a lower price to those consumers for whom occasional interruptions are not too troublesome. Other consumers may be willing to pay for the high costs of supply during peak; for these, we may use either maximum demand meters, switched on during the peak hours of the month, with a charge related to maximum recorded demand (in this system, kilowatt-hours are metered separately and related to fuel and running costs of supply), or time-of-day meters with high kilowatt-hour rates during peak hours. Telecontrol can be used to make timing of the metering more flexible and accurate. Broadly, we have found that the choice between metering maximum demand and metering kilowatt-hour consumption during peak depends on the demand conditions.[4] If the

4. See, in particular, the case study on Tunisia reported in Chapter 4.

peak demands are persistent over many hours, in the form of plateaus, it is worth casting the net widely, so to speak, by applying uniform kilowatt-hour charges over all peak kilowatt-hours during the month; off-peak kilowatt-hours are recorded separately. If, however, the peak demand is spiky, a wide net is too restrictive while a narrow one may miss the peak or cause it to move elsewhere; here, a charge related to observed maximum kilowatt demand during potential peak hours of the month, with a separate meter for kilowatt-hour consumption, is more appropriate.

Turning to small, mainly domestic, consumers, metering and billing costs and the lesser sophistication of the consumer necessitate simple tariffs. (A time-of-day meter, for example, may cost about $50.00 and is only worthwhile for domestic consumption at levels typical of Europe and North America.) Tariffs for small consumers can reflect only one or two of the various features of the cost structure. As there are quite a few features in the cost structure, this raises the problem of choosing which to reflect and which to average out. The theoretical discussions in Chapter 16 and our case studies all elaborate on these problems. Briefly, seasonal tariffs can be applied even if billing is monthly or bimonthly; less frequent billing may preclude their application unless there are only two seasons (wet and dry) within the year. The problem arises with charging for peak–off-peak differentials within the day. At the simplest level, a flat kilowatt-hour rate may be charged, pitched somewhat below the marginal costs of peak demand but somewhat above the marginal costs of off-peak demand to avoid undue discouragement of off-peak consumption or undue encouragement of peak consumption. At a slightly more advanced level, a load limiter tariff can be introduced, where consumers subscribe to a certain maximum demand and are automatically and temporarily disconnected by a small circuit breaker (in the house) if they exceed it; in addition, consumers pay a flat kilowatt-hour rate. Finally, for the larger domestic consumers, it may be worthwhile to have a time-of-day tariff.

This does not exhaust the options open for economic tariff and metering policies—in particular, telecontrol may offer useful new options—but at the current state of the art, these seem to us among the most important ones (at least in developing countries).

There are also some common institutional problems which can have an important bearing on the choice of tariffs and meters. For example, monthly meter reading is labor-intensive, which increases costs. One might expect it to be more usual in developing countries where labor is cheap. But such countries often find great difficulty in recruiting and managing reliable meter readers, and the main reason for monthly billing seems to be that consumers default less on twelve monthly bills than on fewer, necessarily larger bills.

Reliability, whether of meters or of meter readers, is not only a matter of training and maintenance effort. Consumers can cheat, either by tampering with their meters or by suborning the meter readers. Indeed, consumers in some countries are adept at stealing electricity, at some personal risk. Furthermore, billing systems can degenerate so that bills arrive late, are inaccurate, or fail to arrive at all. Collection may go wrong, too.

Finally, it is evident that consumers must have an understanding of what it is they are being charged for. The purpose of a tariff structure is to provide consumers with incentives. A high rate provides both a message that special economy is called for and an encouragement to do something about it. But consumers by themselves may not understand the message and may not know how to do anything about it. They need help, and it is part of the job of the electricity enterprise to provide it. Tariffmaking very much needs to be supplemented by technical advice. For large consumers, the advice of commercial engineers is needed. For small consumers, individual advice is not practicable, and, though tariffs are already simple, a certain amount of advertising still may be required. By helping consumers adapt to the tariff structure, electricity companies help themselves.

Cost Distortions

A tariff structure which fully reflects the enterprise's cost structure may not lead to efficient resource allocation. One reason relates to what is known to economists as the "second-best" problem. Consumers' choices may be influenced not only by the price structure of electricity but also by the prices of other fuels. Again, the prices paid by the electricity industry may not reflect the value to the economy of the resources used. Only if all such prices are right in some sense have we the "first-best" situation where tariffs that reflect cost will lead to an efficient allocation of resources.

One answer to the second-best problem, which may be institutionally necessary although intellectually unsatisfying, is to ignore it. A practical reason for this is simply that the problem may not be in one's terms of reference. The electricity enterprise has been given the job of supplying electricity, not of running the whole economy, and may have to work within the existing framework. If the enterprise thinks that the tax on oil makes oil prices too high, for example, it may nevertheless have to mind its own business. (Another practical reason for ignoring the problem is that distortions elsewhere in the economy should be tackled directly.)

The other answer is, of course, to try to make some adjustments for the distortions. Such adjustments may be called for not only in setting tariffs but also in making investment decisions. It is in this latter context that much has been written about the use of shadow prices as a way of making the adjustments in developing countries. An introduction to the subject is given in Chapter 12. Government directives are sometimes provided to public electricity companies to use appropriate shadow prices for capital, labor, foreign exchange, and material inputs when comparing projects; this, at least, facilitates the institutional problems (not to be underestimated) of deciding on an efficient investment program.

Given that shadow prices are important for determining which projects make up an investment program based on least-cost (see, as one illustration, the case study on Turkey reported in Chapter 8), conflicts may arise when attempting to reflect them in tariffs. In power systems with fuel oil plants, for example, taxes on fuel oil, which are generally heavy, may rightly be neglected when power plants fired by fuel oil are being compared with, say, plants driven by hydro power, since taxes are not a cost but rather the government's share in profits. However, the government will still expect its taxes to be paid, so the enterprise must somehow raise them. This has three implications for tariffs: their structure should reflect resource cost (computed using shadow prices) as far as possible; the revenue which this structure would generate should be computed; and then, if this is too low, the structure should be amended to achieve the desired financial objective by increasing some elements of the tariffs in such a way as to do least damage to the efficiency and equity objectives.

Before passing to the equity and financial aspects of tariffs, there is one final point to make about distortions to costs. Tariffs which reflect resource costs would often lead to considerable financial surpluses in the electricity enterprises in developing countries (fuel oil taxes notwithstanding) because these enterprises are among the heaviest and most intensive users of capital and foreign exchange, both of which may have high shadow prices. These enterprises generally have had small beginnings and have faced very high growth rates of demand, and thus, large expansion programs over long periods, so it is common for them to experience considerable difficulties in meeting financial targets. Thus, strong arguments for the yet higher tariffs suggested by the shadow prices will not always be accepted.

Finance and Equity

We have already noted that considerations about equity and finance as well as about resource allocation are relevant to tariffs. Our view is that it is best to design a tariff that reflects cost, subject to any second-best considerations, and then to modify it if the promised revenue is inadequate or if it seems unfair. This procedure, which keeps resource allocation, equity, and finance separate in the earlier stages, avoids the confusion that afflicts the traditional approach.

We have only two general points to make on the financial side. First, the management of an electricity enterprise often welcomes a requirement that the enterprise earn a certain minimum rate of return, calculated so as to cover its accounting costs and possibly to earn sufficient revenue to finance a certain proportion of future capital expenditure. This requirement helps support financial responsibility, mobilize financial resources for expansion, and may enable management to obtain considerable autonomy in running the enterprise, a valuable spur to innovation and efficiency. Enterprises which rely on having their deficits met by government are usually (though not inevitably) in difficulties, and their capacity to innovate is sometimes noticeably stymied. It is true, we admit, that very high profits may have a debilitating effect, too, but this is a much less common phenomenon.

Our second point is that putting tariffs at a level above that called for by pure cost reflection is equivalent to taxing the supply of electricity. The yield of the "tax" may finance the enterprise's capital expenditure rather than flow into the country's exchequer. Apart from any effect on the enterprise's independence of the sort just noted, if the exchequer would otherwise finance part of the enterprise's capital expenditure, the difference is only one of bookkeeping. What concerns us here is a point relating to second-best resource allocation. Something does have to be taxed and there is no general case against taxing electricity. Indeed, if other kinds of energy are taxed, there is a positive case for taxing electricity as well, so that relative prices including tax reflect relative cost before tax. More generally, in countries where the tax base is limited and the tax system is inefficient, electricity is a good candidate for taxation even if the tax takes the implicit form of a high proportion of self-finance. Although there may be substantial institutional difficulties in raising financial targets, therefore, it is something to be encouraged and is worth striving for.

Fairness in tariff structure is a more contentious topic. We have already argued that there is nothing intrinsically fair in the financial

19

view that tariffs should be set so that revenues from each class of consumer cover the share of accounting costs allocated to that class. Similarly, there is nothing intrinsically unfair in revenues that do not cover accounting costs—as happens in the village electrification programs of many countries. Certainly a tolerant attitude on tariffs to poorer consumers can be defended in such cases when the more appealing methods of redistribution through fiscal policy are not administratively feasible. Having said this, however, we also state our general belief that distortions in the use of economic resources stemming from inequities in the economic system, like those stemming from distortions in the pricing system, are best dealt with directly. (Fairness and income distribution are discussed further in Chapter 11.) Countering inequities through cross-subsidization within services such as electricity is a poor second best.

Returning to less controversial matters, we have noticed that what interests electricity enterprises and governments is often not the fairness of tariff levels in relation to costs but the political acceptability of tariff changes. Since no one ever objects to a reduction in tariffs, our observation is that if a new tariff would noticeably increase the bills of a group of consumers who would create a big fuss, that tariff will be reexamined. A large part of the effort involved in setting a new tariff is spent comparing it with the existing tariff for a sample of consumers in order to estimate the effect on their bills. Thus, in practice, the "fairness" constraint on new tariffs often becomes an implicit stipulation that no consumer shall suffer an increase in his bill of more than so much percent within a certain period. The economist who is advising on tariffs has to take this kind of constraint into account, even if only by recommending a gradual rather than a sudden transition to a new tariff. The people who run electricity enterprises naturally value a quiet life.

CHAPTER 3

Electricity Tariffs in Thailand

Electricity generation in Thailand, which has been expanding with extraordinary rapidity in the past twenty years, is the responsibility of the Electricity Generating Authority of Thailand (EGAT). Distribution is the responsibility of two authorities who purchase electricity in bulk from EGAT: the Metropolitan Electricity Authority (MEA), serving the Bangkok area, and the Provincial Electricity Authority (PEA), which serves all areas except the Bangkok area.[1] This chapter presents an economic analysis of each authority's tariffs.

Introduction and Summary

Tariff policy is always a delicate matter and a constant worry for management. Debt on past investments must be serviced and running costs met. Expansion is generally very rapid and requires internal cash generation in large amounts. For economic, social, or other reasons, service has to be extended to new areas, often at high costs, low revenues, and thus heavy financial debts. The costs of service differ from one region to another but tariffs have to be fairly uniform. Service, in some cases, is expected to be sold below cost on social grounds. At the same time, tariff increases are unpopular and have to be kept to a minimum even though costs and financial needs may be rising rapidly.

---

1. A map of Thailand showing some details of the electricity system appears on the next page. Boundaries and locations of project areas shown in the map are based on the best information available but are necessarily imprecise.

21

Mae Hong Son Project Area

□ Kud dam

Chaing Mai ▲

Chiang Rai Project Area

Nan Project Area

Mae △ Moh

Nam Ngum dam ■

Phrae Project Area

Bhumibol dam ■   Sirikit dam □

Udonthani ▲

Nam Pung dam ■

Phetchabun Project Area

Ubolratana dam ■
Chulabhorn dam □

Yanhee Project Area

Sirindhorn dam ■

Nakhon Ratchasima ▲

Quae Yai dam □

Sai Yai project □

Pathum Thani Project Area

Lam Dom Noi Project Area

Prachin Buri and Nakhon Nayok Project Area

Kang Krachan dam ■

Bangkok Metropolitan Area

○ Chanthaburi

Prachuap ○
Ranong ○
Chumphon ○

THAILAND

PROJECT AREAS OF THE
PROVINCIAL ELECTRICITY AUTHORITY
LOCATION OF POWER PLANTS

		Existing	Proposed or Under Construction
Power Plants			
Hydro		■	□
Thermal		▲	△
Nuclear		Ⓝ	Ⓝ

Krabi Project Area

Surat Thani ▲

Phuket ○   ▲ Krabi

▲ Hatyai

Pattani project □

Lower Southern Project Area

*Bangkok Metropolitan Area
(Served By Metropolitan
Electricity Authority)*

NORTH BANGKOK ▲

BANGKOK NOI ▲   BANGKAPI ▲

SOUTH BANGKOK ▲△

The boundaries shown on this map do not imply endorsement or acceptance by the World Bank and its affiliates.

22

Aims of the study

Since the capital, foreign exchange, and primary energy needs of electric power authorities are substantial, are growing quickly, and are costly, the question arises of how to determine a tariff policy that promotes good use of these resources while recognizing the financial, social, and other obligations and concerns of the authorities. This chapter is addressed to this question. Separate sections analyze the costs and tariffs of EGAT, MEA, and PEA, respectively. The final section presents general conclusions. Technical details of tariff suggestions are discussed in the concluding parts of each section.

A principal finding is that the *cost structure* of all three utilities is very simple. It is a basic energy cost related to the cost of fuel oil, plus a capacity cost related to demand in the peak period that varies with the voltage level of service. Simple time-of-day tariffs for the different voltage levels could be introduced to reflect the cost structure for all but the small consumers; a simple flat rate with adjustments for particular financial and social factors at hand is appropriate for the latter. This measure would enormously simplify and improve the present tariffs, which are rather complicated and do not reflect the cost structure. Moreover, simplifications and improvement could be accomplished without raising delicate problems about *tariff levels*. If, in addition, questions about tariff levels could be addressed, then (a) marginal cost pricing would raise EGAT's revenues above what is normally required for their financial needs, since recent oil price increases have raised marginal cost above average costs; and (b) PEA, on the other hand, would require external financial support, since it is extending service on a large scale to new areas at a high fixed initial cost, and consequently marginal costs are below initial average costs.

It is also apparent that inflation is beginning to affect the costs of the three authorities. The case for a general increase of tariffs when costs rise is a strong one: financial loss undermines the ability of utilities to expand their programs; low prices encourage overexpansion, further exacerbating financial difficulties. More generally, a strong and growing sector of the economy can be weakened.

Approach of the study

The approach of this study begins with an economic analysis of costs and then suggests a decision as to which tariff and metering policy would best reflect them. This procedure gives an "ideal tariff," so to speak. The next step introduces financial, social, and other factors in such a manner as to distort the "ideal tariff" as little as possible.

The economic analysis of tariffs begins by estimating the marginal or incremental costs of supply. These are the costs resulting from a unit increase of supply (also equal to the cost savings from a unit reduction in supply). Since the marginal costs of increasing supply differ according to time, place, and voltage level, it is common to refer to the *structure* as well as to the *level* of marginal costs.

Marginal costs are different from accounting costs, on which tariffs are often based. Accounting costs are calculated by examining records of past expenditure, while marginal costs are calculated by examining expansion plans and how the power system is to be operated as demand increases. Accounting costs, in other words, are backward looking while marginal costs are forward looking.

The relevance of marginal cost is derived from the fact that it is the cost to the enterprise of an extra unit of supply, while price is the cost to the consumer of an extra unit of consumption. It follows that, from an economic viewpoint, to set price below marginal cost is to subsidize extra supply and encourage waste, while to price above marginal cost is to overcharge and restrict demand unnecessarily. Even though, on average, prices may be right, overcharging and undercharging can occur at different times and different voltage levels through defects in the price structure.

EGAT's Costs and Tariffs

In 1962, the sum of the peak demands on the system now run by the Electricity Generating Authority of Thailand (EGAT) amounted to 113 megawatts; by 1973 the peak demand had risen more than tenfold to 1,200 megawatts, an average growth rate of 24 percent a year. The load factor of the system improved from 52 to 64 percent in the same period, reflecting the fact that energy demands grew slightly faster, at about 27 percent a year. In the same period, the installed generating capacity rose from 170 megawatts to 1,400 megawatts. In 1974, with the completion of a large multipurpose hydro scheme at Sirikit, EGAT's installed generation capacity amounts to 2,137 megawatts, of which 909 megawatts (43 percent) is hydro and 1,228 megawatts (57 percent) is thermal:

Power plants	Capacity in megawatts
Hydro	909
Fuel oil	1,028
Lignite	6
Gas turbines	165
Diesels	29
Total	2,137

The rate of growth of demand is such that the peak demand in one month is generally higher than in the previous month (see Figure 3.1) and no seasonality is apparent.

The hydro schemes are dominated by two large multipurpose projects, one at Bhumibol (420 megawatts) and one at Sirikit (375 megawatts); both serve the additional purposes of providing flood control and irrigation in the central plains to the north of Bangkok. To meet the increasing needs for irrigation and electricity, another large hydro project of 360 megawatts is under construction at the Quae Yai Dam, the Ban Chao Nen Project, about 200 kilometers northwest of Bangkok.

Thermal reserves are dominated by the fuel oil plants at South Bangkok (700 megawatts) and North Bangkok (237 megawatts); there are also several small fuel oil, diesel, gas turbine, and lignite plants, and some of the North Bangkok units were converted to burn lignite following the October 1973 rise in oil prices. EGAT plans to increase the capacity of the plant at South Bangkok by 300 megawatts in 1976, and by a further 300 megawatts in 1978. A 150-megawatt expansion of the lignite plant at Mae Moh is also under way.

Most of EGAT's system is interconnected; about 85 megawatts (4 percent of capacity) in the south is isolated but is to be connected to the main system in 1978.

Marginal costs

EGAT's marginal costs comprise four elements; these are the marginal costs of (a) energy; (b) adding to generating capacity; (c) adding to transmission capacity; and (d) maintenance and operation. Each of these is discussed in turn below and then summarized.

Energy. The daily pattern of demand during workdays on EGAT's interconnected system broadly consists of an evening peak; a daytime plateau, with small valleys at lunchtime and at the end of the afternoon; and a light load period at night. (During Sundays and holidays the daytime load is much lower and the evening load a little lower.) Figure 3.2 charts this pattern for July days in 1973 and 1974. To meet this load, all the available capacity, except for diesels and gas turbines, is operating during all twenty-four hours. The small hydro and lignite plants are operated more or less continually. North and South Bangkok steam plants produce at full capacity during the peak, at a fairly constant low level during the night, and at a constant intermediate level during the daytime. The Sirikit hydro plant does the same, while the Bhumibol hydro plant provides the remainder of the load to be met, its output varying continually to follow the

FIGURE 3.1. INSTALLED CAPACITY, PEAK DEMAND, AND ENERGY
GENERATION OF THAILAND'S ELECTRICITY SYSTEM

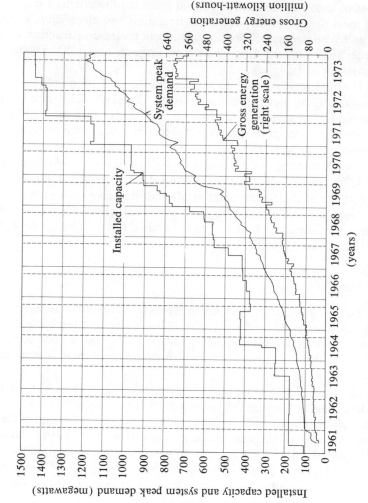

SOURCE: Charted from data supplied by the Electricity Generating Authority
of Thailand

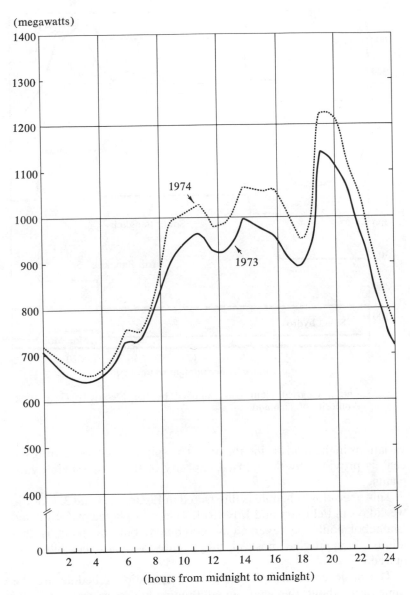

(megawatts)

1974

1973

(hours from midnight to midnight)

SOURCE: Charted from data supplied by the Electricity Generating
Authority of Thailand

FIGURE 3.3. POWER GENERATION SCHEDULE AND SPINNING
RESERVE OF THAILAND'S ELECTRICITY SYSTEM, WEEKDAY
OF FEBRUARY 1974

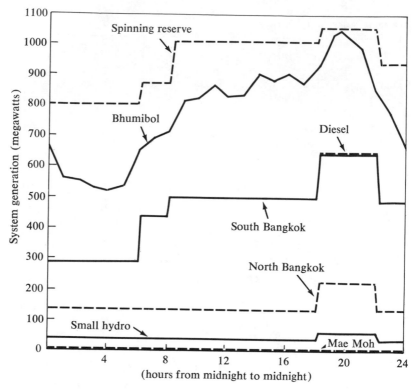

SOURCE: Charted from data supplied by the Electricity Generating
Authority of Thailand

variations in the load during the day. The spinning reserve during the
peak is provided by the unused capacity of these two main hydro
plants.

This operating schedule is illustrated in Figures 3.3 and 3.4 for the
weekdays in February and July 1974. The roles played by Sirikit and
Bhumibol could be reversed or combined, but the point is that
jointly they provide most of the minute-to-minute flexibility required.

The basic characteristics of EGAT's operating schedule are the
same throughout the year, even though hydro reserves are, of
course, much higher at the end of the wet season in December. (Figure 3.5 illustrates typical variations in reservoir levels at Sirikit.)

The hydro inflows need to be stored and discharged to meet irrigation requirements, which are predetermined on a weekly basis. There is no surplus water in the wet season, which would enable hydro to replace thermal on base load at this time. With rare exceptions, there is also no spillage. Moreover, there is unlikely to be a surplus, even with considerably greater runoff than experienced in the catchment areas in recent years.

Since hydro reserve does not imply surpluses for electricity production, EGAT schedules its generation so that (a) fairly steady operation of thermal plant is achieved in each of the three periods of

FIGURE 3.4. POWER GENERATION SCHEDULE AND SPINNING RESERVE OF THAILAND'S ELECTRICITY SYSTEM, WEEKDAY OF JULY 1974

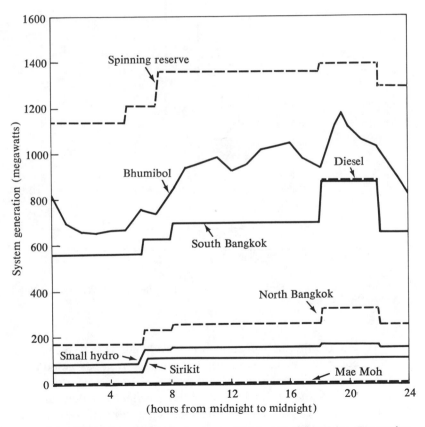

SOURCE: Charted from data supplied by the Electricity Generating Authority of Thailand

FIGURE 3.5. RESERVOIR LEVELS AT THE 375-MEGAWATT SIRIKIT DAM, THAILAND

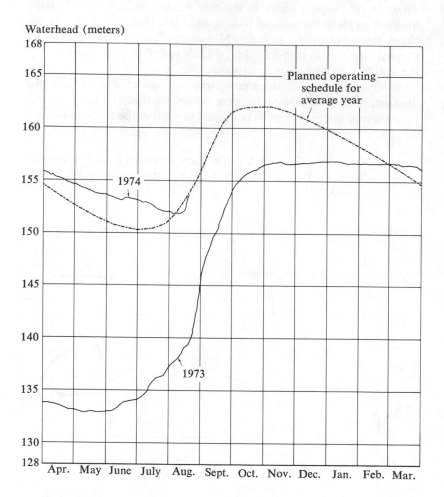

SOURCE: Charted from data supplied by the Electricity Generating Authority of Thailand

the day; and (b) thermal generation is scheduled so as to meet total energy requirements in excess of the (predetermined) amount of hydro energy available. This second practice has an important consequence. It is that extra kilowatt-hours, whenever they are required, ultimately require extra thermal generation. If they are required in the daytime or peak periods they are, at those particular times, met by extra hydro generation. In such instances, however,

there has to be correspondingly less hydro and more thermal generation in the light load period. At whatever time during the twenty-four
hours an additional kilowatt-hour is demanded, or one less kilowatt-
hour is saved, the marginal cost incurred, or saved, is the marginal
cost of thermal generation during the light load period. The marginal
cost of energy consequently is constant throughout the twenty-four
hours.

This situation is the same throughout the year, save only when
transmission or thermal plant outages impose some constraint.
Hence marginal energy cost equals marginal thermal generation cost
at North or South Bangkok during the light load period—not just
over the twenty-four hours of a day, but over the 8,766 hours of a
year. Our data would indicate that, at South Bangkok, the marginal
cost of generation is Bht 0.33 per kilowatt-hour; this is the marginal
energy cost figure used in the present study.[2]

Operation along these lines is likely to continue at least until the
nuclear plant is commissioned in 1980, if not thereafter. The addition
of two new 300-megawatt units at South Bangkok, of Ban Chao
Nen hydro, and of a few smaller new plants, will match the projected growth in the load but will not fundamentally alter the way the
system is operated. The role of hydro power, with its fixed energy
availabilities, will remain unchanged.

Adding to generating capacity. Extra demand at time of peak requires not only extra energy but also extra capacity if the probability
of failure of the supply is not to increase. Conversely, with a reduction in demand. Hence the total marginal cost of supply during the
peak periods includes marginal generation capacity costs in addition
to the marginal energy costs.

To calculate the marginal capacity costs of system expansion, it is
necessary to consider how investment plans have to be changed in
response to an increase in the forecast of peak demand levels. The
possible alternatives are six: advance the investment program and
possibly change the mix (for example, gas turbines for oil); increase
the unit sizes of new plants planned but not yet under construction;
accelerate the completion of plants not under construction; build a
small new fuel oil plant (with a short construction period); install additional gas turbines; or accept a lower reserve margin and an increased probability of failure to meet the peak. Determining which
of these alternatives applies to a given situation depends on how the

---

2. About 1.62 U.S. cents per kilowatt-hour at an exchange rate of Bht
20.375 = US$ 1.00. This exchange rate may be used for the conversion of bahts
throughout the chapter.

TABLE 3.1. INVESTMENT PROGRAM FOR THAILAND, 1974–88: PLANT CAPACITIES AND SYSTEM DEMAND

Year	Power plants (megawatts)					Total planned capacity (megawatts)	Expected demand (megawatts)	Ratio of capacity to demand[a]
	Gas turbine and diesel	Lignite	Fuel oil	Hydro	Nuclear			
1974	194	6	1,028	909	—	2,137	1,421	1.50
1975	194	6	1,028	909	—	2,137	1,614	1.32
1976	194	6	1,328	909	—	2,437	1,840	1.32
1977	194	81	1,328	921	—	2,524	2,040	1.24
1978	194	156	1,628	921	—	2,899	2,265	1.28
1979	194	156	1,628	1,041	—	3,019	2,487	1.21
1980	194	156	1,628	1,321	—	3,299	2,721	1.21
1981	194	156	1,628	1,321	600	3,899	2,980	1.31
1982	194	156	1,628	1,321	600	3,899	3,260	1.20
1983	194	156	1,628	1,321	1,200	4,499	3,600	1.25
1984	194	156	1,628	1,421	1,200	4,599	3,900	1.18
1985	194	156	1,628	1,521	1,200	4,699	4,100	1.15
1986	194	156	1,628	2,021	1,200	5,199	4,400	1.18
1987	194	156	1,628	3,221	1,200	6,399	4,800	1.33
1988	194	156	1,628	3,221	1,200	6,399	5,200	1.23

a. End of September (EGAT's fiscal year is October–September).
SOURCE: Based on information supplied by the Electricity Generating Authority of Thailand.

construction schedule is proceeding, on whether demand is growing as forecast, and on how fast demand is growing (since the effects of slippages on rapidly growing systems are felt sooner). A further factor which affects marginal capacity costs is, of course, the change in the mix of investments over time in response to relative price changes and resource availability.

Evidently, therefore, estimates of marginal capacity costs require a thorough system analysis of the investment program and an examination of how demand is growing in relation to forecasts. Below are a few illustrative remarks and calculations regarding EGAT's program.

In the next fifteen years, EGAT plans to introduce a mixture of hydro and thermal schemes. Those planned for the next six years are fairly firm, though timing may change, while those planned beyond then are still tentative and under review. Table 3.1 shows how the investment program might look.

With the completion of the Sirikit scheme there is now sufficient capacity to meet present day peak demands comfortably. The growth of demand up to 1980 is to be met by two additional 300-megawatt fuel oil units at South Bangkok (units 4 and 5, the former now under construction), the 360-megawatt Ban Chao Nen hydro project, two 75-megawatt lignite-fired units at Mae Moh, and two small hydro schemes of 12-megawatts at Pattani and 40-megawatts at Sirindhorn. EGAT believes that a heavy concentration on hydro and nuclear power will be needed in the 1980s, the need for nuclear power being precipitated by the rise in oil prices.

Though the balance on EGAT's system is likely to shift toward nuclear and hydro, the generating costs of meeting an increment of peak demand are, it seems to us, the costs of adding to fuel oil capacity. The reasons for this are six. (a) There is an upper limit to the rate at which nuclear can be introduced on the system. (b) There is an upper limit both to the extent of hydro resources and to the rate at which they, too, can be exploited. (c) If demand grows faster than forecast, extra demands will probably be met either by a small fuel oil plant or by the larger units at South Bangkok 4 and 5; conversely, if demand grows more slowly than forecast, it would be South Bangkok 5 which might be best postponed. (d) If slippage of, say, nuclear or hydro projects occurs, the main alternative will again be fuel oil. (e) Gas turbines could also be introduced, but there are already enough on the system. (f) Despite the large increase in oil prices, oil still has economic advantages over the alternatives for peak load, and for loads of short duration.

To illustrate this last point, the relative costs of South Bangkok unit 5 and of the First Nuclear Project are compared for loads of

TABLE 3.2. VARIATION OF COSTS WITH LOAD DURATION FOR A FUEL OIL AND A NUCLEAR POWER STATION IN THAILAND

Load duration and cost components	South Bangkok (300 megawatts)			Nuclear (600 megawatts)		
Load duration (hours a year)	2,000	4,000	6,000	2,000	4,000	6,000
Capital cost (millions of bahts)	1,170	1,170	1,170	8,380	8,380	8,380
Capital cost per kilowatt (bahts)	3,900	3,900	3,900	14,000	14,000	14,000
Annual cost per kilowatt (bahts):						
Capital costs[a]	429	429	429	1,540	1,540	1,540
Maintenance costs[b]	28	28	28	50	50	50
Other[c]	50	50	50	100	100	100
Fuel[d]	640	1,280	1,920	140	280	420
Total	1,147	1,787	2,427	1,830	1,970	2,110

a. Annuity of 11 percent taken, corresponding to an interest rate of 10 percent at 25 years.

b. For South Bangkok and Nuclear these are expected to be about Bht 37 and Bht 30 million a year, respectively (South Bangkok = 1,300 megawatts, Nuclear, 600 megawatts). Since maintenance is only about 2 percent of total annual costs, the table neglects the point that some of the maintenance costs vary with kilowatt-hour output.

c. For South Bangkok and Nuclear these are expected to be about Bht 65 and Bht 60 million a year, respectively.

d. Fuel costs of Bht 0.33 a kilowatt-hour for fuel oil, Bht 0.07 a kilowatt-hour for nuclear. Fuel costs per year are calculated as load duration times fuel cost per kilowatt-hour.

SOURCE: Based on information supplied by the Electricity Generating Authority of Thailand.

34

different durations in Table 3.2. (The absolute value of these cost data for EGAT are low, since they do not reflect recent inflation and cost escalation; we were not able to estimate related effects on costs, but do make a general point about inflation and tariffs in the conclusions. Similar points also apply to PEA and MEA data.)

According to these data, nuclear stations become increasingly cheaper than fuel oil stations for load durations of about 5,000 hours and above. For load durations of less than 5,000 hours, fuel oil is cheaper. The relatively low capital costs of oil-fired power stations, therefore, continue to provide cost advantages for short duration loads even though fuel oil costs are very high.

The situation could change over time due to further price changes, large slippages in the construction program for nuclear stations, or demand which is very much higher or lower than forecast. At present and for the next ten years or so, however, it seems that marginal costs of generation capacity will correspond roughly to those of an oil-fired power plant—barring major changes in the energy scene in Thailand. As an estimate of these costs, we take the incremental capacity costs of South Bangkok unit 5:

Capital costs   Bht 1,170,000,000
Annuitized capital costs   (11 percent annuity)   Bht 129,000,000
Capital cost per kilowatt capacity
    Annual   Bht 429
    Monthly   Bht 35.75

One should note that since the peak demand on EGAT's system increases from one month to the next, it is the monthly capital costs that are relevant for pricing policy. Also, the expansion of South Bangkok will not enable other plants to be operated less, so there are no system fuel savings for which allowance can be made.

The costs estimated above are expressed per unit increase of capacity; however, it is the costs induced by increases of maximum kilowatt demand on EGAT's system that are of interest for pricing policy. Two adjustments are therefore required. One adjustment is needed to allow for power losses in the transmission system at system peak; this is estimated by EGAT to be roughly 3 percent. The other adjustment allows for the point that EGAT needs to carry spare capacity on the system for contingencies—demands above expectations, generator outage, or project slippage during construction. During the period from 1974 to 1984, the ratio of planned capacity to system peak demand is 1.27 on average (see Table 3.1).

Thus the marginal capital costs of adding to generation capacity are about $35.75 \cdot 1.03 \cdot 1.27 =$ Bht 46.8 per kilowatt at peak demand per month.

TABLE 3.3. TRANSMISSION EXPANSION PROJECTS IN THAILAND

Year to be completed	Project description[a]	Capital expenditure at completion (million bahts)	Demand (megawatts)	Demand growth (megawatts)
1971	—	—	870	—
1975	TSP	930	1,421	551
1977	TSP 1	861	2,040	619
1978	CST	400	2,265	225
1981	TSP 2	786	2,980	715
1985	TSP 3	847	4,100	1,120
Totals		3,824		3,230

a. TSP denotes transmission and substation expansion project; TSP 1–TSP 3, threee transmission expansion projects; and CST, the Central-Southern Line, which will make the system fully interconnected.
SOURCE: Based on information supplied by the Electricity Generating Authority of Thailand.

Adding to transmission capacity. The effect of an increase in peak demand is to require transmission projects to be brought forward, and of a decrease, to enable them to be delayed. Thus to calculate the incremental costs of, say, bringing forward transmission projects one year, it is necessary to calculate the extra annuities involved. Table 3.3 shows EGAT's projects planned to expand the transmission system.

Since transmission projects are lumpy, it is generally necessary to take an average of the marginal costs. Here we take an average over the fifteen-year period in Table 3.3. Average capital expenditure for each kilowatt increase in demand is: $(3,824 \cdot 10^6)/(3,230 \cdot 10^3)$ = Bht 1.184 per kilowatt. Annuitized capital costs (11 percent annuity) = Bht 130 per kilowatt a year, or Bht 10.8 per kilowatt a month.

Maintenance and operation. A number of other cost components also increase with system capacity. Each new power station incurs fixed costs to maintain it, independent of kilowatt-hour output. There are also the costs of running the stations, of maintaining transmission lines, and of system administration and control, which increase as the system becomes larger. Some expected values for these costs are shown in Table 3.4, excluding power station maintenance and operation, which are discussed separately in the next paragraph. Over the next few years these costs average out at about Bht 133 per kilowatt peak demand per year, not including power station maintenance and operation.

The marginal costs of power station operation and maintenance have variable (kilowatt-hour–related) and fixed (kilowatt-related) components. For estimates of these, we take the costs expected at

TABLE 3.4. ESTIMATED ANNUAL INCREMENTAL COSTS OF COMPONENTS THAT INCREASE WITH INCREASES IN DEMAND, EGAT

	Cost components (millions of bahts)							Increase in demand (megawatts)	Annual incremental cost (bahts per kilowatt)
Year	Operation	Mainte- nance	Adminis- tration	Subtotal	Annual increase	Miscel- laneous plant additions[a]	Total annual increase		
1974	55	27	83	165	—	7.2	—	—	—
1975	63	31	95	189	24	7.7	31.7	194	163
1976	73	33	108	214	25	8.2	33.2	226	147
1977	79	36	116	231	17	8.8	25.8	200	129
1978	84	38	124	246	15	9.4	24.4	225	108
1979	91	41	134	266	20	9.9	29.9	222	135
1980	98	44	144	286	20	10.5	30.5	237	129
1981	105	48	154	307	21	11.0	32.0	256	125
Totals							207.5	1,560	133[b]

a. Annuity of 11 percent applied to actual investment.
b. Average
SOURCE: Based on information supplied by the Electricity Generating Authority of Thailand.

South Bangkok after unit 5 has been completed. The *variable* costs are expected to be roughly Bht 18 million a year; annual output will be about 9,000 gigawatt-hours so that the marginal kilowatt-hour costs of maintenance, on these figures, total about Bht 0.002 per kilowatt-hour.

The *fixed* costs of operation and maintenance at South Bangkok are expected to be Bht 65 million and Bht 18 million, respectively. Scaling these up for losses (3 percent) and the need for spare capacity, and dividing by capacity (1,300 megawatts), these marginal costs total Bht 82 per kilowatt peak demand a year. Adding to the figure of Bht 133 per kilowatt peak demand a year derived above for other system operation and maintenance costs thus gives marginal operation and maintenance costs of system expansion equal to Bht 215 per kilowatt peak demand a year, or Bht 17.9 per kilowatt peak demand a month.

Summary of marginal costs. Marginal energy costs, which are the same at all times of the year, are approximately the costs of extra kilowatt-hour output at South Bangkok, and are likely to remain at this level for several years. These costs are roughly Bht 0.33 per kilowatt-hour, allowing for losses. The variable (kilowatt-hour–related) maintenance costs are roughly Bht 0.002 per kilowatt-hour and are small enough to be neglected. Hence: EGAT's marginal energy costs ≈ Bht 0.33 per kilowatt-hour.

For the marginal cost related to increases in system peak demand, we estimate the following (allowing for losses and spare capacity needs):

Items increasing with increased demand	Costs (bahts per kilowatt per month)
Generation capacity	46.0
Transmission capacity	10.8
Other kilowatt-related	17.9
Total	74.7

Nonmarginal costs

Some costs do not change with increases in kilowatt-hour or peak kilowatt demands; this is a feature of, for instance, certain administrative costs. Also there may be certain historical or sunk costs to be paid. From an economic viewpoint, such costs should be ignored; but from a financial viewpoint they often cannot be ignored. The way to deal with them is, first, to determine if tariffs related to marginal costs would yield revenues sufficient to meet financial obligations. If revenue would be short, then, in the absence of external financial support, one or more elements in the tariff structure would have to be raised above marginal cost. In this event the increases should be confined to the elements of the structure that exert least influence on consumption; this will generally cause least distortion to the economic and social objectives of the tariffs. On the other hand, if revenue would be more than sufficient (as we believe would be the case for EGAT), then three options are open: the revenue could be absorbed in a higher internal rate of finance of new projects; the surplus revenue could be transferred to the public revenue or to other authorities in need of financial support; or there could be an obvious reduction in one or more elements of the tariffs. (While there may be a tendency to prefer the latter, the first two are well worth debating.)

Tariffs

The Electricity Generating Authority of Thailand sells most of its electricity to the Metropolitan Electricity Authority and the Provincial Electricity Authority. EGAT also supplies a few industrial customers, but at different tariff rates.

Bulk rates to MEA and PEA. EGAT charges MEA and PEA for energy as follows:

Kilowatt-hours per kilowatt of maximum demand per month	Charges (bahts per kilowatt per month)
First 120	0.39
Next 290	0.37
Excess above 410	0.32

MEA and PEA are charged, in addition, Bht 42 a month per kilowatt of maximum demand. In the case of MEA this is its aggregate maximum demand, while in the case of PEA it is the sum of the maximum demands at the forty-six terminal substations where delivery is made to PEA. Diversity is apparently so small, however, both within PEA and between it and MEA that, since together they provide 93 percent of EGAT's maximum demands, it comes to the same thing as charging them on their contribution to EGAT's peak. (MEA's peak demand period is more prolonged, however, a point which is important when assessing MEA's tariffs.)

At 70 percent of the terminal substations, PEA takes less than 410 kilowatt-hours per kilowatt so that its marginal cost of energy is Bht 0.37. MEA, and PEA with respect to its remaining 30 percent, on the other hand, face a marginal energy cost of Bht 0.32. It is not clear to us whether or not this difference is justified by differences in EGAT's transmission losses, but the general level of these marginal prices is adequately close to EGAT's Bht 0.33 marginal cost of supplying energy.

It seems natural to regard Bht 42 as the marginal tariff cost of a peak kilowatt. This is incorrect, however, because the effect of the kilowatt-related kilowatt-hour blocks in the energy charges is that an extra kilowatt raises the number of kilowatt-hours charged for on the higher rate blocks. Thus, one extra kilowatt raises the number of kilowatt-hours in the first block by 120 and, for the 70 percent of PEA that is on the second block, lowers the number of kilowatt-hours on the second block by the same amount. Hence, the kilowatt-hour charge rises by $120 \cdot (0.39 - 0.37) =$ Bht 2.4, making the effective marginal cost to PEA $42 + 2.4 =$ Bht 44.4 a kilowatt.

For the rest of PEA and for MEA, where kilowatt-hours per kilowatt exceed 410, an extra kilowatt will raise the number of kilowatt-hours in the first block by 120 and in the second block by 290, while lowering the number in the third block by 410. The net effect of the extra kilowatt on the energy charge is $(120 \cdot 0.39) + (290 \cdot 0.37) - (410 \cdot 0.32) =$ Bht 22.9. The effective marginal charge for a kilowatt is thus $42 + 22.9 =$ Bht 64.9.

To summarize: The marginal cost to EGAT of supplying an extra kilowatt is Bht 74.7. The marginal charge for a kilowatt is Bht 44.4 for most of PEA and Bht 64.9 for the rest of PEA and for MEA. But the impression given by the present tariff structure is that the marginal charge is only Bht 42.

It is difficult to justify the difference between the effective marginal charges of Bht 44.4 and Bht 64.9. Furthermore, both are lower than the true marginal cost of Bht 74.7. Hence the tariff could be simplified by having a *single* kilowatt price and a *single* kilowatt-hour price. This could be accomplished without any effect on EGAT's total revenue, though it would slightly lower MEA's bill and raise PEA's bill correspondingly. (If this latter effect were regarded as undesirable it could be avoided by introducing an annual surcharge on MEA's bill and a corresponding annual deduction from PEA's bill.)

An alternative, which would be equivalent and just as simple, would be to have *two* kilowatt-hour prices, one for EGAT's daily peak period from 6:30 P.M. to 9:30 P.M. on each of the twenty-six days a month when the peak occurs; and one for the off-peak period. The off-peak charge would be for kilowatt-hours only, while the peak charge would cover the costs of kilowatt-hours *plus* the costs of capacity spread over the peak hours, thus: the off-peak charge (9:30 P.M. to 6:30 P.M. the next day) = Bht 0.33 a kilowatt-hour; and the peak charge (6:30 P.M. to 9:30 P.M.) $= 0.33 + 74.7/(3 \cdot 26) =$ Bht 1.29 a kilowatt-hour. This tariff would also require no change in metering, since EGAT currently has digital kilowatt demand recorders at the terminal substations, recording demand every 15 to 30 minutes.

If no change in total revenue were required, the peak kilowatt-hour charge (or the single charge for a kilowatt during peak) could be based on the present effective marginal kilowatt charges, which as just shown lie somewhere between Bht 44.4 and Bht 64.9.

In addition to the simplification of having one kilowatt and one kilowatt-hour price (or two kilowatt-hour prices), which we believe would remove anomalies and avoid confusion, we also believe that the new kilowatt charge should be raised toward Bht 74.7 (or Bht 1.29 per kilowatt-hour during peak). This would make the marginal costs of power to MEA and PEA reflect EGAT's marginal costs in supplying it. It would also, of course, result in a much higher profit to EGAT (which could be absorbed in the form of a higher level of internal finance of new investments, or be transferred to the government). The reason why a higher tariff is suggested is that the costs of increasing the supply of electricity have risen markedly due to the rise in oil prices. Since EGAT cannot avoid burning extra oil to meet extra energy demand, the costs of extra output are now, and will continue to be, much higher than the average costs, which are kept down by the hydro schemes now on EGAT's system. (In addition to this, inflation affects capital costs—a matter that we have so far not discussed.) The rationale for a tariff increase would be that higher oil prices also make scarce hydro resources more valuable; a higher price to encourage conservation of hydro resources on the one hand, and to discourage unnecessary use of oil on the other, seems to be needed. In addition, a higher and restructured tariff would also help to moderate a very high rate of growth of demand, and make useful savings on investment. More on these points, and also on inflation, appears in the conclusion to this chapter.

(Note that, as it happens, the present level of the kilowatt-hour charges is about right, while the kilowatt charge is too low. Before the oil price increases, kilowatt-hour charges were set high implicitly in order to cover the financial losses from low kilowatt charges. This arrangement has the effect, we believe, of encouraging too high a rate of expansion. Had the October 1973 oil price increases not occurred we would have still argued for higher kilowatt charges, but also for lower kilowatt-hour charges, than those prevailing up to that time.)

Industrial rates. Most of EGAT's few customers pay Bht 96,000 monthly for the first 2,000 kilowatts of their own maximum demand and a monthly marginal rate of Bht 48 a kilowatt for the excess.

There is a single monthly rate of Bht 30 kilowatt for those whose demands during peak hours do not exceed 25 percent of their maximum demands outside these hours. Finally, there is a special single monthly rate of Bht 30 kilowatt for electrolytic processes and the steel industry.

The rate of Bht 48 a kilowatt cannot be compared with the marginal cost of Bht 74.7. The former relates to consumers' own maximum demands, which presumably occur during daytime, while the latter refers to their contributions to system peak. Hence the rate of Bht 48 would be appropriate only in the unlikely event that each one-kilowatt change in such consumers' own maximum demands were uniformly and inevitably accompanied by a 0.64-kilowatt change (48/74.8) in their demands at time of system peak.

The Bht 30 off-peak demand charge is equally unlikely to reflect marginal costs. A customer paying this charge will find that an extra kilowatt during peak hours will cost him: zero, if his demand during peak hours is currently less than 25 percent of his own maximum demand; Bht 120, if he has to add another 4 kilowatts to his own maximum demand in order to stay on the tariff; or a very large amount, if the extra kilowatt causes him to be taken off the off-peak tariff. An extra kilowatt added to his own maximum demand, on the other hand, will cost the customer Bht 30 even though EGAT's marginal capacity cost of supplying it is zero.

All these customers have their demands recorded, so there would be no difficulty in changing both the on-peak and the off-peak tariff to reflect the marginal cost of a peak kilowatt. Since the consumers cannot know in advance the hour when the system peak will occur, to charge them Bht 74.7 a kilowatt for their demands in whatever turns out to be the hour of system peak is not the best way of structuring charges. A tariff which averaged Bht 74.7 over all potential peak hours would not involve the same uncertainty, so would have clearer incentive effects. If the potential peak lasts for two to three hours during each of twenty-six working days in a month, an addition to the kilowatt-hour rate of $74.7/(3 \cdot 26) = $ Bht 0.96 during all these potential peak hours would be appropriate (for example, between 6:30 P.M. and 9:30 P.M. weekdays, according to Figure 3.2).

The conclusion is, therefore, that a charge of Bht 0.33 a kilowatt-hour during all off-peak hours and $0.96 + 0.33 = $ Bht 1.29 a kilowatt-hour during all potential peak hours would reflect both the level and structure of marginal costs much better than the present tariffs for EGAT's own consumers.

Future developments. Figure 3.2 suggests that the demand on EGAT's system during the daytime, between the hours of 9:00 A.M.

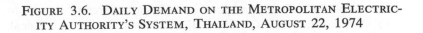

FIGURE 3.6. DAILY DEMAND ON THE METROPOLITAN ELECTRIC-
ITY AUTHORITY'S SYSTEM, THAILAND, AUGUST 22, 1974

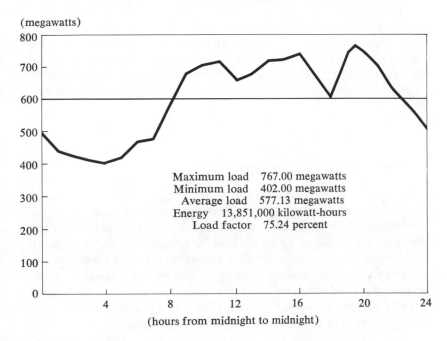

SOURCE: Charted from data supplied by the Metropolitan Electricity Authority, Bangkok

and 6:30 P.M., is large and that nearly 80 percent of the peak demand
occurs at 7:00 P.M. Much of this is due to the business and industrial
loads of MEA, whose peak demand period spans the period from
roughly 9:00 A.M. to 9:00 P.M. (see Figure 3.6). MEA's industrial and
business loads have, in addition, grown faster than other loads. PEA,
in contrast, has a marked evening peak and this is presumably creating the evening peak on EGAT's system. However, the business
demands on PEA's system are also growing rapidly and it is possible
that PEA's load factor will improve as a result.

It is possible, therefore, that EGAT's peak demand period eventually will become more prolonged. If this becomes the case, it would
be desirable for EGAT to anticipate it and reflect it in its tariffs. If,
then, the peak demand period eventually spanned thirteen hours
each day (say, from 8:30 A.M. to 9:30 P.M.), twenty-six days a
month, the appropriate charges to MEA, PEA, and the industrial con-

43

sumers would eventually become: an off-peak charge (9:30 P.M. to 8:30 A.M. the next day) = Bht 0.33 a kilowatt-hour; and a peak charge (8:30 A.M. to 9:30 P.M.) = $0.33 + 74.7/(13 \cdot 26)$ = Bht 0.55 a kilowatt-hour.

Such a shift in tariffs from that presently recommended (with a peak period charge applied between 6:30 P.M. and 9:30 P.M.) would depend, of course, on how the daily demands on EGAT's system developed. The point is that tariff policy, like investment policy, needs to be flexible, and needs to be responsive to changing situations.

MEA's Costs and Tariffs

The Metropolitan Electricity Authority (MEA), which serves the Bangkok metropolitan area, accounts for nearly 70 percent of the electricity demand in Thailand, and 70 percent of EGAT's sales. In 1972, MEA served nearly 400,000 consumers with a maximum demand of 640 megawatts and sales of 3,500 gigawatt-hours. The demand from residential, business, and industrial users has been rising rapidly for many years. Between 1968 and 1972, for instance, the level and growth of energy demands were as follows:

Growth indicators	Level in 1972	Average yearly growth rate (percentage)
Number of consumers	396,543	8
Total energy sales in		
gigawatt-hours	3,500	19
Households	623	16
Business and industry	2,849	20
Street lighting	28	19

Energy is purchased in bulk from EGAT at four substations. Subtransmission lines of 69 and 115 kilovolts link these substations to distribution substations and networks of 12 and 24 kilovolts. A number of large industrial consumers take power directly off the subtransmission system; medium-size industry and business demands are supplied at 12 or 24 kilovolts; small businesses, street lighting, and households are supplied at 220/440 volts.

MEA needs to maintain a large and rapidly expanding program of network reinforcements and extensions. Demand in the Bangkok area is expected to double over a five-year period; in anticipation of such expansion, substation capacity is typically 40 percent above the megawatt demand.

TABLE 3.5. ENERGY AND POWER DEMAND INCREASES BY VOLTAGE LEVEL ON MEA'S SYSTEM

Customers, by voltage	1973 sales (million watt-hours)	1976 sales (million watt-hours)	Increase in daily sales (million watt-hours)	Kilowatts at peak daily (kilowatt-hour)	Demand increase (megawatts)	Peak loss factor	Cumulative loss factor	Increase in EGAT demand (megawatts)
69/115 kilovolts								
Industrial	598,150	908,950	852	.05	43	1.02	1.020	44
12/24 kilovolts								
Industrial	1,110,850	1,688,050	1,581	.05	79	1.02	1.040	82
Business	507,930	845,010	923	.058	54		1.040	56
Low voltage								
Business	1,185,170	1,971,690	2,155	.058	125	1.08	1.123	140
Households	705,900	1,014,300	845	.085	72		1.123	81
Street lighting	34,000	46,000	33	.1	3		1.123	4
Total	4,142,000	6,474,000	6,389					407

SOURCE: Based on information supplied by the Metropolitan Electricity Authority, Thailand.

Marginal capacity costs

Marginal distribution and subtransmission costs can be estimated by relating proposed expenditure on system reinforcement and expansion to the expected growth in the load met by the system.

MEA's maximum demand to be met by EGAT was forecast to grow by 407 megawatts between 1973 and 1976. This figure is at the bottom right of Table 3.5, which shows how it is related to the growth in energy sales to different consumer classes at different voltage levels. The increase in demand by each consumer class during the system's peak period is obtained by multiplying the growth in average daily energy consumption by a ratio: *demand at the time of the system's peak* divided by *daily energy consumption*.[3] This increase in demand is then multiplied by the relevant cumulative loss factor to obtain the equivalent increase in demand to be met by EGAT. The loss factor reflects average, not marginal, losses at the time of the system's peak. (Average losses at time of the system's peak are relevant because capacity is growing along with demand; marginal losses arise when demand served by a given capacity increases.)

The increase in demand served by the low voltage system is $125 + 72 + 3 = 200$ megawatts. Multiplying this by the low voltage peak loss factor of 1.08 and adding the increase in demand at the time of peak of 12/24-kilovolt customers of $79 + 54 = 133$ megawatts gives the increase in peak demand on the primary system of $(200 \cdot 1.08) + 133 = 349$ megawatts. Multiplying this by the primary system's peak loss factor of 1.02 and adding the increase in the demand at the peak of high voltage customers of 43 megawatts gives the increase in peak demand on the 230/115/69 kilovolt system of $(349 \cdot 1.02) + 43 = 399$ megawatts. This, in turn, when multiplied by the high voltage system loss factor of 1.02 gives an increase in demand to be met by EGAT of 407 megawatts.

Table 3.6 shows the proposed capital expenditure at each voltage level. These figures and the demand increases just calculated as shown in Table 3.7, were used to calculate incremental capital cost for each kilowatt at each voltage level. This is converted to an annual cost at 11 percent annuity, and annual maintenance costs are added to obtain marginal annual capacity cost for each kilowatt at each voltage level.

A kilowatt addition to peak demand from high voltage customers

---

3. In practice it is desirable to obtain estimates of the demands by different consumer categories at the time of the system's peak by load research into coincidence and load factors. In the absence of this information, we have simply made a rough guess at the ratio.

TABLE 3.6. CAPITAL EXPENDITURE PROJECTIONS BY VOLTAGE
LEVEL ON MEA's SYSTEM
(millions of bahts)

Distribution units, by voltage	Projections for year			
	1974	1975	1976	Total
230-kilovolt substations	—	—	35.22	
230-kilovolt cables	—	—	66.36	
69/115-kilovolt lines	21.35	37.62	47.42	
Total high voltage				207.97
69/115-kilovolt substations	97.29	74.04	74.52	
12/24-kilovolt lines	31.62	60.02	65.52	
Capacitors	2.04	1.95	1.91	
Total				408.91
Distribution transformers	69.95	80.46	83.91	
Low voltage lines	31.33	39.40	43.06	
Total low voltage				348.11

SOURCE: Based on information supplied by the Metropolitan Electricity Authority, Thailand.

thus costs an extra $1.02 \cdot 88 = $ Bht 90 a year. A kilowatt addition
to peak demand from 12/24 kilovolt customers then costs $164 + (1.02 \cdot 90) = $ Bht 256 a year. A kilowatt addition to peak demand
from low voltage customers therefore costs $239 + (1.08 \cdot 256) = $ Bht
515 a year. Dividing these figures by 12 gives MEA's monthly marginal
capacity for each kilowatt of consumer demand at the system's peak

TABLE 3.7. MARGINAL COSTS OF CAPACITY AND INCREASE IN
DEMAND, MEA DISTRIBUTION NETWORKS

Cost components and demand increase	System voltage level		
	High voltage	12/24 kilovolts	Low voltage
Capital expenditure (millions of bahts)	207.97	408.908	348.114
Demand increase (megawatts)	399	349	200
Marginal capital cost per kilowatt (bahts)	526	1,172	1,741
Annual equivalent at 11 percent annuity (bahts)	58	129	192
Maintenance cost per kilowatt (bahts)	30	35	47
Marginal annual cost per kilowatt (bahts)	88	164	239

SOURCE: Based on information supplied by the Metropolitan Electricity Authority, Thailand.

(*not* for each kilowatt of consumer's own maximum demand, unless it coincides with the system's peak) as: Bht 7.5 for high voltage consumers; Bht 21.3 for 12/24 kilovolt consumers; and Bht 42.9 for low voltage consumers.

It might be thought that these costs should be multiplied by a ratio of demand at the time of peak to own maximum demand in order to obtain the marginal cost with respect to a consumer's own maximum demand. This procedure would be very misleading, however. The marginal costs that have been calculated show the effect on MEA's costs of an increase in demand at the time of peak, for it is this demand which is responsible for sizing MEA's system. An increase in the maximum demand of a consumer whose maximum demand does *not* coincide with system peak will usually require no increase in system capacity and will thus involve only extra energy cost. The only exception to this arises in, for example, an industrial area, where the local distribution system is sized to meet a local peak demand that does not coincide with system peak. In such a case local marginal costs of distribution capacity relate to a consumer's contribution to the peak demand on the local distribution system; and upstream marginal costs of distribution capacity relate to his contribution to the system's peak. This situation would require a slightly more complicated analysis than that presented here.

Apart from this complication, however, it should be clear that the amount of a customer's own maximum demand is of little relevance to system costs. The fact that it is simpler to meter his maximum demand than to record his demand at the time of the system's peak should not obscure this principle.

Total marginal costs of supply

The figures for MEA discussed in the previous section need to be added to EGAT's bulk supply costs to obtain MEA's total marginal costs of supply at peak and off-peak. Total marginal costs of capacity are reflected in the figures in Table 3.8.

TABLE 3.8. TOTAL MARGINAL COSTS OF CAPACITY
(bahts per kilowatt per month)

Customer	Bulk supply	+ Distribution	= Total
High voltage	$74.7 \cdot 1.02$	+ 7.5	= 83.7
12/24-kilovolts	$74.7 \cdot 1.02 \cdot 1.02$	+ 21.3	= 99.0
Low voltage	$74.7 \cdot 1.02 \cdot 1.02 \cdot 1.08$	+ 42.9	= 126.8

SOURCE: Based on calculations discussed in the previous section, "MEA's marginal capacity costs."

TABLE 3.9. MARGINAL PEAK KILOWATT-HOUR COST
(bahts per kilowatt-hour)

Customer	EGAT's kilowatt-hour charge · losses	Total
High voltage	0.33 · 1.02	≈0.34
12/24-kilovolts	0.33 · 1.02 · 1.02	≈0.34
Low voltage	0.33 · 1.02 · 1.02 · 1.08	≈0.37

SOURCE: Based on calculations discussed in the previous section, "MEA's marginal capacity costs."

The marginal kilowatt-hour costs vary between peak and off-peak as a result of differing losses between those periods. We do not, however, have the loss data to make this calculation; in practice, marginal off-peak kilowatt-hour costs will be slightly lower than the estimates of marginal peak kilowatt-hour costs shown in Table 3.9. (In practice, as long as EGAT's marginal cost of energy remains the same at peak and off-peak, it is probably not worth making the distinction between peak and off-peak kilowatt-hour costs.)

Tariffs

The Metropolitan Electricity Authority employs various tariffs or rate schedules according to the class of customer served. Some of these rates are complicated and seem to serve no useful purpose; changing them to reflect marginal costs would both simplify them and have economic merits.

Complicated tariffs for large consumers. A "Medium Business Service" tariff applies to consumers with a maximum demand between 30 and 500 kilowatts and a "Large Business Service" tariff applies to those taking more than 500 kilowatts, with a "Large Business Off-Peak Service" tariff available as an option. Table 3.10 compares the capacity (kilowatt) components of these tariffs with our estimates of marginal costs of capacity.

It is evident that, since the marginal cost of kilowatts supplied outside the peak hours is practically zero, the only rate which is anywhere near to reflecting marginal cost is the on-peak kilowatt charge in the Large Business Off-Peak Service tariff. Other customers appear to pay between Bht 26 and Bht 38 for a kilowatt addition to their own maximum demand, while the marginal cost to MEA is Bht 83.7 to Bht 99.0 or zero depending upon whether their maximum demand occurs during the peak period or not.

Now consider the kilowatt-hour components of the tariffs. In the Large Business Off-Peak Service tariff, all kilowatt-hours are

TABLE 3.10. COMPARISON BETWEEN MARGINAL KILOWATT CHARGES AND COSTS

Maximum demand (kilowatt)	Charge (bahts) per kilowatt of own maximum demand		Marginal cost (bahts) per kilowatt at peak	
	12/24-kilovolts	69-kilovolts	12/24-kilovolts	69-kilovolts
First 50	38	36		
Next 150	34	32		
Next 300	28	26	99.0	83.7
500 to 1,000	34	29		
Over 1,000	29 or 29 off-peak 85 on-peak	25 or 29 off-peak 85 on-peak		

SOURCE: Tariff data supplied by the Metropolitan Electricity Authority, Thailand.

charged Bht 0.34 at 12/24 kilovolt and Bht 0.33 at 69 kilovolt. Otherwise, the rates are all in kilowatt-related declining blocks, ranging between Bht 0.51 to Bht 0.37 a kilowatt-hour irrespective of voltage for medium business consumers and Bht 0.44 to Bht 0.36 for large business consumers. If our estimated marginal energy cost of Bht 0.34 is correct, these are on the high side for the lower load factor consumers. More important, however, declining block rates make the marginal costs of electricity to the consumers differ from one consumer to another when the marginal costs to MEA of supplying them is the same.

Declining block rates have been traditionally justified in terms of elaborate and arbitrary allocation procedures for analyzing accounting cost. In the light of the much more relevant analysis of marginal cost they now can be seen to serve no useful purpose, *except* that a high charge on a small first block is an acceptable alternative to a fixed monthly charge as a way of recovering customer costs (though the size of the first block should not be related to billing demand).

Declining block rates involve not only differences in the cost of an extra kilowatt-hour to different consumers. They also produce curious anomalies in the cost to consumers of an extra kilowatt when, as in Thailand, the kilowatt-hour blocks are kilowatt-related. Thus, consider the Large Business Service tariff for 69-kilovolt consumers:

Demand	Charge
First 1,000 kilowatts of billing demand (bahts per kilowatt)	29.00
Excess kilowatts of billing demand (bahts per kilowatt)	25.00
First 200 kilowatt-hours per kilowatt (bahts)	0.44
Next 280 kilowatt-hours per kilowatt (bahts)	0.39
Excess kilowatt-hours (bahts)	0.36

The total monthly bill of a consumer with a billing demand of 5,000 kilowatts and monthly energy consumption of 2,500,000 kilowatt-hours will be: $(1,000 \cdot 29) + (4,000 \cdot 25) + (1,000,000 \cdot 0.44) + (1,400,000 \cdot 0.39) + (100,000 \cdot 0.36)$, that is, Bht 1,151,000.

Now suppose that this consumer raises his maximum demand by 1 kilowatt and his energy demand by 1 kilowatt-hour. His monthly bill then becomes: $(1,000 \cdot 29) + (4,001 \cdot 25) + (1,000,200 \cdot 0.44) + (1,400,280 \cdot 0.39) + (99,521 \cdot 0.36)$, or Bht 1,151,049.7. This is an increase of Bht 49.7. Thus the extra cost to this customer of the extra kilowatt-hour during his hour of peak demand is higher than might appear at first sight.

Though the capacity charge is higher than a superficial glance at the tariffs may suggest, it still has two basic defects—it is too low, and it is related to the demand at system peak, not at the consumer's own peak. Marginal capacity cost at 69 kilovolts is, to repeat, Bht 83.7 at times of system peak and zero at other times.

In addition, it is probable that consumers think that extra kilowatts cost only Bht 25 or Bht 29; in that case, any incentive effects of kilowatt-related declining block rates do not exist and the rates seem to lack purpose.

Summing up, we first showed that kilowatts at the time of the system's peak are grossly underpriced and at other times are grossly overpriced. This can only result in an unnecessary strain on the economy by encouraging overexpansion and making it provide extra resources in the shape of extra generation, transmission, and distribution capacity the extra worth of which to consumers is less than the extra cost. Second, we showed that the kilowatt-hour charge is very complicated, without serving any useful purpose. We can now discuss a tariff that would remedy these defects and would also be much simpler to understand and administer.

Suggested tariffs for large consumers. It seems to us that the tariffs for the large consumers need to have, at most, only three components:[4] (a) A basic charge for energy costs, of roughly Bht 0.34 a kilowatt-hour if our cost data are right, would be the first component. (b) The next component would be a kilowatt charge to reflect EGAT's capacity charge for bulk supply, with an allowance for losses, to be applied to maximum demand during EGAT's peak period of 6:30 P.M. to 9:30 P.M. This would be in principle: 74.7 · 1.02 = Bht 76.2 a kilowatt at 69 kilovolts; 74.7 · 1.02 · 1.02 = Bht 77.7 a kilowatt at 12/24 kilovolts; though in practice the distinction between the two would hardly be worth making. (c) The last component would be a kilowatt charge to reflect MEA's capacity cost of distribution to be applied to maximum demand during MEA's thirteen-hour peak period between 8:30 A.M. and 9:30 P.M.: Bht 7.5 a kilowatt at 69 kilovolts, and Bht 21.3 a kilowatt at 12/24 kilovolts.

If, indeed, the peak demand periods of MEA and EGAT were coincident and of equal duration, the last two items could be grouped into one, and a *single* kilowatt-hour and a *single* kilowatt charge would prevail. However, as Figures 3.2 and 3.4 show, MEA's peak demand period is more prolonged.

An alternative to this tariff policy—in our opinion a much better alternative—would be to retain the three components but to spread capacity costs over kilowatt-hours consumed during peak. The reason why this is better is that consumers understand kilowatt-hour charges better than maximum kilowatt demand charges. Also, high

4. Cost data used here correspond to those summarized in Tables 3.8 and 3.9.

kilowatt-hour charges provide a more persistent incentive for consumers to economize during peak periods than do maximum kilowatt charges. This alternative tariff would break down as follows: (a) During off-peak hours, a basic Bht 0.34 a kilowatt-hour would be charged to reflect energy cost. (b) During MEA's thirteen peak hours on twenty-six days a month, this charge would be raised to reflect distribution capacity cost as follows: $0.34 + [7.5/(13 \cdot 26)] =$ Bht 0.36 a kilowatt-hour at 69 kilovolts; $0.34 + [21.3/(13 \cdot 26)] =$ Bht 0.40 a kilowatt-hour at 12/24 kilovolts. But during EGAT's three peak hours the charge would be raised further to reflect the capacity cost of bulk supply, with an allowance for losses: $0.36 + [76.2/(3 \cdot 26)] =$ Bht 1.34 a kilowatt-hour at 69 kilovolts; $0.40 + [77.7/(3 \cdot 26)] =$ Bht 1.40 a kilowatt-hour at 12/24 kilovolts. In sum, the charge—in bahts a kilowatt-hour—would differ by voltage level and time of day as follows:

	Charge	
Time	*High voltage*	*12/24 kilovolts*
Off-peak	0.34	0.34
8:30 A.M. to 6:30 P.M.	0.36	0.40
6:30 P.M. to 9:30 P.M.	1.34	1.40

Since the off-peak and the 8:30 A.M. to 6:30 P.M. rates are roughly equal, it may not be worth making a distinction between them; the tariff could, if desired, be simplified into a double time-of-day tariff. This simplification would save metering costs.

For the high voltage consumers, MEA already has the metering capability to apply either of the tariff alternatives discussed above. The consumers' kilowatt demands are recorded digitally each half or quarter hour. Similar metering could be installed for the larger 12 and 24 kilovolt consumers. Alternatively, triple or double register kilowatt-hour metering could be installed.

The cost of recording meters for such tariffs is acceptable for larger consumers. For smaller consumers, who number around 3,000, a simpler alternative would be preferable, because of both the cost of meters and the problem of meter maintenance. One immediately apparent alternative, instead of measuring both kilowatt-hours and kilowatts on separate meters, or on a combined meter, is to measure only kilowatt-hours on time-of-day, two-register kilowatt-hour meters. These can be provided with a spring reserve so that power failures do not upset their timing. They would register kilowatt-hour consumption separately during off-peak and potential peak hours.

Finally, for the smaller 12/24 kilovolt consumers it might prove costly to have the peak hour recording automatically switch off during Sundays and holidays. The thing to do is to apply the peak or off-peak charges on all days for these consumers, perhaps with a slightly lowered peak kilowatt-hour rate for them.

Household and small business tariffs. While many of the arguments elaborated above apply to low voltage consumers, a crucial point of difference is that most of these use so little electricity that anything more complicated than a simple kilowatt-hour meter would be a waste of money. A two-rate time-of-day tariff might be suitable for some of the larger residential and small business consumers; it could, for instance, be made available as an option as in the United Kingdom. But, for the bulk of consumers in these classes, a kilowatt-hour rate plus either a high-rate first block, as at present, or a fixed charge in order to cover customer costs is all that is practicable.

Our estimate of costs is Bht 126.7 a kilowatt during peak plus Bht 0.37 a kilowatt-hour. The figures given earlier for kilowatts at peak for each daily kilowatt-hour (see Table 3.5) are .058 for business and .085 for residential. Using these figures and taking 30.5 days to the month, we can calculate an average marginal cost as: $126.7 \cdot (.058/30.5) + 0.37 = $ Bht 0.61 for business consumers and $126.7 \cdot (.085/30.5) + 0.37 = $ Bht 0.72 for residential consumers.

The ratios of 0.058 and 0.085 are, it should be stressed, unreliable; this last calculation has been included only to illustrate a method. The results are not good enough to be compared with the actual tariffs. At present there are no reliable measurements of daily load curves for different classes of small consumers so that the contribution of each to the system's peak can be ascertained. However, a few qualitative remarks can be made.

The case in principle still exists for setting a tariff which cannot, by its nature, reflect the *structure* of marginal cost such that its level reflects the *level* of marginal cost. However, other considerations—such as income distribution—can be relevant, too, and the current coexistence of rising block rates for residential consumers and declining block rates for small business consumers suggests that this is the case in Thailand. Hence, our suggestions in this area are two: (a) Using the results of load research, the average level of marginal costs should be calculated in the manner suggested above. (b) This average, and information about customer costs, should be used when deciding on kilowatt-hour tariffs that reflect costs, even though upward or downward adjustments or the introduction of blocks may be justified on political or social grounds. These suggestions only apply to simple kilowatt-hour tariffs for small consumers. For larger, low voltage consumers, the provision of a time-of-day tariff as an optional alternative is worth consideration.

PEA's Costs and Tariffs

The Provincial Electricity Authority is responsible for providing electricity supply in the provincial towns and rural areas of Thailand (that is to say, all areas except the Bangkok area). Part of the electricity is supplied from PEA's own diesel generating plants; but most of it (nearly 90 percent) is purchased at 33, 22, and 11 kilovolts from EGAT's bulk supply substations. In 1972, PEA served over 575,000 customers; sold 1,200 gigawatt-hours, with a maximum demand of 340 megawatts (compared with 640 megawatts for MEA); and accounted for 23 percent of EGAT's sales. The demand on PEA's system has grown rapidly—over tenfold in the last ten years—and from many kinds of consumers, as Table 3.11 shows.

The future investment program of PEA is very large, as can be gauged from the fact that only 17 percent of Thailand's 38 million population has access to electricity service, and most of the 6.5 million who do live in the Bangkok metropolitan area. PEA has the responsibility of greatly extending supplies to areas now without service as well as of increasing network capacities to meet rapidly growing demands in areas already served. Their current investment program has six components: (a) Extension of networks in the EGAT grid area (Bht 108 million in the 1972–76 period); (b) extension and revamping of the electric generation and distribution system supplied by PEA's own powerhouses (Bht 259 million in the 1972–76 period); (c) extension of distribution lines from diesel electric gen-

TABLE 3.11. DEMAND ON THE SYSTEM AND SYSTEM GROWTH RATES, PEA

Customer	Demand (gigawatt-hours)		Annual growth rate (percentage)
	1968	1972	
Households	161	359	22
Small business	61	193	33
General business	77	145	17
Medium business	11	72	60
Large business	44	362	69
Waterworks	8	26	34
Mining	89	39	−19
Agricultural pumps	0.75	0.5	−10
Street lighting	6	11	16
Temporary customers	2	4	19
	460	1,212	27

SOURCE: Information supplied by the Provincial Electricity Authority, Thailand.

TABLE 3.12. PEA's Investment Program

Project type and project area[a]	Distribution Equipment			Network investment[c] (millions of bahts)	Investment for each kilovolt ampere (bahts)
	Kilometers of high voltage lines[b]	Kilometers of low voltage lines	New transformer capacity (kilovolt amperes)		
Extensions in EGAT, grid area					
Prachin Buri	262	148	7,570	38	5,020
Ranong	69	27	3,270	18	5,613
Phrae	222	147	5,420	37	6,827
Pathum Thani	127	42	11,370	15	1,319
Phetchabun	131	62	4,250	23	5,412
Extension and revamping of systems fed by PEA generator					
Chiang Rai	735	249	15,170	97	6,394
Nan	167	69	2,870	40	13,937
Chanthaburi	194	112	10,510	52	4,948
Prachuap	170	54	2,360	32	13,559
Chumphon	220	96	4,100	34	8,293
Small diesel extensions	870	226	6,870	88	12,809
Accelerated rural electrification	10,476	9,000	36,000	1,074	29,833
System reinforcement	480[d]	790	325,280[e]	308[f]	947
Rural electrification in remote areas	—	—	—	22	—

a. See map of PEA project areas.
b. 33, 22, and 11 kilovolts.
c. Investment figures relate to different periods and are not strictly comparable.
d. Includes new lines only; 448 kilometers are also being converted from 11 to 22 kilovolts.
e. New transformers only; 54,760 transformers are being changed from 11 to 22 kilovolts on the primary side.
f. Excluding consumer connections and contingency allowances.
SOURCE: Information supplied by the Provincial Electricity Authority, Thailand.

erators to small electric works (Bht 88 million in the 1972–76 period); (d) a program of "accelerated rural electrification" to extend service from the grid to 3,600 villages (Bht 1,074 million in a five-year period); (e) reinforcement and extension of the existing system to meet load growth (over Bht 300 million over a five-year period); and (f) electrification of small villages in remote areas by small diesel generator sets (Bht 22 million). Some statistics on this program appear in Table 3.12.

Marginal capacity costs

The main feature of the marginal or incremental capacity costs of PEA investments is their high variability between one scheme and another. With very large variations in load density, some areas require substantially more circuit kilometers of line per consumer and per kilowatt demand than others. Also, because of very large variations in loads, the schemes to meet larger loads are cheaper for each kilowatt of capacity and demand on account of large economies of scale in equipment costs. The costs of 22/0.4-kilovolt three-phase transformers, for example, vary as follows:

Rating (kilovolt amperes)	Cost (bahts)	Capacity cost per kilovolt ampere (bahts)
50	68,500	1,370
100	75,100	750
250	112,600	450

Similar, often larger, economies of scale are found in overhead lines. Another reason for the high cost variability among PEA schemes is that some involve mainly reinforcement and others mainly extension, the latter being more expensive. Indivisibilities also account for variability; though these are always significant in distribution, they are more so for small schemes. Other factors, such as different construction standards, equipment, and terrain, also play a part. Accordingly it is necessary to take a separate look at the marginal cost of each of a number of projects.

Selected extension and reinforcement schemes. Table 3.13 summarizes our estimates of the marginal cost for a number of PEA schemes (except those for rural electrification, which are discussed separately). For comparison, our estimates of MEA's marginal costs are also included in the table. The estimates, which are rather approximate, were obtained in the following manner. The marginal cost of a kilowatt increase of peak demand on the high voltage system is the investment in high voltage equipment and lines per kilowatt demand increase on the high voltage system. The marginal cost of a kilowatt increase of peak demand on the low voltage

TABLE 3.13. MARGINAL COST ESTIMATES OF SELECTED PEA EXTENSION AND REINFORCEMENT SCHEMES

Project[a]	Peak kilowatt on high voltage system			Peak kilowatt increase[c]		Investment[a] (millions of baht)			Marginal capacity costs[e] (bahts per kilowatt)	
	Start[b]	End[b]	Increase	High voltage consumers	Low voltage consumers	Total	High voltage system	Low voltage plus transformer	High voltage consumers	Low voltage consumers
Ranong	1,300	2,985	1,685	915	670	18	13	5	7,806	16,205
Phrae	1,656	3,844	2,188	375	1,619	37	23	14	10,512	20,420
Phetchabun	1,233	2,364	1,131	181	848	23	16	7	14,147	24,099
Nan	753	1,386	633	300	297	40	29	11	45,813	88,348
Chanthaburi	2,376	6,772	4,036	1,234	3,305	52	34	18	6,888	13,161
Prachuap	758	2,734	1,616	275	1,197	32	25	7	15,470	23,174
Chumphon	1,483	3,151	1,668	334	1,191	34	24	10	14,388	24,511
System reinforcement	—	—	250,000	70,000	161,600	308	138	170	552[f]	1,670
MEA	—	—							1,172[f]	3,054[g]

a. See map of PEA project areas and Table 3.12.

b. Refers to completion of project, after which reinforcement is required.

c. The actual division between high voltage and low voltage demands is unknown; the estimates above were made by considering the various types of consumer (for example, business, commerce, and residential) expecting to be on PEA's system and regarding the larger ones to be high voltage. Note that demand increases at low voltages have been adjusted for local losses.

d. Some of these figures are 1972 data, others are 1973 and 1974; adjustments have not been made for inflation (see the text).

e. Losses of 12 percent assumed in low voltage system, 4 percent in high voltage system. See text for calculations. Note that the figures are not annuitized.

f. Taking 12 and 24 kilovolt lines only. See Table 3.7.

g. 3.054 = 1,172 multiplied by losses (12 percent) plus the marginal cost of low voltage networks (1,741). See Table 3.7.

SOURCE: Based on information supplied by the Provincial Electricity Authority, Thailand.

system is the marginal cost of high voltage supply, grossed up for low voltage losses, plus investment in low voltage equipment, lines, and transformers per kilowatt increase of low voltage consumer demand. For example, the marginal costs shown in Table 3.13 for projects in the Ranong area were calculated as follows: High voltage marginal cost = Bht 13 million/[915 kilowatts + (1.12 · 670 kilowatts)] = Bht 7,806 per kilovolt. Low voltage marginal cost = 1.12 · 7,806 + (Bht 5 million/670 kilowatts) = Bht 16,205 per kilowatt.

Rural electrification. The rural electrification project in ten provinces is a plan for electrifying 246 villages and supplying them from EGAT substations via 22-kilovolt transmission lines. The plan includes cost and demand projections over a period of twenty years. Leaving aside investment in, for example, offices and vehicles (in order to concentrate on the cost of lines and transformers), and leaving aside investment in service drops and meters (which are customer-related rather than kilowatt-related), we consider only costs of the kilowatt-related line and transformers.

The initial investment, which takes place in years 0 and 1, has a value in year 1, using a 10 percent interest rate, of Bht 48.8 million or Bht 198,528 a village. The growth of the load, from 1,832 kilowatts in year 1 to 14,276 in year 20, would necessitate capital expenditure on reinforcement in every year beginning with year 5. This would consist, at first, entirely of additional transformers but would include additional lines at both primary and secondary voltages from year 15 onward. The discounted cost of all this reinforcement expenditure, calculated at 10 percent, is Bht 96.7 a kilowatt. This can be regarded as a weighted average of the marginal cost of distribution capacity for load growth over the whole twenty years, a cost that is zero up to year 5 and is thereafter positive.

The discounted rate per kilowatt can also be calculated including the initial expenditure on establishing the networks. This calculation gives Bht 954.9 a kilowatt. It is, in other words, the revenue per kilowatt per year that would give a present worth of total revenue equal to the present worth of all costs over the twenty years. It is thus a weighted *average* annual cost per kilowatt.

The discounted unit cost per kilowatt is therefore about ten times higher if the initial investment costs are included, illustrating the extreme lumpiness and large economies of scale of village electrification schemes (Table 3.14).[5]

5. It is, of course, very important that pricing policy does not act against efficient use of installed capacity and growth of demand. See also the discussion of pricing policy in Chapter 7, "Rural Electrification in Developing Countries."

TABLE 3.14. DEMANDS AND COSTS OF RURAL ELECTRIFICATION PROJECTS IN THAILAND

Year	Peak demand[a] (kilowatt)	Capital cost[b] (thousands of bahts)	Present worth of demand[c] (thousands of bahts)	Present worth of costs[c] (thousands of bahts)
0	1,832	40,963.8	1,832	45,060.2
1	2,825	3,777.8	2,568	2,777.8
2	4,342		3,588	
3	4,770		3,584	
4	5,078	106	3,468	72.4
5	5,363	227	3,330	140.9
6	5,676	307	3,204	173.3
7	6,197	431	3,180	231.1
8	6,499	501	3,032	233.7
9	7,044	626	2,987	265.5
10	7,484	663	2,885	255.6
11	8,056	613	2,824	214.9
12	8,723	348	2,779	110.9
13	9,309	469	2,616	135.9
14	10,048	8,275.4	2,646	2,179.2
15	10,769	1,168.5	2,578	279.7
16	11,654	1,316.7	2,536	286.6
17	12,327	2,866.4	2,439	567.1
18	13,462	1,189.2	2,421	213.9
19	14,276	802.7	2,334	144.4
20				
Subtotals			56,831	54,343.1
Total, years 5 to 20				5,505.1

NOTE: Total discounted unit cost = 54,343/56.9 = Bht 954.9 per kilowatt a year. Reinforcement discounted unit cost = 5,505/56.9 = Bh 96.7 per kilowatt a year. Total discounted unit cost for each village is: Bht 198,500 a village plus Bht 96.7 per kilowatt a year.

a. Excluding losses.
b. Excluding vehicles, connections, and overheads.
c. Interest rate of 10 percent taken.

SOURCE: Based on information supplied by the Provincial Electricity Authority, Thailand.

Interpretation of PEA's marginal capacity cost

Table 3.15 summarizes our estimates of marginal distribution capacity costs, expressed on an annual basis with an 11 percent annuity. A number of anomalies in the data can only be partly explained. First, PEA's reinforcement costs of Bht 61 a kilowatt (high voltage) and Bht 184 a kilowatt (low voltage) are lower than those of MEA, even though PEA's figures do include some network extensions and MEA has a higher load density. Reinforcement costs less than extension, however, and one can only presume there is less of the latter in the reinforcement program of PEA. Second, the marginal costs of the schemes for provincial towns seem higher than, even, the discounted unit cost of rural electrification; this is probably because these schemes could take a much greater growth of demand (particularly in the subtransmission networks) than the above estimates assume. Third, the figure of Bht 97 per kilowatt a year for the weighted average marginal cost of reinforcing rural electrification schemes is less than that for urban schemes. However, this statement ignores reinforcements beyond the twentieth year (see Table 3.14) and so ignores, probably, quite a large chunk of subtransmission reinforcement cost beyond then. It is possible though we lack the information to calculate it, that the figure would rise to somewhere midway between the discounted unit cost of Bht 955 a kilowatt and the reinforcement cost of Bht 97 a kilowatt. No doubt

TABLE 3.15. MARGINAL DISTRIBUTION CAPACITY COSTS OF PEA

Project	Final kilowatt demand	Marginal costs (bahts per kilowatt a year)	
		High voltage	Low voltage
Ranong	2,985	858	1,783
Phrae	1,656	1,156	2,246
Phetchabun	1,131	1,556	2,651
Nan	633	5,039	9,722
Chanthaburi	4,936	758	1,448
Prachuap	1,616	1,702	2,549
Chumphon	1,668	1,583	2,696
Reinforcement	(250 megawatt increase)	61	184
Rural electrification:	Total discounted unit cost of Bht 955 per kilowatt a year. Discounted reinforcement cost of Bht 97 per kilowatt a year.		
MEA	(407 megawatt increase)	129	336

SOURCE: Based on information supplied by the Provincial Electricity Authority, Thailand.

some anomalies are explained by the fact that the available data relate to different time periods and are not adjusted for inflation, and that the demands of high voltage and low voltage consumers are not accurately estimated.

Nevertheless, three points emerge very clearly from the above estimates: (a) There is invariably a very large, fixed cost in setting up the networks in an area for the first time. (b) The cost of subsequent network reinforcement and expansion, once the backbone network is completed, is much less. (c) The cost for each kilowatt of initial investment, and for subsequent reinforcements, decline with the size of demand (economies of scale effects, as discussed earlier). As a result, for PEA's smaller schemes and for rural electrification, marginal costs are well below average cost; additionally, marginal costs can be expected to decline over time. These points are revealed very clearly in the data for the seven projects (Ranong, Phrae, Phetchabun, Nan, Chanthaburi, Prachuap, and Chumphon) at the top of Table 3.15. There is a strong negative correlation between marginal costs and demand level. The implications of these points for tariff policy are discussed below, after a short review of PEA's tariffs.

Tariffs

PEA's tariffs in the area supplied from EGAT's bulk supply points are summarized in Table 3.16. A very similar schedule exists for areas supplied from PEA's own powerhouses, except that the levels are higher (reflecting the higher costs of supply in these areas) and there are no medium business and industrial consumers. We concentrate first on the tariffs in the EGAT grid supply area.

The two low voltage tariffs, tariffs A1 and A2 for households and small business respectively, both involve kilowatt-hour blocks. Households taking up to 20 kilowatt-hours a month pay Bht 1.10 a kilowatt-hour, and Bht 1.15 a kilowatt-hour for over 20 kilowatt-hours; the minimum monthly bill is Bht 4. The charges to small businesses decline from Bht 1.10 a kilowatt-hour for 100 kilowatt-hours a month to Bht 0.75 a kilowatt-hour for over 10,000 kilowatt-hours; the minimum monthly bill is Bht 100.

Given the difficulties and costs of metering anything more than kilowatt-hours for small consumers, a difference between the charges for small businesses and households is reasonable, even though they are all supplied at the same voltage level. Extra small business consumption is more likely to be off-peak than residential, and thus to have a lower weighted average marginal cost of supply. Also, a minimum charge is a useful way to recover consumer billing and connection costs—though, perhaps, no better than recovering these "nonmarginal" costs out of slightly raised rates to all consumers.

The justification for the five declining blocks on the small business tariff, however, is less clear. The costs to PEA of supplying extra kilowatt-hours are probably independent of consumption for most small businesses; a flat kilowatt-hour rate would probably be better and simpler for low levels of small business consumption (up to, say, 3,000 kilowatt-hours a month). For larger levels, the costs of time-of-day metering becomes comparatively low, and it would be worth considering this as an alternative to a flat kilowatt-hour rate. For example, a two-dial time-of-day meter should certainly cost no more than Bht 2,000 (say, Bht 20 a month); this works out at less than 0.7 percent of the bill of a consumer taking 3,000 kilowatt-hours a month. Thus the present small business tariff could be simplified into a single flat kilowatt-hour rate for, say, consumers taking less than 3,000 kilowatt-hours per month, with an optional time-of-day tariff for consumers taking more than this amount (the off-peak charges would be lower than the flat rate—say about Bht 0.40, to cover energy costs—and the peak charges much higher).

Historically speaking, one justification for declining blocks is that they are promotional and that increases in the sale of electricity, even at prices *below* the extra costs, are a good thing. Similarly, the special tariffs A6, A7, and A8 for waterworks, mining, and pumping, which are all significantly cheaper than the business and industrial tariffs, have been regarded as promotional.

However, it is questionable if subsidized service to the larger consumer is beneficial. It undermines financial returns and thus makes expansion in other areas more difficult, and it provides too little incentive for consumers to economize on the use of PEA's energy purchases from EGAT and system capacity. Also, special concessions to help small business argues for low *first* blocks (as in the household tariffs), not declining blocks.

PEA has only about 300 high voltage customers, but they account for 60 percent of PEA's kilowatt-hour sales. Apart from a few on a special rate, these customers are on the general business, medium business, and industry tariffs, A3, A4, and A5. They pay a kilowatt charge related to their own maximum demand plus a sum for kilowatt-hours calculated on declining kilowatt-related blocks. These tariffs are similar in structure to those of MEA for high voltage consumers, and have the same defects. First, they are too complicated and provide no useful message to the consumer about the costs of supply at different times. Next, the demand charge needs to be related to the demand at the time of PEA's peak (which coincides with EGAT's peak) rather than the consumer's own peak. Last, the cost to

TABLE 3.16. SUMMARY OF PEA's MONTHLY TARIFFS IN EGAT SUPPLY AREA

Tariff category	Consumption	Basic charge (bahts a kilowatt-hour)	Minimum charge (bahts)
A1, households	(kilowatt-hours)		
	<2	—	4
	2–20	1.10	
	>20	1.15	
A2, small business	≤100	—	100
	101–1,000	0.95	
	1,001–4,000	0.90	
	4,001–10,000	0.85	
	>10,000	0.75	
A3, general business[a]	(kilowatt-hours per kilowatt)		
	≤50	0.60	—
	51–200	0.56	
	201–400	0.50	
	≥400	0.42	
A4, medium business[b]	≤50	0.58	—
	51–200	0.54	
	201–400	0.48	
	≥400	0.40	
A5, industry[c]	≤50	0.56	—
	51–200	0.52	
	201–400	0.46	
	≥400	0.38	

64

(kilowatt-hours)

A6, water works supply service[d]	≤200	—	
	>200	0.70	140
A7, mining industry service[d]	≤1,000	—	
	>1,000	0.65	650
A8, agricultural and public water pumping[d]	100	—	
	100	0.50	50
A9, temporary service[e]	(f)	(f)	—

a. Plus a demand charge of Bht 50 a kilowatt-hour.
b. Plus a demand charge of Bht 48 a kilowatt-hour.
c. Plus a demand charge of Bht 46 a kilowatt-hour.
d. There is a minimum charge convenant on this tariff.
e. For example, annual fairs.
f. A connection charge plus Bht 2.50 a kilowatt-hour for metered service, with options available.
SOURCE: Information supplied by the Provincial Electricity Authority, Thailand.

the consumer of extra kilowatts is, in any case, generally more than the kilowatt demand charge because of the effects of extra kilowatt demand on the kilowatt-hour charges. A time-of-day tariff would be simpler and have beneficial effects all around for PEA, EGAT, and the Thai economy.

A general point about the tariffs is that there are probably too many categories. The distinction, on low voltage tariffs, between households and small businesses is probably worth retaining for reasons discussed above. But the larger consumers on tariffs A3 through to A8 are served at high voltage and, apart from connection cost, which might be dealt with contractually or with a local surcharge, these consumers impose similar kilowatt and kilowatt-hour costs on PEA when they increase demand at any particular time. There is a strong argument, in principle, for grouping all these consumer categories into one "high voltage tariff schedule."

Two categories that merit retention are the special tariff A9, for temporary services, and a separate schedule for consumers supplied from PEA's own powerhouses. The latter, as mentioned earlier, is similar in most respects to the tariffs for consumers supplied from the grid, except levels are generally higher. However, it has the same defects as tariffs A1 to A8, and it could be simplified and improved in similar ways. The only problem that might arise is that time-of-day metering might be unreliable if the system is frequently shut down on account of generator failure. In this case, a two-part tariff might be considered for the larger consumers—a kilowatt charge related to *estimated* demand at time of peak, and a flat kilowatt-hour charge related to the energy costs of diesel generation and losses.

Finally, there is one tariff category that has been abandoned but that, it seems to us, might usefully be reintroduced. This was a pumping tariff under which consumption was not allowed between 5:00 P.M. and 9:00 P.M. The use of a time switch to make the control effective might well be justified; the flat kilowatt-hour rate would be related to the off-peak kilowatt-hour costs.

Suggestions for tariffs

First consider the structure and then the levels of PEA's tariffs.

Tariff structure. The daily peak period on PEA's system in the EGAT grid supply area coincides with that of EGAT, and lasts approximately from 8:30 P.M. to 9:30 P.M. (see Figure 3.7). Increases of demand in this period ultimately determine the capacity requirements of the distribution networks and of EGAT's system. Outside this

FIGURE 3.7. DAILY DEMAND ON THE PROVINCIAL ELECTRICITY AUTHORITY'S SYSTEM AT UDONTHANI SUBSTATION, THAILAND, AUGUST 22, 1974

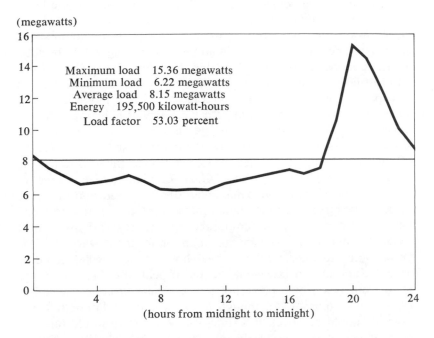

(megawatts)

Maximum load   15.36 megawatts
Minimum load   6.22 megawatts
Average load   8.15 megawatts
Energy   195,500 kilowatt-hours
Load factor   53.03 percent

(hours from midnight to midnight)

SOURCE: Charted from data supplied by the Electricity Generating Authority of Thailand

period, extra kilowatt-hours can be supplied by EGAT at roughly Bht 0.34 a kilowatt-hour. Consequently, there are two marginal cost components to be reflected in the tariff structure, both of which vary with voltage level of service. First is an off-peak marginal cost of about Bht 0.35 a kilowatt-hour for high voltage consumers and Bht 0.40 a kilowatt-hour for low voltage consumers. Second is a peak period cost substantially above this (by a factor of 4 for high voltage and of over 6 for low voltage, at a guess), on account of the extra capacity cost and other kilowatt-related costs of supply. These cost components are roughly the same throughout the year. The capacity cost, and thus the peak period cost, differs remarkably from one region to another as we have shown earlier. But for administrative reasons, and for reasons of acceptability, it is not generally practicable to let tariffs vary correspondingly; some uniformity is obligatory.

A similar cost structure holds for supply from PEA's own powerhouses, except that both peak and off-peak costs are higher, the former on account of higher capacity and maintenance costs, and both on account of the higher energy costs of diesel generation.

Accordingly we believe that a tariff reflecting costs would be as follows for consumption in the EGAT grid area: (a) For households, a flat kilowatt-hour rate (with a low first block if desirable on social grounds). The costs and complications of metering would prohibit anything more complicated than this. Roughly, the rate in bahts a kilowatt-hour would be: 0.40 + (average PEA monthly marginal cost of capacity for each kilowatt)/(average hours in a month). (b) For small businesses on low voltage, a flat kilowatt-hour rate, slightly lower than (a) for those businesses taking less than about 3,000 kilowatt-hours, with a time-of-day option for those taking more, the off-peak rate being about Bht 0.4 a kilowatt-hour, the peak rate being several times higher. (c) For consumers on high voltage, a time-of-day tariff, the off-peak rate being about Bht 0.35 a kilowatt-hour, the peak rate being several times higher [but lower than in (b)]. (d) Special tariffs, as at present, for temporary service. (e) Perhaps a tariff based on interruptible service, as an option for those who would be prepared not to consume during peak hours; a time switch could be used; the appropriate rate would be the off-peak rate. In the area supplied from PEA's own powerhouses, a similar *structure* would in principle be appropriate, though *levels* would be different. However, it should be checked if time-of-day metering would function here; if not, a two part (kilowatt, kilowatt-hour) tariff would be appropriate.

For financial reasons, minimum charges could be retained, or the basic rates could be raised above marginal cost.

Tariff levels. In the tariff suggestions outlined above we have not attempted to indicate appropriate levels of the peak period or capacity charges. Our reason for this, apart from the obvious one that our cost estimates are at best very approximate, is that marginal cost pricing would almost certainly lead to (possibly large) financial deficits for many years. Much of PEA's expansion program involves large initial fixed (and thus high initial average) cost; the cost a kilowatt of subsequent extensions and reinforcements is much less, and continues to decline with growth of demand. The logic of marginal cost pricing is that the growth of demand and the use of capacity should not be held back by high initial charges aimed at quick cost recovery—this is both a waste of investment and contrary to the aims of the program.

However, financial losses would also undermine PEA's ability to extend service. The only way out of the dilemma is either external financial support, or increases in the basic rates where demand is less price elastic, or a combination of both.

Conclusions

There are four main conclusions of this chapter. The first conclusion is one that does not, by itself, require a great deal of new information. It is that the complicated maximum demand tariffs with kilowatt-related kilowatt-hour blocks could both be simplified and altered so that the incentive to customers to keep down their maximum demands is more appropriately timed. As long as the system peak is an evening one, the demand charge (or a high kilowatt-hour rate, which seems easier to understand) should be confined to the evening hours of potential peak.

The fear has been expressed that the reactions of some business and industrial consumers to the new tariff might create a new peak during the daytime. We think it more probable that it would merely slow the growth rate of demand. In time, of course, increases in the air-conditioning and industrial loads may produce a daytime peak on the interconnected system. When this happens, the tariff should reflect it. But realization of that situation is probably a long time off since the extension of the Provincial Electricity Authority (PEA) system is continually adding new consumers whose main demand is in the evening. PEA has a very marked evening peak so that, even though the Metropolitan Electricity Authority's (MEA) daytime demand nearly matches its evening level, the interconnected system has an evening peak of something over two hours and enjoys spare generating capacity the rest of the time. We have in any case suggested that the higher kilowatt-hour charge should apply for three hours a day rather than two, to allow for any possibility that if it were confined to two hours it might create new peaks just before and after the present one.

In the Bangkok metropolitan area served by MEA, and in particular areas of PEA service where most of the load is business and industrial, the peak on the distribution system is a daytime one. This means that, unlike marginal generation capacity costs, marginal distribution capacity costs attach to daytime rather than to evening demands. Hence there are two possibilities. The first recognizes that since (for industrial and business loads on high voltage and megawatt distribution) the marginal generation and transmission capacity costs much exceed the marginal distribution capacity costs, it is better to have a high charge in the evening than in the daytime. There would be a basic kilowatt-hour energy charge for

69

twenty-one hours a day, reflecting only marginal energy cost; and a higher kilowatt-hour charge during the three evening peak hours reflecting the costs of marginal energy, capacity, and capacity maintenance. The second possibility is to reflect marginal costs in more detail at the expense of greater complication. This might be suitable for a number of large consumers and would involve: a low kilowatt-hour energy charge for eleven hours a day, reflecting only marginal energy cost (roughly between the hours of 9:30 P.M. to 8:30 A.M.); a higher kilowatt-hour charge for three evening hours a day, reflecting the sum of marginal energy, marginal capacity, and capacity maintenance cost (roughly between the hours of 6:30 P.M. and 9:30 P.M.); a nominal increase of the basic kilowatt-hour energy charge for ten hours a day to reflect local marginal distribution capacity and capacity maintenance costs (roughly between the hours of 8:30 A.M. and 6:30 P.M.). Where consumers already have their kilowatt demands recorded every quarter or half hour, such a tariff would, of course, involve no extra metering cost.

Our second conclusion is that, in addition to any adjustments required to keep up with general inflation or with the rising price of oil, the charges at the bulk supply points for generation and transmission capacity should be increased. Although they require detailed checking, our figures do appear to show that, quite apart from the defects in their structure discussed above, the *level* of capacity charges lies below marginal capacity costs. (This is an indirect consequence of the rise in oil prices and a faulty tariff structure.) This implies that the tariff of the Electricity Generating Authority of Thailand (EGAT) needs to be increased and that the increase needs to be reflected in PEA's and MEA's tariffs.

This conclusion is founded entirely on considerations of efficient resource allocation. We recognize, however, that to increase the level of tariff would involve various difficulties, while merely to change their structure would be easier. But before examining these difficulties it is worthwhile to examine the resource allocation aspect a little more.

The basic point is that the costs to consumers of more electricity consumed are measured by prices, but the costs to the electricity supply industry are measured by marginal costs. As consumers add to peak load they are, in effect, demanding more generation, transmission, and distribution capacity. They are, in other words, requiring capital expenditure by EGAT and by the distribution authorities. Since electricity is capital intensive, consumers are indeed requiring a great deal of capital expenditure. But as Thailand's capital expenditure on electricity becomes greater, more money must be borrowed from abroad and less can be used as capital expenditure on other development projects. Thus, from a national point of view, a faster growth of the peak entails an increased foreign exchange, interest, and repayment burden and reduced development programs elsewhere.

To make consumers pay the full marginal cost of capacity is to make them implicitly take into account in their private decisions the impact of these decisions upon the rest of the economy. The argument is not that the peak should not grow; it is merely that it should only grow to the extent that, through the tariff, consumers take into account the full consequences for the economy of their additions to peak demand. A tariff that reflects marginal cost and that consumers can understand serves as a signal and as an incentive that enables them to take these consequences into account. A tariff that fails to do this—either because consumers do not understand it, or because it fails to charge peak demand, or because it is too low—will result in excessively rapid growth of electricity consumption at the expense of a foreign exchange burden and ultimately the sacrifice or postponement of alternative development projects.

In calculating the costs of system expansion we have used figures which include taxes. In a sense, then, the figures overestimate marginal costs, both of energy and of capacity, since the tax element represents a financial transfer to government rather than a use of real resources. On the other hand, the fact that many imports are taxed means that the ratio of Thai prices to foreign prices is generally higher than the exchange rate indicates. It is only if import taxes on capital equipment for electricity supply are higher than import taxes on other things that their relative prices falsify their relative costs. We have had neither the time nor the opportunity to study such matters, which involve the working of the whole Thai economy, not just the electricity sector.

If electricity charges were raised to reflect the current level of marginal costs, we would expect EGAT to make large profits. One reason is that the marginal cost of energy is an oil cost, while much of the energy comes from hydro-electric plants. The other reason is that the marginal cost of new oil capacity is higher than the average accounting cost of existing capacity that was acquired at a lower price level. A resultant dilemma is that the price increase which is desirable to avoid excessive foreign exchange burdens and an undue concentration of capital investment in electricity would create immediate unpopularity and discontent. The resource allocation benefits to Thailand would be realized at the expense of an unwelcome financial impact on consumers (though they stand to gain in other ways).

We suggest that this dilemma should not be considered just in terms of the electricity industry but in terms of the public sector as a whole. From this point of view, an increase in the revenue of one part of that sector, the electricity part, can be offset by a decrease in revenue in another part. Some other charges or some taxes could be lowered to offset the increased revenue from EGAT's sales; alternatively the financial gains could be used to finance other projects. Hence the problem is whether the tariff changes for electricity could form part of a wider package. The package as a whole would *not* make people financially worse off but it would improve resource allocation.

Once again, therefore, the consideration of electricity pricing brings in wider issues which we have not been able to examine. As far as the level, as distinct from the structure, of tariffs is concerned, we have to leave the problem open.

Our third conclusion is that, while improved pricing should give EGAT a large profit, we should not expect the same for MEA and PEA. Regarding MEA, increased (and restructured) bulk supply tariffs should be suitably passed on to consumers, leaving MEA's financial returns virtually unchanged. As for PEA, though EGAT's tariffs at the bulk supply points need to be increased (and restructured), there is a strong case for providing PEA with financial assistance; PEA should not be expected to be financially profitable for some time. The reason is that PEA is continually engaged in extending the area of electricity suppply. This involves large initial capital expenditure and low initial revenue on each new extension scheme so that, even when, examining a long future time period, the extensions pay for themselves in discounted cash flow terms, annual revenues will initially fall short of annual accounting costs. To set prices to give good initial financial returns would act against the interest of (a) promoting the new investments, (b) a fuller and more efficient use of them, and (c) to some extent, the social aims of PEA's program. Only in areas more fully electrified by PEA, and where the demand has developed, should financial returns be expected to be normal. (One possibility is for increased EGAT revenues as a source of financial support for PEA.)

Our fourth and last conclusion relates to inflation. It seems that many of the costs with which we have worked, and also the present tariffs of the three authorities, have not felt the full impact of recent inflation. A common reaction of public enterprises to inflation is to keep tariffs down even at the expense of financial performance. Such a policy, it seems to us, only makes the position of public enterprises worse: it undermines their ability to finance and undertake their programs. Low tariffs also encourage yet faster rates of expansion, thus wasting capital and energy resources and exacerbating financial difficulties. Moreover, unless power cuts and brownouts are preferred, the expanding programs would have to be met increasingly out of the public revenue, thus entailing a direct sacrifice of projects in sectors that for many reasons need more public support than electricity. To reduce the adverse consequences of inflation, it seems to us, therefore, that tariffs need to be increased in line with cost.

CHAPTER 4

Electricity Tariffs in Tunisia

In the early 1970s, the Société Tunisienne de l'Electricité et du Gaz (STEG) simplified a morass of tariffs inherited from the seven private companies that it superseded in 1962. By 1972 STEG had established some eighteen tariffs that were both simpler than the old ones and fixed at levels that produce a comfortable financial result. However, STEG has initiated a tariff study to achieve further simplification and to achieve an approximation to marginal cost pricing. This study has been undertaken in the Direction des Etudes Economiques within STEG, with the help of training and advice from Electricité de France.

This chapter surveys the progress that has been made so far and comments on some of the problems that have arisen.[1]

STEG's Marginal Cost Structure

STEG's present system is predominantly thermal, comprising 150 megawatts of steam plant in Tunis, 42 megawatts of small gas turbine and diesel units variously located, and 32 megawatts of hydro plant. The system is interconnected by a 150-kilovolt transmission ring with secondary high voltage branches of 90-kilovolt.

System expansion and system demand

System expansion for several years ahead will be based on a mixture of gas turbines and conventional steam plant (oil, gas, or dual-fired); it will use gas currently being flared at the El Borma oil field, imported oil and, possibly, some domestic oil. Figure 4.1 shows

---

1. Chapter 4 was prepared during a visit to Tunisia in October 1972.

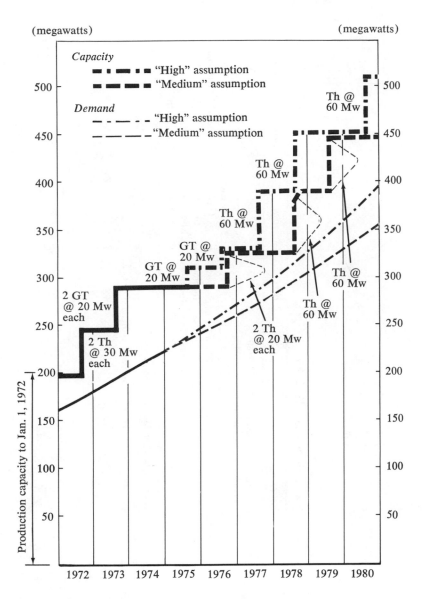

FIGURE 4.1. ACTUAL AND EXPECTED GROWTH OF IN-
STALLED CAPACITY ON TUNISIA'S POWER SYSTEM

SOURCE: Société Tunisienne de l'Electricité et du Gaz

TABLE 4.1. STEG's PLANT PROGRAM, 1972–80

Plant characteristics	1972	1973	. . .	1976	. . .	1978	1979
Maximum demand (megawatts)	180	200		260		305	330
Installed capacity (megawatts)	245	290		230		390	450
New capacity (megawatts)	2 at 30 each	45		2 at 20 each		60	60
Type	Thermal[a]	Gas turbines[b]		Gas turbines		Thermal	Thermal
Location	Rhennouch	Rhennouch		Rhennouch or Sfax		Goulette or Rhennouch	Goulette or Rhennouch

a. Dual-fired, to use either gas from the El Borma field or imported oil.
b. To use gas currently being flared at El Borma.
SOURCE: Based on data provided by the Société Tunisienne de l'Electricité et du Gaz.

TABLE 4.2. ENERGY DEMAND ON STEG's SYSTEM

		Consumption			
		1970		1976[a]	
Voltage level	Consumers (1970)	gigawatt-hours	per-centage	gigawatt-hours	per-centage
Medium	1,246	399	69	690	71
Low	283,000	178	31	280	29
Totals	284,246	577	100	970	100

a. Forecast.
SOURCE: Based on data provided by the Société Tunisienne de l'Electricité et du Gaz.

STEG's firm plans up to 1975 and provisional plans for the 1975–80 period. The plant program, based on the medium forecast, is shown in Table 4.1. Continuing extensions and reinforcements of the 150-kilovolt and 90-kilovolt transmission systems are also planned to provide interconnection and to feed the large markets in Tunis and the east.

A recent study by STEG found that about 70 percent of energy demand came from medium voltage consumers. Figures from this study are shown in Table 4.2. The three largest medium voltage loads are the extractive industries (15 percent of the total), construction industries (12 percent), and tourism (10 percent), all of which are growing at roughly equal rates.

The daily demand curves show weekday peaks that are comparable throughout the year. (See Figure 4.2, the "contour map" of the levels of all Wednesdays' demand curves for 1971.) During the summer months, when the weekday peaks are slightly lower, planned maintenance reduces available capacity commensurately. The result is that the period when demand approaches, or, with a low probability, may even exceed, available capacity includes four hours in practically all weekdays throughout the year. The system's peak thus occupies 1,250 hours a year, compared with only about 500 hours in climates with big seasonal variations in demand.

Marginal costs

The estimation of marginal costs has been undertaken within STEG. Periodic discussions have been held with Electricité de France (EDF) and the approach is apparently similar to that used by

FIGURE 4.2. "CONTOUR MAP" OF ELECTRICITY LOAD DEMAND IN TUNISIA, 1971 (THOUSAND-KILOWATT CONTOUR LINES, DRAWN FROM LOAD CURVES FOR EVERY WEDNESDAY IN THE YEAR)

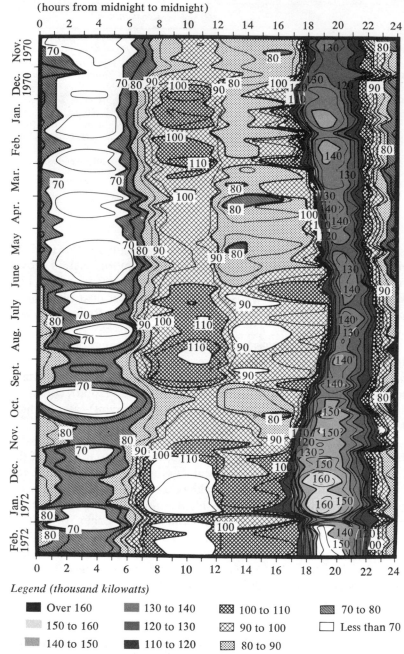

(hours from midnight to midnight)

Legend (thousand kilowatts)

■ Over 160	130 to 140	▨ 100 to 110	▨ 70 to 80
150 to 160	■ 120 to 130	▨ 90 to 100	☐ Less than 70
140 to 150	■ 110 to 120	▨ 80 to 90	

SOURCE: Société Tunisienne de l'Electricité et du Gaz

78

Table 4.3. Marginal Capacity Costs of STEG

Item	Cost for each kilowatt (dinars)	Cost for each peak kilowatt-hour (millimes)[a]
Generation:		
New power stations	18.90	
Coûts d'exploitation[b]	1.20	
Fuel savings due to new stations	−8.00	
Subtotal: generation costs	12.10	
Including allowance for reserve capacity[c]	14.52	
High voltage transmission:[d]		
Extension and reinforcement	6.12	
Coûts d'exploitation[b]	0.08	
Transmission losses[e]	0.51	
Running total: marginal costs at high voltage terminals	21.23	
High voltage/medium voltage substations:		
Extension and reinforcement	3.21	
Coûts d'exploitation[b]	0.54	
Substation losses[f]	0.38	
Running total: marginal costs at substation outlets	25.36	
Medium voltage network[g]		
Extension and reinforcement	11.30	
Coûts d'exploitation[b,h]	0.20	
Medium voltage losses[i]	1.52	
Total marginal costs to medium voltage consumers[j]	38.38	30.70
Low voltage network[k]		
Extension and reinforcement	—[l]	22.70
Coûts d'exploitation[b,h]	—[l]	0.80
Low voltage losses[m]	—[l]	1.84
Total marginal costs to low voltage consumers[j]	70.00[n]	56.04

a. 1,000 millimes = 1 dinar.
b. For example, administration and maintenance.
c. 20 percent, or 1.2 · 12.10.
d. Average for 150 and 90 kilovolts.
e. 3.5 percent, or 0.035 · 14.52.
f. 1.8 percent, or 0.018 · 21.23.
g. Including transformation at medium voltages.
h. STEG's information is incomplete; these are thought to be mainly a fixed nonmarginal overhead (see text following reference to Table 4.3).
i. 6 percent, or 0.06 · 25.36.
j. Not including connection costs.
k. Including transformation at low voltages.
l. Information not sufficient to estimate marginal capacity costs per kilowatt, the kilowatt capacity being unknown. Kilowatt-hour marginal cost data were obtained by dividing investment in the low voltage networks over a period by increases in low voltage peak kilowatt-hour sales over the same period.
m. 6 percent, or 0.06 · 30.7.
n. A rough estimate.
SOURCE: Based on data supplied by the Société Tunisienne de l'Electricité et du Gaz.

TABLE 4.4. MARGINAL ENERGY COSTS OF STEG
(millimes per kilowatt-hour)

Categories of cost	Peak	Day[a]	Night
Generator terminals	7.62	3.38	3.16
Medium voltage supply points	9.09	3.84	3.55
Low voltage supply points	9.64	4.07	3.76

a. Off-peak day hours.
SOURCE: Based on data supplied by the Société Tunisienne de l'Electricité et du Gaz.

EDF in computing what came to be known as the *tarif vert*.[2]. We first summarize the results and then explain and comment on them.

An increase of demand during peak hours involves the marginal capacity costs on STEG's system shown in Table 4.3.[3] These are known as the *coûts d'anticipation*, following EDF terminology. The marginal energy costs are the extra fuel costs per kilowatt-hour, corrected for losses in the system (see Table 4.4).

We can now combine the marginal costs of energy and capacity to obtain the total marginal costs, and proceed in one of two ways. The first is to retain the distinction between kilowatt costs and kilowatt-hour costs. The second is to express the capacity costs on a peak kilowatt-hour basis by adding them to the energy costs during peak. The two types of marginal cost structures are shown in Table 4.5.

Which one of these two ways of describing the cost structure should be reflected in tariffs? This is one of the most important issues facing STEG and is still open to discussion. Later we suggest that the choice between the two should rest on the practical issues of general acceptability and the incentives they present to the consumers. On account of the long period when demand is close to available capacity in Tunisia, we shall be arguing in favor of a time-of-day kilowatt-hour tariff, without separate kilowatt charges, for all but the smaller consumers on low voltage.

Improving cost estimates

STEG's attempt to estimate the structure of marginal costs has been handicapped by certain deficiencies in the information available. STEG is, of course, well aware of this. For the record, the im-

2. See, for example, M. Boiteux, "The 'Tarif Vert' of Electricité de France," in J. R. Nelson, ed., *Marginal Cost Pricing in Practice* (Englewood Cliffs, N.J.: Prentice-Hall, 1964).
3. An exchange rate of D 0.48 = US $1.00 may be used for conversion of dinars in the table and throughout the chapter.

Table 4.5. Marginal Cost Structures of STEG

	Medium voltage consumers	Low voltage consumers
Kilowatt-kilowatt-hour basis		
Marginal capacity costs	38.38	≈70[a]
(dinars per kilowatt per year)		
Marginal energy costs		
(millimes per kilowatt-hour)		
Peak	9.09	9.64
Day[b]	3.84	4.07
Night	3.55	3.76
Kilowatt-hour basis		
Marginal costs		
(millimes per kilowatt-hour)		
Peak	39.79	65.64
Day	3.84	4.07
Night	3.55	3.76

a. Not known with accuracy, as indicated in the text. This figure, obtained by comparing kilowatt/kilowatt-hour capacity costs in Table 4.3, is intended to be illustrative.
b. Off-peak day hours.
Source: Based on data supplied by the Société Tunisienne de l'Electricité et du Gaz.

portant deficiencies are five: (a) The determinants of the *coût d'exploitation* of distribution are unknown, so the extent to which it varies with, for example, kilowatts, kilowatt-hours, and number of consumers, can only be guessed. (b) The costs of reinforcing distribution to meet a growing demand from existing consumers cannot be distinguished from the costs of extending it to supply new consumers, a matter we discuss later. (c) Information on losses is very approximate. (d) Little is known about the low voltage network, its kilovolt-ampere capacity, or the diversity of demands of its consumers; indeed consultants are being paid to map it! (e) The daily consumption patterns of STEG's consumers are unknown (this would be particularly necessary information if kilowatt tariffs were to be introduced). Nevertheless, STEG has made very reasonable, if approximate, estimates of marginal costs and extracted as much as possible from the available information.

There are also a few points of methodology which should be noted, and some revisions to the estimates may be desirable. First, the generators taking up fluctuations in load during both day and night will be comparatively new, namely those installed at La Goulette and Rhennouch after 1970 (see the dispatching schedules for December 1976 in Figure 4.3). Differences in energy costs between day and night and also among seasons will thus be small,

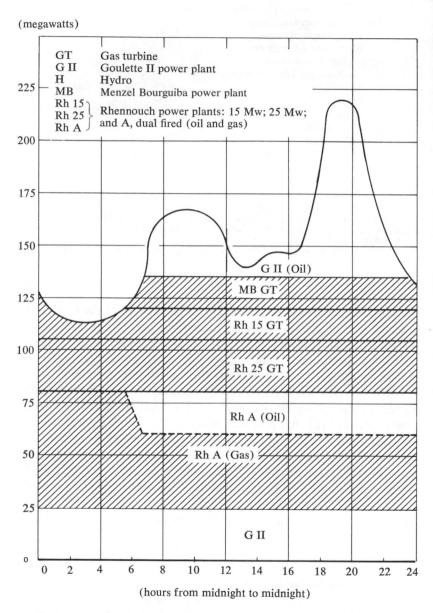

FIGURE 4.3. FORECAST DAILY DEMAND CURVE AND DISPATCHING
SCHEDULES FOR TUNISIA, DECEMBER 1976

(megawatts)

GT   Gas turbine
G II   Goulette II power plant
H   Hydro
MB   Menzel Bourguiba power plant
Rh 15 ⎫
Rh 25 ⎬ Rhennouch power plants: 15 Mw; 25 Mw;
Rh A ⎭ and A, dual fired (oil and gas)

225

200

175

150

G II (Oil)

MB GT

125

Rh 15 GT

100

Rh 25 GT

75

Rh A (Oil)

Rh A (Gas)

50

25

G II

0

0   2   4   6   8   10   12   14   16   18   20   22   24

(hours from midnight to midnight)

SOURCE: Charted from data supplied by the Société Tunisienne de l'Electricité et du Gaz

82

except during peak hours. The energy costs of these generators are high because of the high costs of holding La Goulette I on hot standby, ready for peak load operation. (La Goulette I is to be phased out of service gradually during the next few years, and the marginal costs of energy during the peak will then decline by about 50 percent.) Second, the marginal costs were obtained by estimating the annual equivalent of the capital costs of a given increase of capacity on the system and dividing by the increased capacity. As a point of principle, this procedure is not entirely correct, although under certain conditions it gives the correct answer. Strictly speaking, the marginal costs of an extra kilowatt of peak demand are the present worth of the costs of bringing the program *forward* to meet the demand, as the term *coût d'anticipation* suggests. Third, one consequence of STEG's method of estimating marginal costs is that indivisibilities in their program are neglected.[4] Looking at Figure 4.1 we see that the effect of an increase of kilowatt demand in a given year is not to increase capacity in *that* year, but, on average, to increase the required capacity of the plant to be commissioned one year later (investments are made every two years on average). The result is that the above marginal capacity costs of generation should be discounted for one year at the rate of 10 percent (the opportunity cost of capital). Finally, there is the general point that many of the maintenance and overhead costs are nonmarginal and should therefore be left out of the marginal cost calculations. When the time comes to allow for such costs and for any financial requirements in fixing tariffs, they can be allocated to those components of the tariffs that are politically and economically most convenient.

It is possible therefore that STEG has overestimated the marginal costs of meeting peak demand, though not seriously. Even if the estimates were revised, there would still be a high ratio between peak and off-peak marginal costs. This presents a serious dilemma for STEG. It is evidently not feasible for STEG to mirror such a cost structure in tariffs in the short run, if only because of the likelihood of hostility from consumers. Indeed, it is hardly fair to inundate consumers with new, radically different tariffs when they have bought appliances because the old tariffs, however uneconomic, offered special advantages through cross-subsidies. A slow transition to a new structure will be necessary. Besides, the effects of a new tariff structure on demand are unknown, but may be important (for example, in increasing the number of peak hours). Thus a cautious shift in tariff structure is desirable on this count, too.

---

4. Chapter 17 discusses indivisibilities more fully.

Important Tariff Problems

It is clear that the Société Tunisienne de l'Electricité et du Gaz feels, for political reasons or because of acceptability to consumers, there are a number of constraints upon their ability to reflect the structure of marginal costs in the structure of their tariffs. (These are in addition to the fact that it is too expensive to implement complicated tariffs for small consumers.) In particular, STEG does not dare to have a peak kilowatt-hour price that fully reflects peak marginal costs and thus intend to set some off-peak prices at above marginal costs. This constraint, as we show below, has found expression in the series of calculations made that, proceeding from an analysis of marginal costs, seeks to establish a set of new tariffs.

Acceptability in the short term

The danger of political constraints is that they will affect not only the *levels* of the various components of tariffs, but also the *types* of tariff chosen. Yet this would be a mistake. The types chosen will last for a long time and, over a long period, propaganda and the experience of change will alter consumers' attitudes. Consequently it would seem advisable to proceed as follows: First, choose those tariff types which are best if all such constraints are disregarded—that is, those that reflect the structure of marginal costs correctly. Second, implement these tariff types during the next year or two so as to achieve as much of the desired modulation of consumer behavior as possible while staying within the range of possibilities determined by the constraints. Third, adhering to these tariff types, attack the constraints and gradually change the various components of the tariffs to achieve relativities that do fully reflect the cost structure. If this approach is chosen, it is desirable to start stage one from the fundamental principle that (*apart* from financial considerations) the reason for pricing a kilowatt-hour at more than marginal short-term cost is to prevent demand from exceeding available capacity—that is, to avoid interruptions of supply.

Kilowatt-hours and kilowatts at peak

For many years in the future, the risk of interruptions in STEG's supply, other than those due to distribution failures, will not be negligible during as many as 1,250 hours a year. So a kilowatt-hour price in excess of marginal short-term cost is desirable during all these hours. An annual kilowatt charge for maximum demand (or even a charge one-twelfth as high for monthly maximum demand) is a poor substitute. A few consumers may experience their own maximum demand outside the critical period of, say, 1,250 hours. Also, a consumer who has reached a maximum demand of x kilowatts has henceforth no incentive to keep it below x during the remaining critical hours of the year (or month).

In the case of consumers whose use of electricity can be interrupted on short notice, the problem is different. The aim here is not to make them economize during *all* of the 1,250 hours when demand could potentially exceed available capacity, but only when it seems (on short notice) very likely that, if they do not, demand will exceed available capacity. Thus in their case, during the, say, 50 hours a year when such conditions occur, what is appropriate is an extremely high price per kilowatt-hour or, more simply, an interruption. This can be achieved by telephone for very large consumers and by telecontrol for certain electrical uses of smaller consumers (for example, in water heaters).

The argument thus runs as follows: In the long term, a kilowatt price is not a good idea; consequently, it should not be introduced in the short term if this either gets consumers used to it or necessitates the purchase of new meters. This argument applies to production and transmission costs. Local distribution costs, however, undoubtedly are related to a customer's contribution to local distribution peak. We discuss these costs in the next section.

All of the above discussion applies to medium voltage consumers (there are no high voltage consumers). Some of it applies to the larger low voltage consumers. For the smaller low voltage consumers, both consumer acceptance, even in the long term, and metering and billing costs are naturally much more important.

Local Distribution and Connection Costs

After a general survey of some of the problems and principles relevant to STEG's tariffmaking, we need to get down to more detail. First, however, we shall devote some space to the relation between charging consumers for connection to the supply system and charging them for their consumption once they are connected. Since electrification is proceeding apace and still has a long way to go, this is an important issue. Some definitions will be helpful:

> *Branchement:* Individual connection of low voltage consumer to nearby low voltage line, that is, a "service."
> *Raccordement:* Individual connection of medium voltage consumer to nearby line or transformer.

Reinforcement: Increase in the capacity of the distribution system made necessary by saturation of existing lines, cables, and transformers.

Extension: Increase in the capacity of the distribution system without which *branchements* and *raccordements* for a group of new consumers are not physically possible.

From the technical point of view, STEG must at least exercise technical supervision over all four operations defined above. Given this requirement, the juridical and accounting points of view should be subordinate to the economic requirements to which we now proceed. Note that these relate to the Tunisian national economic interest, not to a narrow, STEG profit-making point of view.

Unless there is good reason for a subsidy, individual new consumers should meet the costs of their individual *branchements or raccordements.* If these are installed by STEG, two sets of choices must be made: (a) Single payment versus a series of installments. The latter may be preferred for poor consumers; otherwise, the choice does not matter much. (b) Forfeit versus an individual estimate of cost. Various combinations are possible, for example, extra payment for a distance of more than x meters. The aim must be to seek a suitable compromise between simplicity and certainty, and making customers bear the actual costs. Consideration (b) is relatively more important for medium voltage than for low voltage consumers.

Reinforcement

Reinforcement is necessitated both by a growth in the load of existing consumers and by the individual connections—*branchement or raccordement*—of new consumers in areas already covered by a distribution network. In principle it is a function of the contributions of consumers to local distribution peak. Hence a marginal capacity cost or *coût d'anticipation* of reinforcement is appropriately included in tariffs in one or more of three ways: (a) in a charge per kilowatt of maximum demand (or per kilowatt of maximum demand within peak hours for the odd consumer whose own peak falls outside the local distribution peak); (b) in a charge per kilowatt of subscribed demand (with a similar complication) where a fuse or load limiter is set to reflect it; and (c) in the charge per kilowatt-hour of peak-period consumption for time-of-day tariffs and in the kilowatt-hour price for simple tariffs.

Inclusion of marginal reinforcement costs in a peak kilowatt-hour charge for consumers on a time-of-day tariff may be superior to a kilowatt charge or subscribed demand charge. It saves the cost of a demand indicator or a load limiter and simplifies the tariff. Also, the relation between a contribution to local system peak and a peak-period kilowatt-hour may be more relevant than the relation between a contribution to local system peak and a customer's own maximum demands; the former is in fact a closer relation as well as one easier to estimate.

The reinforcement cost of an individual consumer can only be ascertained in the case where he individually adds a new load that by itself is sufficient to cause saturation of the local distribution system. While such a consumer ought to pay any cost of reinforcing his individual *branchement,* there is no reason why he should be made to pay separately for the local reinforcement that he makes necessary unless there is some occasional and rare reason why this costs substantially more than the reinforcement costs already included in his tariff.

One way of ascertaining reinforcement costs is to compare past or predicted reinforcement expenditure with past or predicted peak-hour kilowatt-hour or peak kilowatt in areas already covered by distribution networks. This is difficult, however. Even if this load growth can be distinguished from load growth due to system extension, drawing a line of distinction between expenditure on reinforcement and expenditure on expansion is not presently possible (though it may be worth attempting in the future).

The other way of ascertaining reinforcement costs is to use engineering planning data, relating the cost of a number of reinforcement schemes to the increase in capacity provided.

Extension

Extensions are desirable if: (a) the present worth of what the new consumers in question would be collectively prepared to pay for connection and consumption plus the amount, if any, that (on social or other grounds) other people are prepared to pay on their behalf, exceeds: (b) the present worth of the costs of connecting and supplying them. Once the new consumers in question (for instance, the inhabitants of a village that is to be electrified) are connected and have a total load of x, they will, if the principles set out above are applied, be paying not only the (marginal) costs of producing x but also the national average of the marginal costs of a reinforcement of magnitude x. Thus, unless on social or other grounds it is desired to sell electricity at tariffs below marginal costs, the principle above can be restated as follows: Extensions are desirable if (a) what the new consumers are prepared to pay for connections plus the amount, if any, that on social or other grounds other people are prepared to pay on their behalf, exceeds: (b) the cost of connecting them *less* the national average of the marginal costs of a reinforcement of magnitude x.

All of this means that there is a problem of obtaining participation in the costs of extension (apart from individual low and medium voltage connections—*branchements* and *raccordements*) only to the extent that the costs of extension exceed the costs of reinforcement. Presumably they do in fact exceed them, although STEG has no reliable figures to show this.

If the difference is ignored and if, therefore, the tariffs include a national average of the marginal costs of both extension and reinforcement, then: (a) consumers on the existing network will pay more than their own marginal costs in order to subsidize electrification—that is, extension of the network—and (b) to charge anything for electrification (apart from charging for individual *branchements* and *raccordements*) will involve double charging. Regarding the first of these points, it is not obvious why any subsidy of extension (if there is to be one) should be borne by other electricity consumers. Nor, if it is decided that any should bear such a subsidy, is it obvious why the proportion of the subsidy borne by each of them should be related to peak consumption in particular.

If, to take the opposite case from that just discussed, the difference between the costs of extension and reinforcement is not ignored, then pricing requires a participation in the costs of the former by the new consumers or, on social or other grounds, by others on their behalf. This total participation will equal the *coût d'anticipation,* or marginal capacity cost, of the electrification minus the reinforcement component of the expected tariff payments by the new consumers averaged over, say, the first two or three years after electrification. The problem then arises, to the extent that the whole amount is not provided by a subsidy, of splitting the sum involved among the new consumers. These new consumers include both those who are connected immediately upon electrification and those who only ask for connection somewhat later. This problem of splitting a joint cost has no perfect solution. Any proposals for dealing with it can only be a compromise among the aims of: (a) relating payments to benefits; (b) keeping payments low enough not to discourage potential consumers; (c) securing simplicity, certainty, and avoiding unacceptable discrimination between consumers; and (d) obtaining the desired total.

The whole of the preceding discussion relates to cases where the new consumers brought in by electrification will pay for their consumption according to tariffs that include a component reflecting marginal costs of reinforcement. In the case of a tariff that reflects the marginal cost of off-peak pumping, this will not be so, and the whole of the *coût d'anticipation* should therefore be met by or for pumping consumers. There seems to be no other reason for treating these consumers differently, however.

STEG already appreciates most of the principles discussed above, but we have nevertheless set out our views at length because a piece by piece examination of the few differences between us would have been less clear. We can now leave these problems on one side and concentrate on tariffs for electricity alone.

STEG's Provisional Tariff Proposals

The Société Tunisienne de l'Electricité et du Gaz is formulating triple time-of-day tariffs that vary according to the consumer's transformer rating. These tariffs reflect marginal costs only in a limited sense, as will be discussed below.

A high voltage tariff that reflects cost

To examine STEG's approach to tariff construction, we begin by considering only generation costs, ignoring for a moment the costs of transmission and distribution that also need to be reflected in consumers' tariffs. The only seasonal variation involved is a change in the timing of the three periods into which STEG divides the day and week: *pointe* (otherwise, *P*) is the peak period of four hours daily, six days a week; *jour hors pointe* (*J*) is the off-peak daylight period of eleven hours daily, six days a week; and *nuit* (*N*) includes nights and Sundays. The 1,250 hours constituting *P* are peak periods both in the sense that demand is high throughout these hours and in the sense that any one of them may turn out to be the hour of annual system peak.

Marginal energy costs per kilowatt-hour for 1976, the year of reference, are put at: P = 7.62 millimes; J = 3.38 millimes; and N = 3.16 millimes.[5] The *coût d'anticipation*—that is, the marginal capacity cost, including a 20 percent plant margin—is D 14.5 or 14,500 millimes a kilowatt.

Thus a cost-reflecting tariff, in addition to J and N prices per kilowatt-hour of 3.38 and 3.16 millimes, respectively, would be achievable in three ways: a kilowatt-hour price of 7.62 millimes and

5. It is frequently easier to think of these costs in millimes, the Tunisian monetary subdivision equal to one thousandth of a dinar.

a price per kilowatt of measured maximum demand during P of about 14,500 millimes; the same, with a monthly maximum demand charge of about 1,208 millimes; or a kilowatt-hour price during P of $7.62 + (14,500/1,250) = 7.62 + 11.60 = 19.22$. In the first two alternatives, the word *about* is used to allow for the possibility that the coincidence factor may be a little less than unity even within the daily four-hour peak period.

In terms of their incentive effects, the three ways of reflecting capacity costs are arranged in ascending order of appropriateness. Once a consumer has registered a demand of x kilowatts, he retains an incentive during the rest of the year or month not to exceed x but has no incentive to keep his demand below that level. The high kilowatt-hour charge, on the other hand, provides an equal incentive during all the hours in P.

Note that we are concerned with measured kilowatts during P and not with subscribed demand. The latter is relevant only to the capacity of the consumer's *raccordement*.

Imposition of any of these tariffs might flatten and extend the peak or even create a new peak during J. In such a case, the costs and periods would have to be recalculated. In principle, one can conceive of a process of iteration between demand and costs. But the final shape of the tariff would be similar. The basic principle is to charge more than marginal generation costs only to the extent necessary to restrain demand sufficiently to keep the risk of power cuts down to an acceptable level.

STEG does not have high voltage consumers. For their medium voltage consumers, transmission and distribution costs and losses would naturally lead to higher levels of tariff than mentioned above. It is not necessary to examine their calculations of these items at this point, no additional matters of principle being involved. We merely note that these items add proportionately more to marginal costs of capacity than, by way of losses, to marginal costs of operation. This raises the gap between the two. Thus in terms of the third alternative, the difference between the kilowatt prices for P and J would be even bigger than between 19.22 and 3.38, as is shown later (and also in Table 4.5).

Acceptability

It has been STEG's view that a gap between kilowatt prices for different periods such as that described above is too big to be acceptable in the early 1970s. Similarly, a kilowatt price per year or month well in excess of 14,500 or 1,208 millimes (to include transmission and distribution capacity costs) is regarded as too big compared with present kilowatt charges (*primes fixes*) to be acceptable. This is so even though the present charges relate to subscribed demand rather than to measured maximum demand.

STEG's views on this point must naturally be respected. Sudden and violent changes in tariff patterns do indeed create serious difficulties. As suggested earlier, a *gradual* change toward new tariffs of this sort is desirable over a period of years. A strategy is needed, first, for introducing the new *type* of tariff to replace the old ones, and, next, for changing the relativities within each tariff toward a pattern that ultimately reflects the structure of marginal costs.

Proposals for the first stage, the new (1973) tariffs, should be judged by three criteria: Do they constitute a movement toward reflecting the structure of marginal costs as described above? Do they avoid the introduction of elements that do not form part of this ideal structure toward which they are aiming? Do they avoid unacceptably large increases or decreases in typical consumers' bills?

STEG's arithmetic

We have some doubts about the extent to which the approach followed by STEG meets the first two criteria just described (of reflecting the structure of marginal costs and of avoiding extraneous elements). In order to discuss this, we consider their proposals for large consumers. Thus we disregard two (agreed) points: (a) Interruptible supply tariffs, with somewhat different terms, may be a desirable option for some consumers. (b) Tariffs have to be simple for small consumers.

What STEG has done in formulating its proposals is first to spread marginal capacity costs between a kilowatt charge and P (the peak period of kilowatt-hour demand) and then to spread only a fraction of them, denoted by g, in this way, spreading the rest, $1 - g$, over J (the off-peak daytime kilowatt-hour demand). This involves two departures from marginal cost pricing, although the result is still described as such.

The first step, that of spreading marginal capacity costs between a kilowatt charge and P, *could* have been done without falsifying the structure of marginal costs. Instead of a kilowatt charge of 14,500 millimes or an addition to the kilowatt-hour price in P of 11.6 millimes, a fifty-fifty split of 7,250 millimes a kilowatt and an addition to the kilowatt-hour price of 5.8 millimes would have spread the costs as desired. But STEG has calculated *three* optional alternative tariffs such that one will be chosen by consumers with annual use totaling

91

between 8,760 and 4,000 hours; a second will be chosen by consumers with annual use totaling between 4,000 and 2,000 hours; and a third will be chosen by consumers with less than 2,000 hours use.

Each succeeding tariff has a lower kilowatt charge and a higher kilowatt-hour charge in P than the one before. The calculations rest upon some estimates of coincidence factors and of the number of hours of use during P for consumers with total uses of 8,760, 4,000, 2,000, and 1,000 hours. Thus the first of these options is calculated so that both for a consumer with 8,760 hours of use and for one with 4,000 hours of use; kilowatt charge + (hours of use during P · capacity-cost element in kilowatt-hour price) = (coincidence factor · marginal capacity costs). Similarly, the second and third options are calculated using the estimated figures for the second and third pairs of typical consumers, namely those with 4,000–2,000 and 2,000–1,000 hours of use.

This has the result that if a consumer within any of the three intervals increases *both* his maximum demand *and* his kilowatt-hour consumption during P in the same proportion, the increase in his bill will approximately equal marginal cost, that is, $14,500 \cdot \Delta kw + 7.62 \cdot \Delta kwh$. In this limited sense, the three tariffs do all reflect marginal cost. Yet if we compare, say, the first and second options, we find kilowatt charges of 9,700 millimes and 2,000 millimes and peak kilowatt-hour prices of 11.45 millimes and 26.82 millimes, respectively. Such differences do *not* reflect the structure of marginal costs.

It must be explained that STEG is not actually proposing such tariffs for two reasons, both already hinted at. The first is that these cost figures exclude transmission and distribution costs, so they relate to imaginary high voltage consumers situated next door to generation. The tariffs actually proposed are thus higher. This introduces no new problems of principle, however. The second reason is that they proceed to the second step of putting half ($g = 0.5$) of marginal capacity costs onto off-peak daytime kilowatt-hours. Thus, for the imaginary high voltage consumers on the first of the three optional alternatives, instead of the figures given in the preceding paragraph (kilowatts at 9,700, P at 11.45 a kilowatt-hour, and J at 3.38 a kilowatt-hour), STEG would propose kilowatts at 8,710, P at 9.78 a kilowatt-hour, and J at 4.27 a kilowatt-hour. The only part of the tariff structure that still would reflect marginal cost is the price of 3.16 millimes a kilowatt-hour during N, nights and Sundays.

The corresponding possible tariff on medium voltage that STEG has constructed for large consumers involves the three alternatives in Table 4.6. The differences in kilowatt-hour prices do not reflect differences in marginal costs, and the kilowatt charges, not being

TABLE 4.6. ALTERNATIVE MEDIUM VOLTAGE TARIFFS FOR
STEG's LARGE CONSUMERS

		Kilowatt-hour price (millimes)		
Alternatives	Kilowatt charge (millimes)	Peak	Day[a]	Night
Tariff A	23,040	14.22	6.21	3.55
Tariff B	13,280	22.26	9.06	3.55
Tariff C	6,730	34.07	11.85	3.55

a. Off-peak day hours.
SOURCE: Based on data supplied by the Société Tunisienne de l'Electricité et du Gaz.

proportional to coincidence factors, do not do so either. On the other hand, the proposals do succeed in limiting the increases and decreases that such consumers would suffer or gain in their bills from the change from existing tariffs.

Metering costs

In their proposals for standardizing the metering for medium voltage tariffs, it appears that STEG would confine the above triple time-of-day tariffs to consumers with transformer ratings in excess of 315 kilovolt-amperes. At present there are only 150 such consumers. The total capital cost of metering them is, according to transformer rating, D200, D410, or D770 per consumer. If maximum demand were not measured, there would be a considerable saving. Such consumers could be given a better type of tariff than STEG is considering, at a lower cost! This follows from the superiority of a high kilowatt-hour price over a kilowatt charge in providing consumers with an incentive to keep down their consumption during the peak period P.

STEG's proposals for the 1,210 medium voltage consumers with smaller transformers are different. These proposals involve only single kilowatt-hour meters and, in most cases, maximum demand indicators. With this kind of metering, they would naturally tend to have kilowatt-related block tariffs of the type at present in force. As we argue below, such tariffs are less suitable for a (simplified) representation of the structure of marginal costs than are time-of-day tariffs. We therefore obtained figures of the capital costs of different metering systems, as shown in Table 4.7. These costs may not be exactly comparable; for instance, the D105 in the third case includes D24 for a reactive energy meter. Nonetheless, the smallness of the cost difference is very striking. It suggests that many of these consumers ought at least to be given the option, if not compelled, to

TABLE 4.7. CAPITAL COSTS TO STEG OF DIFFERENT METERING SYSTEMS (1972 data)

Medium voltage consumer's transformer rating (kilovolt amperes)	Cost of metering proposed by STEG (dinars)	Cost of metering only peak and off-peak energy (dinars)	Cost of metering only peak, day[a], and night energy (dinars)
≤40	30	55.5	58.5
40–100	77	84.0	89.0
100–315	105	112.5	117.5

a. Off-peak day hours.
SOURCE: Based on data supplied by the Société Tunisienne de l'Electricité et du Gaz.

have a double or triple time-of-day tariff without any kilowatt price for either measured demand or for subscribed demand (apart, of course, from payment for a connection or *raccordement*).

Our conclusions so far, then, concerning STEG's still tentative proposals for medium voltage tariffs are that: (a) they fail significantly to reflect the relative levels of marginal costs; (b) for the largest medium voltage consumers a triple time-of-day tariff would both be a somewhat better type of tariff and be cheaper to meter than what is proposed; and (c) for medium-size medium voltage consumers a triple or double time-of-day tariff would be a much better type of tariff but would cost somewhat more than what is proposed.

A medium voltage tariff that reflects cost

It seems sensible to construct double and triple time-of-day tariffs (without any kilowatt charges) that reflect the structure and relative levels of marginal costs as closely as possible. We are not necessarily suggesting that these tariffs should be introduced immediately. They should be viewed as the ideal tariffs for medium-size and large medium voltage consumers, the aim of efforts over a long period. In the short run proposals for tariffs should be: modifications of the ideal, necessary to achieve acceptability, and judged in terms of the ideal and in terms of acceptability. This approach fits in with what was said above in the section on "Acceptability" about the criteria for introducing new tariffs.

The main sort of modifications that are available for use in avoiding unacceptably large increases or decreases in the bills of existing medium voltage consumers are four: temporary continuation of kilowatt charges for those consumers who already have maximum demand indicators; fixed annual charges greater or less than annual metering costs and per-consumer *coûts d'exploitation;* temporary block prices; and optional continuation of existing tariffs for existing consumers, but at increasing prices. It would be a good idea to have a plan for the gradual phasing out of such of these temporary modifications as STEG decides to choose.

At our request, STEG has calculated the ideal tariffs (in millimes) as follows for the peak, daylight off-peak, and night periods—*P, J,* and *N* respectively:

$$
\left.\begin{array}{ll} P & 39.79 \\ J & 3.84 \\ N & 3.55 \end{array}\right\} \begin{array}{l} \text{or, on a} \\ \text{double-rate} \\ \text{basis} \end{array} \left.\right\} \begin{array}{l} \text{33.02 for five hours per weekday} \\ \text{3.68 for all other hours} \end{array}
$$

Annual metering costs vary between 11,300 and 61,800 millimes, according to transformer rating, for the triple time-of-day tariff and about 1,000 less for the double tariff. As this difference is fairly small, reflecting differences in the capital costs of the two kinds of meters of some 5,000 millimes, it might be worthwhile to insist on the triple time-of-day tariff for all medium voltage consumers above a certain size.

Low voltage tariffs

For the smallest consumers, there is no practicable alternative to a single kilowatt-hour meter accompanied by a load limiter. The latter costs little more than fuse protection and enables the tariff to contain a subscribed demand component in addition to the kilowatt-hour component. Seasonal variations in the kilowatt-hour price, though possible, are not needed.

For larger low voltage consumers, STEG proposes an optional double time-of-day tariff to replace the simple one or an optional off-peak tariff (with a second meter) to supplement it. In either case, since telecontrol will cover the bulk of the system, these will be controlled by relays rather than, as hitherto has been the case, by time switches. This has a number of advantages: for instance, if the morning peak grew toward equality with the evening peak, the peak price could be applied to both periods.

Block tariffs

At the present stage of STEG's tariff studies, there are no detailed proposals for low voltage tariffs. However, for both small medium voltage consumers and small low voltage consumers not on time-of-day tariffs, the tariff types contemplated for the future include some kilowatt-related block prices for kilowatt-hours. We recognize that since these already exist, their sudden abolition might cause any new set of tariffs to involve such large changes in the bills of individual consumers as to make them unacceptable. Nevertheless, in accordance with the basic philosophy of choosing tariffs with an eye to their development over time toward an ideal system, we wish to discuss some problems of principle involved in block tariffs.

Consumers' hours of use (annual kilowatt-hours divided by maximum kilowatts) are clearly related to their coincidence factors (kilowatts at system peak divided by maximum peak) since when the former is 8,766 the latter must be unity. In any case, empirical studies of samples of larger consumers in some countries have displayed the existence of a statistical relation.

More generally, there is probably not merely a relation between annual number of hours of use and contributions to system peak kilowatts, but also between the former and the whole time pattern of consumption. STEG has very little information about such relationships. For the sake of getting the principles clear, let us suppose, however, that: albeit with some dispersion, there is a relation between consumers' hours of use and the division of their annual kilowatt-hours between the three periods of STEG's day and week, P, J, and N; this relation has been statistically estimated; and the marginal costs of kilowatt-hours during P, J, and N are all known for the type of consumers in question.

Under these assumptions, a statistical relation can be calculated between annual hours of use on the one hand and the weighted average of the marginal costs of consumers' kilowatt-hours on the other. If this relation shows that the latter declines (or rises) as a function of the former, then it can be approximated by a series of kilowatt-hour prices. Thus it will be approximately true for each of these consumers that, if they pay this block tariff, their *average* price per kilowatt-hour will cost them the average of the marginal costs of all the kilowatt-hours they take. Alternatively, the block tariff could be constructed to make their *marginal* price per kilowatt-hour (the price of the block they are on) equal the average of the marginal costs of all the kilowatt-hours they take. Note two features of these two block tariffs: (a) the second gives a cruder approximation than the first unless there is a large number of small blocks; and (b) if prices of successive blocks decline, the marginal price will be below the average price—the converse also being true, and in neither case is it possible for marginal and average price to coincide.

The second of these tariffs will make the consumer's marginal cost for a change in his consumption approximately equal to the marginal costs of supplying that change *only if* the division of that *change* among P, J, and N is the same as the division of his *total* consumption among them. The first of these tariffs will achieve this result only if the division of the change among P, J, and N differs from the division of his total consumption among them in a certain, systematic fashion (which could be calculated).

It is true that the first of these tariffs does make the *total* bill of a consumer equal the total cost saving that would result if he ceased to consume. But this is less useful than equating the marginal cost of a kilowatt-hour to the consumer with the marginal cost of supplying it, because tariffs exert much more influence on how many kilowatt-hours a consumer uses than on whether he consumes anything at all. In other words, the sense in which a block tariff of the first sort does reflect costs is not a relevant one. Its arithmetic charm leads people to forget this!

We now proceed to bring in a possible kilowatt charge and kilowatt-related block tariffs. The marginal costs to the consumer of changes in his consumption now become both more complicated and even more difficult to relate to the marginal costs of supply. In addition to the points already made, the marginal cost to the consumer of a kilowatt now can show an arbitrary pattern. Suppose that: there are only two blocks, the size of the first one per kilowatt is B, the kilowatt-hour prices of the first and second blocks are f and s, respectively, and the kilowatt charge is k. For consumers on the first block, with consumption per kilowatt less than B, the marginal cost of a kilowatt is k. For consumers on the second block with consumption per kilowatt sufficiently in excess of B, the marginal cost is: $k + (f - s)B$. It seems extremely unlikely that it would ever be possible to design a block tariff in such a way that the relations among such marginal tariff costs reflect differences in coincidence factors.

Summing up this discussion of block tariffs, it is clear that even if they do reflect marginal cost, they do so in an irrelevant way. What they can very rarely do, especially when the kilowatt-hour blocks are on a per-kilowatt basis, is to make the consumer's marginal cost for changes in his electrical behavior equal the electricity supplier's marginal cost of these changes.

Conclusions

STEG has done a very good job in analyzing the structure of marginal costs, even though minor defects exist, notably regarding expansion versus reinforcement costs and the treatment of *coûts d'exploitation*. These defects rest solely on a lack of information and STEG is fully aware of them.

STEG's tariff proposals, which are still in course of formulation, seem less satisfactory. They sometimes reflect marginal costs only in an irrelevant way. But as we fully recognize that the need for the new tariffs to win governmental and public acceptance imposes constraints upon STEG's *espace de manoeuvre,* making this a quasi-political problem, we have not attempted to put forward any immediate proposals of our own. Our main points have related to kilowatt pricing versus kilowatt-hour pricing, interruptibility, metering systems, and block tariffs.

Two final points remain. One of them is that once a new tariff system has been designed, it will be necessary to see whether it provides sufficient revenue to meet STEG's financial targets. If it does not, so that some or other tariff components have to be adjusted upward, it is desirable to minimize the effects upon resource allocation of the necessary changes. This means picking upon fixed annual charges (meter rents) and upon items with a particularly low elasticity of demand.

The other final point is that pricing related to marginal costs ensures efficient resource allocation only when substitute forms of energy (charcoal, kerosene, town gas, liquified petroleum gas, and even camel power) are priced at their marginal costs. We have not examined their pricing, however, merely relying upon the presumption that this second-best problem is not of major importance.

CHAPTER 5

Electricity Tariffs in Sudan

This chapter presents a study that illustrates an approach to electricity tariffmaking and metering in Sudan. The aim is to determine an electricity tariff and metering policy that would best reflect the costs of providing supply. The study concentrates almost wholly on the Blue Nile Grid, although a note is added on pricing in the isolated microgrids in various parts of the country.

The present tariffs, designed with only financial objectives in mind, follow a traditional declining-block pattern, invariant with time of day or season, and are typical of the type one might find in, say, Chicago. But many kinds of tariffs can satisfy financial objectives, so it seems desirable to choose from among them those that can satisfy something additional and important: namely, a proper and fuller use of capital and a more efficient use of energy resources. These are the aims of cost-reflecting tariffs that, with a few adjustments, can meet financial objectives—and social ones too, if desired.

The idea of cost-reflecting tariffs rests on a simple premise. This is that, if costs are signaled to consumers in prices, then consumers, who adjust consumption levels to the point where the benefits they derive at the margin equal or exceed the price they pay, will adjust consumption to the point where derived benefits exceed or equal the costs of supply. When energy is cheap and capacity is spare, extra supply can be provided at little cost, so it makes sense to have low prices in such times; when energy becomes more costly, but capacity is spare, prices need to be higher; and when energy is costly and the growth of demand requires further capacity, prices need to be much higher.

For the Blue Nile Grid we aim to show that, in the *flood* and *wet* seasons: (a) There are times of day (off-peak times) when hydro energy is being sluiced or spilled in substantial quantities, when capacity is spare. It is possible therefore to provide extra energy at very low—almost zero—cost. (b) There are times of the day (peak times) when demand is pressing against capacity, particularly in the flood season on account of low heads in the reservoirs, and the costs of supply increase substantially.

In the *dry* season: (a) There are times of the day in the early months of the season (off peak) when energy is still being sluiced because water requirements for irrigation exceed the amount being passed through the turbines. Again, extra energy in these times can be supplied at very low costs. (b) In the late months of the season, less water is available so thermal plant is needed to supply extra energy and supply costs rise. (c) In the peak hours of the day, there is a continual (but not a high) pressure on available capacity, and supply costs therefore rise further.

Accordingly there are seasonal and time-of-day patterns in the costs of supply. The details depend on the expansion plans (which are still unsettled), but, with certain exceptions, broadly similar seasonal and time-of-day patterns would exist under all the alternatives now being analyzed by the Central Electricity and Water Corporation (CEWC) of Sudan.

For the larger agricultural and industrial consumers, these variations in costs can be reflected in time-of-day metering with seasonal adjustments to prices. Some consumers, however, might prefer the option of interruptible supplies with lower peak prices. Metering to improve power factors can also be contemplated for such consumers. The advantages and disadvantages of various cost-reflecting types of tariff vary according to the consumer, who could well do with assistance from a commercial engineer within CEWC.

For smaller consumers, time-of-day metering is not feasible, and only seasonal variations in kilowatt-hour charges can be contemplated. This could be employed in conjunction with kilowatt load limiters, possibly operative only during certain times of the year, with a charge related to the kilowatt setting.

The transition from the present types of tariff to more desirable ones is best achieved by giving people options between old and new in the short run; by gradually tightening the terms of the old ones in the medium run; and then by removing options in the long run.

Illustrative calculations of tariffs are provided in this chapter, but the actual numbers are still in question for several reasons. The development plan for the system has still not been finalized, and we could only consider two of the three plans now being evaluated. Also, financial targets have not been settled, and the data on costs, losses, and consumer demands all need a more thorough analysis.

Sources of Electricity Supply

Electricity supply in Sudan, which is entirely the responsibility of CEWC, has two main sources. The Blue Nile Grid, with a present rated capacity of 176.44 megawatts, serves Khartoum and the Blue Nile Valley.[1] It is a mixed system, comprising twenty-one diesels, ranging in capacity from 0.3 to 3.8 megawatts; a gas turbine; steam turbines; and two multipurpose hydro projects. Many of the diesels are old and cannot operate at full capacity or be relied on at all. The practical generating capability of the system is estimated to be:

Power station location	Practical capacity (megawatts)
Burri	
Diesels	14
Steam turbines (2 @ 5 + 2 @ 10)	30
Kilo X	
Gas Turbine	11
Wad Medani	
Diesels	5
Sennar	
Dual-purpose hydro	15
Roseires	
Dual-purpose hydro	90
Total	165

Actual output of the dual-purpose hydro schemes, as will be seen later, depends on water levels and river flows. Note that the present maximum demand on the grid is about 80 megawatts.

Isolated microgrids, mainly diesel fed, in various parts of the country, are the second main source of electricity supply. The practical generating capability of these is estimated to be:

Grid location	Capacity rating (megawatts)
Northern area (Atbara, Berber, El Damrer, Shendi, Dongla)	10.5
Eastern area (Kasala, New Halfa, Kashm, El Girba, El Gedaref)	17.5
Port Sudan	8.1
El Obeid	1.6
El Fasher	0.5
Juba	0.6
Malakal	0.7
Wau	0.4
El Dueim, El Gelena, El Quarashi	1.9
Total	41.8

1. A map of the Blue Nile Grid appears on the next page.

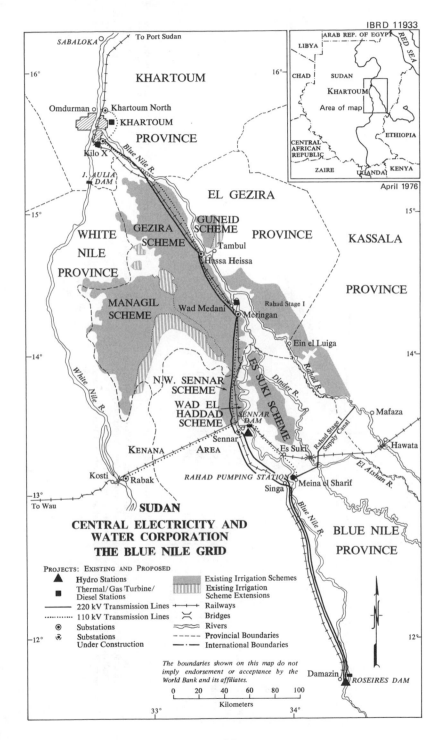

TABLE 5.1. CONTRACT DATA FOR VARIOUS POWER PLANTS IN SUDAN

Plant	Type	Year	Capacity (megawatts)	Costs (thousands of Sudanese pounds)					Cost (Sudanese pounds per kilowatt)
				Capacity	Transmission			Total	
					Common	Specific[a]			
Roseires 1,2,3	Hydro	1971/72	90	6,800	. . .	5,000		11,800	133
Roseires 4,5	Hydro	1976	60	2,898	505[b]	2,778		6,181	103
Sennar[c]	Hydro	1962	15	1,425	. . .	. . .	n.a.	1,425	95
Kilo X	Gas turbine	1969	15	950	. . .	. . .	n.a.	950	64
Burri[c]	Oil steam	1957/71	30	2,531	250[b]	—		2,781	93
New thermal[d]	Oil steam	1975	60	6,656	505[b]	—		7,061	118

a. Specific costs are for the 220-kilovolt reinforcement of the line to transmit the output of Roseires about 500 kilometers to the main load centers in the Khartoum area and the Blue Nile Valley.

b. The common costs are mostly those of reinforcing the 110-kilovolt transmission network in the Khartoum area.

c. The costs of Sennar and Burri would be about 60 percent higher in 1973 prices.

d. Proposed alternative to expansion of units 4 and 5 at Roseires.

SOURCE: Based on data supplied by the Central Electricity and Water Corporation of Sudan.

One might note that the El Girba grid includes a small multipurpose hydro; the possibility of using microhydro has been discussed for Juba; and El Quarashi is an isolated microgrid, but within the area of the Blue Nile Grid. The locations of these various plants and the areas irrigated can be found in the map in this chapter.

Load is growing very rapidly on both kinds of systems, and some of the diesel powered microgrids—particularly the Eastern and then the Northern areas—will eventually be absorbed into the Blue Nile Grid. But this is not likely to happen within the current planning horizon, given the still small loads and the long distances between towns in Sudan. Many of the isolated units, which comprise about 20 percent of Sudan's capacity, and which are situated in large population centers (for example, in Juba and Port Sudan), will continue to be isolated for a long time.

Accordingly, any tariff study asks two questions: what tariffs are appropriate for the Blue Nile Grid; and what are appropriate for the isolated microgrids? It is the Blue Nile Grid, on account of the complexity of its operations, that has occupied almost all of our attention.

Capital Costs of the Blue Nile Grid

Normally the derivation of cost structure should be preceded by a description of the operations of and the expansion plans for the system. This is indeed what we eventually do. But first we need to estimate and measure the costs of the various elements involved in operations and expansion, before putting them together to derive the cost structure and the setting for tariff policy. This turns out to be a long task, because of the large number of elements involved and the large uncertainties in costs. In addition, the results of a certain amount of experimentation are needed, for example, with respect to losses and the efficiency and running costs of thermal plant. Readers not interested in such details can pass directly to the end of this section, where the capital costs are put together in a brief form.

Generation and transmission

Expansion plans for the foreseeable future will involve a further oil-fired thermal plant, located in Khartoum; expansion of capacity at Roseires, which has room for four more generators each of 30 megawatts (or possibly more, if the dam's height were increased); or some phased combination of thermal and Roseires hydro expansion. (The contract data for various plants are shown in Table 5.1.)

The costs that are most relevant for pricing policy are those that are about to be incurred. Will consumers be prepared to pay for the costs of expansion if these are reflected in the prices? If so, expansion is clearly worthwhile. Or will they *not* be prepared to pay? If so, expansion, at least to the extent contemplated, is in question. It is the costs of expansion therefore, as opposed to past costs, that are relevant for pricing policy.

If Roseires 4 and 5 are accepted, the costs of expansion are about £S 103 a kilowatt, or £S 110 a kilowatt allowing for losses in transmission.[2] The costs of the new thermal plant are £S 118 a kilowatt, and the costs for some combination of these alternatives are likely to be in this range. Only expansion with gas turbines would cut expansion costs significantly below these levels (at the expense, of course, of very high energy costs). At the moment gas turbines are not being contemplated—the capacity of Kilo X and five 3-megawatt modern diesels at Burri together provide over 25 megawatts of fast startup, which is quite sufficient for contingency in the next planning period.

Hence, in round numbers, allowing for some cost uncertainties, and also for losses of about 2 percent in the 100-kilovolt subtransmission network and substations, the capital costs of expanding generation and transmission capacity works out at roughly £S 120 a kilowatt.[3]

Distribution

The costs of expanding and reinforcing a system's distribution networks are always dificult to ascertain, and Sudan offers no exception. The reasons are three: first, piecemeal reinforcement, extension, and replacement are always taking place; next, indivisibilities are large, and demand is near capacity in some places, well below it in others (it is usual to allow for eight to ten years of growth of demand when reinforcing or extending networks); and last, while some areas permit overhead lines, others permit only underground cables, which are much more expensive. Except in special cases, such as extension to outlying schemes or villages, it is rarely easy to identify individual expansion costs at a point in time, and even then costs are found to vary erratically. Some kind of average incremental cost of expansion must be struck for each voltage level at which electricity is served.

2. An exchange rate of £S 2.872 = US$ 1.00 may be used for conversion of Sudanese pounds throughout the chapter.
3. The allowance for reserves will be constant at 30 megawatts for the next decade, since reserve allowance in Sudan is not proportional to system size but is determined by the size of the largest unit (30 megawatts at Roseires).

The following is a rough classification of consumer types:

Consumer	Voltage Level of Service
Residential	
Commercial	240 volts phase to neutral or 415 volts
Light industrial	phase to phase (three-phase supply)
Street lighting	
Heavy industrial	11 kilovolts
Light and heavy	11 kilovolts plus 11/0.415 kilovolts
irrigation consumers	transformer

We have tried to estimate the marginal costs of distribution in two ways. One is to inventory distribution equipment in the Khartoum area and divide that by capacity. This gives, of course, average capacity costs, but these seem to be near enough to incremental capacity costs.[4] The other way is to cost out specific schemes; the results are predictably erratic, but some at least are useful in confirming that our estimates are of the right order.

Following are inventory data for service at 11 kilovolts and 0.415 kilovolt (December 1968 figures):

Service at 11 kilovolts	Costs (thousands of pounds)
33 Kilovolt lines	
Poles	22
Overhead lines and protection	29
Underground cables	207
Miscellaneous	35
33/11 Kilovolt substations	446
11 Kilovolt lines	
Poles	100
Overhead lines and protection	111
Underground cables	580
Total	1,530

Service at 0.415 kilovolt (250 line to neutral)	Costs (thousands of pounds)
11/0.415 Kilovolt substations	560
11/0.415 Kilovolt pole transformers	87
0.415 Kilovolt lines	
Overhead lines and protection	290
Poles	553
Underground cables	70
Street lighting	120
Total	1,680

4. It would be desirable, however, to attempt to determine incremental capacity costs independently.

Note that we do not inquire, in this report, into the issue of separate charges for street lighting because of the costs of providing poles.

The total load in the Khartoum area in 1968 was about 30 megawatts, so that the capacity cost per kilowatt supplied by the 11 kilovolt networks was roughly 1,530/30 = £S 51 a kilowatt demanded. The total load flowing through the low voltage networks (that is, total load minus heavy industrial loads) was roughly 20 megawatts, so that the capacity costs of the low voltage networks was roughly 1,680/20 = £S 84 a kilowatt demanded.

These figures have to be adjusted for losses—which we do shortly—and for inflation. An adjustment is also required for the very large level of spare capacity in the distribution networks. While provision of spare capacity is normally a part of the cost of expansion, it is thought that the inventory data displayed above indicate much more spare capacity than usual (because of the smallness of the system at that time) and in the future the amount may drop. It has been suggested to us that the capacity of Khartoum's networks is currently about twice the load. But typically, at higher loads, spare capacity is usually sufficient to accommodate the expansion of seven to ten years. Since some older installations will be nearly fully loaded at any point in time, while for the new installations it will be, say, eight years before they are fully loaded, spare capacity on the system is roughly sufficient to cover four years of growth *on average*; at present growth rates, this amounts to about 40 percent spare capacity, on average. The above capacity figures should thus be adjusted downward by about 1.4/2.0 = 0.7. Making a 20 percent allowance for inflation, we therefore adjust the above figures by 1.2 × 0.7 to get: (a) capacity costs for distribution at the 11 kilovolt level ≅ £S 43 a kilowatt demanded; (b) extra capacity costs of 11/0.4 kilovolt transformers for heavy load ≅ £S 4 a kilowatt demanded; and (c) extra capacity costs, over (a), of low voltage distribution ≅ £S 72 a kilowatt demanded. These are the figures used in this report, but they are obviously very tentative.

Independent checks on these figures were not too successful, largely on account of the reasons given earlier. Our estimates of (a) + (c) = £S 115 a kilowatt seem low compared with contract data to extend supplies to two areas in Khartoum, which showed costs in the range of £S 130 to £S 150 a kilowatt.[5] But extension is more expensive than reinforcement, and the above figures include something of each; hence they *should* be lower.

5. This information was obtained by Hassan Bashir.

Losses and miscellaneous costs

Precise measurement of losses was also not available, and attempts to calculate losses did not match the general impression of engineers in CEWC as to what they were. We decided, after some discussion, on the following percentages:

Losses in	Peak percentage of loss	Off-peak percentage of loss
Subtransmission	2	2
High voltage and 11 kilovolt distribution	10	7
11/0.415 kilovolt transformation	2	2
Low voltage distribution (including transformation)	10	7

These are rough estimates, of course, but are useful for illustrative purposes.

Finally, there are a number of other costs to be considered. Some of these, like administrative costs and wages and salaries, are neither kilowatt nor kilowatt-hour related and are not relevant for marginal (or incremental) cost pricing. Others, like maintenance costs, do vary with system capacity and are thus increased as demand increases (see Table 5.2). We can now combine all the above data to get capacity costs of service.

Total capacity costs of service

We put the above costs on a yearly basis in Table 5.3, using an 11 percent annuity, which is equivalent to a 10 percent interest rate for a twenty-five–year plant life (10 percent is the currently recommended rate for public investments in Sudan).

The costs of supply at 11 kilovolts and 0.4 kilovolt seem somewhat high—about US$ 600 a kilowatt at 11 kilovolts, in 1973 prices, and US$ 850 a kilowatt at 0.4 kilovolt—but we have to allow for the load densities in the Khartoum area, which is widely spread with a low density population.

Energy Costs of the Blue Nile Grid

Our estimated incremental energy costs are:

Plant	(Millimes per kilowatt-hour)
Steam at Burri	4.5
New 60-megawatt steam	3.67
Diesel	5.5
Gas turbine at Kilo X	12.5

TABLE 5.2. MISCELLANEOUS COSTS OF THE BLUE NILE GRID, FISCAL 1972/73

Item	Costs (thousands of Sudanese pounds)			Incremental costs (Sudanese pounds per kilowatt per year)[a]
	Khartoum area	Blue Nile area	Total	
Headquarters and offices[b]	385	81	466	—
Generation				
Salaries and wages	233	109	342	—
Maintenance and operation	100	57	157	0.95
Distribution				
Salaries and wages	233	64	297	—
11-kilovolt maintenance and operation			190[c]	1.15
	259	131		
Low voltage maintenance and operation			200	1.21

a. Kilowatt capacity, recall, is 165 megawatts. There is an error of principle here, not corrected in this study. Maintenance costs depend on capacity levels, but capacity levels depend on demand, and so maintenance costs increase with demand. Since we are interested in the effect of an increment of demand on costs, our incremental maintenance costs per kilowatt should be related to demand, not capacity levels. The above estimates of incremental maintenance costs are therefore too low.

b. 50 percent of total headquarters costs (which latter are also shared with water supply).

c. Only aggregate figures are known; this split between 11 kilovolts and 0.415 kilovolts is our guess.

SOURCE: Based on data supplied by the Central Electricity and Water Corporation of Sudan.

We tried to undertake an experiment at Burri in which the fuel consumption rate was to be plotted against kilowatt-hour output at various levels. The slope of such a curve would give marginal energy costs at Burri. Unfortunately, the load conditions did not permit such an experiment. Average costs there are about 6.5 millimes per kilowatt-hour,[6] but this includes a large amount of fuel consumption during the year incurred because of the extensive use of Burri for spinning reserve. The estimate of these marginal energy costs is therefore a guess based on a judgment of the thermal efficiency of that plant's size and vintage compared with the efficiencies of newer and larger plants. (Burri's cost should naturally be well below the costs of a diesel plant.)

6. It is frequently easier to think of these costs in millimes, the Sudanese monetary subdivision equal to one thousandth of a pound.

TABLE 5.3. CAPACITY COSTS OF ELECTRICITY SERVICE IN SUDAN ACCORDING TO VOLTAGE LEVEL
(Sudanese pounds per kilowatt per year)

Voltage level	Incremental capacity costs
Bulk supply	
Generation and transmission	13.20
Maintenance	0.95
Total	14.15
11-kilovolt distribution	
Bulk supply costs	14.15
10 percent allowance for power losses	1.41
Costs of networks	4.73
10 percent allowance for power losses	0.47
Maintenance	1.15
Total	21.90
11-kilovolt distribution plus 11/0.4-kilovolt transformer	
11-kilovolt supply costs	21.90
2 percent allowance for power losses	0.44
Transformer costs (approximate)	0.50
Total	22.84
Distribution at 0.415 kilovolts (250 volts line-neutral)	
11-kilovolt supply costs	21.90
10 percent allowance for power losses	2.19
Costs of 0.415-kilovolt network, including transformer	7.91
10 percent allowance for power losses	0.79
Maintenance	1.21
Total	34.00

SOURCE: Based on data supplied by the Central Electricity and Water Corporation of Sudan.

For a diesel plant nearer the coast, costs are about 25 percent lower than shown in the informal table above because of lower transport costs. These costs include taxes on fuel oil and diesel oil, which amount to about 30 percent of the figure shown.

We now adjust the figures for losses in various parts of the system at peak and off-peak (see "Losses and miscellaneous costs," above). Tables 5.4 and 5.5 give energy costs of supply according to voltage level.

A word about the mean expected energy costs at peak might be useful. With demand varying randomly and with occasional equipment failures, a less efficient plant is often called in to meet peak demands. So the guesses in Table 5.5 as to the mean expected value of energy costs during peak periods are higher than the energy costs of the plant normally operating. For the Roseires hydro alternative, these costs are put somewhat higher than for the thermal alternative

TABLE 5.4. OFF-PEAK ENERGY COSTS OF THE BLUE NILE GRID (millimes per kilowatt-hour)

Cost component	Station	Bulk supply	11-kilovolts	11/0.415-kilovolts	0.415-kilovolts
Losses (percentage)	included	2	7	7[a]	2
Hydro	0	0	0	0	0
New steam plant	3.67	3.75	4.01	4.09	4.29
Burri (steam)	4.50	4.59	4.91	5.01	5.26
Diesels	5.50	5.60	6.00	6.11	6.42
Gas turbines	12.50	12.75	13.65	13.90	14.60

a. Includes 11/0.415-kilovolt transformation.
SOURCE: Based on data supplied by the Central Electricity and Water Corporation of Sudan.

because the peaking plant would be Burri, with diesels and gas turbines for standby.

This completes our work of estimating the various elements in the costs of the Blue Nile Grid. We now proceed to analyze system operations and the growth and variability of demand and supply (particularly of hydro power and energy supply) in order to derive the cost structure. Then we can turn our attention to tariffs.

System Operations of the Blue Nile Grid

While Roseires and Sennar dams in the Blue Nile Grid offer considerable potential for power and energy generation, their primary purpose is to regulate river flows and irrigate the fertile land schemes spreading out from Khartoum. We begin our analysis of

TABLE 5.5. PEAK ENERGY COSTS OF THE BLUE NILE GRID (millimes per kilowatt-hour)

Cost component	Station	Bulk supply	11-kilovolts	11/0.415-kilovolts[a]	0.415-kilovolts
Losses (percentage)	included	2	10	2	10
Hydro	0	0	0	0	0
New steam plant	3.67	3.75	4.13	4.21	4.54
Burri (steam)	4.50	4.59	5.05	5.15	5.56
Diesels	5.50	5.60	6.16	6.28	6.78
Gas turbines	12.50	12.75	14.03	14.30	15.43
Mean expected values at peak					
Roseires alternative	—	5.00	5.50	5.61	6.05
Thermal alternative	—	4.50	4.95	5.05	5.45

a. Includes 11/0.415-kilovolt transformation.
SOURCE: Based on data supplied by the Central Electricity and Water Corporation of Sudan.

system operations by examining the multipurpose nature of these dams.

River flows

The river flows of the Blue Nile, regulated by the dams at Sennar and Roseires, serve among the largest irrigation schemes in Africa. Before the introduction of the much larger Roseires Dam in 1966, about 756 million hectares were already irrigated in the Blue Nile Valley. Following this project, irrigation in the area has increased to over 966 thousand hectares, of which the Gezira Managil Schemes occupy 840 thousand hectares (see the map of the Blue Nile Grid appearing earlier in this chapter).[7] Extension of irrigation is continual. The largest project now under development is the Rahad Scheme, to be developed in two stages, of which the first will irrigate 126 thousand hectares, and the second, a further 126 thousand. The first stage of the Rahad Scheme will draw on water pumped from the Blue Nile and delivered along an 84–kilometer canal to a barrage on the River Rahad. The waters for irrigation will also be augmented slightly by the flows of the Rahad itself and by storage at the barrage.

The needs of irrigation in the dry seasons impose firm restrictions on the storage-discharge schedules of Roseires and Sennar dams. Nevertheless, even when operating within these restrictions, there is scope for substantial power and energy generation. Ultimately, a capacity of 210 megawatts is possible at Roseires, in seven 30-megawatt generators, of which 90 megawatts have been installed, and up to 15 megawatts are available from Sennar.

From records of river flows at Roseires between 1912 and 1962, we have compiled a histogram:

River flow range 10^9 cubic meters per year	Number of years when flow was in this range
21–35	1
26–30	0
31–35	0
36–40	5
41–45	7
46–50	11
51–55	13
56–60	6
61–65	4
66–70	3

7. In Sudan this hectarage is commonly thought of in terms of feddans, which are Egyptian units of area each roughly equal to 0.420 hectares or 1.038 acres. Sudanese sources would normally cite this increase in irrigated land as being from 1.8 million to 2.3 million feddans.

Given this large variance in flows, planning for contingency is of crucial importance. Current plans generally relate to an "80 percent dry year"—the chance being that, in four years out of five, flows will exceed this level, which is about 41 billion cubic meters per year. Equally, river flows exceed the median year flows half of the time, yielding substantial benefits to irrigation and electricity generation. Hence calculations for median and "20 percent wet years" are also included in the analysis.

Roseires

The river flows shown in Figure 5.1 for 1972 at Roseires have three phases:[8] (a) The flood season, lasting roughly from mid-June to mid- or late August (later still in wet years). The flows increase at enormous rates in this period, reaching over a hundred times the dry season flows. (b) The wet season, lasting roughly from early September (just after the peak of the flood season) until the beginning of December. The flows decline quickly in this period but are always large. (c) The dry season, lasting roughly from the beginning of December until the latter part of May.

In the flood season, the river carries substantial quantities of silt, and no storage can be contemplated. Reservoir levels are kept as close as possible to the absolute minimum, the sluice gates are fully open, and the maximum amount possible is passed through the turbines. The low waterhead during this period results in a reduction of turbine power capacity by about 30 percent. A further factor keeping turbine power down in this period is the increased height of water at the tailrace, resulting from high water discharge rates at the sluices and the turbines. The result of this flood season situation is that the system's maximum demand—74 megawatts during this period in 1972—exceeds the available power capacity of the Roseires generators, which is down to 20 megawatts or less per generator, and the steam plant at Burri is needed to provide the extra capacity. Sennar's megawatt capability is low in this period, too, for the same reason.

In the wet season, after the peak of the flood has passed, the river's silt content decreases and storage begins. The river flow is such that the reservoir can be filled within the month (of September, in this case) and can be maintained at this level until the river flow reaches a low level at the beginning of December. Continuous maximum power output from all turbines is possible during all of this period if needed, without any reduction of reservoir levels. It is in-

8. Incidentally, 1972 was drier than the "80 percent dry year." Profiles of the river flow and levels appear at the end of this chapter in Table 5.11.

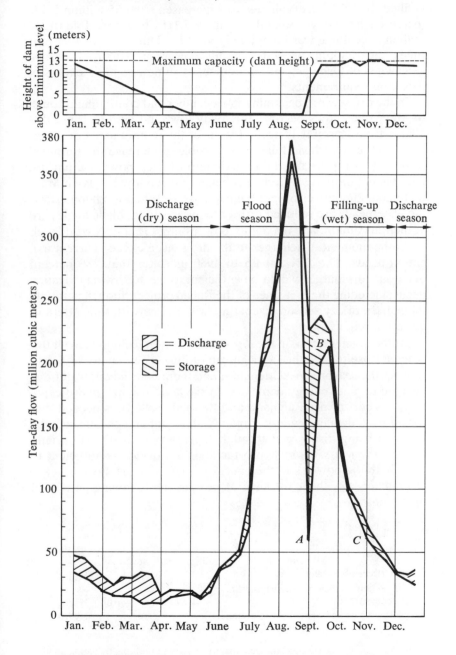

FIGURE 5.1. FLOW, STORAGE, AND DISCHARGE PATTERN AT
ROSEIRES DAM, SUDAN, 1972

SOURCE: Charted from data supplied by the Central Electricity and
Water Corporation of Sudan

deed evident that sluicing or spillage is substantial once the reservoir is filled. In 1972, reservoir releases increased from 65 million cubic meters each ten days (point A on Figure 5.1) by over threefold to 210 million once filling was completed (point B). This figure is over four times the amount needed for full power output from the 90 megawatts of turbines, and, of course, at all times well in excess of irrigation requirements.[9]

In the dry season, beginning in December and continuing through to May, river flows become relatively low, and continual net discharge from Roseires is needed to meet the requirements of irrigation. As the waterhead falls, it is possible to increase the turbines' blade angles (up to a certain maximum) to keep power output up, and it is not until the waterheads begin to reach low levels, in May, that maximum power output begins to drop. When the floods start, the waterheads are reduced further to avoid silting, blade angles are at their maximum, and maximum power output is at its lowest level.

At the moment, discharges in the dry season exceed current irrigation needs. The forecast up to 1980 indicates that "80 percent dry year" discharges would be sufficient to meet growing irrigation needs, including the first stage of the Rahad project, though naturally the pattern of dry season discharges will change with the pattern of irrigation requirements.

At the moment, too, in the *dry season,* the three 30-megawatt turbines at Roseires and the 15-megawatt turbine at Sennar are sufficient to meet the season's peak demand, and there is sufficient water discharged to meet energy demands. In the *flood season,* hydro capability is short of peak demand and thermal capacity is needed, but for off-peak demand energy is plainly abundant and cheap since the water is being discharged through the reservoir at the maximum rate. In the *wet season,* hydro facilities are evidently sufficient to meet both the power and the energy demands of the system.

Summing up, then, we have at present the following pattern of operations:

	Plant in operation	
Season	*Daily peak*	*Daily off-peak*
Dry (December–May)	Hydro	Hydro
Flood (June and July–August and September)	Thermal and hydro	Hydro
Wet (August and September–December)	Hydro	Hydro

9. An option of increasing storage capacity is open to both the irrigation and the electricity authorities in Sudan, and the design of the dam has an allowance for this option.

FIGURE 5.2. DAILY DISPATCHING SCHEDULE FOR SUDAN'S BLUE
NILE GRID, NOVEMBER 1, 1972

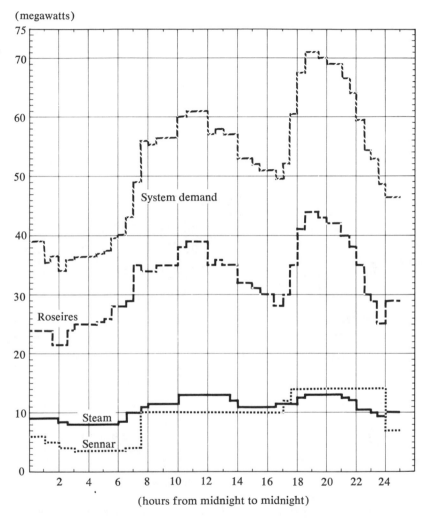

(megawatts)

(hours from midnight to midnight)

SOURCE: Charted from data supplied by the Central Electricity and Water
Corporation of Sudan

Since there is sluicing when hydro is operating, (marginal) energy
costs are near zero in all but, paradoxically, the daily peaks of the
flood season.

This pattern is not quite so evident from the curves of daily demand and the operating schedules shown in Figures 5.2, 5.3, and 5.4

FIGURE 5.3. DAILY DISPATCHING SCHEDULE FOR SUDAN'S BLUE NILE GRID, FEBRUARY 8, 1972

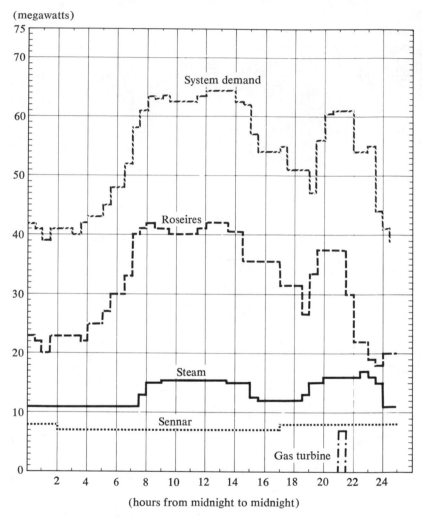

(hours from midnight to midnight)

SOURCE: Charted from data supplied by the Central Electricity and Water Corporation of Sudan

(examples of a weekday taken from each season). One oddity is that the steam plant is operating and delivering power at peak and off-peak in all seasons![10] It turned out that the Central Electricity and Water Corporation was behind on its plans for expanding the capac-

10. Steam plant is used as spinning reserve in the event of a failure of Roseires or its transmission lines.

FIGURE 5.4. DAILY DISPATCHING SCHEDULE FOR SUDAN'S BLUE NILE GRID, JULY 6, 1972

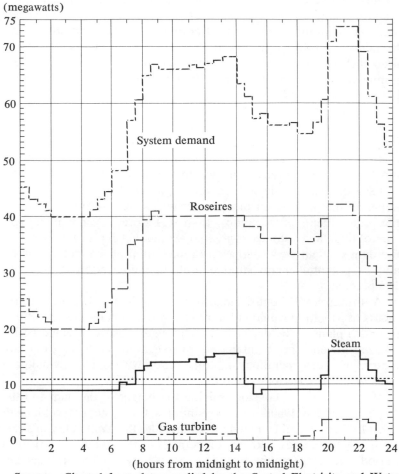

SOURCE: Charted from data supplied by the Central Electricity and Water Corporation of Sudan

ity of one of the feeders to North Khartoum, so that even though CEWC wished to use the energy available from Roseires, it could only use some. The only way of supplying the energy was by way of a parallel feeder from the Burri power station. Once allowance is made for this, the dispatching schedules and energy costs of supply fall into the pattern just described.

Expansion Plans

Clearly as demand grows and further expansion takes place, the pattern of operations and costs will change too. At present three plans are under review: (a) expansion of Roseires (two 30-megawatt sets); (b) addition of an oil-fired thermal plant (60 megawatts); and (c) addition of 30 megawatts at Roseires and 30 megawatts of oil-fired thermal plant. Below we consider the first two alternatives, noting that the third alternative will probably fall somewhere in between the results we obtain.

All three expansion plans relate to the 1970s and have not considered options and operations beyond then, on the assumption that they will all be the same. Yet this assumption does appear to be restrictive. Even in the dry years the reservoir is filled within a month, and for the remaining two to two and a half months of the wet season, water is sluiced at a very high rate. From Figure 5.1, it is apparent that in 1972 far more water was sluiced—over and above the requirements of irrigation—than was stored. A minimum measure of this "lost" storage is given by the area $A B C$ in Figure 5.1. If the dam's height were increased (a maximum of ten meters can be added), potential energy storage could be increased by up to about 150 percent.

A further point about raising the dam's height is that the requirements of irrigation would not impose a restriction on the operations of hydro plant in the dry season. The water reserves would be increased beyond the requirements of irrigation; outflows from any pattern of hydro operations, in conjunction with sluicing, would exceed or meet irrigation requirements.

If CEWC were to consider raising the height of the dam—in the 1970s or in the 1980s—the possibilities for system development open to them would be extended to include: the availability of year-round hydro energy (except, of course, in the flood season) for a period extending into the 1980s; the possibility of higher ratings, because of the higher heads, for the turbines occupying the last two or three places on the reservoir (recall that up to seven turbogenerators can be installed); and the eventual possibility of uprating the present turbogenerators.

This is not to suggest, of course, that these alternatives are better than those presently being considered. It *is* to suggest, however, that the assumption that developments in the 1980s will or should be identical whichever of the three addition or expansion alternatives are adopted is untrue. Perhaps, too, the restrictions on hydro system development set by irrigation have been taken too seriously, in the sense that a fuller development of hydroelectric potential would make them redundant.

Cost Structure of the Blue Nile Grid

We are now in a position to derive the cost structure of the grid, looking forward some years. To the cost structure of bulk supplies—that is, of generation and bulk transmission—we then add in the cost structure of distribution at various voltage levels. At that point we can consider the problems of translating this into cost-reflecting tariffs that meet the constraints of, for example, feasibility, simplicity, metering limitation, and finance.

Bulk supplies

The important feature of CEWC's hydro production is that each day's releases of water at Sennar and Roseires are determined for it, not by it. All CEWC can do is to choose (a) how much of the releases is sluiced and how much is passed through the turbines, and (b) the time-pattern of turbining over the twenty-four hours of the day. The power capability of the turbines and their electrical output per cubic meter of water depends upon the net waterhead and this, too, varies in a way that is outside CEWC's control. Thus, given the behavior of the river and given the Irrigation Department's decision about water releases, for each separate day there is a certain maximum number of megawatts and a certain maximum number of gigawatt-hours available to CEWC from Sennar and Roseires.

Thermal plant will be operated for a large proportion of the year in order to provide a spinning reserve. However, this thermal plant will contribute little energy, merely involving a constant hourly cost that is independent of the load being met from hydro. In the following discussion this fact will be disregarded. We are interested here only in those costs that vary with output, so when we now speak of thermal production we mean that the thermal plant is doing more than merely providing a spinning reserve. Such thermal production may be required for any of four reasons, apart from emergency outages: (a) Transmission and switching limitations prevent full use of hydro capability; (b) maintenance of hydro plant and of transmission lines is required; (c) system megawatt demand exceeds hydro capacity; and (d) system gigawatt-hour requirements exceed the day's hydro capability. We neglect the first two of these possibilities. The present switching limitations should soon be overcome and hydro plant can be taken out of service for annual maintenance between January and the end of May, one set at a time. Very little hydro energy is sacrificed since water availability is low then.

It is, then, roughly correct to say simply that thermal production in the second half of the 1970s will sometimes be required for demand reasons and sometimes for energy reasons. Simulation studies show that the times will be as follows:

Reasons	Roseires alternative	Thermal alternative
Demand	Mid-July to the end of October	All year.
Energy	May	May and August to September.

The first column, relating to the Roseires alternative, is illustrated in Figures 5.5 and 5.6. These forecasts are for 1977/78; the curves showing the monthly average available megawatts and gigawatt-hours indicate the average expectation. (They combine wet, median, and dry years, using weights of 1, 2, and 1.)[11] In a dry year, thermal production would be required for energy reasons for a much longer period, extending from mid-March to mid-June, while in a wet year it might not be required at all. The length of the period during which thermal production would be required for demand reasons would also vary according to whether the year were dry or wet, though not as much. But while such variability is relevant both for system planning and for system operation, it is the average expectation that is relevant for tariffs. This is so for two reasons. One reason is that tariffs are fixed in advance, before actual river flows can be known, and the other reason is that, being fixed for several years at a time, they would in any case have to reflect average conditions over a number of years.

Demand reasons necessitate thermal generation most of all in August and September, under both alternatives. This is when mean maximum available hydro megawatts fall sharply (because of the emptying of the reservoirs), so that the margin between system demand and total available megawatts reaches its annual minimum. System demand is predicted to rise to its annual peak in October, but rapid refilling of the reservoir normally restores hydro capacity, too, so that the demand reason for hydro generation will be much weaker.

In principle, the hours of an average year can be divided into two groups: (a) Hours when water is being sluiced so that extra kilowatt-hours can be produced at no extra cost; the marginal cost of energy,

11. See the end of this chapter, Tables 5.12 and 5.13 on pages 142–144.

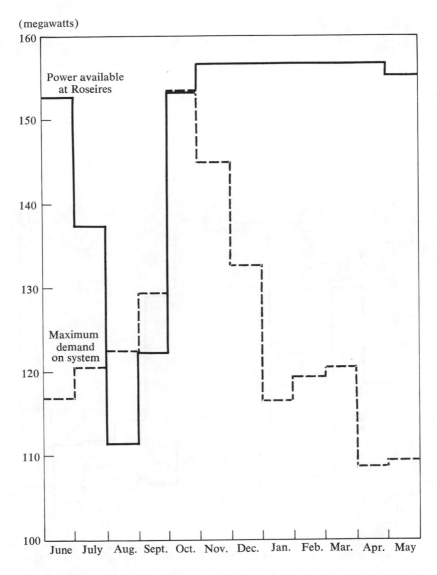

FIGURE 5.5. EXPECTED POWER AVAILABLE AT ROSEIRES WITH FIVE 30-MEGAWATT TURBINES IN 1977–78, CONTRASTED WITH TOTAL POWER DEMAND ON THE SYSTEM

(megawatts)

Power available at Roseires

Maximum demand on system

June July Aug. Sept. Oct. Nov. Dec. Jan. Feb. Mar. Apr. May

SOURCE: Charted from data supplied by the Central Electricity and Water Corporation of Sudan

123

FIGURE 5.6. EXPECTED ENERGY AVAILABLE AT ROSEIRES WITH
FIVE 30-MEGAWATT TURBINES IN 1977–78, CONTRASTED WITH
ENERGY DEMAND

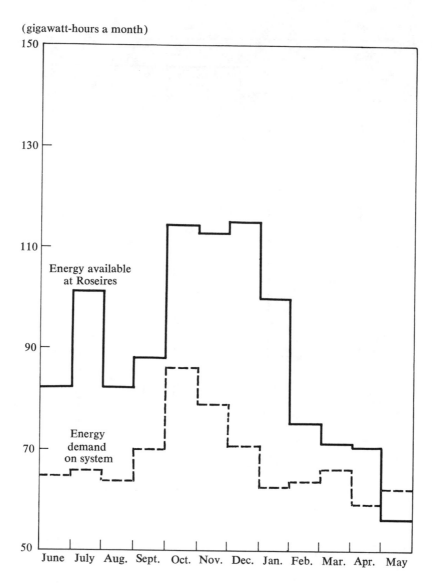

(gigawatt-hours a month)

Energy available
at Roseires

Energy
demand
on system

June July Aug. Sept. Oct. Nov. Dec. Jan. Feb. Mar. Apr. May

SOURCE: Charted from data supplied by the Central Electricity and Water
Corporation of Sudan

in other words, is then zero. (b) Hours when thermal plant is providing more than just spinning reserve, so that extra kilowatt-hours demand the use of more fuel; the marginal cost of energy is then the incremental (marginal) fuel cost of thermal generation. This has to be grossed up to allow for successively higher losses at 110 kilovolts, 11 kilovolts, and 0.415 kilovolt. Group (b) naturally applies when available daily hydro energy is fully used so that an increase in energy demanded necessitates more thermal generation. It may be that the increase is not met directly in this way but indirectly, in the sense that the additional supply is provided by Roseires, which then generates correspondingly less at some other time during the twenty-four hours. It is then the marginal thermal cost of the replacement energy at this other time that is relevant.

Group (b) also applies when hydro capacity is less than system demand, as noted above. Such demand reasons for thermal generation only apply during peak hours. We assume these to be from 7:00 A.M. to 2:00 P.M. throughout the year and 6:00 P.M. to 9:00 P.M. except in winter, when 5:00 P.M. to 8:00 P.M. is a closer approximation (see Table 5.6).

Marginal thermal generating costs will be an average of the incremental fuel costs of the various sets. We use the following figures per kilowatt-hour: new megawatt thermal sets, 3.75 millimes; existing Burri steam plant, 4.59 millimes; and gas turbine, 12.75 millimes. (These figures make a small allowance for transmission losses.) The correct average to use for peak hour generation is one where the weights are the proportion of the peak hours for which each type of plant will be running, but at less than capacity. This is because a plant that is either running at capacity or not running at all cannot produce an incremental kilowatt-hour. Since we do not know what these running times will be for an average year we have guessed the weighted averages to be 5.0 millimes for the Roseires alternative and 4.5 millimes for the thermal alternative, as explained above in the section on "Energy Costs of the Blue Nile Grid."

The relevant marginal generating cost for off-peak hours is the lowest obtained during those of the twenty-four hours when Roseires is generating since, as explained above, this is the time when extra energy will be produced. Hence, the figures we use are: 4.59 millimes per kilowatt-hour for the Roseires alternative; and 3.75 millimes per kilowatt-hour for the thermal alternative.[12]

To obtain a table of marginal energy costs, we can combine these cost figures with the list of months when thermal generation is re-

12. Compare with Table 5.4.

TABLE 5.6. DAILY PATTERNS OF DEMAND ON THE BLUE NILE GRID FOR 1972

Month	Morning peak			Evening peak		
	Commences at hour	Duration (hours)	Maximum Megawatts	Commences at hour	Duration (hours)	Maximum Megawatts
January	7:30 A.M.	6½	45.0	5:00 P.M.	3	57.0
February	7:00 A.M.	6½	47.0	5:00 P.M.	2½	48.0
March	7:00 A.M.	7	54.0	6:00 P.M.	3	60.0
April	7:30 A.M.	7	62.0	6:30 P.M.	3	69.0
May	7:00 A.M.	6½	58.5	6:00 P.M.	3	66.0
(Friday)[a]	(8:00 A.M.)	(5½)	(63.0)	(7:00 P.M.)	(2½)	(69.0)
June	7:00 A.M.	7½	68.0	8:00 P.M.	2½	74.0
July	7:30 A.M.	6½	58.0	7:00 P.M.	3½	61.0
August	7:00 A.M.	8½	65.0	7:00 P.M.	2½	62.0
September	7:30 A.M.	6½	58.0	6:30 P.M.	3	63.5
October	6:30 A.M.	7	64.5	5:30 P.M.	3½	69.0
(Friday)[a]	(7:00 A.M.)	(9)	(49.0)	(5:30 P.M.)	(4)	(57.5)
November	7:30 A.M.	6½	61.0	6:00 P.M.	4	71.0
December	7:00 A.M.	7	53.0	5:00 P.M.	4	69.0
Mean	7:00 A.M.	7	—	6:30 P.M.; earlier in winter	3	—

a. Day of rest. All other daily demand data for work days.
SOURCE: Based on data supplied by the Central Electricity and Water Corporation of Sudan.

TABLE 5.7 MARGINAL ENERGY COSTS OF THE BLUE NILE GRID, FISCAL 1977/78 (millimes)

	Roseires alternative						Thermal alternative					
	11-kilovolt		11/0.415-kilovolt		0.415-kilovolt		11-kilovolt		11/0.415-kilovolt		0.415-kilovolt	
Month	Peak	Other	Peak	Other	Peak	Other	Peak	Other	Peak	Other	Peak	Other
January	0	0	0	0	0	0	4.95	0	5.05	0	5.45	0
February	0	0	0	0	0	0	4.95	0	5.05	0	5.45	0
March	0	0	0	0	0	0	4.95	0	5.05	0	5.45	0
April	0	0	0	0	0	0	4.95	0	5.05	0	5.45	0
May	5.05	4.91	5.15	5.01	5.56	5.26	4.95	4.01	5.05	4.09	5.45	4.29
June	0	0	0	0	0	0	4.95	0	5.05	0	5.45	0
July	5.50	0	5.61	0	6.05	0	4.95	0	5.05	0	5.45	0
August	5.50	0	5.61	0	6.05	0	4.95	4.01	5.05	4.09	5.45	4.29
September	5.50	0	5.61	0	6.05	0	4.95	4.01	5.05	4.09	5.45	2.29
October	5.50	0	5.61	0	6.05	0	4.95	0	5.05	0	5.45	0
November	0	0	0	0	0	0	4.95	0	5.05	0	5.45	0
December	0	0	0	0	0	0	4.95	0	5.05	0	5.45	0

Note: Peak hours are 7:00 A.M. to 2:00 P.M. and 6:00 P.M. to 9:00 P.M. (5:00 P.M. to 8:00 P.M. in winter).
SOURCE: Calculations based on discussion in the text.

TABLE 5.8. CAPACITY COSTS OF THE BLUE NILE GRID
(Sudanese pounds per kilowatt per year)

Cost component	Level of supply voltage		
	11-kilovolt	11/0.415-kilovolt	0.415-kilovolt
Generation transmission			
(high voltage/11-kilovolt)	15.55	15.86	17.04
11-kilovolt distribution	6.35	6.48	6.95
11/0.415-kilovolt transformation	—	0.50	—
11/0.415-kilovolt transformation			
and 0.415-kilovolt distribution	—	—	10.01
Total	21.90	22.84	34.00

SOURCE: Based on data supplied by the Central Electricity and Water Corporation of Sudan.

quired (see Table 5.7). The losses by which the costs given above are grossed up to obtain energy costs at supply voltages are the same as those given earlier. In order to keep to complete months, the whole of July, and not just its second half, is treated as a period when demand reasons require thermal generation under the Roseires alternative.

Marginal energy costs are zero whenever there is both sufficient water and sufficient hydro capacity for extra kilowatt-hours to be producible without recourse to thermal plant. At other times, such recourse is necessary either because of water insufficiency or because of insufficient hydro capacity or (under the thermal alternative during May, August, and September) for both reasons. The costs, where they are positive for the same period under both alternatives, are lower in the thermal alternative because the new thermal sets would have a higher efficiency than the existing ones.

Other voltage levels

Capacity costs expressed in pounds per kilowatt per year of maximum demand have been derived earlier and are here repeated to complete the list of marginal costs. (See Tables 5.3 and 5.8.)

Derivation of Tariffs that Reflect Cost

To get from the cost structure to actual tariff proposals involves several steps that are usefully kept separate from each other. These steps are three: (a) Design practicable tariffs that reflect but, where necessary, simplify the cost structure. (b) Estimate the revenue from these tariffs and, according to whether it is too low or too high, adjust the tariffs downward or upward so that they would yield the desired revenue. (c) Work out a phased program for the transition from existing tariffs to the adjusted practicable tariffs. Below we concentrate on step (a), leaving some aspects of the other two steps to brief discussion at the end of the chapter.

Large consumers at 11 kilovolts

A discussion of the design of a practicable tariff that reflects cost finds a convenient starting point by concentrating on 11-kilovolt supplies and by taking the Roseires alternative. Since 11-kilovolt consumers are large, metering costs are relatively small. Since such consumers are few, complex metering systems are administratively practicable. So, for both reasons, it is possible to have a fairly complicated tariff for such consumers.

Take generation and transmission capacity costs first. An 11-kilovolt consumer's responsibility for these is a matter of his share of system demand at the time when this is closest to system generating capacity. His responsibility for 11-kilovolt distribution costs, on the other hand, is a matter of his share in the local distribution peak. Thus, charges that would reflect costs are approximately: £S 15.55 a kilowatt at time of system peak in August or September, and £S 6.35 a kilowatt at time of local distribution peak, that is, October in irrigation areas and June in Khartoum (see Table 5.8).

Such kilowatt charges, however, are neither practicable nor sensible. They are not practicable because the exact timing of these peaks is not known in advance. They are not sensible because such tremendous charges levied during just one or two hours a year would probably cause the peak to shift. This second and basic difficulty suggests the fundamental point that the design of a practicable tariff requires *not only* information about costs *but also* consideration of consumer reaction to tariffs.

This point can be looked at from both short-run and long-run points of view. From the former, what matters is that charges damp down consumer demand, on the principle that rationing by power cuts is worse than rationing by price. So price needs to be high at all times when there is a danger that demand might press upon capacity, being higher when the danger is greater and lower when it is lesser. In other words, the aim is to make the load curve flatter, so keeping the risk of supply failure to tolerable levels.

But this does not mean that the aim should be to chop off the peaks completely. On the contrary, consumers should be allowed to add to the peak to the extent that they are prepared to meet the extra costs involved. This brings us to the long-run point of view. The tariff should spread the 𝔖S 15.55 and the 𝔖S 6.55 over all *potential* peak hours so that the consumer meets the extra capacity costs of increasing his consumption during them. Thus the combination of the two points of view is that the tariff should provide some incentive to flatten the peak while spreading over it the incremental capacity costs. The more the tariff succeeds in flattening the load curve, the wider should be the spread; the less it succeeds, the narrower should be the spread. But only in the improbable event that the tariff has practically no effect at all upon consumer behavior, even in the long run, should charges all be concentrated upon one or two hours.

The 𝔖S 15.55 and the 𝔖S 6.55 can be charged to consumers either by means of a kilowatt-hour price (added to the energy price) or by means of a kilowatt charge. Taking these in turn, let us suppose, in order to provide an arithmetic example, that it has been decided to spread half of the 𝔖S 6.55 in June and the other half over the other eleven months; and to spread one quarter of the 𝔖S 15.55 in August, one quarter in September, and the other half over the other ten months. The addition to the kilowatt-hour energy price during each of the 310 potential peak hours in August would be: $\{[(1/11) \cdot 0.5 \cdot$ 𝔖S $6.55] + [0.25 \cdot$ 𝔖S $15.55]\}/310 = 13.5$ millimes or 𝔖S 0.0135. Alternatively, assuming that the sum of individual maximum demands of such consumers is, say, 1.2 times their contribution to system peak, there would be an August maximum demand charge per kilowatt of: $\{[(1/11) \cdot 0.5 \cdot$ 𝔖S $6.55] + [0.25 \cdot$ 𝔖S $15.55]\}/1.2 =$ 𝔖S 3.488.

These are only numerical examples. The two main issues are (a) how to spread the amounts between different hours and months, and (b) how to choose between kilowatt and kilowatt-hour charges. Something can be said about both. (a) The more that consumers are expected to react to incentives to alter the time-pattern of their consumption, the wider should be the spread. In practice one has to proceed by experience, starting with a moderate differential between different months and increasing it if the response is limited. (b) Where the number of hours of potential peak is large, a kilowatt-hour charge provides an equal incentive to the consumer to economize during all of them, while a kilowatt charge provides no incentive to reduce demand below the maximum so far attained during the billing period; kilowatt-hour charges during peak hours which vary from month to month may well fit in with variations in kilowatt-hour energy charges.

Both these last two remarks may be helpful to CEWC. The number of peak hours in August and September is 610 and in these months kilowatt-hour energy charges are necessary. Thus, if half the 𝔖S

TABLE 5.9. POSSIBLE MARGINAL COST REFLECTING TARIFF AT 11 KILOVOLTS
(millimes per kilowatt-hour)

Month	Off-peak cost of energy	Peak costs			
		Energy	Generation	Distribution	Total
January	0	0	2.41	1.10	3.42
February	0	0	2.41	1.10	3.42
March	0	0	2.41	1.10	3.42
April	—	—	2.41	1.10	3.42
May	4.91	5.09	2.41	1.10	8.47
June	0	0	2.41	5.37	7.78
July	0	5.90	2.41	1.10	8.92
August	0	5.50	13.50	1.10	20.10
September	0	5.50	13.50	1.10	20.10
October	0	5.50	2.41	5.37	13.28
November	0	0	2.41	1.10	3.42
December	0	0	2.41	1.10	3.42

SOURCE: Calculations based on discussion in the text.

15:55 were spread at 13.5 millimes a kilowatt-hour in August and September and the other half at 2.41 millimes over the other 3,040 peak hours, and if the £S 6.55 were similarly spread at 5.37 millimes a kilowatt-hour in June and October and 1.1 millimes over the other 3,040 peak hours, the kilowatt-hour tariff in Table 5.9 would result. This tariff, which compromises between regarding 11-kilovolt distribution capacity as determined by June and by October demands, could readily be simplified: for example, 18 millimes for peak hours August–October, 8.4 millimes for peak hours May–July, 4.9 millimes for off-peak hours May, 3.4 millimes for peak hours November–April, and 0.1 millime for off-peak hours except May. This would require only a two-rate time-of-day meter read at least four times a year, though for control purposes a simple maximum demand meter might also be useful.

A similar simplification is not easily obtainable with the thermal alternative. But, if the £S 6.55 were reflected in a suitable pattern of monthly maximum demand charges, while the £S 15.55 were treated as above, a possible set of kilowatt-hour charges would be: 18.4 millimes for peak hours August and September, 7.4 millimes for peak hours October to July, 4.0 millimes for off-peak hours May, August, and September, and 0.1 millime for all other off-peak hours.

What we suggest that CEWC should actually consider for its 11-kilovolt tariffs and for its larger 11/0.415-kilovolt consumers can only be spelled out in more general terms since the details would have to be worked out once the system's expansion plans are finally decided. But the approach illustrated above should be followed. Our proposals are: (a) a higher kilowatt-hour rate for about ten peak hours each day than for the remaining fourteen; (b) the highest kilowatt-hour rate to apply when demand is pressing upon effective available capacity *and* when hydro energy is insufficient to meet the twenty-four–hour energy requirement; (c) an intermediate kilowatt-hour rate, or more than one, at times when only one of these constraints applies; (d) a purely nominal kilowatt-hour rate when neither of them applies; and (e) kilowatt charges to be introduced only if treatment of either generation or of distribution capacity costs this way enables the tariff to be simpler. It ought perhaps to be added that the last principle is not meant to exclude the use of kilowatt charges to reflect the cost of any final feeders or transformers which are dedicated to a particular consumer. Such installations as are dimensioned to his individual needs ought to be charged to him, and a kilowatt charge is one way of achieving this—though not the only one. For example, the consumer at 0.415 kilovolt who is served directly by a transformer (a case for which separate cost figures are given above) could pay a kilowatt charge on his monthly maximum demand, he could rent the transformer, or he could pay a capital contribution toward it.

The suggestions made above can be applied to any consumer who is sufficiently large that the cost of providing and maintaining a two-dial meter with a time switch and, where relevant, a maximum demand indicator is a reasonable cost to bear in relation to the value of his consumption. In the case of 0.415-kilovolt consumers, the higher costs appropriate to this voltage level would, of course, be used in constructing the tariff.

Large consumers and interruptible supplies

Hitherto, all our discussion has related to tariffs that are to be fixed on the basis of expected average conditions where, except for faults, the consumers' requirements will be met peak and off-peak in wet and in dry years. For a minority of large consumers, the existence of interruptible supplies as an option may be a good idea. Such an option would offer them lower rates at times when power cuts are possible—that is, when they are most probable, in return for an understanding that they would be the first to be cut. The gain from such agreements would be either a reduction in capacity requirements or an increase in the security of supply of all other consumers. Both of there are well worth paying for, so concessions should be made to reflect this value.

Commercial policies for large consumers

It is not sufficient to promulgate interruptible tariffs and do nothing more. Consumers who might on balance benefit from them would need the advice of a commercial electrical engineer. This raises a more general point. The purpose of tariff structure is to provide consumers with incentives. A high rate both provides a message that special economy is called for and an encouragement to do something about it. But consumers by themselves may not understand the message, may undervalue the encouragement, and may not know how to do anything about it. They need help, and it is part of the job of the electricity industry to provide it. Tariffmaking very much needs to be supplemented by technical advice. One or more commercial engineers are essential to advise consumers and so the establishment of a post and training for it need to be part of the tariff reform. By helping consumers to adapt to the tariff structure, CEWC will be helping itself.

Large consumers and reactive power tariffs

For large consumers, metering reactive power, or—what amounts to the same thing—metering megavolt-ampere and megawatt demands, is worthwhile where it can be seen to lead to beneficial improvements in power factors. (The value of a commercial engineer is particularly evident in this area.) There are two effects of poor power factors: (a) Increased capacity costs of generators (but not, of course, of turbines) and of transmission and distribution equipment when poor power factors occur during the hours of peak megavolt-ampere demands. (To a good approximation these hours will be the same as the hours of peak megawatt demands.) That is, poor power factors lead to higher ratings of the electrical equipment. (b) Extra energy losses at peak and off-peak is the second effect. A built-in allowance for power factors of 0.8 (that is, ratios of megawatt to megavolt-ampere of 0.8) is implicit in the preceding cost and tariff calculations since the system is planned on an average power factor of 0.8. Also, the energy losses at peak and off-peak are (guesses of) *measured* losses on the system, and they too, therefore, reflect average power factors occurring at the time of measurement.

For consumers who are in a position to improve their power factors, some refunding is desirable if they are higher than 0.8 and some penalty is desirable if they are lower than 0.8. The issues in the choice of tariff types for reactive power or megavolt-ampere metering during peak hours are exactly the same as those spelled out and discussed above for active power or megawatt metering. Since

133

the number and occurrence of peak hours is nearly the same in both cases, and the problems of billing are the same, then if tariffs for capacity are on a kilowatt-hour basis, tariff penalties or refunds for reactive power should be on a kilovolt-ampere–hour basis; but if tariffs for capacity are on the basis of kilowatt demands during peak, then the tariff penalties or refunds for reactive power should be on a kilovolt-ampere basis. Taking the former basis, and denoting kilovolt-ampere–hours and kilowatt-hours during peak by *(KVAh) peak* and *(KWh) peak,* respectively, and peak hour capacity charges per kilowatt-hour by *C peak,* the formula for penalties or refunds would be: $C\ peak\ [1.0 - 0.8 \cdot (KVAh)\ peak\ /\ (KWh)\ peak]$. To take an example from Table 5.9, *C peak* during August would be 14.6 millimes per kilowatt-hour in this expression.

Actually, this overstates the desirable level of refunds or penalties somewhat since our capacity costs also include turbine costs, as well as those of electrical equipment, and such costs are not, of course, related to reactive power.

Regarding penalties or refunds for reactive energy at peak and off-peak, the appropriate formula is: $E\ [1.0 - (0.8 \cdot KVAh/KWh)^2]$, where E is the weighted average marginal energy cost over peak and off-peak hours, and the terms kilovolt-ampere–hours $(KVAh)$ and kilowatt-hours (KWh) are totals over all hours.

These two formulae can be used to design a power factor tariff offering refunds for improvements above 0.8 and penalties for power factors below. Tables or graphs can be designed showing the percentage penalties and refunds per kilowatt-hour as a function of power factor improvements at peak and off-peak, in which the penalties and refunds are zero for power factors of 0.8.

Small consumers at 0.415 kilovolts and 250 volts

In the case of tariffmaking for smaller consumers, both the cost of metering and billing and the lesser sophistication of the consumer necessitate simple tariffs. It follows that the tariffs can at the most reflect only one or two features of the cost structure, averaging out all other cost differences. As there are quite a few features in the cost structure, this raises the problem of choosing which of them to reflect in the tariff, and which to average out. There is a clear answer to this, at least in principle. It is that the cost difference should be chosen for reflection where the product of the cost difference and consumer reaction to it are greatest.

In order to show how a simple tariff can reflect only a simplified version of the cost structure, consider low voltage supplies under the thermal alternative. We start by merely describing costs and

TABLE 5.10. LOW VOLTAGE PEAK AND OFF-PEAK COSTS OF
CEWC
(millimes)

Month	Off-peak cost of energy	Peak Costs			
		Energy	Generation	Distribution	Total
January	—	5.45	—	—	5.45
February	—	5.45	—	—	5.45
March	—	5.45	—	—	5.45
April	—	5.45	—	18.70	24.15
May	4.29	5.45	—	18.70	24.15
June	—	5.45	—	18.70	24.15
July	—	5.45	—	—	5.45
August	4.29	5.45	28.0	—	33.45
September	4.29	5.45	28.0	—	33.45
October	—	5.45	—	—	5.45
November	—	5.45	—	—	5.45
December	—	5.45	—	—	5.45

SOURCE: Calculations based on discussion in the text.

therefore spread capacity costs only over the months when demand is likely to press upon capacity. Thus: £S 17.05 a kilowatt of generation and transmission capacity is spread over the 610 potential peak hours of August and September—28 millimes a kilowatt-hour; £S 6.98 + £S 10.01 a kilowatt of distribution capacity is spread over the 910 potential peak hours of April–June—18.7 millimes a kilowatt-hour. Earlier on, such costs were spread more widely because of possible consumer reactions causing a substantial change in consumption time-patterns, but Table 5.10 is different since it is a cost table, not a tariff table.

We can now illustrate two alternative ways in which these cost figures could be turned into a two-rate tariff. (The figures seem oddly low for reasons that will be discussed shortly, but let us take them seriously for a minute.) (a) Peak kilowatt-hour, 14.8 millimes; off-peak kilowatt-hour, 1 millime. (b) All April–September kilowatt-hours, 11.3 millimes; all October–March kilowatt-hours, 2.3 millimes. Neither of these represents the cost structure particularly well, but each does at least represent one aspect of it. If the choice lay only between them and (c) a single kilowatt-hour rate all the year round, the relevant considerations would be: the extra cost of a dual-rate meter and time switch for (a); and whether consumers would react more to a peak–off-peak differential of 13.8 millimes or to a seasonal differential of 9 millimes.

For the great majority of small consumers, the cost consideration would dominate, so that the effective choice among these three would lie between (b) and (c). With monthly meter reading, a seasonal tariff is little more expensive than a single-rate or block-rate tariff. Since it reflects costs better, a seasonal tariff should be preferred. However, it may be thought that consumers would not react very much to a seasonal tariff, so there is another possibility that deserves to be considered either as an additional complication or as an alternative. This is a load limiter tariff, where consumers subscribe to a certain maximum demand and are temporarily disconnected if they exceed it. In addition, they pay a flat kilowatt-hour rate. For the simple case with no seasonal variation, and assuming a diversity factor of 1.3, the monthly kilowatt charge would be: £S 34.04 · (1/1.3) · (1/12) = £S 2.18, though the available steps might well be in tenths or fifths of a kilowatt. The kilowatt-hour charge would then be considerably lower than that in the simple kilowatt-hour tariff. Thus the idea might be to have three optional tariffs available for small and medium-size low voltage consumers: a simple kilowatt-hour tariff (possibly with a cheap, small, first block to look after the needs of the poorest consumers); a load limiter tariff as just described; and a time-of-day tariff, possibly with seasonal variations, as described earlier. All of the smallest consumers would be on the simple tariff, while many medium-sized ones would opt for the load limiter tariff, and still larger consumers would opt for the time-of-day tariff. Initially, choice would be free, but as experience developed, some maximum kilowatt-hours might be set to the simpler tariff and some maximum kilowatts might be set to the load limiter tariff. (Alternatively, a cheap time-switched off-peak kilowatt-hour rate might be made an optional addition to the load limiter tariff.)

Illustrative figures were given above for the two-rate time-of-day tariff and for the two-rate time-of-year tariff, but none has been given for the simple kilowatt-hour tariff or for the load limiter tariff. Nor can such figures be given here, for reasons to which we now turn and that indeed suggest that the figures of 14.8/1.0 and 11.3/2.3 millimes were wrong.

To see this, consider the figure of 2.3 millimes for each kilowatt-hour calculated for all kilowatt-hours taken in the October–March season. Marginal cost for peak hours, under the thermal alternative, has been put at zero. Each figure was weighted by the hourly length of the period to which it relates: $[(5.45 \cdot 10) + (0 \cdot 14)]/24 = 2.3$. Some such weighting is necessary to obtain an average. But the number of hours is probably a bad set of weights. It seems unlikely that people will react 1.4 times as much to the rate in off-peak hours as they will to the rate during the ten peak hours. Yet how much they will react determines what the weighting should be. Perhaps the

nearest guess we can make is that the weights should be proportional to the kilowatt-hours consumed during the ten and the fourteen
hours. If the proportions were six to four, the right average would
be: $[(5.45 \cdot 6) + (0 \cdot 4)]/10 = 3.3$. It is interesing to note that this
weighting problem, which requires load curves of different consumers, did not arise earlier when we were discussing 11-kilovolt
tariffs. Because these tariffs simplified the cost structure much less,
we were there only averaging like with like. The peak ten hours on
each day of three successive months present no problem because
both the length of the period and total kilowatt-hours are pretty well
the same in each of the three months. So the rule is that complicated
tariffs present simple weighting problems, while simple tariffs
present complicated weighting problems. The design of good, low
voltage tariffs is an art as much as a science and actually requires
more load curve information than does the design of high voltage
tariffs.

There is a special point to be made about agricultural tariffs designed for farmers with small pumps. Since the horsepower rating in
effect measures maximum demand, a maximum-demand charge can
be combined with a kilowatt-hour charge without the expense of a
maximum-demand indicator. But if this is the only tariff available to
the farmer, the incentive it gives him is to buy as small a pump as he
can and to run it for as long as he can, including the peak hours. So
the charge per horsepower, in kilowatt terms, should equal the full
marginal capacity cost of £S 34.04 a kilowatt. An alternative that is
worth considering, if only as an option, would be to supply the energy at a low rate, with a time-switch to prevent use of the pump
during peak hours.

Finally, there is the rather obvious point to be noted that since we
have not looked at connection, metering, and billing costs we have
said nothing about devices for recovering these "customer" costs.

Finance

Earlier we distinguished three steps in tariff formulation, of which
only the first, the design of a practicable cost-reflecting tariff, has so
far been discussed. On the second step, two simple remarks will
suffice. The first is that it is probably sensible for Sudan's Central
Electricity and Water Corporation to make a handsome profit on electricity. For a public corporation to make a big profit is not very different from the levying of a tax on its output. And in Sudan, where
tax revenues are limited, it may well make sense to tax electricity.
There is also the point that not only will it be difficult to finance the

expansion of the systems in the most backward areas, particularly in the south, if good profits are not made from the more advanced areas but the financial constraint may create an undue restriction on the development and use of resources in the backward areas.

Our second point is that where, on financial grounds, it is necessary to set tariffs in excess of marginal costs, the aim should be to do this in a way that minimizes the effect on consumers' decisions. A fixed charge in excess of customer costs (or some variation of it such as a high-rate first block) may do this, though care must be taken that it does not discourage new consumers. More generally, the point is that those elements of the tariff which least affect consumer behavior should most exceed marginal costs.

Transitional Problems

The third step in tariff formulation concerns the transition from the present tariff structure—which, though simple, fails to reflect costs adequately—to the new structure. This will probably take some years, so it is important that it be planned. During the transition the types of meter appropriate to the new system can be chosen and, where they fit existing tariffs, can actually be installed. Temporary tariff changes must be carefully chosen so that they involve a movement toward, not away from, the new structure. A more general requirement, of course, is that the current problems of meter reading and of billing are overcome.

An important way to tackle the transition problem is to introduce the new tariffs as options. We have suggested this as a permanent part of the new structure in the case of interruptible tariffs and of low voltage tariffs. But it is also a useful device when a new tariff is meant to supersede the old one completely. First, the new tariff is introduced as an additional option and commercial engineers persuade those customers whom it would benefit to shift over to it. At subsequent tariff revisions, the old tariff is raised relative to the new one so that still more consumers shift over to the new one. When, finally, the new tariff is made compulsory, only a small number of consumers will make a fuss.

Pricing in Isolated Systems

The kind of pricing approach developed above can be applied, albeit more simply, to isolated diesel systems. The cost of more consumption in potential peak hours consists of an increased probability of supply failure in the short run and the cost of expanding capacity in the long run. Outside potential peak hours, marginal cost consists of fuel cost only. Hence any tariff that is more complex than a single kilowatt-hour rate should seek to make potential additions to peak-hour consumption more expensive than additions to consumption at other times.

When diversity is small, a load limiter tariff is suitable and is probably the cheapest alternative available. A two-rate, time-of-day tariff might also be suitable, though the greater cost and complexity of metering may rule it out for all but a small number of the largest consumers; also, one would have to be sure that the meters would function reliably on the small systems (supply failure being a problem)—if not, two-part tariffs would be more appropriate.

In considering the potential peak, it is important to remember that, just as with a hydro system, what matters is the peak of demand in relation to capacity. Thus, times when plant is out for maintenance may be included even though the absolute level of demand is not then near its maximum.

Optional tariffs should be considered, too. For example, the system might offer a single low kilowatt-hour price for pumping that is time-switched to stop it during potential peak hours.

TABLE 5.11. BLUE NILE FLOW
(period totals in 10⁶ cubic meters)

Period		80 percent year	1972 yield	1972 dam releases at Roseires	Ten-day mean levels at Roseires, 1972	Water height relative to minimum level
January	1–10	250	340	470	479.03	12.0
	11–20	213	290	458	478.20	11.2
	21–31	199	275	390	477.29	10.7
February	1–10	157	206	303	476.43	9.4
	11–20	132	177	251	475.88	8.9
	21–29	91	140	300	474.53	7.5
March	1–10	105	140	291	473.83	6.8
	11–20	88	97	343	472.77	5.8
	21–31	89	105	320	471.12	4.1
April	1–10	73	91	162	469.98	3.0
	11–20	73	131	200	469.28	2.3
	21–30	70	145	207	468.07	2.1
May	1–10	67	184	197	467.47	0.5
	11–20	94	154	134	467.36	0.4
	21–31	164	233	189	467.34	0.3
June	1–10	238	388	385	467.27	0.3
	11–20	371	440	408	467.32	0.3
	21–30	546	510	487	467.14	0.1

Month	Period				
July	1–10	841	967	701	467.02	0
	11–21	1,370	1,953	1,947	467.00	0
	21–31	2,764	2,159	2,350	467.04	0
August	1–10	3,925	2,976	2,780	467.03	0
	11–20	4,404	3,626	3,760	467.01	0
	21–31	4,988	3,264	3,231	467.38	0.4
September	1–10	3,939	2,275	606	474.93	7.9
	11–20	3,425	2,381	2,000	479.11	12.1
	21–31	2,916	2,264	2,148	479.87	12.9
October	1–10	2,207	1,455	1,491	479.99	13.0
	11–20	1,555	1,006	969	480.00	13.0
	21–31	1,166	886	818	479.99	13.0
November	1–10	978	697	606	480.00	13.0
	11–20	696	588	495	480.00	13.0
	21–30	553	484	438	479.96	12.9
December	1–10	437	363	354	479.69	12.7
	11–20	361	286	322	479.49	12.5
	21–31	326	244	361	479.01	12.0

SOURCE: Sudan Ministry of Irrigation.

TABLE 5.12. POWER AND ENERGY AVAILABLE FROM ROSEIRES IN 1977–78 WITH FIVE TURBINES

End of period		Maximum megawatts			Weighted average maximum megawatts, 5 percent losses	Maximum gigawatt-hours per day (and load factors[a])			Weighted average maximum gigawatt-hours per day, 5 percent losses
		Dry year	Median year	Wet year		Dry year	Median year	Wet year	
June	10	150.0	147.5	146.5	140.0	1.59 (44)[a]	2.18 (62)[a]	2.95	2.11
	20	148.5	146.5	143.5	139.0	2.38 (67)	3.10 (88)	3.44 (100)[a]	2.85
	30	144.0	143.0	139.5	135.0	3.45 (100)	3.43 (100)	3.34 (100)	3.24
July	10	141.0	137.5	136.0	131.0	3.38 (100)	3.30	3.26	3.14
	20	136.0	128.5	121.5	122.0	3.26 (100)	3.08	2.92	2.93
	31	123.0	114.5	108.0	109.0	2.59 (88)	2.75	2.59	2.54
August	10	112.5	107.5	101.0	102.0	2.70 (100)	2.58	2.42	2.44
	20	111.0	104.5	99.0	100.0	2.66 (100)	2.51	2.38	2.39
	31	111.0	105.0	99.5	100.0	2.70 (100)	2.52	2.39	2.41
September	10	121.0	110.0	104.0	106.0	2.90 (100)	2.64	2.50	2.54
	20	150.0	115.5	109.0	116.0	3.60 (100)	2.77 (100)	2.62 (100)	2.79
	30	150.0	141.5	117.0	131.0	3.60	3.40	2.81	3.14
October	10	150.0	150.0	150.0	142.5	3.60	3.60	3.60	3.42
	20	150.0	150.0	150.0	142.5	3.60	3.60	3.60	3.42
	31	150.0	150.0	150.0	142.5	3.60	3.60	3.60	3.42

November	10	150.0	150.0	150.0	142.5	3.60		3.60		3.60		3.42
	20	150.0	150.0	150.0	142.5	3.60		3.60		3.60		3.42
	30	150.0	150.0	150.0	142.5	3.60		3.60		3.60		3.42
December	10	150.0	150.0	150.0	142.5	3.60		3.60		3.60		3.42
	20	150.0	150.0	150.0	142.5	3.60		3.60		3.60		3.42
	31	150.0	150.0	150.0	142.5	3.42	(95)	3.54	(98)	3.60	(100)	3.35
January	10	150.0	150.0	150.0	142.5	3.02	(83)	3.09	(86)	3.20	(89)	2.94
	20	150.0	150.0	150.0	142.5	2.96	(82)	3.01	(84)	3.11	(86)	2.87
	31	150.0	150.0	150.0	142.5	2.60	(72)	2.78	(77)	3.07	(85)	2.67
February	10	150.0	150.0	150.0	142.5	2.37	(66)	2.58	(72)	3.07	(85)	2.52
	20	150.0	150.0	150.0	142.5	2.21	(61)	2.38	(66)	3.07	(85)	2.38
	28	150.0	150.0	150.0	142.5	2.00	(56)	2.23	(62)	2.98	(83)	2.24
March	10	150.0	150.0	150.0	142.5	1.81	(50)	2.07	(57)	2.78	(77)	2.07
	20	150.0	150.0	150.0	142.5	1.71	(47)	2.00	(56)	2.73	(76)	2.00
	31	150.0	150.0	150.0	142.5	1.41	(39)	1.97	(55)	2.59	(72)	1.89
April	10	150.0	150.0	150.0	142.5	1.17	(32)	1.88	(52)	2.48	(69)	1.76
	20	150.0	150.0	150.0	142.5	1.13	(31)	1.79	(50)	2.34	(65)	1.67
	30	150.0	150.0	150.0	142.5	1.06	(29)	1.68	(47)	2.20	(61)	1.57
May	10	150.0	150.0	150.0	142.5	1.01	(28)	1.58	(44)	1.98	(55)	1.46
	20	150.0	150.0	150.0	142.5	0.96	(27)	1.49	(41)	1.88	(52)	1.38
	31	148.0	147.5	148.0	140.0	1.10	(31)	1.98	(44)	2.10	(59)	1.51

a. Load factor (percentage units) uses weighted average maximum megawatts (fifth column of this table) as its base.
SOURCE: Central Electricity and Water Corporation of Sudan.

TABLE 5.13. MEAN EXPECTED MAXIMUM MEGAWATTS AND GIGAWATT-HOURS FROM HYDRO COMPARED WITH LOAD FORECAST, FIVE TURBINES AT ROSEIRES

Month	Weighted maximum megawatts of hydro power available with 5 percent transmission loss	Maximum megawatts of power available with 5 percent transmission loss (weighted average expected)	Total megawatts	System maximum demand (megawatts)	Maximum monthly gigawatt-hours available with 5 percent transmission loss (weighted average)	Monthly average gigawatt-hours available with 5 percent transmission loss (weighted average)	Total gigawatt-hours per month	Energy demand (gigawatt-hours per month)
June	138.5	14.25	152.8	117.0	72.825	9.73	82.6	65.0
July	124.25	13.4	137.7	120.7	91.84	9.33	101.2	65.9
August	102.75	8.65	111.4	122.4	75.80	6.15	82.0	63.9
September	113.25	8.90	122.2	129.5	81.60	7.04	88.6	70.0
October	139.6	13.45	153.1	153.5	103.85	10.33	114.2	86.3
November	142.5	14.25	156.8	145.0	102.6	10.26	112.9	79.3
December	142.5	14.25	156.8	132.8	105.5	9.63	115.1	70.6
January	142.5	14.25	156.8	116.4	41.7	8.32	100.0	62.6
February	142.5	14.25	156.8	119.3	68.7	6.87	75.6	63.6
March	142.5	14.25	156.8	120.7	63.6	7.5	71.1	66.6
April	142.5	14.25	156.8	108.8	61.7	8.95	70.7	59.7
May	142.25	14.25	155.5	109.5	45.9	10.15	56.1	62.2

SOURCE: Central Electricity and Water Corporation of Sudan.

CHAPTER 6

An American
Tariff Structure

An examination of the tariff structure of an American electric utility will show, by example, how to suggest improvements in tariffs even when cost information is fairly limited. The example also shows the extraordinary and unnecessary complexity of some traditional tariffs, a complexity that can produce curious incentive effects. It is the neglect of such effects—that is, a failure to look at tariffs in terms of their effects on resource allocation—that is a major defect of the old-fashioned approach to tariffs.

The system in question has a summer peak, largely on account of the air-conditioning load, with maximum demand usually occurring on a July or August weekday afternoon. Demand is also fairly high in June and September. While scheduled outages for maintenance are confined to the other eight months, the resulting decline in available generating capacity is much less than the fall in demand. It follows that the incentive to customers to keep down demand ought to be much lower during these eight months than during the four summer months. One can say this even in the absence of information about incremental capacity costs.

Hourly incremental energy cost figures are available for one typical day in each of the last twelve months. No clear seasonal pattern is shown by these figures; in any case, for the study of such variations one would require incremental cost figures averaged over groups of similar days rather than for individual days. The diurnal variation, on the other hand, is both marked and consistent for all of the twelve typical days, incremental cost from 8:00 A.M. to 10:00 P.M. averaging almost double its level from 11:00 P.M. to 7:00 A.M. Thus, although one cannot say exactly how large a difference between night and day kilowatt-hour rates would best reflect costs, it is perfectly plain that a big differential is better than none at all.

The residential tariff, subject to a minimum monthly charge of US$ 1.31, is shown in the tabulation below:

Kilowatt-hours a month	Tariff (cents a kilowatt-hour)
For the first 40	6.28
Next 110	4.27
Next 150	3.21
Next 200	2.70
Over 500, for billing periods:	
Mid-May to mid-October	2.70
Mid-October to mid-May	1.71

This is a declining-block tariff. The high price of the first two blocks fulfill the same function as would a fixed monthly charge in respect to consumer costs. It is the decline in the third block onward that is of doubtful usefulness. It makes the incremental cost to a large consumer of an extra kilowatt-hour less than for a small consumer when there can be no systematic difference in the marginal costs of supplying them. Once upon a time there may have been such a systematic difference, when small residential consumers used electricity for little more than lighting, when lighting created the peak, and other uses were not concentrated similarly in the evenings. In the United States of today, however, tariffs developed to meet this situation are merely an anachronism.

The seasonal variation in the 500-plus kilowatt-hour follow-on rate (tail-block rate) is a relatively recent development. This rate was introduced in response to the emergence of a summer peak in order to develop the winter space heating load. Apparently the move has been successful, thus demonstrating that consumers can be responsive to price incentives. While the extra consumption is presumably daytime rather than nighttime, the concession only relates to the seven winter months when, as we have seen, there is no pressure on capacity. Since residential consumers do not pay any kilowatt charge, such seasonal variation in their kilowatt-hour charges is entirely appropriate. The criticism of this seasonal variation is merely that it does not extend to all residential consumers, but only to large ones. Once again, the marginal cost of electricity varies between consumers in a way that reflects no systematic difference in the marginal costs of supply. One cannot help noting that such price discrimination in favor of consumers whose additional consumption is likely to be particularly price elastic is precisely what one would expect of a profit making enterprise.

The tariff structure attempts to encourage space heating more specifically in the cases of commercial consumers. Since they are fewer and larger than are industrial consumers, it is feasible for the utility to ascertain the connected load of their space heating equipment for tariff purposes. Thus the demand charges for commercial consumers are:

Kilowatts of billing demand	Each month per kilowatt
First 60	$0.
Next 440	$2.41
Excess over 500	$2.27

Space heating attracts a rebate on these demand charges: The measured demand used in determining the billing demand in October through May is reduced by 75 percent of the excess over 25 kilowatts of the total connected load of the heating equipment, where this equals or exceeds 150 kilowatts. Thus, consider a consumer whose winter monthly billing demand is 300 kilowatts. He will pay a demand charge of $240 \cdot \$2.41 = \$578.40$. Now, suppose that he puts in 165 kilowatts of space heating. His monthly billing demand will be reduced in winter by 75 percent of the excess of this over 25 kilowatts, that is, by 105 kilowatts. This will save him $105 \cdot \$2.41 = \$253.05$ a month and will go a fair way toward paying for the increase in his billing demand which use of the heating will entail. Thus while the addition of electric heating to his load will cost him the same for the extra kilowatt-hours as will any other use, the extra kilowatts are cheaper than for other uses. Once again there is price discrimination, though this time it is both between uses and between customers; consumers taking more than 500 kilowatts would obtain a smaller reduction in their kilowatt charge than in the example. There is a similar feature in the tariff for industrial consumers.

A second feature common to both commercial and industrial consumers is the ratchet clause that, in certain cases, provides another complicated form of seasonal variation in demand charges. For commercial consumers the clause runs: Billing demand is the maximum measured demand in the twelve months ended in the current billing month if such demand is less than 75 kilowatts; otherwise, it is the maximum measured demand for the month but not less than 75 kilowatts; and, in either event, not less than two-thirds of the maximum billing demand, up to 200 kilowatts, in the months of June to September, inclusive, of the preceding eleven months plus one half of the excess (if any) of such maximum billing demand over 200 kilowatts.

In order to work out what this ratchet clause means, take a consumer whose maximum demand always exceeds 75 kilowatts but falls below 500 kilowatts. Such a consumer, it appears, will be charged on whichever is the *greater* of two measures. The first is his actual maximum demand during the month. The second is two-thirds of his previous summer maximum demand up to 200 kilowatts plus half of its excess over 200 kilowatts. Thus, if his previous summer maximum demand was 450 kilowatts, this second measure will be two-thirds of 200 plus half of 250 = 258 kilowatts. In this case, his billing demand in any nonsummer month will be his maximum demand in that month or 258 kilowatts, whichever is greater.

Suppose, to start with, that in nonsummer months this consumer's maximum demand always lies above 258 kilowatts. Then the ratchet provisions will not apply and there will be no seasonality in the demand charge at all.

Suppose, alternatively, that in nonsummer months the consumer's maximum demand does lie below 258 kilowatts. Then, the amount he pays in respect to nonsummer months will not vary with maximum demand in those months. In other words, the incremental cost of a kilowatt to the consumer in those months will be zero. An increase in his maximum demand during summer months, on the other hand, will raise not only his summer bills but also the amount he pays in the rest of the year. The effective incremental cost to the consumer of a summer kilowatt will then be very high indeed. Thus, suppose that his summer maximum demand of 450 kilowatts occurs in July. An increase in it from 450 to 451 kilowatts will cost him an extra $2.41 in that month. In addition, it will raise his billing demand in the seven nonsummer months from 258 kilowatts to 258.5 kilowatts, adding $1.205 (or half of $2.41) to his demand charge in each of those months. Hence the extra July kilowatt will cost the consumer $2.41 plus 7 · $1.205, a total of not less than $10.845.

The effective prices per kilowatt for this customer will be as follows: July, $10.84; June, August, and September, $2.41; all other months, zero. Hence, for the minority of commercial consumers to whom the ratchet provision applies, seasonal peak pricing exists. But do they understand and respond to this absurdly complicated provision?

A simple seasonally varying kilowatt charge would be much superior to the space heating and ratchet provisions. It would be simpler to understand, it would involve no more metering or meter reading than at present, and it would avoid the present unjustified discrimination between uses and between consumers.

We now turn to a feature which is peculiar to the tariff for large high voltage supplies, that is, for industrial consumers. Apart from its ratchet and space heating provisions, its monthly demand and energy charges are:

Demand charges

First 200 kilowatts	$384
Next 1,800 kilowatts	$2.10 per kilowatt
Excess over 2,000 kilowatts	$1.79 per kilowatt

Energy charge

First 50,000 kilowatt-hours	1.66¢ per kilowatt-hour
Next 250,000 kilowatt-hours	1.52¢ per kilowatt-hour
Next 300 kilowatt-hours per kilowatt	1.23¢ per kilowatt-hour
Next 200 kilowatt-hours per kilowatt	1.07¢ per kilowatt-hour
Excess	0.96¢ per kilowatt-hour

Here, the third and fourth blocks in the energy charge are kilowatt-related so that the amount paid depends upon billing demand as well as upon kilowatt-hours consumed. This can cause the effective marginal cost of a kilowatt to the consumer to differ from its nominal cost. To show this, we now work out the total monthly bill of two consumers who have the same billing demand but different energy consumptions.

Billing demand, denoted D, is in excess of 2,000 kilowatts. Energy consumption, denoted C, is sufficiently in excess of 900,000 kilowatt-hours to put the consumers in the 1.07-cents energy block. Demand charge = $384 + (1,800 \cdot \$2.10) + (D - 2,000) \cdot \$1.79$. Energy charge = $(50,000 \cdot \$0.0166) + (250,000 \cdot \$0.0152) + (300D \cdot \$0.0123) + (C - 300D - 300,000) \cdot \$0.0107$. Adding all this up and simplifying gives a total charge = $\$2,004 + \$2.27D + \$0.0107C$. Hence for this customer an extra kilowatt of billing demand costs an extra $2.27 and an extra kilowatt-hour of energy consumption costs 1.07 cents.

The second customer has a billing demand, and hence demand charge, the same as the first, but an energy consumption which is only sufficient to put him in the 1.23-cent energy block. His energy charge = $(50,000 \cdot \$0.0166) + (250,000 \cdot \$0.0152) + (C - 300,000) \cdot \$0.0123$. In this second case: total charge = $\$1,524 + \$1.79D + \$0.0123C$. Hence, for this customer, an extra kilowatt of billing demand costs an extra $1.79 and an extra kilowatt-hour of energy consumption costs an extra 1.23 cents. This means that his effective marginal charge for a kilowatt is 21 percent lower than it is for the previous consumer. There seems to be no possible justification for this; it probably is an entirely unintended consequence of the tariff. A simple kilowatt charge, uniform for all consumers at the same voltage level and varying seasonally, would be much better.

For industrial consumers the demand charges, at least, do vary between daytime periods and the low demand periods of nights, weekends, and holidays. This variation is achieved by reducing the measured demand during these periods by one-third in ascertaining billing demand. Thus, a firm with a daytime maximum demand of 6,000 kilowatts will pay $1.79 for an extra kilowatt of daytime demand and either nothing for an extra kilowatt of night, weekend, and holiday demand (if demand then is below 9,000 kilowatts) or $1.19 (if demand then exceeds 9,000 kilowatts). The incentive to keep down daytime demand is appropriately much higher than the incentive at these other times.

This system of charging for maximum demand requires a continuous measurement of consumption. If the integration period is say, thirty minutes, the result is a record on tape of the consumer's consumption summed over thirty-minute intervals. It follows that without any extra metering cost the same record could be used to allow diurnal variation in the kilowatt-hour rate. Since, as noted above, the night-day change in marginal running cost is substantial, such variation is desirable. For commercial and residential consumers, on the other hand, night-day variation in kilowatt-hour rates would involve substantial extra metering costs, so that its desirability cannot be assessed without more information.

The main changes in the tariff structure that would improve it can now be set out simply. Declining blocks (except at the beginning, as an alternative to a fixed charge) should disappear and the seasonal variation in the kilowatt-hour rate should be extended to all residential consumers. For commercial and industrial consumers, the space heating incentives, the ratchet clause, and the kilowatt-related kilowatt-hour prices should be replaced by a seasonally varying kilowatt charge and much simpler kilowatt-hour charges. The latter should vary diurnally where existing metering permits.

The optimal levels of the various charges in a new structure along these lines would require a great deal of calculation. But even with only the very limited information available as described in the second and third paragraphs of this chapter, a move in the right direction can confidently be recommended. The extra metering and billing costs which in other cases might argue against this are negligibly small in the present case. Finally, the greater simplicity and comprehensibility of the new tariffs would constitute an additional advantage.

CHAPTER 7

Rural Electrification in Developing Countries

Rural electrification is a comparatively new field of investment in developing countries. In common with other initiatives to invest in new areas, particularly areas where living standards and productivity are very low, rural electrification raises a number of basic questions for investment analysis. For example: What are the prospects for successful investment? What project justification procedures are appropriate given that the investments are intended to serve both economic and social aims? In particular, is the economic rate-of-return calculation a suitable basis for project appraisal in low income areas? If so, how do we estimate economic costs and benefits? What pricing and financial policies are appropriate?

This chapter inquires into such questions. It begins with a general discussion of rural electrification in developing countries—the extent of investment, the technology and costs, and the aims and the outlook for successful investment. It then discusses project justification procedures and pricing and financial policies.

Program Development and Returns

Rural electrification in developing countries is intended to serve both economic and social aims. To understand these aims and how they might best be achieved, it is first useful to know something about the extent and growth of village electrification in developing countries and the costs and the uses to which electricity is put.

A somewhat expanded version of Chapter 7 appeared as *Rural Electrification* (Washington, D.C.: World Bank, October 1975). This booklet is available on request from the Publications Office, World Bank, 1818 H Street, N.W., Washington, D.C. 20433, U.S.A.

TABLE 7.1. EXTENT OF RURAL ELECTRIFICATION IN SELECTED REGIONS

	Population in 1971			Village and rural population served in 1971 [a,b]	
	Total	Village and rural [a]	Village and rural [a] (percentage)	Millions of persons	Percentage
Region	Millions of persons				
Africa	182	165	91	7	4
Asia	934	700	75	105	15
Latin America	282	140	50	32	23
Selected countries in Europe, Middle East, and North Africa [c]	143	87	61	45	15
Total	1,541	1,092	71	189	12

a. Definitions of *village* and *rural* vary among countries. Generally, villages are conglomerations of 5,000–10,000 persons, or fewer; rural refers to low density populations outside the villages, often persons living in clusters close to large farms.

b. Electrification data are not available for each country and the percentages should be taken as typical levels for countries in the region, about which there may be considerable variance.

c. Algeria, Cyprus, Egypt, Iran, Morocco, Saudi Arabia, Tunisia, and Turkey.

SOURCE: Electrification data are compiled from miscellaneous documents and correspondence with countries, and are not official statistics. Population data are from United Nations documents.

Extent and growth

Countries are putting increased resources into rural electrification. As one might expect, the resources countries allocate to it increase with their per capita incomes, with the result that rural electrification is more extensive in Latin America than in Asia, and more extensive in Asia than in Africa (see Table 7.1). Total cumulative investment in rural electrification by developing countries was about US$10 billion by 1971,[1] or about 10 percent of total investment in the electric power sector. This figure includes generation, transmission, and distribution.

Future investment in electrification is likely to be much larger. Many countries indicate that the rate of investment is generally likely to be higher than in the past and to form an increasing proportion of total investment.[2] Some countries, including Iran, Egypt, Turkey, and Thailand have announced major new initiatives, while others, in particular India and most of Latin America, are to continue and often expand on theirs.

The information is not good enough for a precise forecast of the level of investment, nor of the population likely to be affected. But it does seem that the total new investment (in 1972 prices) is likely to exceed $10–$15 billion in the next ten years—which is over 10 percent of total new investment—bringing supplies within the reach of 300 million more people. Up to about half of these people, comprising 15 percent of the village or rural population, may be able to afford service. Thus a total of, say, one-quarter of the village or rural population would be served ten years from now, compared with about three-quarters in urban areas at the present time.

Technology and costs

Electricity is introduced into rural areas in three ways: through (a) autogenerators serving single consumers; (b) autogenerators serving several consumers on a local network; and (c) public supplies from the main grid system. The term *autogeneration* refers to isolated generators powered by diesel engines, small steam turbines, or microhydro turbines. They range in size from about 5 kilowatts, sufficient to meet minor needs of, for example, refrigeration and lighting on a farm, to over 1,500 kilowatts, sufficient to meet the motive power needs of a large sugar processing plant.

---

1. The American billion—10^9 or 1,000 million—is used here and throughout the chapter.

2. United Nations Inter-Regional Seminar on Rural Electrification, New Delhi, December 1971. Papers never published; draft papers available.

Public supplies from the main grid consist of medium voltage (typically 11- to 40-kilovolt) subtransmission links to transmit electricity from the grid to the larger demand centers of an area, plus low voltage distribution within the demand centers.

Investment in rural electrification is mostly in public supplies from the main grid; at a guess, over 80 percent of rural electrification is supplied in this way. For small loads in remote localities, however, utilities often find that it is cheaper to meet electricity needs by installing small autogenerators. In the absence of public supplies, shops, farms, and agro-industries will often install their own autogenerators to meet their own particular needs in lighting, refrigeration, heating, and motive power; often, they also supply a few local consumers and provide public lighting if such demands occur when their equipment would otherwise be unused. Autogeneration, serving single or several consumers, is very common in rural areas.

Evidently, the utility must often make a decision whether to provide electricity from the grid or from local autogenerators. This decision depends on a number of factors: for example, the expected level and growth of demand; the expected utilization of the investment; the distance from the main network; and the difficulty of terrain, which can affect costs enormously. Table 7.2 displays some typical cost data at two levels of demand.

The capital costs of supplies from the grid are much higher than those of autogeneration, but the fuel, operation, and maintenance costs are much less. When the use of the project is high, and is reflected in high load factors (the ratio of average to peak rates of consumption), this strongly favors the more-capital, less-fuel intensive investment in supplies from the grid. Taking the 50-kilowatt projects, the relative annual costs of the two projects at various load factors are as shown in Table 7.3.

The fuel bill heavily penalizes autogeneration. In general, it compares well with public supplies from the grid only at low load factors—except when the demands are remote. This last point is important, since to extend a subtransmission link by 25 kilometers to an isolated demand point may cost around $100,000 ($10,000 a year at 10 percent annuity), with the kinds of effect on the capital costs of public supplies shown in Table 7.4. Such cost increases are sufficient to make autogeneration the better alternative for all but high load factor demands. To see this, it is useful to consider the effect of distance, shown in Table 7.5, on cost comparisons, presented in Table 7.3. To judge from these figures, it is extravagant to extend networks to meet small demands in areas remote from the grid. However, the same subtransmission networks can be used to meet much larger demands, so that if a good demand develops from

TABLE 7.2. TYPICAL COSTS OF AUTOGENERATION AND
PUBLIC SUPPLIES, 1972

Item	Autogeneration[a]		Supplies from grid[b]	
	50-kilowatt project	25-kilowatt project	50-kilowatt project	25-kilowatt project
Consumers served	140	70	140	70
Capital costs (thousands of U.S. dollars)	34	25	56	38
Fuel, operation, and maintenance (cents per kilowatt-hour)	6	6	0.5	0.5
Billing and administration (thousands of U.S. dollars per year)	2	1	2	1

a. Includes one standby motor generator.
b. Average length of subtransmission line for each village is assumed to be 4 kilometers.
Note the economies of scale in capital costs. The 50-kilowatt and 25-kilowatt projects could
serve fully developed loads in villages of about 2,000 and 1,000 persons, respectively. Demands
from farms and agro-industries outside the village may add anything from 20 to 100 kilowatts or
more to total capacity demands. Capital costs, it can be seen, range from $400 to $550 per customer in the above case of supplies from the grid (or $40 to $55 per capita in the village served).
However, for large villages of 5,000–10,000 population, these costs may drop to $200 per con-
sumer ($20 per capita) or less.
SOURCE: World Bank, *Rural Electrification: A World Bank Paper* (Washington, D.C.,
October 1975), p. 19.

farms, agro-industries, and several villages, average costs may decline very quickly to about 4–8 cents a kilowatt-hour.

It is now possible to explain how electrification schemes evolve
in rural areas. It is a fascinating process that has three or four
phases. The initial phase is one of private generation, in which only
a few scattered, isolated businesses may need and be able to afford
electricity. They obtain electricity by installing their own generators, and it is common to find them used for such purposes as refrig-
erating milk on farms, lighting and heating egg and chicken farms,
refrigeration and lighting in shops, refrigeration on a large scale in
slaughterhouses, or meeting the motive power needs of large agro-
industries such as sugar processing. During this phase, the motive
power needs of small farms and businesses are generally met
directly by animals or by small diesel engines.

In the second phase, the need to meet small collective demand for
electricity may develop from several households and businesses that
require, for example, public lighting and private lighting, and from
large and small businesses and farms that make further demands.
During this phase, small local networks or "microgrids" are often

155

TABLE 7.3. RELATIVE ANNUAL COSTS OF 50-KILOWATT PROJECTS

Cost components	Autogeneration (thousands of U.S. dollars)			Supplies from grid (thousands of U.S. dollars)		
	10 percent load factor	25 percent load factor	50 percent load factor	10 percent load factor	25 percent load factor	50 percent load factor
Annual capital costs[a]	4.5	4.5	4.5	5.6	5.6	5.6
Fuel, operation, and maintenance	2.6	6.6	13.2	0.2	0.5	1.0
Billing and administration	2.0	2.0	2.0	2.0	2.0	2.0
Total	9.1	13.1	19.7	7.8	8.1	8.6
	(cents per kilowatt-hour)			(cents per kilowatt-hour)		
Average	21	12	9	18	7	4

a. Annuity of 10 percent used on electrical components, 15 percent on mechanical components of autogenerators (taking their shorter lifespan into account).
SOURCE: World Bank. *Rural Electrification: A World Bank Paper* (Washington, D.C., October 1975), p. 20.

TABLE 7.4. CAPITAL COSTS OF PUBLIC SUPPLIES: 25-KILOMETER EXTENSION OF A SUBTRANSMISSION LINK
(thousands of U.S. dollars)

	50-kilowatt scheme	
Cost components	4 kilometers from grid[a]	29 kilometers from grid
Generation and transmission	24.0	24.0
Subtransmission	18.0	118.0
Local distribution	14.0	14.0
Total	56.0	156.0
Annual capital costs	5.6	15.6

a. The 4-kilometer case corresponds to the data in Tables 7.2 and 7.3.
SOURCE: World Bank, *Rural Electrification: A World Bank Paper* (Washington, D.C., October 1975), p. 21.

extended from local autogenerators installed through public or private initiative.

If the collective demand becomes large enough, and offers good use of equipment, the second phase may be by-passed or lead to the third phase—full-fledged electrification from the grid system. The microgrids are taken over and extended; subtransmission links replace the old autogenerators, which are scrapped or used elsewhere; and small and large businesses begin to turn to electricity as a source of motive power in preference to animals or diesel engines (often creating a useful second-hand market in the latter), and may even introduce some new processes as a result. During this third phase, a number of major demand centers can be identified in a region, stem-

TABLE 7.5. AVERAGE COSTS OF AUTOGENERATION AND PUBLIC SUPPLIES BY LOAD FACTOR
(cents per kilowatt-hour)

		Public supplies	
Load factor	Autogeneration	4 kilometers from grid	29 kilometers from grid
10 percent	21	18	40
25 percent	12	7	17
50 percent	9	4	8

Note: Since average costs in urban areas are about 3 cents a kilowatt-hour, it is extravagant to extend networks to meet small demands in areas remote from the grid. However, the same subtransmission networks can be used to meet much larger demands. If adequate demand develops from farms, agro-industries, and several villages, average costs decline very quickly to about 4–8 cents a kilowatt-hour.
SOURCE: Data and calculations in Tables 7.2, 7.3, and 7.4.

ming from the larger villages and the farms and agro-industries that lie outside of them. A design has to be worked out to route the electricity network so as to economize on the heavy costs of subtransmission and distribution lines.

Once the networks have been established, a fourth and final phase follows quite naturally. Now close to the networks, centers of *low* demand can be connected up at very low marginal cost. Whereas the initial thrust into a region may cost $50,000 to $200,000 for each demand center, secondary thrusts into areas of low demand may now cost only $5,000 to $20,000. (Many areas of low demand, however, remain remote from the main networks, and for this reason it is never worth electrifying them from the main grid; even in North America and Europe, where rural electrification programs were substantially completed twenty years ago, many areas continue to be served by local autogenerators.)

Practically every country has some degree of rural electrification, but different countries are in different phases. Broadly speaking, African countries are largely in the first phase of private generation, but are gradually beginning the second and third phases of meeting the larger collective demands from the grid or local autogenerators. Asian, Middle Eastern, and North African countries are mostly in the midst of the third phase, of connecting the main demand centers to the grid. Most Latin American countries are in the fourth and final phase, or connecting low demand centers to networks already established in rural areas.

As we remarked earlier, the term *rural electrification* is normally associated with electrification from the grid system, that is, with the third and fourth phases of electrification. The relative magnitudes of each phase may be gauged from Table 7.1 and also from the statistics for Mexico in Table 7.6, which show that over 50 percent of the rural population live in areas of low demand. Similar distributions in the sizes of village, and in the areas of high and low demand, can be observed in most countries.

Uses of electricity

There is a surprisingly wide range of electricity uses in rural areas, for both household and productive needs. Generally speaking, the total demand stemming from productive needs is higher than that stemming from households, as can be seen in Table 7.7. These data refer to typical situations and understate the productive uses since many small business demands creep in under domestic and general tariffs.

TABLE 7.6. POPULATION DISTRIBUTION OF VILLAGES
IN MEXICO

Population of village, by category	Number of villages	Population	
		Number	Percentage
Low demand areas (25 percent electrified)			
Less than 100 persons	55,376	1,823,900	7
100–499 persons	28,494	6,944,500	26
500–999 persons	7,346	5,091,900	19
Medium to high demand areas (30 percent electrified)			
1,000–4,999 persons	5,207	9,681,800	37
5,000–9,999 persons	416	2,894,300	11
Total	96,839	26,436,400	100

SOURCE: Comisión Federal de Electricidad, Mexico.

The relative demands from households and producers vary markedly from one area to another. Often, the demand in an area may be dominated by one large consumer, as with irrigation or cotton processing. Though some areas may use electricity for a wide range of productive purposes, others may use it for little more than domestic and public lighting.

In addition to the various agro-industrial demands that develop from the local agriculture, it is not uncommon to find demands developing from twenty or more commercial activities in a single village, such as for light and refrigeration in shops and services, and for light, heat, and motive power in workshops (carpentry, welding, and repair shops are typical examples). Community demands may include public lighting and demands from a local church, a water pump, a police station, a school, and a health center. Growth in local agriculture and wages, and improvements in complementary infrastructure, can thus generate all kinds of uses for electricity.

Consumption levels in rural areas are, of course, much less than in urban areas. But again it is surprising that there is often a strong response to rural electrification from consumers, reflected in high, sustained rates of growth of demand once an area is electrified (see Table 7.8). Average demand for each consumer varies among areas largely because of variations in the type of productive uses (and also with the age of the project because of the growth of demand). Irrigation pumpsets, for example, consume about 5,000 kilowatt-hours a year in India, while a large agro-industry may consume 100,000 kilowatt-hours a year or more.

To sum up, there is often a surprisingly strong response to rural

TABLE 7.7. DISTRIBUTION OF ELECTRICITY DEMAND IN RURAL AND URBAN AREAS FOR VARIOUS COUNTRIES, 1971 (percentages)

Country	Rural areas					Urban areas	
	Producers' demands			Total	Household demand	Producers' demand	Household demand
	Farms	Agro-industry	Commercial-community				
Chile	9	26	32	67	33	n.a.	n.a.
China, Republic of	10	. . .16 . . .		26	74	80	20
Costa Rica	—	—	—	70	30	43	57
El Salvador	—	—	—	45	55	60	40
Ethiopia	—	. . .21 . . .		55	45	44	56
India	59	. . .21 . . .		80	20	89	11
Nicaragua	15	. . .45 . . .		60	40	30	70
Pakistan	23	. . .17 . . .		40	60	90	10
Tanzania	—	—		75	25	80	20

SOURCE: Rural data have been compiled from correspondence and miscellaneous documents provided by the countries; urban data have been compiled from similar sources and from restricted World Bank appraisal reports.

TABLE 7.8. CONSUMER DEMAND IN URBAN AND RURAL AREAS FOR VARIOUS COUNTRIES, 1971[a]

Country	Demand per consumer (kilowatt-hours per year)		Annual growth rate of demand (percentages)	
	Rural[b]	Urban[c]	Rural	Urban
Costa Rica	1,900	6,000	20	10
El Salvador	1,000	4,000	20	10
Ethiopia	800	2,000	40	15
India	1,000	n.a.	15	10
Thailand	200	4,000	12–20	22

a. Estimates that are purely illustrative and not averages.
b. For selected areas.
c. For capital cities except Thailand data, which is an average.
SOURCE: Rural data are estimates based on various documents and project reports provided by the countries; urban data are inferred from World Bank appraisal reports.

electrification projects. This is reflected in high rates of growth of demand, though they start from very low initial levels. This response stems from a wide range of uses of electricity.

Aims and net returns

Having discussed both demand and supply sides, it is now useful to put the two together and discuss the net returns—social, economic, and financial—that are expected from the investments.

Most countries stress the social importance of their rural electrification programs, in particular, the need to raise the standard of living in rural areas and to provide a counterweight to excessive urbanization. But many of the returns, as illustrated above, are of economic importance since they stem from the voluntary demands of communities, houses, and businesses for a cheaper or superior form of energy. Indeed, many countries state that unless the programs are set in an economic context, the results are disappointing. For this reason, they stress the importance of both economic and social aims.

Where the economic content of rural electrification programs is large, it may seem reasonable to expect satisfactory financial returns—electricity increases energy use in the area, often reduces energy costs, and is far superior in quality to the alternatives. But this is not the case, at least for a period of years. Three factors account for this: (a) the high initial investment costs associated with low density populations, often remote from the main networks; (b) the low initial demand levels in relation to the capacity of the networks,

161

TABLE 7.9. COMPARATIVE DATA FOR URBAN AND RURAL
AREAS, 1972

Item	Urban	Rural
Consumption (kilowatt-hours per consumer per year)	4,000	600[a]
Load factor (percentage)	50	20[a]
Investment in subtransmission and distribution per consumer (approximate U.S. dollars)	100	300
Average costs (approximate cents per kilowatt-hour)	2.5	6–10[a]
Average price (approximate cents per kilowatt-hour)	2.8	4
Mean per capital annual income (U.S. dollars)[b]	800	125

a. Typical initial conditions.
b. Data for El Salvador, 1973.
SOURCE: World Bank, *Rural Electrification: A World Bank Paper* (Washington, D.C., October 1975), p. 26.

which have large indivisibilities and which may take over 10 years to develop fully in relation to capacity; and (c) the arguments for keeping tariffs low in relation to costs to meet the social aims of cheap energy to low income households and small businesses. Table 7.9 illustrates these factors. The initial average costs are over two or three times those incurred in urban areas, and though average prices are nearly 50 percent higher, this is not, of course, sufficient to make up the deficit. As both load factors and the level of demand rise, average costs decline very quickly, though the possible financial gains from this are often undermined by the system of declining-block tariffs widely adopted in many countries.

Financial assistance is generally considered to be necessary, therefore, at least in the early years. This assistance takes several forms, including low interest capital from internal or international sources, special depreciation provisions, preferential tariffs, and contributions in kind from the rural areas, such as voluntary labor. (It is also interesting to note that when it was desired to promote rural electrification in the United States in the 1930s, it was considered necessary to finance it on concessionary terms in accordance with the Rural Electrification Act of 1936.)

Outlook

As long as the investment programs are expanding, the fact is that continued financial assistance is required. Accepting this, however, three other facts are becoming clear: (a) In many electrified rural areas, the financial returns are improving markedly over time, though from very low initial levels. One reason is that there are substantial economies of scale as demand and consumer density increase. (b) Although existing projects are mostly in the better developed areas, extensions to less developed areas in the same region need not undermine overall financial or economic performance; the better developed areas have absorbed the brunt of the high initial costs and, as explained earlier, subsequent extensions cost much less. (c) Financial performance can often be improved significantly by appropriate attention to pricing policy. Low prices often exist in places where they are unnecessary on account of ill-structured tariffs. The consumption of large farms and agro-industries is often subsidized, for example, even though they are able and willing to pay more for the service.

Taking a long perspective and a constructive attitude toward tariff policy, it therefore seems that there are good prospects both for continued expansion and improved financial performance. Nevertheless, the prospects of low financial returns in the initial years, and the arguments for subsidizing small businesses and low income households, invalidate any simple criterion for project selection based on financial profitability. A broader basis for project selection is called for and is being sought by many countries and institutions.

Project Justification

In the social and economic justification of rural electrification projects, it is useful to begin with a study of economic returns and then work social factors into the analysis. Confusion between social and economic aims is then avoided and trade-offs (to the extent that they occur) can be examined. This approach is followed below. The starting point is a discussion to clarify the nature of the economic benefits. Following is a discussion of the practical aspects of benefit measurement; forecasting demand and benefits; cost analysis; and cost–benefit (economic rate-of-return) calculations. This covers the economic side. This is a traditional analysis involving forecasting benefits and comparing them with the costs of the (least-cost) project in an economic rate-of-return calculation. The social side is then brought into the picture in the discussion of criteria for project acceptability.

The economic analysis of costs and benefits, it should be noted, has two main purposes. One—the usual one—is to provide a consistent guideline for an efficient allocation of investments among the various sectors in urban and rural areas, and some indication, therefore, of economic priorities. The other is to provide some measure of the economic costs of investments when social aims are strong, economic returns low, and conflicts arise. (Conflicts do not always arise, however, and some investments are *socially and economically desirable*.) Economic rate-of-return calculations can be very helpful for these purposes, and are suggested here. They only break down when social arguments are overwhelmingly strong, as with water supply projects in drought areas. But this, in our experience, is *not* the case for rural electrification.

The nature of economic benefits

There is a very close relationship between the level of use of electricity and the level of benefits derived from it, in the sense that when use is low only a few people may be benefiting marginally from the service, and the converse is true when use is high. The benefits most frequently quoted, and which are all related to use, are that electricity: (a) increases productivity and output in rural areas by reducing the costs of energy and thus increasing the profitability and output of farms, agro-industries, and commerce; (b) adds to the standard of living in village homes and communities; (c) and, on account of these two benefits, helps stem migration from rural areas to cities. (The latter—the problem of urban-rural balance—is related to use because, to the extent that people and businesses are attracted to rural areas by electricity, they will use it.)

There is, in fact, little hard evidence as to the effect of electricity on migration. Most investigations have revealed, as one might expect, that older people migrate mainly in search of jobs, while the younger ones migrate in search of jobs and education or to begin families.[3] Also, the countries with the largest rural electrification programs generally are the most urbanized (see Table 7.1, for example).

Nevertheless, despite migration to the cities, and whatever its causes, the economic output of farms, agro-industries, and rural commerce is increasing, large numbers of villages are increasing in population and are in a process of modernization. As a result, demands for electricity, and the range of uses to which it is put, are also increasing. Hence, there are positive benefits to look for, even if electricity by itself has little or no effect on stemming migration to cities.

In monetary terms, and ignoring complications about shadow prices and income distribution for the moment, the benefits of electricity to families and businesses are to be measured by the amount

3. Dennis Anderson, Mario Bicard, Maria Luisa Calderon Sol, and Antonio Orellana, with Xabier Beltran de Heredia, Maria Cristina de Cabrera, and others, "Costs and Benefits of Rural Electrification: A Case Study in El Salvador," a joint report (restricted circulation) by the World Bank Public Utilities Department and Universidad Centroamericana José Simeón Cañas (Washington, D.C., February 1975).

of their income that these families and businesses are prepared to allocate to it. This is the monetary value placed by individuals on the service. Small businesses and low income families, in particular, make this allocation decision very carefully. The decision is made in the light of the many complex and varied circumstances of the family or business and consideration of the alternative uses for this portion of family or business income.

The estimation of benefits, in monetary terms, can begin by adding up these monetary valuations over all family and business consumers. For practical purposes, it is useful to divide the monetary benefits into two parts: actual revenues (the "direct consumer benefits"), and surplus monetary benefits ("consumers' surplus benefits"), where the latter simply reflects a general tendency of consumers to value service by more than the amount they may be asked to pay for it.

Revenue estimation presents no new problems, apart from the difficulties of forecasting. But, what is the nature of the surplus benefits, and how can they be estimated?

For farms, agro-industries, and commerce, there is normally a substitute for publicly supplied electricity in the form of, for some examples, autogenerators for large agro-industries; diesel engines for many purposes, including irrigation, corn grinding, and motive power in small agro-industries; often, animal power; small autogenerators for refrigeration on farms; or kerosene refrigerators. The surplus benefits are the net advantages of electricity over these alternatives. In many activities the same output can be produced by the substitute, so the net advantages are cost savings. This is commonly the case, for example, with electricity used for motive power, as in irrigation pumping and corn grinding, where diesel engines can do the same job, though often at a higher cost. It is also the case for many large farms and agro-industries that can also produce the same output using diesel powered autogenerators, though again, often at a higher cost.

In other activities, however, electricity is far cheaper or of higher quality, and extra output also results; the benefits constitute the net increase in the profits of the activity. As one example, this is often the case for small businesses using electricity for motive power or refrigeration. The alternatives (including associated capital and maintenance costs) are often too expensive or unreliable, and the business cannot make a profit with them. So new business activities can and do spring up if costs are cut sufficiently for them to become profitable. Refrigeration in shops and corn grinding are common examples in Central America.

By taking a representative sample of such activities, covering different types and sizes, it is possible to estimate a typical ratio of surplus benefits to actual amounts paid for electricity. From these ratios, and knowing the number of different types and sizes of business consumers, it is possible to calculate total surplus benefits directly. The level of these benefits rises commensurately with the number and total demand of these consumers.

On the household side, the surplus benefits of some uses, such as for lighting and ironing, are also the net advantages over substitutes. The benefits of others, such as refrigeration and television, are generally the household's valuation of a new product, practical substitutes not being readily available. As we remarked earlier, the total monetary benefits would be the amount of income the households are prepared to allocate to such goods.

It is exceptionally difficult to estimate the monetary value of surplus benefits to households, however, even with well-conceived sample surveys and elaborate econometric analysis. The problems of randomness, of specifying a correct algebraic model of household behavior, and of identifying the separate influences on household behavior, have so far precluded reliable estimation. What we do know, however, is that when service is benefiting many households, there will be a strong demand for it, reflected in quite good revenues (the direct benefits). So it is still revealing to look at the direct benefits even if the surplus benefits cannot be estimated—though the point that such monetary benefits are omitted from the economic rate-of-return calculations means that tolerance is needed for projects with returns somewhat below the opportunity cost of capital.[4]

Practical aspects of benefit measurement

In practice it is necessary to confine cost–benefit analysis to what can be measured, and to supplement data as necessary by descriptive analysis. The benefits that can be measured will generally be three: the direct benefits to households, reflected in the revenues; the direct benefits to farms, agro-industries, and commerce, again reflected in the revenues; and the surplus benefits to farms, agro-industries, and commerce, reflected in the net effects on profits and output of electricity to these activities. Descriptive analysis of households, and of household demand, can be couched in terms of indications of living standards, the number and percentage of the people demanding service, and what these people are likely to use electricity for. Analysis of the growth of the area, its history,

---

4. See the discussion below, under "Criteria for project acceptability."

whether people are likely to move into it or remain there or both, are also important.

Where there is a strong demand for "productive uses," the above basis of benefit estimation will be more than sufficient to justify a good project. The revenues from farms and agro-industries should boost the project, unless tariffs are low. Counting in the surplus benefits to productive uses will boost justification further. If, for example, 80 percent of demand is from productive uses, and surplus benefits are (typically) 50 percent, then benefits are $1.5 \cdot 80 = 120$ percent of revenues, not counting household demand, and 140 percent in total. This can make a large difference in rate-of-return calculations. Where, on the other hand, there is a small demand for productive uses, coupled with low tariffs and a low level of demand from households, justification will be difficult—as perhaps it should be in these situations.

Forecasting demand and benefits

Because of information shortages, demand forecasting in areas hitherto without service involves more uncertainty than it does in areas with service. Forecasting therefore requires a good deal of judgment and guesswork. This points to the importance of flexibility in project design and investment planning, and to the need to collate information from several sources and to experiment, as discussed below.

Evidence from other projects. The most concrete basis for a forecast is provided by projects already functioning in other areas of the country. Most countries in Latin America, the Middle East, and Asia, and several in Africa, have had pilot projects and sometimes extensive programs for several years. The thing to do is to examine how both domestic and nondomestic consumers have responded to these projects. There are five things to look at: the growth in the number of consumers; the growth in consumption per consumer; the types of consumers, including a breakdown by, for example, large and small, irrigation, various agro-industries, and various levels of household consumption; the changes in load factor; and, if possible, the kinds of uses to which electricity is put. This information should not be difficult to obtain in a well-run program; if it is, there should be some self-questioning both about whether projects are properly monitored and about whether recordkeeping is systematic.

An elementary understanding of the areas in which these projects are located is also necessary in order to understand the factors that affect the returns of the projects. Often, a look at the living conditions in an area, the area's infrastructure, and the growth of local agriculture, agro-industries, commerce, and wages may be sufficient for this purpose.

In building up forecasts from experience with other projects, it is desirable to use information from areas that are comparable with the area under consideration. Such areas should have comparable population and income levels, and be comparable with respect to local infrastructure, housing quality, and levels of activity in agriculture, agro-industries, and commerce. More generally, they should be areas comparable in size and levels of development.

Such coincidences in size and levels of development do not always occur, even within broad limits. However, to obtain an impression of how size and levels of development interact with the project, it is a good idea to look at how projects have functioned in larger and smaller areas, and in both more and less developed areas. This will provide a range to the forecasts and a basis for interpolation.

Evidence from neighboring countries. If such evidence is scarce or is not available within the country, either because there are no pilot projects or because they are new and it is too early to form a judgment, the experience of neighboring countries is often highly relevant. (Indeed, one can often go even further afield.) Again, the aim is to see how people and businesses have responded to projects in different situations.

The use of pilot projects. Where there is absolutely no local precedent for the forecast, it is difficult to justify a full-scale program. The case for pilot projects—developing a base for forecasting, as well as providing experience in project design and management—is a strong one. It should be noted, too, that pilot projects can often be provided out of a very small fraction of a utility's budget. Typically about five villages can be electrified for $250,000, depending on their size and location.

Evidence from low income areas of cities. Household demand is related to income, so evidence can be sought among groups having similar incomes. Often many households in villages are really no poorer than many electrified households in low income areas of cities. Analysis of the latter may give some indication of the likely response from households in villages (even though the costs of serving villages are higher).

Economic and social analysis of the area. Any evidence carried over from experience in other localities and countries needs, of course, to be supplemented by local inquiry. On the nondomestic side, items to look at are five: the type and growth of local agriculture; the development of local agro-industries; the extent of local commerce (strong correlations with the population of the area appear here); quality of local infrastructure, such as roads, schools, water, and health centers; and any government plans on projects for the area. Apart from its importance for forecasting, this information is important for determining priorities.

On the domestic side, items to look at are four: family income data (if available or ascertainable); quality of housing; history of the area; and migration in the area. There are some empirical points to be made about each of these.

The main factor that determines household demand is household income. Electrical appliances and the costs of running them can be expensive for a low income family, even if large subsidies are offered on electricity costs. Table 7.10 illustrates these points.

Family income and costs are not the sole determinants, of course. A large proportion of families in rural areas often can afford electricity but nevertheless do not request it. One reason for this is that there is a high propensity for families to move between regions in search of jobs, the opportunities for which may vary seasonally in the case of agriculture and agro-industries. Illiteracy, fragmentation of the family unit, and a lack of incentive to develop the home are also important. Generally, although there are exceptions, it is those families seeking better housing who are also likely to seek electricity; some kind of solidity or permanence in house structure is an important indicator of the likelihood of demand.

Turning to the history of the area, this too can provide indications of the likelihood of demand. Many villages, for example, have long (if scantily recorded) histories, with long traditions in commerce and socialization; for this reason they can and do form points for growth.

Related to this is the possibility of migration into an area. Despite migration from rural areas to cities, rural populations often do not decline. Furthermore, there is evidence from several countries to show that villages are frequently able to attract people out of rural areas on a par with cities. (Nearly all the villages we have studied in El Salvador also showed a general increase in the number of homes.[5]) Evidence of this kind is exceptionally important in indicating the regard people have for the future of the village; it also indicates whether demand can be expected to grow.

5. United Nations Inter-Regional Seminar on Rural Electrification. See also Anderson and others, "Costs and Benefits of Rural Electrification."

TABLE 7.10. FAMILY INCOME AND EXPENDITURE ON ELECTRICITY

	Family income[a] (in U.S. dollars)		Costs[b] (in U.S. dollars)				Annual cost ÷ family income (percentage)
Use of electricity	Total	Per capita	Connection[c]	Appliances	Electricity	Annual total[d]	
Lights (L)	430	72[e]	13	2	6	9	2
L + Iron (I)	550	90	18	15	8	15	3
L + I + Refrigerator (R)	850	140	18	270	22	81	10[f]
L + I + Television (T)	1,000	170	18	240	10	62	6
L + I + R + T	2,300	380	18	600	40	160	7[f]

a. Group means; family size of six taken in computing per capita family incomes.
b. Note that the data are based on sample surveys, and appliance prices vary with type and quality. For this reason, the expenditure on an appliance varies with income group.
c. Includes house wiring.
d. Using a 20 percent annuity on connections and appliances.
e. The actual threshold income, at which families begin to consume, was about $50.00 per capita.
f. Refrigerator sales often used to augment family income by unascertainable amounts; family income is probably underestimated.
SOURCE: A sample survey of rural household consumers in El Salvador reported in World Bank, *Rural Electrification: A World Bank Paper* (Washington, D.C., October 1975), p. 35.

This list of items for economic analysis is not exhaustive, nor is such information always available. But analysis of what is known about the development of the area will add substance to the forecasts decided upon.

Evidence on energy use. Further evidence on the potential demand for electricity can be obtained by a sample study of energy use by households and businesses in the area. Items to concentrate on are four: types, costs, and extent of motive power (generally animal and diesel) for various purposes; sources and costs of refrigeration; sources and costs of light in businesses and homes; and sources and costs of heating for various purposes. This information is not only useful for forecasting but also for benefit calculations. Although it is not often available, it is not too difficult or costly for the utility to obtain, and it is all part of good recordkeeping and an institutional interest in the program. When it is not available, no harm is done by suggesting that someone should look into it, even if only on a sample basis.

Building up a forecast. While attempts are being made to interpret data econometrically or through other statistical models, forecasts generally have to be made in a rough and ready way.[6] In practice, it is most straightforward to begin with concrete evidence from other electrified areas within the country and, if possible, from other countries. Next, an economic analysis of the area should indicate whether the demand data obtained from these areas should be revised up or down; such revisions will be strengthened further by the studies of energy use. If there are concrete plans for the development of the area, the revisions can be made fairly precisely; otherwise they can be based only on judgment, the bounds of which can be determined by studying areas of higher and lower levels of development than the one considered.

Demand for community purposes. Street lighting and service to schools and health centers are among the community purposes for which demand needs to be forecast. Data can be estimated directly from technical coefficients.

Forecasting benefits. From demand forecasts, the forecasts of revenues follow rather easily to give the *direct* benefits. To calculate

6. For one example of statistical approaches to forecasting, see N. R. Prasad, J. M. Perkins, and G. Nesgos, "A Markov Process Applied to Forecasting the Demand for Electricity," Power Engineering Society Paper C74 146-7 (New York: Institute of Electrical and Electronics Engineers, January 1974).

the surplus benefits to consumers, it is first necessary to distinguish between various types of consumers: various sizes and types of farms, agro-industries, and commerce; demand for community purposes; and various levels of household demand. An idea of what electricity is used for, and of the costs of the substitutes, will then give a basis for estimating surplus benefits per unit of demand. As we remarked earlier, it will only be practicable, in general, to estimate surplus benefits for consumption for productive uses. But information about uses of electricity in households will give some qualitative idea of the benefits. Also, as will be apparent later, this information is particularly important (a) for shadow price adjustments, and (b) for analyzing income distribution issues in pricing policy.

Cost analysis

Once demand and benefits have been forecasted, the next steps are to determine what are the least-cost means of meeting demand, and whether costs can be reduced further by lowering design standards and accepting an increase of supply interruptions. The main alternatives to be considered in the least-cost exercises are: (a) public supplies from the main grid; (b) the same, but with different network layouts, equipment capacities, and expansion plans; and (c) local autogenerators serving local microgrids. The third alternative needs to be considered before the initial decisions are taken to bring electricity into an area, and also, of course, for obviously small demands in remote areas. In areas close to the grid, or close to existing subtransmission networks, the main alternatives to be considered are (a) and (b), that is, alternative plans for public supply.

Both the least-cost studies and the comparisons of costs (of the least-cost proposal) with benefits require a dynamic analysis over a long time horizon. Discussion earlier in the section on "Program Development," illustrates the point that costs change enormously over time with the growth of demand and use of equipment (load factors). Since the electrical equipment in the networks lasts about thirty years, this is the sort of time horizon needed for the study of costs and benefits.

Although there are periodic needs to reinforce and extend networks as demand increases, the costs of service per consumer and per unit of power and energy demand decline in real terms. This is the case for both autogeneration and public supplies, for four reasons: (a) There is a large initial fixed cost in setting up the local networks and installing local autogeneration or, in the case of public supplies, of setting up the subtransmission links to the main grid.

172

TABLE 7.11. EFFECTS OF INCREASED KILOWATT DEMAND ON
COSTS, 1971[a]

Item	1st year	7th year	14th year
Peak demand (kilowatts)	100	425	1,120
Capacity (kilowatts)[b]	150	1,150	1,500
Total investment (U.S. dollars)	104,000	254,000	288,000
Investment per kilowatt demand (U.S. dollars)	1,040	598	257
Investment per kilowatt capacity (U.S. dollars)	693	221	192
Average costs per consumer (U.S. dollars)	870	320	72

a. Data relates to the Ghimbi district of Ethiopia, 450 kilometers from Addis Ababa, with a rapidly increasing population marked at about 10,000 in 1971. Forecasts were based on experience with a similar project in Shashemene district, which was of "similar economic status."

b. Local autogeneration comprises one generator of 150 kilowatts in the first year, one generator of 150 kilowatts plus two each of 500 kilowatts in the seventh year, and three generators each of 500 kilowatts by the fourteenth year.

SOURCE: Data supplied by the Ethiopian Electric Power and Light Company.

Also, equipment costs per unit capacity decline very quickly with size. Data in Table 7.11, taken from a project in Ethiopia, illustrate these points. (b) Related to (a) is the fact that costs decline as consumer density increases. The Kenya Light and Power Company reports initial investment costs (in 1971 prices) of $1,700 a kilowatt for a rural center with 500 persons a square mile, compared with $250 a kilowatt for a center of three times this population density. (c) Fixed costs of administration, billing, and maintenance also decline in relation to demand. Again, this is illustrated by data supplied by the Ethiopian Electric Power Company (see Table 7.12). The costs, it can be seen, are dominated in the initial stages by the fixed costs of capital and administration. Later the fuel costs predominate. The factors underlying cost structure thus shift markedly over time. (d) As the demand per consumer increases, load factors improve. This means that peak demands, and thus the investments in more capacity, do not rise as quickly as energy demand. Typically, load factors may rise from 10 to 20 percent initially to 30 to 40 percent after ten years, thus doubling the returns only at the cost of extra fuel.

The changes in demand, load factor, and cost structure over time have an important bearing on both the least-cost and the cost-benefit analysis. In most cases, it will be necessary to estimate a time-stream of costs for running costs related to kilowatt-hour sales (fuel and variable costs of maintenance and administration); capacity costs related to kilowatt peak demand (generators, local distribution networks, and, in the case of public supplies from the grid, transmis-

173

TABLE 7.12. EFFECT OF INCREASED KILOWATT DEMAND ON FIXED COSTS[a]

Item	1st year	7th year	14th year
Peak demand (kilowatts)	100	425	1,120
Energy demand (kilowatt-hours per year)	120,000	629,000	3,307,000
Costs (U.S. dollars per year)			
Capacity[b]	15,600	38,000	43,200
Fuel	5,400	28,200	148,400
Fixed administration[c]	13,600	13,600	15,100
Variable administration[d]	5,000	11,000	28,000
Total	39,600	90,800	234,700
Costs (cents per kilowatt-hour)			
Average	33.0	14.4	7.1
Administration	15.5	3.9	1.3

a. Same project as that noted in Table 7.11; all cost data are presented here for purposes of comparison.

b. 15 percent annuity applied to capital costs appearing in Table 7.11.

c. Mainly comprising salaries of the branch manager, clerk, cashier, production foreman, four mechanics, a distribution foreman, four electricians, and guards.

d. Meter readers and miscellaneous.

SOURCE: Data supplied by the Ethiopian Electric Power and Light Company.

sion and subtransmission capacity); and fixed administrative overheads.

Cost–benefit calculations

As in other projects, the time-streams of costs and benefits need to be calculated on a present worth basis. Calculations of internal economic rates of return and cost–benefit ratios also follow customary practices.

Shadow price adjustments, as usual, are required to allow for distortions in the pricing system. We have found that the four most important adjustments to be made are for: (a) Net tax revenues, which are part of the government's profit stemming from sales of electrical appliances and equipment, and also of electrical energy if the utility pays taxes on inputs or sales. These taxes should be counted in on the benefit side (or deducted from the cost side); often they can be quite large if appliances are heavily taxed. These revenues are offset to some extent by reduced tax revenues due to a reduced use of substitutes. Mainly, this is only significant for farms and agro-industrial demands that otherwise would use autogenerators, diesel engines, and alternative sources of refrigeration. (b) Foreign exchange, for which the usual shadow price adjustments need be calculated when the balance of payments is in disequilibrium, or there is heavy protection, or both. The penalty applies to electrical appliances and equipment as well as to the production of electricity. The penalty is partly offset because substitute sources of energy and equipment are often imported. Again, the most significant cases are generally to be found in the demands of farms and agro-industries—autogeneration, diesel engines, and substitute sources of refrigeration. (c) Capital, because a specific adjustment may often be needed to allow for scarcity of credit. This mainly affects the sales of appliances and equipment and the costs of connection. Local inquiries may sometimes show effective rates of interest above the opportunity cost of capital. The profits made from this do not, of course, accrue to the consumers but to the sellers; nevertheless, they are part of the monetary benefits. (d) Labor, the principal element of which here is found in construction of the networks, where unskilled labor costs may constitute about 25 percent of initial investment costs, depending on the difficulty of terrain. The excess of wages over the shadow wage of labor can be deducted from cost-streams. Since it is linked to investment rather than to operations, the adjustment will be lumpy.

Evidently the calculation of shadow price adjustments requires good records and data about consumers. Items (a) and (b) directly above, for example, require some knowledge of what consumers use electricity for, and item (c), a study of credit. It is desirable for utilities to record and take an interest in such data. It is useful not only for cost–benefit calculations and investment decisions but also for efficient running and promoting of electrification programs.

The assumptions of the analysis becomes clearer if each of the time-streams of benefits, costs, and shadow price adjustments are listed separately, so that the cost–benefit tableau contains, for example, benefit streams, cost streams, and shadow price adjustment streams. *Benefit streams* comprise direct benefits to households (revenues); direct benefits to agro-industries, farms, and commerce (revenues); and surplus benefits to agro-industries, farms, and commerce. *Cost streams* comprise generation (capital costs); transmission and subtransmission (capital costs); local distribution networks (capital costs); generation (energy costs); and administration and maintenance costs. *Shadow price adjustment streams* comprise net tax revenues (deducted from costs, or added to benefits); net foreign exchange penalties; profits from credit rationing; and shadow wage adjustments to labor costs. The cost-streams, of course, refer to the least-cost project. Some demand statistics—on total demand, its division between productive and domestic uses, load factors, and numbers of consumers—might also be added to the tableau for explanatory purposes.

Criteria for project acceptability

Most of the economic factors discussed so far increase the calculated returns to electrification. The economic picture is thus somewhat more optimistic than the financial one. Taking a long-run view, for example, shows benefits rising faster than costs. (This is not as apparent in the financial analysis, which is heavily preoccupied with financing the initial investments, low short-run returns, and high risks.) Counting in the surplus benefits to farms, agro-industries, and commerce will, if the demands for these "productive uses" are high, add quite significantly to the calculated returns. The shadow price adjustments will generally be favorable toward the project because tax revenues, and the shadow price adjustments for capital and labor, are likely to be greater than the penalties on foreign exchange costs.

After all such adjustments have been made, what should be the criterion for project acceptability? Strictly speaking, it should be somewhat lower than the opportunity cost of capital, because some social and economic benefits generally cannot be quantified but are nevertheless considered important. Among these benefits are: the surplus benefits to households; the value judgment that rural poverty is unacceptable and some degree of subsidy is desirable; and institutional benefits, in that a new project is a stimulus to public and private institutions, as well as to the area itself, to take a stronger interest in the area's development.[7] A further point to consider is that the expected returns may be lower than the optimistic returns, but an *optimistic* view of the project should be taken: the social consequences of neglect in rural areas far outweigh the risks of limited success. (Related to this last point is the observation by many countries that demand is often higher than expected.) Such matters are sufficiently important to urge tolerance when the quantified economic returns are somewhat lower than the opportunity cost of capital. The degree of tolerance depends on the country and in particular on its fiscal strength.

How much lower than the opportunity cost of capital the internal economic rate of return (IER) can be permitted to go is a matter of judgment; only experience and discussion can decide. But there are several related arguments for not permitting IER to go too low.

First, if rural electrification is to contribute toward the economic

7. This benefit should feed back positively on the returns to the project, but to an immeasurable extent—an example of Albert O. Hirschman's dictum that the benefits of unintended side effects on institutions are often more far-reaching than those of the intended effects of policy. See *A Bias for Hope: Essays on Development and Latin America* (New Haven: Yale University Press, 1971), pp. 34ff.

output and wages in rural areas, it must be developed with productive applications in mind. Where it is so developed, the demands from agriculture, agro-industries, and commerce will be large, and the revenues and surplus benefits from these should provide a good economic return to the investment. In this respect, electricity is simply a factor input to agriculture and rural commerce, so the economic returns should be comparable with those of other investments in these sectors. Indeed, on a good project with strong demands from these consumers, the IER may often exceed the opportunity cost of capital, and there will be no need to invoke the above arguments. On the other hand, where the IER is low it is a sign that demands for productive uses may be low and that its contribution toward raising productivity and incomes in the areas is limited.

Second, and closely related to this, is that a low IER may signal insufficient attention to the development of local infrastructure and agriculture—poor or no credit, for example, or bad roads. Electricity is only one of many factor inputs needed for development. If the complementary inputs are neglected, the contribution of electricity to development is diminished.

Third, low economic returns can also lead to disillusionment among both investors and, perhaps more important, consumers. One reason for this is that even subsidized electricity and the appliances to use it often cost far more than consumers anticipate. This is an unwelcome setback for low income households, and a high rate of disconnection—and cynicism—may result.

Fourth, where there is a strong demand from households and businesses, a low IER probably indicates that tariffs are too low and incorrectly structured. Many of the larger household consumers in villages often have above average per capita incomes, while many of the larger farm and business consumers make quite good profits. It is invariably the case, however, that subsidies continue, even though such consumers are able and willing to pay more. Tariffs can be restructured to give more help to the lower income groups while enabling the utility to earn a better financial return and extend service more widely.

Fifth, the basic reason for a low IER is a low level of use on a high cost project. It is possible in such a case that a least-cost solution has not been found. Low demand stemming from simple uses like lighting, ironing, and one or two refrigerators in village shops, can be met at relatively low costs by small diesel powered or microhydro autogenerators. When such alternatives are adopted, the economic rate of return is not only good, but the schemes are often financially profitable.

Finally, of course, a low IER signifies an inefficient investment and, perhaps, wrong priorities. For the $250,000 or more that it may cost to electrify about five villages, good water supplies may be provided. Alternatively, respectable improvements to the access roads can be contemplated (this has the added advantage of cutting the costs of electrification significantly). Schools and health centers can be built. Villagers invariably place these projects higher in their list of preferences.

In sum, the economic return calculation provides some useful messages. A high IER signifies a good investment. An IER somewhat below but approaching the opportunity cost of capital deserves tolerance since there are several benefits of importance that cannot be quantified. Low and very low IERS on the other hand may signal an ineffective project, wrong priorities, and the possibility of disillusionment.

It should be added that postponement or rejection of electrification projects until priorities are sorted out need not lead to disaster—as with rural water projects in drought areas, for example. Farms, agro-industries, and commerce can and do turn to useful substitutes in the form of diesel motors and autogenerators, and households are well adapted to using substitutes and to doing without electricity.

Defining project areas

One particular problem of identifying and appraising projects is posed by the very large number and interconnection of projects to be considered. It is particularly troublesome if the village is to be the unit for project evaluation, instead of a larger unit. Even small countries have several thousand villages. Roughly speaking there are 2,000 to 4,000 villages for each million rural inhabitants, so that a country with a rural population of 30 million may have about 100,000 villages (as in Mexico, for example). It is too much to expect (or to ask) that appraisal be rigorous and comprehensive in each of these cases; it is also unnecessary.

It is generally better to think instead in terms of the best way to introduce electricity into a *region,* and then to calculate the overall costs and benefits of electrifying the region. One reason is that most of nondomestic consumers of electricity are outside the villages. Irrigation schemes are an obvious example, but also the processors of rice, sugar, coffee, and cotton. Villages are major demand nodes, of course, but so are the areas outside of the villages. The region is the appropriate unit for economic analysis because a study of its demography, agriculture, wage levels, agro-industries, commerce, and general infrastructure will give the main indications of the desirability of introducing rural electrification.

There are also technical and administrative reasons for thinking in terms of a region. Plans have to be made regarding the locations and capacity of substations and transformation points, the various voltage levels of subtransmission and distribution, the type of automatic protection equipment, and the routing and interconnection of the circuits between the various demand nodes. (Most lines and substations in any case serve not one but several demand nodes.) Administration, maintenance, and billing procedures also need to be worked out on a regional basis. Costs can be reduced considerably by coordinated planning rather than by ad hoc, piecemeal extensions in a region.

Enlarging the definition of the project to relate it to the problem of electrifying a region does not, of course, imply electrifying the whole region. There will be many demands not worth bothering with because they are too small and too remote from the main demand nodes. Other demands can wait until the networks have been constructed to meet the more important demands; after this, extensions to neighboring demand nodes can be accomplished at low marginal cost.

Pricing and Financial Policies

Pricing policy generally requires compromises among economic, social, and financial aims. Economic aims require a forward-looking view with prices related to the marginal costs of expanding investment and output, ignoring the large initial sunk costs. The need to encourage people to use electricity also requires a forward-looking view, with a promotional element in tariffs in the early years. Social aims require provisions for small consumers. On the other hand, to provide the resources for an expanding program, and to limit pressures on the public revenue, financial analysis may suggest higher prices for consumers who are larger and better off, even above the prices suggested by economic analysis of marginal costs. In practical terms, these various considerations should have five results: prices that are higher in rural than in urban areas; prices below average costs in the early years, because of the high initial fixed costs and also the need to encourage people to use the service; low prices only for small consumers; generally, prices that substantially exceed operation and maintenance costs; and recovery of investment costs in later years, to an extent depending on the financial

179

goals (as discussed later). Often, however, these requirements are not met. Low prices, for example, are often charged to large consumers who are able to pay more, while cost recovery is often undermined by prices that decline unduly with the volume of consumption.

General approach

To reconcile the various requirements of pricing policy, it seems appropriate to proceed in three steps (as outlined in Chapter 2): (a) estimate the structure of marginal costs, and decide on the form of a metering and tariff policy that may practically reflect this structure, in order to meet efficiency aims; (b) incorporate any fairness aims into the pricing structure; and finally, (c) place any further financial burden on those elements of tariff structure so as to minimize any adverse impact on fairness and efficiency. A few remarks can be made on each of these steps.

The marginal costs of reinforcements and extensions to capacity, in order to meet increased demand, are well below (less than 50 percent of) average costs for the first ten to twenty years of a project on account of the high initial fixed costs. Economies of scale and increasing consumer density also act to reduce the long-run marginal costs once an area is electrified (note again the cost estimates provided earlier in this chapter). For many years there is also excess capacity in the subtransmission and distribution networks. In principle, efficient use of the services should not be held back by high sunk costs. Hence, there is an economic rationale for *not* demanding too high a financial return on assets, at least in the early years. (Forgoing high financial returns is also desirable in the interest of promoting the project.)

As far as possible, there should be some consistency over time in pricing policy. For this reason, it is best to take estimates of the long-run marginal costs (or average incremental costs) of future reinforcements and extensions and expansion—of generation, transmission, subtransmission, and distribution—as an initial basis for pricing policy calculations.

Metering and tariff policies have to be simple for most consumers. Complicated tariffs bewilder most people, and advanced metering is often too expensive. For most domestic consumers in rural areas, and for a good number of small business consumers, a flat-rate tariff will suffice, accompanied as necessary by a fixed charge (which could serve revenue-raising purposes or be an incentive to economize on capacity demand). Where metering and billing costs are very high, a device to reduce them involves eliminating meters and introducing a fixed charge, related to the setting on a simple load limiter, for very small consumers. This arrangement is only suitable, however, if fuel costs are not high, for it encourages wastage of energy. Seasonal variations in tariffs—for "wet" and "dry" seasons—may be contemplated if there tend to be energy shortages in the dry season. For the larger farms and agro-industrial consumers, more complicated metering (such as time-of-day for irrigation and other uses) may be considered.

The widely adopted system of declining-block tariffs to all consumers has several defects, and its application in rural areas should be questioned. Small household consumers do not understand it, it does not exploit willingness or ability to pay and so keeps financial returns down, and it has no readily apparent economic merit.

Fairness aims can be incorporated by providing concessions on one or more of the elements of the tariffs at low levels of consumption. Devices that can be used are a low first block followed by a higher flat rate in excess, say, of 50 kilowatt-hours a month, a low connection cost to small consumers, and concessions on fixed charges.

Devices to raise financial returns while minimizing the impact of tariff increases on efficiency and fairness include, of course, increasing the fixed charges to large consumers, or raising the flat rate at high levels of consumption or both. It is often appropriate to use these devices if one bears in mind that the larger businesses are often making good profits and there is no need for concessions. Larger businesses are often willing and able to pay more, and, by being expected to do so, will help financial performance. Also, as we remarked earlier, many household consumers in rural areas are also able and willing to pay more.

Financial goals

The financial characteristics of new or expanding programs are such that the initial investments need to be financed by some combination of debt, grants, equity, or internal funds of the utility that results in a relatively "soft" blend for the capital structure of the program. The reasons for this are two: (a) the long gestation period before demand and revenues build up to reasonable levels, and (b) the various economic, promotional, and social constraints acting on pricing policy. Often, these factors are made more difficult, and the financial returns worse than they need to be, by ill-structured prices. But even with suitable reforms in pricing policy, funding on soft terms, especially with long grace periods, is necessary. In practice, the kind of financial goals that might be achieved evolve with the level and growth of demand. Initially—say, during the first three or four years—revenues can generally be expected to cover operating and maintenance costs quite comfortably. In the next phase—say, up to ten years—revenues can additionally be expected to service debt (assuming the soft blend as suggested above). In subsequent years, revenues may generally be sufficient to make an increasing contribution toward the costs of expansion (sufficient in magnitude, on some projects, to meet a good proportion of the capital required, and to give a good internal financial rate of return to the project). But such achievements, as often noted, depend on the level and growth of demand, reforms to pricing, well-prepared and well-run projects, and also on a systematic follow-up on projects to ensure that financial targets are raised as soon as circumstances warrant. As a matter of principle, then, it should not be assumed that costs cannot be recovered over the life of the investment. But whether or not they are will be determined by (a) the financial needs of the program, (b) the effect of the program on the utility's overall financial performance, (c) the fiscal strength of the country, and (d) the economic and social objectives of the program.

Sources of finance

In most cases, a portion of the capital requirements has to be provided by the government or the profits of the central electricity utility or both. The profits of the utility can be a substantial source of finance, and using them has the added advantages of giving the utility some autonomy in expanding and running the program and reducing the strain on the public revenue—which might be better used on such projects as water, education, and health, where funding problems are more severe. Also, providing funds from taxes may be unpopular, while price increases to provide funds can be accommodated during inflationary adjustments, or may even be acceptable if the intent of the increase is announced. Internal cash generation through the occurrence of cost reductions as the system expands may even pass unnoticed.

Government funding, on the other hand, has particular advantages in large countries where the supply and distribution of electricity may be undertaken by several independent regional utilities. It can be used to help the less developed regions, to influence the expansion plans of utilities, and to promote cooperation among regions. This system is used in India, under the administration of the Rural Electrification Corporation. Apart from its success in deflecting capital to the less developed regions, it has also promoted some degree of coordination in policy, including equipment standardization, and a considerable interchange of ideas and experience.

From an economic viewpoint, there are no distinct advantages to using one source of funds or another. The choice depends on institutional factors, the fiscal strength of the country, and the political acceptability of one arrangement or the other.

CHAPTER 8

Electricity Development in Turkey: A Case Study Using Linear Programming

Turkey, in common with many other countries, is experiencing a sustained high rate of growth of demand for electricity. The forecast rate of growth is about 11 percent a year, with the expectation that 1974 peak demands of 3,000 megawatts will be over 8,000 megawatts by the mid-1980s and approaching 30,000 megawatts by the mid-1990s. To meet such demands, Turkey will have access to four resources:[1]

- Hydro-electricity—there are over 160 as yet untapped hydro-electric sites, several being multipurpose, having an aggregate capacity of about 13,000 megawatts and 60,000 gigawatt-hours a year, and ranging in size from 1 megawatt to a 3,700-megawatt multidam, multipurpose scheme on the River Firat (Euphrates);
- Lignite—there is a 3 billion-ton deposit at Elbistan, in central Anatolia, and small deposits in the west, capable of supporting perhaps 6,000 megawatts of plant;
- Residual fuel oil processed in Turkey from imported crude oil; and
- Nuclear energy.

This chapter is extracted from Dennis Anderson, Orhan Tarkan, and Narong Thananart, "Optimum Development of the Electric Power Sector in Turkey: A Case Study in Linear Programming," Economic Staff Working Paper no. 126 (Washington, D.C.: World Bank, February 1972). No attempt has been made to revise the cost data, which are now completely out of date on account of inflation and cost escalation (as will be evident if one looks at the oil prices in the section of the chapter describing results of the model). The principles of the analysis still hold, however.

1. A fuller description of Turkey's energy resources can be found in the World Energy Conference study, "General Energy Report of Turkey" (Ankara, November 18–20, 1968).

At present, hydro, oil, lignite, and coal resources (which are rather limited) are used in combination; plans for a nuclear program have been discussed for several years. Eventually there must be a transition to nuclear plant or fuel oil plant or both, since the potential hydro and lignite resources are capable of supporting, according to current estimates, no more than 15,000 to 20,000 megawatts. Demand will very likely exceed the capacity of these resources by the late 1980s.

There are two important requirements of a study that is to examine the least-cost development of these resources. First, dynamic (or time-dependent) optimization is required. Most electric power plants are designed to operate for thirty years or more, so how these plants are operated (and thus their total operating costs) depends on what other plants are on the system during this period. For example, the lifetime savings on system fuel costs of a hydro plant are greater, the greater the extent of fossil plant on the system, and less the greater the extent of nuclear plant. The second requirement is that a comprehensive scan of alternative combinations (or mixes) of resources is needed in each time period. Generally, it is economical to use resources in combination. Gas turbines, for example, are costly to run but comparatively cheap to build, and so are ideal for short-duration peak loads. Lignite plants are cheaper to run but more expensive to build, and are suitable for longer duration and often base loads. Nuclear plants, on account of low running costs, are also suitable for base loads if the scale of demand is sufficient to justify large reactors (per unit capacity costs are very high for small ones). Finally, hydro may be used for long-, medium-, or short-duration loads depending on the water availability and the storage capacities of the schemes.

Both of these requirements can be met by a linear programming (LP) model of the sort used in this chapter; it is particularly convenient for scanning, costing, and then selecting the optimum mix of resources over a long time period. This chapter first outlines the LP model, then discusses the data input and finally examines the results. The chapter concludes with a short discussion on the least-cost analysis of a specific project within the program when data input is uncertain.

A Linear Programming Model

Taking a long time-horizon (thirty-five years in the present case), the planner's objective is to choose plant capacities and plant outputs so as to minimize the present worth of total costs. This objective function can be formulated as follows.[2] Let the load duration curve be broken down into $p = 1, 2, \ldots, P$ discrete blocks of power demand of magnitudes Q_{tp} in year t, each lasting for a time interval of Θ_p. Also let: X_{jv} = decision variable denoting capacity of plant type j $(j = 1, \ldots, J)$, vintage v; C_{jv} = corresponding capital cost per unit of capacity; U_{jtvp} = decision variable denoting power output of plant j, vintage v, in year t, and block p on the load duration curve; and F_{jtv} = corresponding operating cost (which is taken not to vary with p). Then the objective is to choose X_{jv} and U_{jtvp} so as to minimize

$$\sum_{j=1}^{J} \sum_{v=1}^{T} C_{jv} \cdot X_{jv} + \sum_{j=1}^{J} \sum_{t=1}^{T} \sum_{v=-V}^{t} \sum_{p=1}^{P} F_{jtv} \cdot U_{jtvp} \cdot \Theta_p. \qquad (8.1)$$

Note that only new vintages of plant enter the investment decision, but that old vintages of plant, denoted by $v = -V, \ldots, 0$, also need to be operated and thus are included in the second term; replacement is neglected.

The sets of constraints to be satisfied are as follows. First, available installed capacity needs to be sufficient to meet the expected peak demand plus an allowance for demand above expected levels,

$$\sum_{j=1}^{J} \sum_{v=-V}^{t} a_{jv} \cdot X_{jv} \geq Q_{tp} (1 + m), \qquad \begin{array}{l} (t = 1, \ldots, T; \quad (8.2) \\ p = 1), \end{array}$$

where Q_{tp} (for $p = 1$) is the peak demand in year t; m is a margin for demands above expected levels; X_{jv}, for $v = -V, \ldots, 0$, defines the known, initial capital stock, that is, the inherited plant; and a_{jv} is the availability of plant j,v.

The second set of constraints refers to operation; it is that the total plant output must be sufficient to meet the instantaneous power demand levels (defined by Q_{tp}),

$$\sum_{j=1}^{J} \sum_{v=-V}^{t} U_{jtvp} \geq Q_{tp}, \qquad \begin{array}{l} (t = 1, \ldots, T; \quad (8.3) \\ p = 1, \ldots, P). \end{array}$$

Also, the output from each plant cannot exceed its available capacity (that is, the actual capacity less that fraction that is shut down for maintenance or due to faults),

---

2. The notation is similar to that used in Chapter 13.

$$U_{jtvp} \leq a_{jv} \cdot X_{jv}, \qquad\qquad (t = 1, \ldots , T; \; (8.4)$$
$$p = 1, \ldots , P;$$
$$v = -V, \ldots , t;$$
$$j = 1, \ldots , J).$$

(To cut down on the number of these constraints, the Us are transformed into Z-substitutes (as described in Chapter 13) in the "matrix generator" for the computer input, and then transformed back into Us in the "report writer" for the computer output.)

The third set of constraints refers to hydro operation. In any year, the output from a hydro plant cannot exceed the energy available in the water supplies, as follows:

$$\sum_{p=1}^{P} U_{jtvp} \cdot \Theta_p \leq b_j \cdot X_{jv}, \qquad\qquad (t = 1, \ldots , T; \; (8.5)$$
$$j = \text{hydro};$$
$$v = -V, \ldots , t).$$

Here b_j is the load factor of the hydro plant, that is, its average annual output divided by its maximum, or capacity output (note that we define Θ_p in time units of years).

The fourth set of constraints stems from the seasonal fluctuations in hydro output. Most hydro plants are only capable of producing full, continuous output in the winter and spring; output in the summer and autumn is restricted by the storage capacities of the hydro sites, so thermal backup is needed in this period; thermal backup is also needed in event of low water supplies in dry years. The result is that there is an upper limit to the amount of hydro capacity that can be permitted on the system. Let this limit be expressed as a fraction, R, of the peak demand (R, which can be ascertained from studies of river flows and hydro storage capacities, is about 50 percent for Turkey); then

$$\sum_{j=1}^{J} \sum_{v=-V}^{t} X_{jv} \leq R \cdot Q_{tp}. \qquad\qquad (t = 1, \ldots , R; \; (8.6)$$
$$p = 1;$$
$$j = \text{hydro}).$$

Strictly speaking, of course, a seasonal model is needed to study this problem. However, seasonal data were not good enough for a seasonal model, which is why the above approach was used. It follows that (a) only the average annual position of each hydro plant on the dispatching schedule is computed, and (b) implicitly, system operating costs are overestimated in the filling-up periods when hydro is operating on base load, and underestimated in the discharge periods when hydro is operating on peak or intermediate-duration loads. To a large extent, these over- and underestimations offset each other.

The fifth set of constraints relates to resource availability. Let $X_{j\text{max}}$ denote the maximum potential capacity of plant type j that remaining resources can support. Then

$$\sum_{v=1}^{T} X_{jv} \leq X_{j\text{max}}. \qquad\qquad (j = 1, \ldots, J) \ (8.7)$$

Referring to the introductory discussion, for example, $X_{j\text{max}}$ is about 6,000 megawatts for new lignite plant, 13,000 megawatts for all hydro plant, and in principle is unlimited for nuclear and fuel oil plant.

Often it is required to set maximum or minimum limits to the capacities of certain plant on the system. For this purpose optional constraints can be introduced that limit the capacity of any plant to within predefined maximum and minimum limits. In the analysis of a single project, for example, it is useful to consider the system's development with and without the project. In this case, two computer runs can be undertaken, one with the minimum constraint activated and set equal to the project's capacity, the other with the maximum constraint set equal to zero. There may also be a need, for example, for a minimum level of gas turbine capacity on the system, because gas turbines are useful in emergencies; pilot nuclear projects may be included; or, more generally, certain projects may be included in the plan for reasons other than least-cost objectives. In these situations, the following kinds of constraint can be used:

$$X_{jv\text{min}} \leq X_{jv} \leq X_{jv\text{max}}. \qquad\qquad (8.8)$$

$X_{jv\text{min}}$ and $X_{jv\text{max}}$ are predefined constants setting upper and lower limits to the installation of plant j in year v. (These constraints are also useful for dealing with indivisibilities and for investigating the optimum timing of projects.)

Having set out the model, we conclude with a discussion of the cost coefficients. The capital costs of new plant decline more or less continuously with time because of technical progress and economies of scale. Economies of scale, for example, are a direct function of system size, since it is the system size which sets an upper limit to the size of plant that, for system security reasons, can be installed. As a result, the present worth of the capital cost coefficient can often be expressed in the simple form:

$$C_{jv} = C_j(1 + r)^{-v}(1 + g)^{-v}, \qquad\qquad (8.9)$$

where r is the discount rate and g is annual rate of decline of per unit capital costs of new vintages of plant.

The present worth of the fuel and running cost coefficient can be expressed in a similar form:

$$F_{jtv} = F_j(1 + r)^{-t}(1 + g^*)^{-v}, \qquad (8.10)$$

where g^* is the annual rate of decline of fuel and running costs of new vintages of plant brought about, for example, by improved thermal efficiencies.

Data Input to the Model

Now we can illustrate the way the model works, using a particular set of data on demand, costs, and technical coefficients, and on various restrictions regarding system expansion. In practice, such data and assumptions change continually, necessitating continual (if sometimes minor) changes in plans. This is, of course, all part of system planning, and utilities that have planning models tend to use them almost continuously.

Demand data

The load duration curve, in this example, is divided into four discrete blocks: one for peak demand periods, another for base load demand, and the other two for demands of intermediate duration (referred to as "off-peak demands"). The planning period considered is thirty-five years, broken down into five investment periods of five years each, and one end condition of ten years. The form of the input is shown in Table 8.1.

The idea of dividing the planning period into such coarse invest-

TABLE 8.1. FORM OF DEMAND DATA FOR THE LP MODEL

Demand period on load duration curve	Duration of demand (hours a year)	Demand in median year of investment period (megawatts)					
		1978	1983	1988	1993	1998	2005
Peak	526	4,500	7,740	13,066	22,018	37,101	77,028
Off-peak	3,066	3,406	5,864	9,902	16,686	28,117	58,376
Off-peak	6,132	2,740	4,715	7,960	13,415	22,604	46,930
Base load	8,760	2,020	3,493	5,902	9,946	16,760	34,797

SOURCE: Turkish Electricity Authority.

189

TABLE 8.2. COSTS AND TECHNICAL DATA FOR THE MODEL

Power scheme	Capital cost coefficient (millions of Turkish lira per megawatt)	Operating cost coefficient (millions of Turkish lira per megawatt a year)	Annual rate of cost decrease		Initial capacity (megawatts)	Availability	Load factor limit	Maximum new capacity (megawatts)
			Capital	Operating				
Hydro 1	1.40	0.090	0.0	0.0	0.0	0.9	0.40	684.0
Hydro 2	4.00	0.090	0.0	0.0	0.0	0.9	0.40	1,484.0
Hydro 3	6.50	0.090	0.0	0.0	0.0	0.9	0.40	844.0
Hydro 4	7.00	0.090	0.0	0.0	0.0	0.9	0.40	250.0
Hydro 5	3.00	0.090	0.0	0.0	1,829.0	0.9	0.60	2,000.0
Hydro 6	6.80	0.090	0.0	0.0	0.0	0.9	0.60	814.0
Hydro 7	4.30	0.090	0.0	0.0	0.0	0.9	0.80	890.0
Hydro 8	2.70	0.090	0.0	0.0	0.0	0.9	0.40	1,366.0
Hydro 9	4.60	0.090	0.0	0.0	0.0	0.9	0.40	656.0
Hydro 10	6.10	0.090	0.0	0.0	0.0	0.9	0.40	192.0
Hydro 11	3.90	0.090	0.0	0.0	0.0	0.9	0.60	1,002.0
Hydro 12	5.60	0.090	0.0	0.0	0.0	0.9	0.60	947.0
Hydro 13	6.10	0.090	0.0	0.0	0.0	0.9	0.80	81.0
Gas turbines	2.50	1.700	0.0	0.005	120.0	0.8	1.00	99,999.0
Fuel oil	4.50	1.100	0.010	0.005	847.0	0.9	1.00	0.0
Lignite 1	5.00	0.600	0.010	0.005	960.0	0.8	1.00	0.0
Lignite 2	7.00	0.200	0.010	0.005	0.0	0.8	1.00	2,500.0
Lignite 3	7.00	0.200	0.010	0.005	0.0	0.8	1.00	3,500.0
Nuclear	9.00	0.300	0.020	0.005	0.0	0.8	1.00	99,999.0

Note: There are nineteen plant types, and thirteen hydro plants. Peak reserve requirements (proportion of peak demand) = .050. Maximum aggregate hydro capacity in any year (proportion of peak demand) = .500.
SOURCE: Turkish Electricity Authority.

ment periods is to cut down on computing time and expense, both of which rise faster than with the square of the number of investment periods chosen for study. The LP algorithm computes the optimum investments for the middle year for each period and the associated plan operating schedules; investments and operating schedules for intermediate periods can be estimated by interpolation. (This approximation is a simple and economical device to use at the beginning of investment analysis when many sensitivity studies are needed to test assumptions and the effects of changes in, for example, costs, demand forecasts, and water inflows into the hydro schemes. As a picture of the optimal program begins to emerge, these approximations can be reduced, particularly for the analysis of the optimal timing and capacities of the more immediate investments; typically, the thirty-five–year investment period may then be divided into nine investment periods: the first five each of one year, four each of five years, and one end condition of 10 years.[3] A good matrix generator program to translate the basic data into a standard LP form can make light work of such adjustments to data input and the sensitivity analysis.)

Cost and technical data

Cost and technical data, listed in Table 8.2, follow logically from the definitions and formulae of the model, expressed in relationships (8.1) to (8.10). Nuclear plant, for example, is listed as having a 1975 capital cost of TL 9 million a megawatt, decreasing at 2 percent a year, and an operating cost of TL 0.3 million a megawatt a year (0.034 lira per kilowatt-hour) decreasing at 0.5 percent a year.[4]

Turkey's hydro sites in this particular example are classified into thirteen groups as follows. First, they are divided into schemes that are practicable before 1985 and schemes that are not practicable until after 1985; the former have mostly been the subject of technical feasibility studies, while the latter have only been reconnoitered, or are too small or remote for early inclusion in the program. Second, they are grouped according to three ranges of load factors: 20 to 50 percent (taking an average of 40 percent); 50 to 70 percent (average of 60 percent); and over 70 percent (average of 80 percent). Next they are grouped according to capital cost. Figure 8.1 illustrates how this is done for schemes in the group with load factors which average

3. In addition, some utilities may also undertake simulation studies, as explained in Chapter 13.
4. An exchange rate of TL 15 = US$ 1.00 may be used for conversion of Turkish lira throughout the chapter.

40 percent and in the group that can be installed before 1985. These schemes are first ranked according to capital costs per unit capacity, giving a discontinuous cost curve; this curve is then approximated by three steps, the three schemes labelled Hydro 1, 2, and 3 in Table 8.2. The decision to include one scheme with a 40 percent load factor (Hydro 4) had already been made at the time of the study, and so this scheme is classified separately. Hydro 5 and 6 represent schemes with average load factors of 60 percent; Hydro 7, a scheme with an 80 percent load factor. All of these schemes are potentially available before 1985. Hydro 8 through 13 are schemes not practicable until after 1985.

The lignite resources are divided into three groups: the first represents existing power stations; the second, resources that might feasibly be exploited before 1985; and the third, resources that cannot be exploited until after 1985. Note that the operating costs of the new lignite plant are quite low; the reason is that the power stations are to be built on-site with capital-intensive mining equipment; the mining equipment costs are included in the capital cost estimates for the power stations.

Maximum-minimum policy constraints

Table 8.3 shows the max-min policy constraints, that is, constraints that set upper or lower limits, or both, to the amount that can be installed of a given type of plant in a particular year. 1975–85 vintages of Hydros 8 to 13 and of Lignite 3 are not feasible, as explained in the preceding section, and so the max-min constraints are set to zero for this period; Hydro 4 is already in the program, so the constraints are set equal to the scheme's capacity. Additions to gas turbine capacity are kept within lower and upper limits on engineering grounds. Finally, it is thought that, whatever the cost advantages of nuclear plant may be, the transition to a large nuclear program will have to be gradual and begin with pilot schemes. An expanding upper limit is thus placed on the additions to nuclear capacity in each investment period, beginning with 600 megawatts in the 1980–85 period, increasing in successive periods to 2,500 megawatts, 5,000 megawatts, 10,000 megawatts, and unlimited thereafter.

Results of the Model

The output includes (a) the optimum investment program and the present worth of total costs; (b) the plant operating schedules; (c)

TABLE 8.3. MINIMUM-MAXIMUM POLICY CONSTRAINTS
ON THE MODEL

Type	Vintage	Minimum capacity (megawatts)	Maximum capacity (megawatts)
Hydro 4	1	250.0	250.0
Hydro 8	1	0.0	0.0
Hydro 8	2	0.0	0.0
Hydro 9	1	0.0	0.0
Hydro 9	2	0.0	0.0
Hydro 10	1	0.0	0.0
Hydro 10	2	0.0	0.0
Hydro 11	1	0.0	0.0
Hydro 11	2	0.0	0.0
Hydro 12	1	0.0	0.0
Hydro 12	2	0.0	0.0
Hydro 13	1	0.0	0.0
Hydro 13	2	0.0	0.0
Gas turbines	1	0.0	230.0
Gas turbines	2	100.0	390.0
Gas turbines	3	200.0	650.0
Gas turbines	4	360.0	1,110.0
Gas turbines	5	600.0	1,580.0
Gas turbines	6	1,600.0	3,580.0
Lignite 3	1	0.0	0.0
Lignite 3	2	0.0	0.0
Nuclear	1	0.0	0.0
Nuclear	2	0.0	600.0
Nuclear	3	0.0	2,500.0
Nuclear	4	0.0	5,000.0
Nuclear	5	0.0	10,000.0

the dual variables to the demand constraints, represented by constraints (3) (these are, of course, the marginal costs or, more strictly, the marginal savings resulting from a unit reduction in these constraints); (d) the dual variables to the constraints on resource availability, represented by constraints (7); and (e) the dual variables to the hydro-thermal balance constraints (6).

The optimum investment program corresponding to the data just discussed is outlined in Table 8.4. The ranking of the hydro schemes can be deduced straightforwardly from curves like that appearing in Figure 8.1 once the optimum groups shown in Table 8.4 have been found; also, by interpolation, the optimum capacities of the thermal plant can be deduced for intermediate years (indeed, it is not difficult to write suitable interpolation procedures into the "report writers"). The optimum dispatching schedules for each type and vintage

TABLE 8.4. RESULTS OF A POWER SYSTEM PLANNING MODEL
FOR TURKEY: MEGAWATTS OF INSTALLED CAPACITY ON
POWER SYSTEM
(minimized total costs = 73.01 billion Turkish lira)

Power scheme	Median year in investment period						
	1975	1978	1983	1988	1993	1998	2005
Hydro 1	0	171	513	0	0	0	0
Hydro 2	0	0	0	0	1,484	0	0
Hydro 3	0	0	0	0	0	844	0
Hydro 4	0	250	0	0	0	0	0
Hydro 5	1,829	0	217	1,783	0	0	0
Hydro 6	0	0	0	0	0	814	0
Hydro 7	0	0	890	0	0	0	0
Hydro 8	0	0	0	880	486	0	0
Hydro 9	0	0	0	0	476	180	0
Hydro 10	0	0	0	0	0	192	0
Hydro 11	0	0	0	0	1,002	0	0
Hydro 12	0	0	0	0	947	0	0
Hydro 13	0	0	0	0	81	0	0
Gas turbines	120	230	390	650	1,110	1,580	3,580
Fuel oil	847	0	758	464	1,456	5,991	10,953
Lignite 1	960	0	0	0	0	0	0
Lignite 2	0	1,218	1,282	0	0	0	0
Lignite 3	0	0	0	2,880	620	0	0
Nuclear	0	0	0	0	3,528	9,942	37,871
	Total megawatts by groups						
All hydro	1,829	2,250	3,870	6,533	11,009	13,039	13,039
Gas turbines	120	350	740	1,390	2,500	4,080	7,660
Fuel oil	847	847	1,605	2,069	3,526	9,516	20,469
Lignite 1	960	960	960	960	960	960	960
Lignite 2	0	1,218	2,500	2,500	2,500	2,500	2,500
Lignite 3	0	0	0	2,880	3,500	3,500	3,500
Nuclear	0	0	0	0	3,528	13,470	51,341
Total	3,756	5,625	9,675	16,332	27,522	47,065	99,469
Peak demand		4,500	7,740	13,066	22,018	37,101	77,028

of plant in each of the twenty-four demand periods are too numerous
to be listed here. Figures 8.2 and 8.3, however, bring out some features of the schedules: new lignite takes most of the base load and is
joined by nuclear in the later years; fuel oil takes the peak load, with
gas turbines acting as standby plant only; existing lignite plant is on
base load in the early years but is eventually shifted to peak load service; hydro takes a range of loads, varying from peak to near-base
load service, depending on load factor.

The results reveal what is essentially the main feature of Turkey's

FIGURE 8.1. COSTS AND CAPACITIES OF POTENTIAL HYDRO SCHEMES IN TURKEY [a]

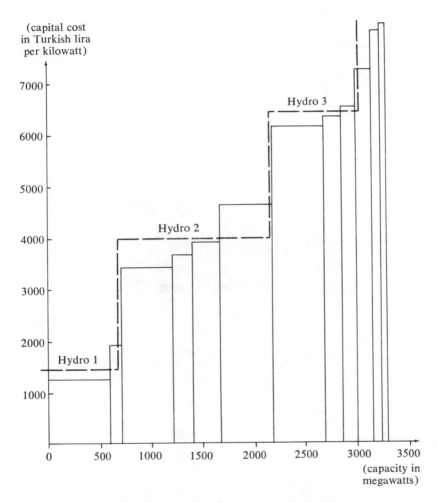

a. Each of the schemes shown is in the group with load factors averaging 40 percent, and also in the group that are practicable before 1985. Schemes are represented by blocks and ranked in ascending order of capital cost per kilowatt. For definition of Hydro Groups 1, 2, and 3, see the text.

investment policy: a heavy reliance on a balanced use of the better hydro and lignite resources for the next ten years, followed by a gradual transition to a balanced use of oil and nuclear power. The timing of the transition and the balances struck will depend, of course, on how both demand and relative prices change over time.

FIGURE 8.2. DISPATCHING SCHEDULES FOR THE FIRST INVESTMENT PERIOD, 1978

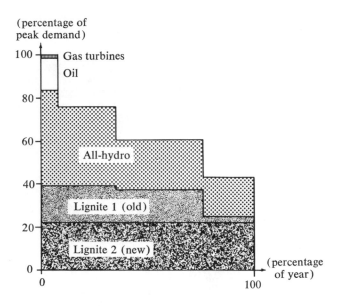

FIGURE 8.3. DISPATCHING SCHEDULES FOR THE FOURTH INVESTMENT PERIOD, 1993

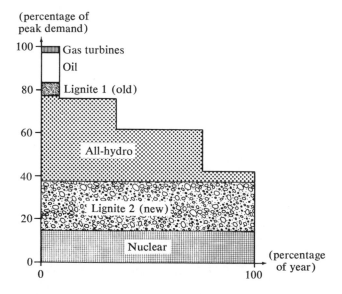

TABLE 8.5. DUAL VARIABLES TO RESOURCE AVAILABILITY
CONSTRAINTS IN THE MODEL
(Turkish lira per kilowatt)

Power scheme	Dual variable	Scheme	Dual variable
Hydro 1	977	Hydro 10	50
Hydro 2	325	Hydro 11	484
Hydro 3	5	Hydro 12	178
Hydro 4	0	Hydro 13	228
Hydro 5	696	Gas turbines	0
Hydro 6	29	Fuel oil	0
Hydro 7	555	Lignite 1	56
Hydro 8	559	Lignite 2	592
Hydro 9	217	Lignite 3	213
		Nuclear	0

But some indication of how robust the policy is in the presence of these uncertainties is provided by the dual variables to the constraints on resource availability, shown in Table 8.5. The dual variables for nuclear, gas turbines, and fuel oil are, of course, bound to be zero because the extent of these resources was taken to be unlimited. It is apparent that there are quite large gains to be made from exploitation of some of the hydro schemes and lignite resources, since the marginal costs of reducing these resources, which is what the above variables measure, are often quite high. (Note that the dual variable for Lignite 3 is lower than for Lignite 2, even though the costs of the two schemes are the same. One reason for this is that Lignite 3 is not available until ten years after Lignite 2 is first exploited, so in present value terms, it is worth much less.)

Some inkling of how the picture changes over time can also be obtained by inspecting the dual variables to the constraint on hydrothermal balance. These dual variables show that the economic case for new hydro gradually diminishes in importance, though over a long time period.

Investment period	Dual variables (Turkish lira per kilowatt)
1975–80	1,364
1980–85	1,150
1985–90	451
1990–95	187
1995–2000	0

Note, however, that the dual variables naturally decline over time in present value terms.

The dual variables to the demand constraints are not quite so useful from the viewpoint of least-cost studies, though, of course, they are enormously useful for studies of pricing policy.[5] For the 1975–80 period of the study they are computed in terms of kilowatt-hours as:

Demand period	Turkish lira per kilowatt-hour
Peak	0.72
Off-peak	0.26
Off-peak	0.26
Base load	0.20

To obtain the marginal cost of an increment of peak demand, the marginal cost of carrying standby capacity (corresponding to constraint (2), above) needs to be added to the above dual variable for the peak period; this roughly equals the annuitized capital cost of gas turbine capacity times the reserve margin, $(1 + m)$, divided by the availability of gas turbines.

Uncertainty

A continually occurring problem with investment analysis is that the results change kaleidoscopically with changes in data inputs; special procedures based on Monte Carlo analysis, or those propounded by Wagle and Hillier are called for to handle this problem.[6] The idea is to consider probability-weighted ranges of the data inputs and compute a probability distribution of the returns to the decision in question; the consequences of accepting it are evaluated to determine whether it is desirable to act on expected values or to err on the "optimistic" or "pessimistic" side. An example of this approach is outlined below.

The problem is to examine the desirability of a 1,200-megawatt lignite power plant for base load operation, with oil as an alternative, when there are uncertainties about (a) the availability of the lignite plant, and (b) fuel oil prices. With low grade lignite, it is possible that the plant might be shut down for as much as four months per year (65 percent availability) for plant maintenance and boiler

---

5. Since the system is predominantly hydro, the dual variables would be more interesting, however, if the model were seasonal.

6. See J. M. Hammersley and D. C. Handscomb, *Monte Carlo Methods* (London: Methuen, 1965); B. Wagle, "Statistical Analysis of Risk in Capital Investment Projects," *Operational Research Quarterly* 18 (March 1967):13–33; and F. S. Hillier, *The Evaluation of Risky Interrelated Investments* (Amsterdam: North-Holland, 1969).

cleaning. Availabilities of 75 to 85 percent are expected, however, and in some countries availabilities are sometimes found to be over 90 percent. Such differences in availability levels are enormously important: a drop from 85 percent to 65 percent, for example, is equivalent to capital cost escalation of over 30 percent. In such circumstances it seems reasonable to consider a range such as:

Availability (percentage)	Probability of occurrence
65	0.1
75	0.5
85	0.4

Similarly it might be decided that oil prices have the following ranges:

Prices (dollars per ton)	Rate of growth each year (percentage)	Probability of price occurring
20 (low)	0	0.1
22 (medium)	1.5	0.3
25 (high)	3.0	0.3
28 (very high)	3.0	0.3

If, then, low oil prices occurred with low availabilities of the lignite plant, oil would most likely be favored, but there would be only a 1 percent chance of this situation occurring; the chance of good lignite availability and high oil prices, on the above data, is 12 percent.

For each combination of occurrences the present worth of total system costs is calculated, first with the lignite plant included, then with the oil alternative (see Table 8.6). A discount rate of 11 percent

TABLE 8.6. PRESENT WORTH OF TOTAL SYSTEM COSTS

Case		Probability of occurrence	Present worth of cost difference between lignite and oil (millions of U.S. dollars)	Rate of return, r (percentage)
Lignite availability	Oil prices			
0.65	low	0.01	348	3.4
0.65	medium	0.03	321	4.1
0.75	low	0.05	253	5.4
0.75	medium	0.15	222	6.0
0.65	high	0.03	217	6.5
0.85	low	0.04	182	6.8
0.65	very high	0.03	158	7.7
0.85	medium	0.12	147	7.8
0.75	high	0.15	102	8.9
0.75	very high	0.15	34	10.3
0.85	high	0.12	11	10.9
0.85	very high	0.12	−67	12.4

was used in the calculations of present worth. The rate of return is the interest rate that makes the present worth of cost differences zero. (Note that the cost data used were not the same as in Table 8.2.) Grouping the figures into 3 percent ranges for the rate of return gives the following results:

Range of r (percentage)	Probability of occurrence
Below 3	0.0
3 to 6	0.24
6 to 9	0.37
9 to 12	0.27
Over 12	0.12
Expected value, 8.6	

The final question to be answered is: Which of these rates of return should be considered for assessment if the lignite project is desirable? An approach that is commonly used, on the one hand, is to work with "conservative" assumptions, and take it that things may turn out below expectations. But this seems unduly biased—oil prices are risky, too. Suppose, on the other hand, that the cost of the risks are symmetrical. If we accept lignite, and performance is good, or oil prices rise above expectations, hindsight will show that the better project will have been chosen. If performance is bad, and oil prices are lower than expected, the lesser project will have been chosen. If oil is chosen, and oil prices turn out lower than expected, the better project will have been chosen; conversely, if oil prices rise above what is expected. But one or the other has to be chosen, so the best thing to do, it seems, is to opt for the project with the better expected returns. This appears sensible, however, only assuming that risks are symmetrical. If oil is thought to have more risk, as has manifestly been the case in recent times, it follows that lignite deserves added weight, and decisions should be based on the assumption that returns will be *above* expected values (above an 8.6 percent rate of return, in the above example). How much above is something—in this as in many other cases—that is difficult to quantify, and final decisions may require political judgments. However, in pinpointing the range of uncertainties and their effects on the economic returns, the approach can be helpful for decisionmaking.

PART TWO

Studies of
Principles and Theory

CHAPTER 9

How to Study Tariffs

This chapter highlights practical questions that are often useful to ask in studying the pricing policy of electricity enterprises from the points of view of economic efficiency and fairness, given a need to meet a certain revenue requirement. This study frequently demands investigation of the structure of marginal costs. The reason is that *price* is what it costs the consumer to acquire an extra unit of output, but *marginal cost* is a measure of the value of the extra resources required to provide it. While there may be very good reasons for not equating these two things—that is, strong arguments against pure marginal cost pricing—price and marginal cost should at least be looked at in relation to one another. To set a price below marginal cost is to make the cost to the consumer less than the related cost imposed upon the enterprise (or the economy as a whole), and vice versa. Also, the consumer's individual decision for or against purchase is then not related to the use of resources that his purchase will involve, or to the savings in resources gained by his abstention. This idea needs justification in terms of its effects.

It is logical to study pricing policy in two major steps. First, the structure of marginal costs should be investigated, and then the pros and cons of setting prices higher or lower should be studied. But setting prices unequal to marginal costs may not always be the best procedure. In some cases, at least where only the immediate future is considered, the barrier to expansion of output is not a high marginal cost but a physical or administrative limitation on capacity. In such circumstances, a high price is one way of determining who shall have a share in the limited supply; waiting lists, priority rules, and bribery constitute other ways. The problem is to determine the best mix in the particular circumstances.

One reason for setting prices above marginal costs—and a reason that will arise when marginal costs are below unit accounting costs—is the need to provide a certain revenue. If in any particular case this were the only reason, the aim should be to raise the extra revenue with the least possible effect on resource allocation. This would mean concentrating most of the excess of price over marginal costs on those components of demand least sensitive to price and on those parts of the price (rate) structure that least affect consumers' behavior.

A possible reason for setting prices below marginal cost is a desire to subsidize consumers. This may rest upon political or social judgments, and the responsibility of making such judgments may or may not rest with the analyst. At the very least, it is important to distinguish whether a subsidy is proposed primarily to encourage consumers to consume more, or to leave them with more money to spend on other things. (It can be argued, though not in each and every case, that a public enterprise's responsibilities should not include the second of these two. There are many other ways of redistributing income.)

A third possible reason for setting prices unequal to marginal costs is that other prices may convey a distorted message and it may seem right to attempt to offset them. Thus, marginal cost to the producer may fall below marginal cost from the point of view of the whole economy when extra output requires extra foreign exchange and when foreign exchange is particularly scarce. The prices that consumers are willing to pay for the output may similarly be distorted by, say, heavy taxation of substitutes. The range of such possibilities is large, with regard to both costs and demand; in any particular case, those that are significant must be listed and examined. Here, only one general point should be made—that a distortion can be dealt with either by accepting its existence and offsetting it or by denouncing it and remedying it directly.

There may be other reasons for charging prices that neither equal marginal costs nor serve to limit demand for the available supply. But in all cases the particular circumstances of the particular public enterprise must be considered. The following text, therefore, does not attempt to give general answers to most of the questions posed. The importance and relevance of these questions vary from case to case, and the only general and positive recommendations relate to the method of inquiry: (a) Consider the effects of prices upon resource allocation—that is, the incentives they provide to consumers in relation to the structure of costs. (b) Look for alternatives and weigh their advantages and disadvantages as systematically as possible. (c) Avoid both ''conventional wisdom'' and the assumption that the best practices in developed countries are also best in

less developed countries. (d) Be explicit about the political and social judgments involved, whoever makes them.

Cost Analysis of Generation and Transmission

Once the plans are given for the future development of a power
system to meet the projected development of the load (the shape of
the system over the next few years is known in any case), the appropriateness of the present tariff structure can be considered. This, at
its most general, is a question of whether existing tariffs adequately
discourage loads with characteristics that impose a heavy cost upon
the system or, conversely, encourage those that involve a low cost.
If they do not have such effects, then it may well be desirable to
change their structure to introduce incentives of this kind. To charge
a little for a load that imposes heavy costs may encourage wasteful
use of electricity, while to charge a lot for a load that can be met easily and cheaply is to signal the consumer incorrectly. Hence it is necessary to relate the incentive effects of the tariff structure to the cost
and availability of supply. The relations of the tariff structure to income distribution and to financial requirements—both very important—are left aside to start with.

What concepts of tariffs and costs are relevant? Regarding tariffs,
the answer is simple. From the point of view of incentives to consumers, what matters is how much they actually pay and not what
the electricity supply authority receives. Hence, any taxes that consumers pay should be included in the study. Regarding costs, in the
present context of analysis in terms of the national interest, what
matters is cost to the nation as a whole and not what the electricity
supply authority pays for its inputs. This means that, where relevant, shadow prices rather than actual prices must be used and that
taxes on inputs must be deducted and subsidies added back. If capital is scarce, its opportunity cost rather than the supply authority's
borrowing rate should be used in discounting future costs in order to
obtain their present values.

Starting with costs, consider generation and transmission, leaving
distribution on one side for the moment. Information is required
about three areas: (a) the incremental cost of energy delivered to the
distribution system at times when an increase in generation will not
run up against the security constraints; (b) the times at which an increase in generation would bring the system up against the security
constraints (by lowering the generation reserve below its target
level, by involving an unacceptably large loss of load should a trans-

mission outage occur, or by drawing down all water storage below the rule curves); and (c) the addition to all system costs resulting from adding to generation, transmission, or storage in order to make increased generation possible at such times without infringing the security constraints. In short, information is required about incremental energy costs, bottlenecks or capacity limitations, and the cost of removing bottlenecks by increasing capacity. In a partly or wholly hydro system, capacity may have a kilowatt-hour as well as a kilowatt dimension.

Consider first the incremental costs of delivering more or fewer kilowatt-hours at a time when a small increase in output will not infringe the security constraints. These costs usually vary with the level of the load and, in a mixed hydro and thermal system, may also vary with the season. The aim should be to group together times within a season when the load will be approximately at the same level (for example, winter nights and weekdays from noon to 2:00 P.M.). Each set of such times, in effect, constitutes a "step" on a daily, weekly, seasonal, or annual load duration curve. Each will have an average incremental generating cost, and it is this that needs to be estimated.

At times when an increase in demand would be met by increased thermal generation, incremental generating cost simply depends upon the incremental cost of the plant or plants that would provide the extra power and upon incremental transmission losses. The times in question will occur when thermal plant is on load: generating more than the minimum required by a decision to avoid shutdown or to provide spinning reserve, but leaving more than sufficient to provide the desired reserve margin. The incremental cost, then, is what is termed *system lambda* in discussions of economic dispatching (system operation), that is, incremental generating cost per unit sent out, divided by one minus incremental transmission losses.

Normally, information about future incremental thermal generating costs should be available from the work of the engineering consultants who have costed the operation of the system over a period of years in order to choose the least-cost alternative for its future development. But whether or not the program is optimal, once it is known which plant will be operating at what levels of system load and at what times of the year, then the incremental costs can be estimated. Note that where there are several load centers and long transmission lines, these costs may differ between load centers.

When thermal plant is not in use, except at some minimum level, or when it is running at capacity, extra generation requires extra use of water. Incremental cost is then the incremental value of water, where water is measured in terms of the kilowatt-hours it will generate. Here, too, the right figures emerge from the sort of simulation of future system operation that is a necessary part of any sophisticated system planning study designed to select the best development program. Where cruder methods have been used, a more direct approach must be taken. Since the information available and the system configuration vary so much from case to case, generalization is difficult. Two examples relating to a mixed hydro and thermal system will show what is involved, still confining the analysis to times when there is spare generating capacity:

- Extra hydro generation during a period when reservoirs are not spilling will require either extra thermal generation at some other time during that period or less spillage once the reservoirs are full. In the first case, the incremental cost is that of the extra thermal generation; in the second case, it is zero. The first case is typical of the "dry" or "discharge" season; the second, of the "wet" or "filling" season.
- It is also zero at times when water is being spilled.

Note that the right answer, in principle, is an average of all the conditions that could occur, each weighted by its probability.

Turn now to the second lot of information that was said to be necessary, that relating to bottlenecks. This is a matter of the times or load centers or both when it is anticipated that, under typical or average circumstances, a future increase in some customer's load would necessitate at least one of three things:

- a corresponding reduction of other customers' loads;
- a reduction in security below the chosen threshold; or
- more generating, transmission, or storage capacity.

In an all-thermal system with a seasonal swing large enough to accommodate all planned maintenance in the slack season, the only such time will be that of system peak. But where planned maintenance is spread throughout the year, many daily weekday peaks may be such times. In mixed systems, energy (kilowatt-hours) as well as capacity (kilowatts) may be involved too, over periods when it is planned to use all the water that is available under normal conditions without drawing down the reservoirs below the levels chosen to give the selected degree of security. Thus, just as in the case of incremental energy costs, the information required will reflect both the operating characteristics of the system and the time pattern of the load. In practice, the information may relate only to anticipated normal conditions but, in principle, it is again a probability calculation of mean expectations which is the ideal.

The third lot of information required is the cost of adding to generating, storage, or transmission capacity in order to meet extra load during the times just specified without either reducing other customers' loads or infringing on the security constraints. Such an addition to capacity will often involve bringing forward projects that are planned anyway to meet a growing load, but it could, for example, simply involve a plant specially designed for peaking. The point is to ascertain the extra costs of removing the bottlenecks. This may be difficult in cases where the engineering consultants who chose or designed the scheme have not used a proper system-planning model. The net cost of such additional capacity is the cost of adding to capacity, or bringing forward plans for new capacity; the net cost must also be corrected for its effects on the subsequent costs of running the system over the next few decades. Only construction cost estimates and a little discounting are involved in adding to capacity, but correcting for subsequent costs involves a simulation or optimization model. Since many consultants do not always provide such a model, one must accept the fact that, at present, an adequate systems analysis of the net cost of capacity additions will not always be available. Hence, the evaluation of a tariff structure may have to proceed using the first two sets of information plus only rough estimates of net incremental system capacity costs.

The need for the three sets of information can now be summed up in three questions:

(1) In the light of the anticipated future mode of operation of the system under normal conditions as a function of the shape of the load curve and, where relevant, of hydrology, how can the year be divided into periods and points of time?

(2) What are the incremental costs (measured from a national point of view) of additional kilowatt-hours delivered to the distribution system at periods and places when supplying extra power under normal conditions will not infringe on the security constraints?

(3) What are the periods or points of time and places where extra power cannot be supplied without infringing on the security constraints? And what would be the net addition to discounted system costs of expanding capacity to avoid such infringement?

These questions and, indeed, all the others suggested in this chapter may appear to demand impossibly precise answers. That is a false deduction. Precise questions are intended to avoid ambiguity, and a rough and ready answer to them is all that can reasonably be expected from a brief investigation. Even lengthy investigation may not produce better answers because of an irremediable lack of basic data. An analysis that is logical but quantitatively crude can suggest tariff improvements that are important and well justified, even though they depart, to an extent, from the unascertainable optimum tariff.

Bulk Tariffs

Given the answers to questions (1), (2), and (3), posed at the end of the preceding section, it is possible to ask a fourth question:

(4) What bulk tariff structure would accurately reflect the cost and availability structure revealed by those answers?

This question implies that a bulk tariff ought to reflect the cost and availability structure of generation and transmission in some detail. In contrast with the use of retail tariffs, the necessary metering involves too small a cost in relation to the size of the supply to constitute an obstacle. The positive reasons for a detailed cost-reflecting bulk supply tariff are two: first, an incentive is provided to the distribution management both to consider some reflection of the bulk tariff in retail tariffs and to concentrate load-building efforts in suitable directions; second, information is communicated pithily.

This last point is important in many ways. For example, it enables distribution management to cost transformer losses, examine the case for reactive power compensators, and estimate one of the main cost elements in rural electrification schemes. Even for a generating authority with no bulk sales, calculation of a notional bulk tariff is essential for any examination of retail tariff level and structure.

In constructing such a bulk tariff one can start with the answer to question (2), that is, kilowatt-hour rates equal to incremental kilowatt-hour costs for the various periods when, under normal conditions, there is spare capacity, so that extra energy can be supplied without infringing the security constraints. Periods that turn out to have fairly similar incremental energy costs can be lumped together. At other periods and points of time, kilowatt-hour rates will have to exceed incremental energy costs or kilowatt rates will have to exist such that either they jointly make the tariff as high as is necessary at these times to keep the load just below the level that would infringe on the security constraints, or they jointly measure the net addition to discounted system costs of supplying more power in such periods without infringing on security constraints, or both.

The first of these, the tariff that rations energy and capacity demands to match the bottlenecks, is more relevant both as information and incentive for the next few years. The second of these, the incremental kilowatt-hour and kilowatt costs of removing bottle-necks, is more relevant for subsequent years. If the two differ, then the more difficult are tariffs to alter, the more should the second form the basis of tariff determination—though means of encouraging or discouraging demand other than price may have to be used in the next year or two. What any particular level of rates will do to limit demand is naturally difficult to measure. However, it must be recalled that the load forecasts for the next year or two usually continue recent experience. If, to make up an example, the load has recently been pushing against some security constraint on winter weekday evenings, then it should be possible to predict whether the rise in capacity already under way for the next few years is going to outpace the growth in load at these times. If it is, then a reduced tariff component with respect to such loads may be indicated. Conversely, if the bottleneck in question is likely to become worse, then a tariff high enough to keep these loads within the security constraints will become higher than the existing one. Thus, even without any definite knowledge about the responsiveness of sales to tariffs, at least a little can be deduced.

What has just been said about existing tariffs really applies to any mix of kilowatt-hour and kilowatt rates in force during the relevant period that adds up to the same total charge for loads during that period. Given this total, the problem is to get them right separately as well, remembering that while a kilowatt-hour charge measures incremental cost or signals scarcity of energy during a period, a peak kilowatt charge measures incremental system cost or signals scarcity of capacity at a point in time when system demand matches capacity less required reserves. While the period can be dated in advance—for example, winter weekdays from 5:00 P.M. to 7:00 P.M. from December 15 through February 28, excluding public holidays—the actual peak point of time cannot. Such a point can be ascertained only retrospectively. This makes unacceptable a system-peak kilowatt charge when there is more than one bulk customer, as no customer would know (until afterward) when he was paying for system-peak kilowatts. This difficulty will not arise if each such customer is charged on his own peak, but only in the rare event of a complete lack of diversity will this provide exactly the desired incentive. Since what is needed is a message conveying information and incentive to the bulk customers in advance, the kilowatt charge could alternatively be spread out over all the potential peak hours. The charge on any one of these hours should then be proportional to the probability of its turning out to be the actual peak hour. This would amount to an extra high kilowatt-hour charge during potential peak hours, and the case for it is stronger as the number of such hours in the year becomes larger.

When a bulk tariff has to serve not only as a means of conveying information and incentive but also as a source of funds for the generating authority (for distributional or financial reasons, which have yet to be discussed), a conflict may exist between the two sets of purposes. Suppose that a bulk tariff constructed along the above lines has to be supplemented by a certain total amount in order to provide the requisite cash flow or rate of return. Then the aim should be to achieve this with the least possible disturbance to its signaling and incentive functions. Three devices suggest themselves, of which the first necessarily exerts the smallest such disturbance: (a) sharing out the excess charge between bulk customers on nonelectrical variables, such as population or book value of net assets if they are distributing authorities; (b) concentrating the excess on those components of the bulk tariff whose signaling and incentive effects are at least, that is, spreading the excess in such a way that all outputs are reduced by the same percentage; and (c) spreading the excess uniformly over all components of the bulk tariff, increasing them all in the same proportion, so that its relativities are undisturbed. No general solution is possible, but it should be noted that providing an adequate answer to question (4) at the head of this section demands the exercise of ingenuity.

Distribution Cost Analysis

Proceeding from the bulk level to the retail level, requires an examination of distribution costs. Here, too, our concern is with engineering estimates of future costs and not with the accounting records of past expenditures. A fifth question then is:

(5) What is the structure of distribution costs?

A first step in answering this question is to estimate incremental losses at different supply voltages and at different load levels in order to convert the bulk tariff rates into their retail equivalents. The second step is to estimate customer costs, a topic about which no more is said here. The third step is to examine the annuitized capital costs, plus associated future operations and maintenance costs involved both in reinforcing the distribution system per kilowatt of load growth in areas currently served and in extending the system to new areas per kilowatt of new load. While the latter may have to be an ad hoc calculation, there are three approaches to the former. In order of decreasing crudeness they are:

- relating past capital expenditure on distribution (corrected for changing price levels minus guesses of the cost of major system renovations and extensions) to the growth in retail demand at the time of distribution peak in areas currently served;
- relating growth in total length of each type of feeder, number of terminations, and transformer capacity at each voltage level to the growth in maximum demand at that voltage level, leaving out system extensions (the average growth in equipment per kilowatt of demand is then costed at current price levels); and
- finding the average cost per kilowatt of reinforcement of each voltage level by costing a weighted sample of reinforcement schemes and then multiplying by the ratio of demand to capacity implicit in the chosen provisioning period to get the average incremental cost per kilowatt of demand of distribution peak.

In all three cases, the annuitized capital costs plus the associated annual operations and maintenance costs can be set out per kilowatt of the relevant maximum demand, without specifying exactly when the maximum is going to occur. Alternatively, they may be spread over kilowatt-hours in all the hours when the maximum is likely to occur. In this case, as with the similar bulk tariff analysis, the result is to be interpreted probabilistically. Thus, if a kilowatt cost of $10 is equally likely to relate to any one of 100 specified hours, the resulting figure of 10 cents applicable to each of them signifies that there is a 99 percent chance that the cost is zero and a 1 percent chance that it is $10 in any one of them.

Schedule of Rates for Costing

Combining the notional bulk tariff with the information on distribution losses and costs makes it possible to reply to a sixth important question:

(6) What is the schedule of rates that can be used for costing retail loads? In other words, the schedule of rates that measures (a) the extra cost of delivering extra power to consumers at times when this neither infringes on the security constraints nor requires extra capital expenditure; (b) the charges that would have to be levied at other

times to keep the load within the security constraints; and (c) the extra cost to the nation as a whole of expanding production, transmission, and distribution capacity to meet an increased load at such other times.

Note that if (b) exceeds (c) there is a strong case for expanding capacity. But it is more useful to look at (b) as having different time dimensions; (b) is a matter of restraining the load to match the capacity over the next few years while (c) is a matter of the cost of subsequent system expansion. As argued earlier, which of them is relevant when they differ is a question of tariff flexibility and of the importance of signaling a short-term or a long-term message to consumers. If physical rationing (load shedding) commonly occurs at certain times, then (b) is in excess of that incremental charge for extra electricity which the existing retail rate structure would involve. It is worth repeating, too, that in the cost studies used to answer (a) and (c), rough but relevant information about the future is more relevant than precise data from the past. Great care must be taken in using accounting records to ascertain which prorated overheads are included in particular items of costs, since such allocations may—not surprisingly—be inappropriate for the present analysis, for which they were not designed.

The schedule of rates used for the costing of retail loads is no more than a collection of information necessary for examining tariffs. Metering and billing problems alone would prevent its implementation as an actual rate structure for all consumers. But this schedule does provide necessary information for constructing feasible retail tariffs and for costing new loads. Before we get on to tariff construction it is worth pausing to note that a distribution undertaking can influence its customers not only through retail tariffs but also by encouragement or discouragement of particular loads. An "active marketing" posture of this latter sort may be uncommon among electricity authorities, but is to be commended for all that.

Load Analysis

The next step in studying pricing policy is to find out as much as possible about the composition of the load—that is, who uses how much electricity, for what purposes, and when? The seventh question is

(7) What information can be assembled about the separate load curves of the different groups of customers, the split of their consumption among different uses, and the time pattern of these uses?

When quantitative information is lacking, merely qualitative information must suffice. Knowledge of factory hours, people's eating habits, and the time it gets dark are of some use. Suggestions that quantitative techniques ought to be applied in the future may not be amiss.

Price Distortions

Using information about the load, it is then necessary to ask which of the various uses are affected by the availability and price of other fuels, and electrical appliances. Thus, one can find out, for example, whether gas competes with electricity for cooking, whether some industrialists generate their own electricity, how important other sources of motive power are, and whether a tax on air-conditioners is important. The aim is, first, to understand these matters as factors helping to determine the pattern of electricity usage and, second, to see whether they would be substantially different if these prices were corrected to allow, for example, for taxes and shadow exchange rates. If so, they constitute misleading incentives. If nothing can be done to change them, it may be worth considering ways in which the incentives provided by electricity tariffs could be slanted to produce an offsetting effect. Two imaginary examples will show what is meant. In the first example, if gas competes with electricity for certain peak-intensive uses, if rates for gas are heavily subsidized, and if nothing can be done about it, any case that there might otherwise be for charging high peak rates for these uses of electricity may be weakened. In the second example, if private enterprises obtain generous tax relief on all capital expenditure including autogeneration, then perhaps there is a case for lower electricity tariffs for large industrial users than there otherwise would be. Summing up, the questions must be asked:

(8) Are price distortions in other parts of the economy likely to affect electricity sales importantly? If so, can and should these distortions be remedied? If they cannot or should not, should electricity tariffs be slanted in order to offset these distortions?

Slanting the tariffs in this way may well prove to be too complicated, may conflict with notions of fairness, or may interfere with other broad government policy objectives. Nonetheless, it is right to consider such slanting and include it as one of the factors in a critique of the present tariff structure. The difficulties involved in slanting furnish an argument in favor of tackling the distortions directly. The same applies to distortions that make marginal cost to the electricity supply undertaking differ significantly from cost from the national economic viewpoint.

Existing Tariffs

Next, the present tariff structure must be described. Such problems of administration as cost, complexity, and fraud must definitely be considered, but in the present context the main question is:

(9) What incentives does the present tariff structure provide to consumers?

Another way of expressing this is to ask what are the partial derivatives of consumers' electricity bills with respect to their electrical behavior. A few examples will show what is meant by such a description: (a) extra kilowatt-hours cost the same by day and night; (b) a uniform monthly maximum demand charge offers no greater incentive to keep demand lower in the peak months of demand than in the rest of the year; (c) penalties for low power factor apply only below 0.8; (d) a lower domestic rate for "heating" than for "lighting" with separate meters and circuits makes extra kilowatt-hours dearer for lighting than for other domestic uses; (e) a flat rate of 3 cents for users consuming up to 150 kilowatt-hours a month, and one of 4 cents for users consuming more, strongly encourages small users to keep their monthly consumption below 150 kilowatt-hours; and (f) descending block rates make the cost to the small consumers of an extra kilowatt-hour 5 cents, compared with 3.5 cents for large consumers. These examples are purely anecdotal, to show what sort of incentive effects can exist, but what is required by way of answer to the question above is naturally a systematic description.

Tentative New Tariffs

With all the information collected in answer to the earlier questions, it is now time to ask:

(10) How can the tariff structure be changed so that the incentives it gives correspond more closely to the schedule of rates developed for the costing of loads?

This question will not produce a final proposal for a new structure since income distribution and financial problems are still being left on one side, as are the problems of transition to a new structure. But at this stage it is certainly necessary to allow for two considerations. The first is any strong arguments for slanting the tariff structure developed under question (8). The second is practicality and cost—if the existing tariff is difficult to administer, conducive to disputes, or prone to fraud, ideas for making it better in these respects will be useful and must be allowed to help determine the choice of the new tariff structure.

There is, of course, a trade-off between the cost of administering a tariff structure (which depends largely on the cost of metering and billing) and the extent to which it can reflect the structure of the schedule of rates for the costing of retail loads, so providing appropriate incentives. Five rather general but useful propositions about this trade-off can be advanced:

- As the extra cost of more complex metering has to be justified by the effect of the superior incentives it can present, and as this extra cost rises but little with the size of the consumer while the absolute response to incentives rises quite fast with the size of the consumer, the case for more complex metering is relatively stronger the larger the consumer.
- As the response to incentives is greater for uses that are not time-bound and where there are alternative sources of energy, complex metering is best justified for consumers for whom such uses are important.
- The option between a simple tariff and a more complex, more expensive one can often be left to the consumer by allowing him a choice of tariff. With such options, the consumer who could respond strongly to the incentives of the more complex tariff should find it to be the cheaper one, even though he has to bear the extra cost of the more complex metering.
- There is often a choice between a larger number of simple tariffs and a smaller number of more complex ones. Thus, if nighttime kilowatt-hours are shown by the schedule of rates for the costing of commercial loads to be, on average, much cheaper than daytime kilowatt-hours, and if nighttime kilowatt-hours form a smaller proportion of commercial than of domestic consumption, a two-rate night and day tariff will cope with both. The alternative would be to have a separate single-rate tariff for each, with a higher unit charge for shops.
- With monthly meter reading, seasonal kilowatt-hour tariffs can always be introduced at a negligible extra cost. There-

fore, such tariffs should always be considered when demand and costs display a significant seasonal pattern.

An improved tariff structure, once achieved, should be designed to last for a number of years, apart from adjustments to inflation, since the responses to incentives involving the design and the growth in ownership of appropriate appliances are spread out over time. This, it will be seen, is an argument for concentrating on the cost (c) rather than the charge (b) in question (6), that is, for looking at long-run costs—at least when there is no acute shortage of capacity necessitating a lot of load shedding. A statement that 40 percent of residential consumers buy less than 100 kilowatt-hours a month, for example, is less interesting than a forecast that, in five years' time, the figure will be only about 15 percent. The incentives should be directed at tomorrow's consumers rather than at today's, except when today's problems are particularly acute. When they are not, an attraction of optional tariffs becomes important. Suppose, for example, that a time-of-day tariff can give much more relevant incentives than a straight energy tariff; however, it does cost more, so that its immediate introduction for all consumers would not be worthwhile. In these circumstances it might be introduced as an option to which, initially, only a minority of consumers might subscribe. As individual loads grow, then, with effective marketing, more and more consumers might subscribe and the relation between the two tariffs could gradually be tilted so as to favor it. But if the course of events showed that its wider adoption was not worthwhile after all, it could be discouraged or even suspended (subject to a right for existing consumers on it to continue) and little would have been lost. Options, therefore, must be seriously considered.

Except possibly for large industrial consumers, the revised or new tariff structure proposed will not be expected to reflect most of the details of the schedule of rates for the costing of retail loads by which it is inspired. Thus, the new tariffs will contain only a very few of all the possible incentives to economize in the use of electricity more at some times or in some uses than at other times and in other uses. It is, therefore, important to see that those few incentives that can be put in the tariffs are those that matter most. What matters most is proportional first to the size of the incentive suggested by the schedule of rates for the costing of retail loads, and second to the magnitude of the response.

Therefore charging for marginal capacity costs with, for example, the use of maximum demand metering may be less effective than with peak kilowatt-hour metering, since consumers more readily respond to the latter system. If water heating is the most promising subject for domestic tariff incentives, however, telecontrolled water heaters with a special cheap rate and a separate kilowatt-hour meter may be more appropriate. Similar sorts of considerations affect decisions about industrial tariffs. Thus, if shift-working is insensitive to electricity charges, it may be better to concentrate on selling interruptible supplies to industry than on cheap nighttime kilowatt-hours. In most cases, as argued in the previous paragraph, the response that is relevant is not the immediate one but rather the response over a period of years, so that the relevant schedule of rates for costing retail loads must relate, correspondingly, to the average over a future period of years. Only when power shortages are acute and are not going to be remedied for a few years is concentration on short-run load-restraining tariffs to be preferred.

Finance and Income Distribution

Any set of new tariffs and the new consumer classification that they may well involve tentatively developed along the foregoing lines still has to be modified. Allowances are needed for (a) financial requirements, (b) any desired income redistribution, and (c) the problems of making the transition. Although these interact, it is expositionally convenient to consider them separately.

The financial requirements are that the electricity tariffs generate sufficient cash flow, a requirement often translated into rate-of-return terms. In addition, a government may wish to tax electricity consumers to provide general revenue. This is perfectly reasonable; indeed, if other fuels are taxed, it may be necessary to tax electricity too in order to avoid a distortion in the relative prices of electricity and other fuels.

Circumstances vary between countries too much for generalization to be possible, but the first step is to inquire:

(11) If the tariffs tentatively developed so far were applied, how much revenue would they yield, and is that sufficient?

It may be thought that tariffs based on the schedules of rates for the costing of retail loads, including connection charges or fixed charges to cover customer costs or both, will normally fall below accounting costs, so that the revenue produced would be sufficient. But this, in fact, is far from necessary. For one thing, if inputs are valued at shadow prices, costs looked at from the electric utility's point of view may be exceeded considerably. But such national economic refinements may be outside the scope of a tariff investigation. The main point, which applies to all systems which have existed for any length of time, is that accounting costs reflect past capital expenditure and the chosen depreciation rules, whereas any capital costs entering into the analysis relate to expected future expenditure. There is an ongoing race between inflation and technical progress, the one raising and the other lowering future capital costs relative to past capital costs. Furthermore, even when the schedule of rates for the costing of retail loads reflects only generating costs plus losses, these are incremental costs. With plant loaded in "order of merit," these will usually exceed average generating costs, so a tariff based on them will yield an excess of revenue over generating costs that may or may not suffice to cover all other costs. Thus, there is no general presumption either way about the answer to question (11).

If more revenue is required, then the argument follows similar lines to those set out earlier concerning bulk tariffs. Subject to any reservations relating to income distribution, the aim should be to increase the level of tariffs with the least possible disturbance to incentives that they present to customers to go easy on consumption at times or places when incremental costs of energy are high, or when extra kilowatts push against the security constraints or necessitate extra capacity, or both. This involves concentrating the increase on those components of the tariffs that will elicit the smallest response by way of change in consumption. Fixed charges are an obvious first target. They do not necessarily have to be uniformly high. For example, they could be related to property value as assessed for tax purposes. The same considerations apply if less revenue is needed.

Income distribution decisions are difficult for individuals since they involve political and social judgments that may be outside their competence. But someone, depending upon the circumstances of the case, must make these decisions and, once made, they should specify who is to benefit and who is to pay; the problem is to decide how. Such decisions can be elicited, and justification of them sought, by asking what distributional objectives entered the existing tariffs, if any. Two cases must be distinguished: (a) where the aim is to stimulate the consumption of a particular group of consumers, that is, to achieve an incentive effect; and (b) where the aim is merely to reduce the bills of a particular group. An example of a subsidy is the provision of rural supplies at tariffs below the costs that can be calculated for rural loads using the schedule of rates for the costing of retail loads (which embodies the capital costs of extending the distribution system). This may be done simply by requiring rural tariffs to be the same as urban tariffs, in which case there is no more to be said. But in other cases, where the nature of the subsidy is an open question, the aim must be to provide any desired incentive without producing other unwanted incentives. Thus, a low rate on a first block of energy will reduce the bills of the consumers on the tariff. This will have different incentive effects according to whether the consumers on the tariff in question use less or more than this block of energy. Hence a lower fixed charge might be considered if what is aimed at is merely a financial benefit.

The changeover from one tariff structure to another is always difficult, since customers who did well under the old tariff tend to regard themselves as having a vested interest in it. Hence, some importance is attached to the impact effect of the changeover and possible tactics for making it more acceptable. The transition may need to be made in several stages, and it may be a good idea for the new tariffs to be introduced only as options.

All these matters deserve thought and investigation. To sum up, one must ask:

(12) Given the answer to question (11) and given the amount of any overt subsidies, how can the tentatively determined customer classifications and tariffs be modified to provide the required revenue and implement the desired subsidies with the least possible distortion of incentives?

The phrasing of the question is not meant to imply that all proposals for income redistribution and subsidization should be accepted automatically. For example, while nationally uniform tariffs are simple and appear to be fair, it is not at all obvious that the resulting equal incentives to load growth make sense in terms of resource allocation. Perhaps electricity-intensive industries should have an incentive to locate near generation centers. The magnitude of regional differences in the schedule of rates for the costing of retail loads should at least be set out and considered before any decision is made to ignore them. Another example of conventional wisdom which requires a second look is the notion in some countries that poor electricity consumers should be subsidized. Poor people without electricity are worse off than poor people who have it. Hence, the idea of subsidizing the poor in some way other than with electricity deserves attention.

Security of Supply

Developing countries cannot afford the same quality of service as can developed countries. An application of this point relates to the provisions made to ensure the security of electricity supply.

Any project for the expansion of power capacity normally constitutes the next step in a whole proposed program for the development of a power system. This program is asserted to be the minimum-cost way of meeting the projected load, subject to certain constraints relating to the security of supply. Two simple illustrative examples of such constraints are: (a) there must be enough generating capacity to withstand the loss of the largest single generating unit without having output fall below the predicted peak demand; and (b) water storage capacity and thermal capacity must together be sufficient to meet predicted energy requirements in the critical period, even if the inflow is as low as in the driest season experienced since records began.

The probability of interruptions of supply is often not calculated by the engineering consultants responsible. This would require data about the weather sensitivity of consumption, the risks of plant outage, and the range of forecasting errors, as well as about the variability of water flows (where hydro power is involved). Nevertheless, even without a probability calculation, if the constraints were less stringent there would be a cheaper minimum-cost program to meet the projected load and the probability of interruptions of supply would be greater.

Hence the question arises of whether this saving in cost (which can be calculated readily) outweighs the disadvantages of the greater probability of interruptions. Even if the latter is also calculated, this question cannot be answered in purely objective terms because of the problem of putting money values on interruptions of supply. But this does not justify ignoring the question. It is necessary to gather whatever information can be obtained and use it to form a judgment. Continuing the simple example given above, more relaxed constraints could be considered, such as the ability to withstand outage of the second-largest unit; or meeting energy requirements in the second-driest season experienced in the past.

The resulting cost-saving could then be calculated and estimates made of how much load shedding would be required if outage of the largest unit occurred, or if a season as dry as the driest experienced in the past occurred, assuming correctness of the load forecasts. This would give a rough idea of the order of magnitude of the possible disadvantages of the reduction in security. It might be expressed in value terms by using a "penalty price" per kilowatt-hour of supply failure. A judgment could then be made as to which of the two levels of security was the better choice in the circumstances of the country in question. The system's arrangements for load control and load shedding surely figure among these circumstances, and their adequacy would have to be investigated.

Generalizing from this example, the following question can be formulated:

(13) How do the possible consequences of a lower degree of security compare with the cost savings involved, given that load shedding arrangements are the least damaging possible?

This question should be applied to investment in transmission and distribution as well as to investment in generation. It might lead, for example, to a judgment that suburban distribution networks should be provided with relatively less security than urban networks.

Final Remarks

The reader of the preceding pages of this chapter will have noticed the prominent point that the questions proposed will often be rather too general to match the particular circumstances of any particular study. But while the letter of the analysis will need modification from case to case, the spirit of it applies everywhere. Prices can and do affect the attractiveness to consumers of alternative courses of behavior and so need to be related to their consequences for resource use—consequences measured in terms of a forward-looking concept of costs. This is as much, or more, a matter of the structure of prices and costs as of their levels.

Simple and general propositions about pricing cannot be made. But it is usually a good idea to ask whether prices should not be cut at times and places when more electricity could be supplied easily because capacity is underused. Similarly, when capacity limits are strained, it is worth considering whether a rise in prices might limit demand more efficiently than interruptions of supply, rationing, and the like.

Pricing, as well as being a means of raising revenue, is about *future* choices in relation to *future* costs. This means that the relevant figures are only estimates and are subject to uncertainty. There is, therefore, a temptation to go back to accounting cost figures. But an accurate record of the past is not relevant; rough and uncertain estimates about the future are unavoidable in decisionmaking. Accounting costs, on the other hand, are relevant for total revenue requirements.

Politics may demand that pricing policy should aim to achieve some measure of income redistribution. This may have to be accepted, but the analyst should at least ask whether other methods of income redistribution are not better.

CHAPTER 10

The Rate of Return on Projects—and Relations between Pricing and Investment

An economic rate of return on an electric power project indicates whether it is a good one or not. If the rate is high, the time-stream of benefits from the project is large in relation to the time-stream of costs. The benefits and costs constitute what is gained and what resources are used in undertaking the project versus not undertaking it. *The rate of return thus compares the two alternatives, to undertake the project or not, from an economic point of view.* A financial rate of return, with which we are not here concerned, would compare receipts and payments in a similar way.

Rate of return calculations of this kind are often required in the electric power sector, as in other sectors, to justify projects. There are, however, two difficulties with the calculation, and the interpretation of it, which require clarification. One is, given that many areas are highly adapted to service, the electric utility often does not have the option of rejecting a project—severe rationing and breakdowns in supply may result, disrupting economic activity on a large scale. Generally, rejection of a project to provide service is a realistic alternative only in areas accustomed to doing without service. The other difficulty is that the calculated rate of return may reflect more on the pricing policy than on the project—that is, a poor rate of return may argue for reforms in pricing policy rather than rejection of the project.

For purposes of analyzing the economic returns to an electric power project, we find it convenient to draw a distinction (though it is not absolutely clear-cut) between projects serving established markets and those serving new markets. One reason is that there is a technological difference between projects serving each type of market. Projects in established markets consist largely of additions to the capacity of an existing and growing system, making it possible to increase both the consumption of existing consumers and the number of consumers within the same geographical area. Examples are the addition of a new generating plant or the reinforcement of a distribution network to meet load growth. In such cases, a project forms only one component of a whole sequence of additions to the capacity of the system and its functioning has to be integrated into the operation of the total system. A new generating plant may be used for base load, with some corresponding reduction in the output of older plants. Where such interdependence exists, the increase in total system output following the introduction of the new project may well be different from the output of the new project itself.

Such interdependence does not occur in the type of distribution project that brings supplies to areas previously lacking them. Here, the output of the project and the increase (from zero) in consumption are one and the same thing. Such projects usually draw on a central generating system already serving established markets as a source of supply, so any consequential addition to the costs of the central system naturally must be taken into account.

While projects to serve new markets may be rejected—or at least postponed for quite some time—this generally is not a realistic alternative for projects intended to serve established markets. To reject projects that will add to the capacity of an electricity supply system in the face of a growing load from existing customers requires the analysis of *a growing likelihood of voltage fluctuations and power cuts, while saving the costs of the project*—an alternative that could be reformulated as *a tariff increase sufficient to choke off the growth of consumption so that voltage fluctuations and power cuts are obviated*. Neither of these alternatives seems useful, however, at least in established markets. Industrial and domestic consumers are usually highly equipped to use public supplies of electricity. Sometimes the entire choice and location of a manufacturing technique may be based on the expectation of reliable public supplies. Once such adaptations to public supplies have taken place, investments can be wasted if (increasing) demands are not met with a tolerable level of continuity. Rejection of new projects soon leads to physical rationing and to a deterioration in the quality and continuity of supply, disrupting output on a large scale. On the other hand, tariff increases, which would have to be large to ration demand, may be unacceptable—and also ineffective, since short-run elasticities are small once consumers are adapted to service. At least in established markets, a totally different approach is required.

Established Markets

In a growing system the response of consumers to prices is a long-term and gradual one. The problems to consider with such a system are three: (a) What should the rate of expansion over a period be—that is, should growth be slow or rapid? (b) What should the target standard of security be (the risk of voltage fluctuations and power cuts or, in sum, the quality of supply)? Here there is a trade-off between planning a higher or lower ratio of capacity to projected demand (which involves higher or lower costs), on the one hand, and a lower or higher risk of power failure, on the other. (c) What is the minimum-cost method of achieving the expansion at the chosen target level of security?

This chapter addresses questions about the rate of expansion and the standard of security, but it does not have anything additional to suggest regarding minimum cost methods of achieving the desired balance of expansion and security, a topic that is discussed at length in Chapter 13. An answer to question (c) requires a systems analysis of costs alone, disregarding benefits, and involves comparison of the cost of a chosen project as part of a sequence of capacity expansions with the cost of alternative possible sequences.

The rate of expansion

Once the target standard of security has been chosen, electricity planners attempt to meet the predicted growth of consumption. Except for the extension of electricity supply to new areas (discussed separately below), planners do not decide directly what this consumption shall be. But though the utility does not fix consumption, it does influence it. The utility fixes tariffs to which the consumers adjust when determining their consumption. The level and pattern of consumption responds, albeit slowly, to the level and structure of electricity tariffs (as well as, of course, to many other things). Thus, the practical problem facing the utility is not: What should the growth and pattern of consumption be? Instead, the practical problem is: What should the level and structure of tariffs be? In considering this question, the utility aims to fix tariffs so that consumers' decisions about consumption result in an efficient use of the country's resources.

Above and beyond the purely financial concern with the adequacy of tariff levels, an appraisal of the level and structure of tariffs is required as an essential and necessary part of the examination of capacity expansion plans. While investigation of a single project may furnish the occasion for such a tariff appraisal, this appraisal re-

225

lates to the future expansion of the whole enterprise and not to the single project considered in isolation. Tariffs help determine growth, so they are of central importance. They are not a separate and optional aspect of operating efficiency.

General guidelines for tariff appraisals have been set out in Chapters 2 and 9, with case studies in Chapters 3 through 5. The underlying principle is that, subject to any subsidies or taxes that may be appropriate, the costs to the country of variations in consumers' level or pattern of consumption should be reflected in the tariffs imposed on consumers. If, for example, additional peak power is expensive, then the tariff should make consumers pay a lot for additions to peak consumption. The tariffs, however, should reflect the expected future cost structure over a whole period of years because consumer reactions to them, almost always involving capital investment, take time.

How can the rate of return calculation be modified to examine this alternative of tariff reform and a changed growth and pattern of consumption? The answer is that, instead of comparing costs and benefits or revenues with and without the project, *it is more appropriate to make a comparison between implementing the project when planned, and implementing it one year later (or earlier)*. The cost difference between these alternatives comprises four elements: (a) one year's interest and depreciation on capital cost, plus (b) the first-year operating cost, less (c) the first-year fuel savings, plus (d) one year's interest and depreciation on the capital cost of any other equipment needed to provide the input to the project or to transmit its output to consumers.

The latter element in costs reflects the dependence of the project on the rest of the system. If the project is a power station, and we are to consider postponing it, then expansions to the transmission and distribution network capacity needed to transmit the power station's output can also be postponed (indivisibilities complicate the calculation here and are best treated by taking average incremental costs). If the postponed project is a distribution network element, then the supporting extensions to generation and transmission capacity can be postponed. Finally, if it is a transmission project that is postponed, either for interconnection or bulk transmission, then the costs of supporting generation and distribution also are avoided. (In the case of interconnection, the dispatching schedules of the generating plant are also altered by postponement of transmission.) All such changes in costs result from postponing the project in question and need to be considered.

The revenue difference between these alternatives is as follows. It is the net increase in system output provided in the project's first full year valued according to how much consumers pay for it. If the net increase is confined to, say, 2,000 hours in the year, then the relevant value is the extra amount that, under existing tariffs, consumers would pay for that net increase in consumption during those extra hours. In the case of power station projects, the difference in revenues will depend on the type of system. A thermal project in a thermal system will make possible an increase in peak demand revenues. A hydro project will often make possible an increase in revenues both at peak and during the "critical periods" of energy shortages in the dry season. Finally, a thermal project in a predominantly hydro system may also make possible revenue increases at peak and in the critical periods. Examination of system constraints and dispatching schedules is therefore necessary before estimates of the revenue differences can be made.

The prices to be used are those prevailing at times when the system's output is reduced by postponement of the project. Peak demand and capacity charges are the ones relevant when peak demand output is reduced; "critical period" or "dry season" prices are relevant when dry season energy output is reduced. Generally, these prices will, and should, differ from the average price.

If the comparison of one-year costs and revenue on the lines discussed above produces a very low or negative return, what does that signify? A low revenue in relation to costs suggests that consumers ought not to get the extra output, or that they ought to pay more for it, or both. But as discussed earlier, sudden tariff increases may be unacceptable and, in any case, may have little effect in the short run. The practical conclusion is that the project—which should, of course, be the minimum-cost solution—is implemented and that tariffs are changed to make peak period (or dry season) consumption more expensive. This will gradually slow down the rate of growth of peak period (or dry season) consumption. Conversely, a very high rate of return would argue for tariff reductions and faster growth.

Of course, this calculation of the rate of return will not be sufficient for a full appraisal of tariffs. Nevertheless, it can be made fairly readily and it does throw light on this important issue.

The standard of security

If it is impracticable to restructure prices when rate of return calculations and subsequent tariff studies show that it is desirable to do so, then the only formal way of showing that the growth of demand is worth meeting, from an economic viewpoint, is to consider what happens if part of the growth of demand is not met. Again, it is best to consider the economic effects of marginal reductions in capacity by postponing the project for one year. This is the same thing as looking at the economic effects of a marginal reduction in the standard of security—a question which in any case deserves investigation in its own right, even if tariff policy is satisfactory.

Decisions about the target level of security are often taken by applying rules of thumb. For example, it may be proposed that there should always be sufficient reserve to cope with a forced outage of the largest single generating set in the system. But where, either directly or by analogy with other systems, information is available about (a) plant outage rates, (b) weather variability, (c) weather sensitivity of demand, and (d) forecasting uncertainty, it is possible to do better, even if only by rough approximation. The probability of load shedding can be calculated. Estimates can be made of the effect of different levels of plant provision upon this probability. Hence the choice between more plant, higher costs, fewer power cuts, or less plant, lower costs, more power cuts, can be made explicit. This is preferable to the applications of rules of thumb, since such rules may be rather expensive for a developing country. If such a country can shield its process industries, hospitals, and so on, from power cuts, a fairly low standard of security in comparison with that in high income countries may be sensible.

The evaluation of power cuts is difficult, which may explain why rules of thumb are a popular way of avoiding the issue. Yet the nature of the costs involved is clear enough; they include the costs of: (a) keeping kerosene lamps and candles; (b) voltage regulators installed by individual consumers; (c) emergency generators; (d) autogeneration, which is less dear than public supply, except in remote areas; and the less measurable costs of inconvenience and of interrupting production.

Sample case studies of the various consumer groups affected by power cuts will often yield rough but useful estimates of these costs. These estimates can then be grossed up over the consumer population. A rate of return can be calculated, based on a comparison of (a) the expected value of such costs, with (b) the cost savings if the project is postponed for one year (where the cost savings of postponement are calculated as just outlined). If a low rate of return is calculated, it suggests that the enterprise is providing too high a standard of security from an economic viewpoint.

When, as is most likely, no "penalty value" per kilowatt-hour of power cut or voltage drop has been estimated, it still may be possible to make a useful calculation by turning the question around. One then asks how big the penalty value would have to be for the costs and benefits of a one-year postponement to be evenly matched. If the penalty value comes out unreasonably high, it also suggests that the standard of security is too high from an economic viewpoint.

New Markets

New markets are fully, if not always efficiently, adapted to the use of substitutes and to doing without public supply. Irrigation, for example, may use diesel pumps if electricity is not available; and small communities and small businesses can and do turn to autogenerators to provide electricity on a small scale. While public supplies to new markets may spur development and introduce new activities into an area, projects often can be postponed or rejected without creating new problems.

In new markets, therefore, the ''with and without'' comparison is a meaningful basis for project justification. In the rate of return calculation, the time-stream of *all* revenues should be calculated—since there would not be revenues without the project—and compared with the time-stream of costs. Then,

- if the rate of return is high, the project is a good one;
- if the rate of return is low, the project *appears* to be a bad one but might possibly become a good one if the tariff structure were made to reflect costs better.

This asymmetry is a little confusing. To illuminate it, imagine a silly tariff which gives free kilowatt-hours (and charges for kilowatts only). Under this tariff, if the new customers provide a revenue in excess of costs, then they would do so under any sensible tariff; if they provide only a revenue below costs, they might nevertheless provide one in excess of costs under a sensible tariff. For new areas, therefore, something like the conventional rate of return calculation is meaningful, but the case for a tariff appraisal—and a low rate-of-return may signal the need for such an appraisal rather than project rejection—remains.

As with established markets, it is necessary to investigate the security (or quality) of supply. Indeed, the returns at lower standards can be quite considerable in such areas as village electrification, where large cost savings have been reported by utilities working to lower design standards, single-wire systems, and interruptible supplies offered to consumers at lowered tariffs.

Conclusion

To sum up, an orthodox economic rate of return should be calculated in power project appraisals only to the extent that the project extends the system to new areas as distinct from meeting load growth in established markets. For the latter, the rate of system growth and the standard of security require attention, and we have shown how rate-of-return calculations can be brought to bear on both of these matters if the alternative of postponing rather than rejecting projects is considered. Regarding the rate of system growth, which is most appropriately modulated by tariffs, the rate of return will indeed provide some information about the adequacy of tariffs—whether they need to be raised or lowered or restructured. Regarding the standard of security, the rate of return will indicate if the standard needs to be raised or lowered by advancing or postponing projects.

CHAPTER 11

The Willingness-to-Pay Criterion

This chapter discusses an old precept of economic analysis that we find frequently troubling economists and others alike when working in developing countries: it is whether, in low income areas of developing countries, the consumers' willingness to pay for a product is an appropriate basis for deciding on pricing and investment policies. We confine ourselves here to the electric power sector, though the issue is, of course, much wider than this. We do believe, however, that the issue can best be resolved through case-by-case examination of the precept in each of the many different fields to which it is now applied. (We would abandon it, for example, for water supply projects in drought areas of extreme poverty, but would accept it, as will be apparent, for electric power projects.)

Having already spoken in Chapter 10 of established and new markets, we now distinguish in more detail: *established markets,* covering (a) nondomestic consumers, and (b) domestic consumers (high and low incomes); and *new markets,* broken down into cases where (a) incomes and productivity are relatively high, (b) incomes and productivity are low, and (c) incomes and productivity are extremely low. Established markets take the bulk of the investment in developing countries and, relatively speaking, are predominantly prosperous; new markets, in contrast, are predominantly poor. Also, investment to serve low income markets is only a recent initiative in most developing countries.

Established Markets

The justification for expanding an existing system's supply to an area already served rests largely upon the gains that can be provided to individual consumers through increased supplies. There may also be some community benefits from public lighting. But most of the benefits are gained by individual consumers, domestic and nondomestic. Consider nondomestic consumers first.

Increased industrial use of electricity is a necessary condition for industrial growth. For lighting, small motive power units, and some chemical processes on the one hand, the substitutes for electricity are so inferior that any check to availability would retard the expansion of industrial output. For heating and large motive power units, on the other hand, firms can often use coal, gas, or oil as alternative sources of energy. The choice is one of cost-effectiveness; if firms are to make choices that are sensible from a national economic viewpoint, the prices they face should reflect the national economic costs of supply. This requires, among other things, that industrial electricity tariffs have a structure, for example, as between peak and off-peak power, that reflects the structure of supply costs. If, in addition, the general level of electricity tariffs relative to the price levels of other forms of energy reflects their relative costs as seen from the national economic viewpoint, the cost-saving incentives presented to firms will lead them in the direction of making sensible choices. Thus it makes sense to allow the rate of expansion of industrial electricity consumption to be determined by firms' own choices.

Consumers equip themselves to use the public supply at considerable expense. Expenditures on electric motors, for example, may exceed the costs of purchasing electricity to run them. Once the market is established and is adapted to public services, maintaining the continuity and the quality of service becomes important. A deterioration in the continuity of electricity supply due, for example, to large backlogs in the investment program, disrupts business activity on a large scale. Where this has happened in some countries, firms have been driven to installing autogenerators to maintain service, even though the costs of doing this are greater than the costs to the country of expanding public supply. Continuity and quality of supply to industry and commerce in expanding markets need to be maintained, provided that prices reflect costs.

It is with respect to the domestic consumption of electricity that difficulties arise with the idea that, provided tariffs reflect costs, the pace of expansion should be determined by the growth of demand. The use of more electricity by higher income groups in developing countries may well be considered less important than, say, housing for the poor or new rural roads. But, in accepting this, it is necessary to recognize that simply refusing to meet the demands of the higher income groups would create problems. Some mechanism for transferring resources must be introduced. One such mechanism is to provide the electricity but to tax it. This would simultaneously dampen demand and provide revenue for expenditure on other development projects.

Otherwise, simply depriving the higher income groups of service leads to all kinds of difficulties and inequities. In some electric systems, the only way to ration supply is to shed it in a manner that may also entail the shedding of loads to industry and to low income consumers (because they are connected to the same network). Thus, physical deprivation of services is usually inefficient and often inequitable. Finally, a useful basis for raising the public revenue is lost.

It is better, therefore, to meet the growing demands of higher income consumers than to ignore them. Taxes can be introduced if appropriate. The choice of taxes is a broad issue, of course, and cannot be settled solely within the context of public utility projects. There may be a better case for taxing other goods. But once the tax policy is decided upon, there is no other sensible alternative open to the utility than that of meeting the demands of all consumers at a satisfactory level of quality and continuity of service.

There are, of course, some cases where a project that raises the capacity of an existing system to meet demands in existing markets can be postponed temporarily. These instances occur either when the adverse effect upon the quality of service is marginal or when prices that are too low can be raised sharply, with the prompt effect of checking the growth in demand. But these cases are uncommon; the quality of service is seldom too high, and the short-term effect of prices upon demand is usually very limited. Adjustments to higher prices often require new plans and new equipment and appliances and so take place gradually.

In general, therefore, continued system expansion is necessary. But this most emphatically does not signify that public utilities should be allowed to display an unlimited demand for capital. The proposition that system expansion should not be stopped suddenly in the short run leaves open the question of its rate in the long run. It is here that the real options lie. We have already considered in Chapter 10 how rate-of-return calculations can be brought to bear upon this issue of the rate of expansion of the system.

New Markets

A significant portion of the increasing demand for electricity in developing countries stems from newly constructed areas in cities, housing relatively high income families or being centers of expanding industrial, commercial, and governmental activity. Much of what has been said above applies to projects to serve such new areas. The projects are worthwhile if consumers are prepared to pay prices that reflect the costs of the projects and their outputs, plus any taxes that are considered appropriate. Since many similar consumers are supplied currently, there is generally ample precedent for the demand forecast. A comparison between forecast revenues (including taxes) and the opportunity costs of the project and its output will testify to the project's desirability (if tariffs reflect costs plus any appropriate taxes). If the revenues are below opportunity costs, this is almost certainly because the tariffs are too low, as discussed in Chapter 10.

In all new markets—and this is a general point—an alternative to simply accepting a project may be to offer service at a lower quality in order to supply lower cost service to more customers at lower prices. But as noted above, it is important that the utility should not reverse decisions suddenly and significantly reduce the quality of supply once the market has become established and has adapted to the quality of supply first agreed upon.

Major difficulties arise in the extension of service to low income areas in villages and cities where domestic consumers are poor and where the demand for productive purposes, on farms, small industry, and commerce, may be on a small scale. Low levels of demand, low revenues, and high initial costs on account of low economies of scale and low density demands are an obstacle to investment in these areas. (There is, however, a tendency to understate the extent and growth of demand for electricity in these areas. Research in village electrification suggests that many potentially desirable and productive projects are not being considered for this reason. See Chapter 7.)

First, consider conditions of low income and low productivity rather than conditions of extreme poverty and extremely low productivity. At a guess, the border line between these two conditions might be around $50 per capita a year (1972 conditions), though the border line is more evident on sight than in income statistics. Since poverty is not uniformly distributed, both kinds of conditions exist on a large scale in most regions.

The experimental electrification projects of most countries have been directed mainly toward areas of low income and productivity rather than to those of extreme poverty. It is generally the larger villages, for example, that receive electricity first; village electrification programs are generally associated with the needs of farms, irrigation, and agro-industries. In these areas, there is generally a strong response to the investments from both households and businesses. When such consumers purchase electricity, it is apparent that it is because the benefits to them outweigh the price they have to pay for the service. Often the benefits outweigh the price considerably—that is, consumers' surpluses are high. When this occurs, the demand for the service is particularly strong and remains so, even if prices are raised substantially. These benefits take one, two, or some combination of three forms:

- Resource saving, when the price of the utility's service is much cheaper than can be obtained from a substitute or from a private source of supply. Electric motors, for example, are often cheaper to operate than diesel motors. Public electricity is cheaper than electricity from autogenerators for all but low levels of demand in remote areas.
- Higher quality energy supplies, which are valued by the consumer. Electric lighting and electric ironing, though more expensive than substitutes, are valued more highly by households because they are of far higher quality; electric motors are also valued more highly than diesel motors on account of reliability.
- Extra output, which may be generated by reduced prices of the service (relative to substitutes), or by extra quality, or both. More lighting, more ironing, more motive power, and more business activity, for example, may all be induced by the cheaper or higher quality of service that the project can offer. In addition, new activities, such as refrigeration, may be introduced as a result of the project.

In addition to these benefits, there may be a benefit to the community from public lighting, as mentioned earlier. (A fuller discussion of the benefits from rural electrification appears in Chapter 7.)

Because of the importance of these benefits, a satisfactory return on the investment may often be expected. Electricity is a factor input in nondomestic consumption in industry and agriculture, and this indicates the kind of returns that can be expected. When service is desired by nondomestic consumers, it is because it contributes to profits and, apart from the smaller of these consumers, supply costs can be met. Moreover, it is desirable that revenues do meet costs. For example, in irrigation (which shows good profits) a particular problem is to encourage efficiency in the choice between diesel and electric pumping; this can be done if the prices of electric pumps and of electricity reflect the costs of supply, on the condition, of course, that the prices of diesel pumps and energy also reflect the costs of providing them.

Furthermore, since incomes are not uniformly low, a number of households can often afford and are indeed prepared to meet the costs of service. Where electricity serves productive purposes, and where enough domestic consumers are in this "less poor" category, prices can be set to reflect costs and a satisfactory return to the investment can be expected. If the returns are low, this may be because the tariffs are too low or because the quality is too high (and costly). In this case there are two alternatives to simply accepting the project as it is: (a) raise tariffs, or (b) lower the quality (and costs) of the service for some consumers. Alternatively, if it is desirable to assist low income business and domestic consumers in the area, a degree of subsidy may well be acceptable. Such subsidy could take the form of, for example, a low first block in the kilowatt-hour tariffs, or reduced connection costs for low capacity supplies, as discussed in Chapter 7.

The central precept suggested for the economic evaluation of electrification projects is that the desirability of these projects in the circumstances so far described is revealed in the consumer demand at prices that are a compromise between fairness and efficiency. Even in low income areas—say, down to about $50 per capita— where development is just beginning, it seems that this precept holds quite well. In fact, a major obstacle to a successful investment seems to be that the demand for the services generally is underestimated and that the factors that relate to successful investment are not well understood. These include the management of prices, subsidies, and credit policies; the institutional framework; the promotion of and institutional interest in the service; proper monitoring and evaluation of project performance; the indirect influences on the project of public investments and support for local agriculture and industry; and the trade-offs between quality of service and the number of people who can be supplied.

In areas of poverty and extremely low productivity, however, the precept of relying on people's demand for the service and their willingness to pay for it at "fair and efficient" prices breaks down, for the simple reason that these people lack the incomes to purchase service. What can be done in such circumstances? One answer, though it has obvious defects, is for the government to subsidize the service very heavily. In the case of electricity, this does not seem very useful; for the service to be of any use, electricity requires substantial complementary investments in electrical machines and apparatus. Aid to extremely poor areas requires a broad program of investments and economic and institutional reforms and initiatives.

Electrification projects can form no more than a part of such programs.

With the exception of such extremely poor areas, and subject to the possibilities of taxes and subsidies mentioned above, our conclusion is that consumer willingness to pay for electricity is an adequate monetary measure of its economic benefits, and a good basis for pricing and investment decisions.

CHAPTER 12

A Layman's Guide
to Shadow Pricing

A "financial" appraisal of a project is made either to determine its capacity to service debt and contribute to subsequent investment by the borrower, or to determine the return to the investor. An "economic" appraisal or "cost–benefit analysis" is aimed at determining whether or not the project is in the national interest.

In his "economic" appraisal, the analyst may consider that the price paid by the borrower for, say, a ton of cement or for a week's labor is a poor measure of the sacrifice made by the country in using that cement or labor on a project instead of in some other way. So, in costing them, he may multiply the tons of cement used by a shadow price per ton and the weeks of labor employed by a shadow wage per week. Shadow prices and wages are what prices and wages *ought* to be, with one enormous qualification: that they take as given all the limitations to efficient resource allocation and to improvement in the distribution of income in the context of the specific project. The cost analyst considers the shadow figures more relevant than the actual ones in terms of the national interest, even though they are less relevant in terms of cash flows. Similarly, the benefits arising from a project's outputs may be better measured by using shadow prices than by using actual selling prices.

Simply, what a price ought to be depends very much upon circumstances. If a silly government has created a fantastic and totally unnecessary shortage of zinc, for example, in a country where the ground is almost pure zinc, one would want: a very high shadow price of zinc in cost–benefit analysis of a project under circumstances where the silly policy will continue, and a very low shadow price of zinc if the project involves or is conditional upon its reversal. A more realistic example is given by the shadow price of foreign exchange. This could simultaneously be high for a single project, medium for the development of a major export industry, and low if the terms of reference allow a new economic policy.

A certain proportion of the writings of economists about shadow pricing is devoted to the last kind of circumstances, that is, to a generally optimal economic policy (which is not helpful to the appraisal of just one project). This can only concern itself with what have been called *ceteris paribus shadow prices*—all relevant factors being equal—or *second-best shadow prices*. These can reflect distortions in the economy along a continuum between the particular and the general. At the two extremes we have, for example: particular distortions, such as a tax on petrol but not on diesel fuel; and economy-wide distortions, such as urban wages that are kept artificially high by minimum-wage laws, too little investment, or an overvalued exchange rate. Most of the writings of economists about shadow prices relate to the latter end of the spectrum for the reason that it is easier to generalize about general phenomena than about particular phenomena.

It is a feature of economywide distortions that they reduce the usefulness of money as a common denominator. Thus if:

- there is too little investment relative to consumption;
- foreign exchange is very scarce;
- income ought to be, but in practice cannot be, redistributed from rich to poor;

we can say that:

- more currency units, say 100 pesos, of investment is "worth" more than 100 pesos of extra consumption;
- 100 pesos of extra export production is "worth" more than 100 pesos of extra production for the home market; and
- 100 pesos of extra consumption by the poor is "worth" more than 100 pesos of extra consumption by the rich.

Under such circumstances we cannot simply add up pesos of the one kind and pesos of the other. We have to choose *one* kind of expenditure as numéraire—or unit of account—and express other kinds of expenditure in related terms.

An imaginary example will make this clear. Suppose that an extra peso's expenditure on dollar imports, peasants' consumption, and government expenditure use are not all "worth" the same, but that distortions cause their relative values to stand in the ratios 14:9:11. Then we can express costs and benefits in terms of any of the three numéraires:

- pesos of dollar imports, valuing a peso of peasant consumption at $9/14$ and of government consumption at $11/14$;

239

- pesos of peasant consumption, valuing a peso of dollar imports at $^{14}/_9$ and of government expenditure at $^{11}/_9$; or
- pesos of government expenditure, valuing a peso of dollar imports at $^{14}/_{11}$ and of peasant consumption at $^9/_{11}$.

The choice of numéraire (which should be a matter of convenience) is inextricably bound up with the choice of the discount rate used in cost–benefit analysis. The reason is that development will, we hope, gradually reduce distortions and move the economy toward a position where all of the above kinds of ratio are unity. Thus if at present 80 pesos of extra investment is judged to be worth just as much as 100 pesos of extra consumption, the aim will be to increase investment at the expense of consumption until a peso of each is worth the same. So if pesos of investment constitute the numéraire, the shadow price of consumption will gradually rise; if pesos of consumption constitute the numéraire, the shadow price of investment will gradually fall. The discount rate in terms of investment will be higher than the discount rate in terms of consumption: if 80 pesos of current investment is worth 100 pesos of current consumption, and if the latter is worth 110 pesos of next year's consumption (a consumption discount rate of 10 percent); but if this will be worth more than 88 pesos of next year's investment, then 80 pesos of current investment is worth more than 88 pesos of next year's investment (an investment discount rate exceeding 10 percent).

We can now define the numéraire as the kind of peso's-worth which we set at unity; the discount rate or accounting rate of interest as the percent excess over one peso of the amount of future numéraire which we value equally with one peso's-worth now; and the shadow price of a unit of X as the ratio of our marginal valuation of a unit of X to our marginal valuation of the numéraire.

Some shadow prices involve only descriptive information and value judgments. Thus, the ratio between our marginal valuations of a peso's worth of extra peasant consumption and an extra peso's worth of consumption by urban laborers depends upon how well off they are, what prices they pay for consumer goods, and how well off we think they ought to be. But other marginal valuations and the discount rate depend not only upon these things but also upon prediction or understanding of how the economy works. For example: What would be the consequences of hiring more labor? How would the rest of the economy react to making do with less cement? How much greater will consumption be next year? It follows that choosing shadow prices involves judgment in two senses: (a) value judgment and (b) guessing or estimating descriptive facts and how the

240

economy works. They are thus inevitably arbitrary and inaccurate. Indeed it is tempting to say that shadow prices can only be calculated in economies that are sufficiently developed for the use of such prices to be unnecessary! In these circumstances it is sensible to choose as the numéraire something that is easy to think about (that is, something homogeneous, such as dollars, desirable for its own sake and importance, such as government funds available for investment) and to give things shadow prices only when a peso's-worth of them is obviously and importantly worth more or less than a peso's-worth of the numéraire.

One of the general distortions in resource allocation that most excites academic writers on development economics was used as an example three paragraphs above, namely, that too small a proportion of a country's output is devoted to investment. If this is the case, it means that projects ought to be favored that will generate a lot of savings—that is, a lot of future extra investment—while projects ought to be penalized that will reduce savings by employing workers who can only be attracted by giving them a higher level of consumption than they currently enjoy. Thus the right type of project to choose and the right labor intensity for it are affected by the following facts: the government wants to increase investment at the expense of consumption; but cannot do as much as it wants to achieve this by means of fiscal policy; so it tries to get part of the way either by counting savings from profits as extra valuable (when consumption is chosen as the numéraire) or by treating labor whose employment adds to consumption as extra expensive (when investment is the numéraire).

A second general distortion in resource allocation thought to justify the use of a shadow price again relates to the employment of workers in building or operating a project. This time the point, a separate one, is that the amount that workers have to be paid on the project exceeds what their labor is worth to the economy elsewhere. Then workers should be counted in with a shadow wage less than their actual wage. Everyone agrees that this will be appropriate if a minimum-wage law or collective bargaining is the cause of the (relatively) high wage. But there is more disagreement about whether the worth of workers to the economy when they are employed in traditional agriculture is measured by what they consume there. There is also disagreement about the significance of a pool of urban unemployed in working out what labor is worth to the economy when not employed on the project. An uneasy suspicion arises that most contributors to the discussion are right and that the only problem is to discover the times and places to which their various assertions relate!

Tariffs, quotas, subsidies, multiple exchange rates, and other impediments to trade also often cause general distortions in resource allocation and justify the use of: a shadow exchange rate for valuing imports and exports when the numéraire is domestic currency, or, when foreign exchange is the numéraire, the opposite, called "conversion factors." Economists appear to disagree less about these matters than about the ones referred to above, probably because they are more unanimously clear about the nature and effects of the distortions involved. Furthermore, better statistics are usually available about these things.

In appraisals of foreign-financed projects the practice has often been to note the direct foreign exchange cost. This is interesting in a financial appraisal, but for cost–benefit analysis matters can be a bit more complicated. The appraisal consists of comparing a number of alternatives. Taking one of them as the reference case (usually the Do Nothing alternative, if there is one), the appraisal tries to predict the difference between that alternative and the others in the time-stream of foreign exchange payments and receipts. When a lender will lend the direct foreign exchange requirements for all the Do Something alternatives and where there is a Do Nothing alternative, these direct requirements must be replaced by the time-stream of interest and repayment to the overseas lender over the life of the loan. Thus the foreign exchange payments ($-$) and receipts ($+$) to be estimated are:

- indirect foreign exchange component of construction costs,
- direct foreign exchange operating costs,
- indirect foreign exchange component of operating costs,
- loan payments,
+ indirect contribution to exports or import replacement or both,
+ direct exports or import replacement or both.

These have to be multiplied by the shadow exchange rate to convert them into the numéraire (unless foreign exchange has been chosen as the numéraire). Note that some of the receipts and payments are difficult to estimate, involving the marginal import content of hundreds of different kinds of expenditure and the effects upon export earnings of all sorts of different changes in supply conditions.

If the tax system is in a mess, the government may be short of revenue and may value an extra peso's-worth of government domestic expenditure at more than an extra peso's-worth of private consumption. This is rather like the earlier argument that, with saving less than the government would wish and can achieve by taxation, the government may value an extra peso's-worth of investment at more than an extra peso's-worth of private consumption. In the first case the argument is that projects that raise government income rather than private incomes confer important side benefits. In the second case the argument is that extra employment involves extra consumption that imposes a side cost of diminishing saving. In both cases it is assumed that the project evaluator thinks there is a shortage and predicts or accepts the impossibility of remedying it by direct means.

As well as the general distortions in resource allocation relating to investment, labor, foreign exchange, and government revenue, there may also be general distortions regarding the distribution of income. These, too, if deemed incurable by direct means, can be reflected in shadow prices that give a higher weight to extra consumption by the deserving than to extra consumption by the relatively undeserving. Politicians often think of such groups in social or class terms, while economists tend to argue in terms of the marginal social utility of income as being a declining function of the income of the recipient. If either view is to be reflected in shadow prices, explicit judgments about fairness are required.

This chapter has endeavored to explain the justification for using shadow prices in project appraisal and to indicate their meaning. It has not, however, attempted to explain how to derive them, a subject which needs book-length treatment; a delightfully concise exposition on this is to be found in recent research on project analysis by Lyn Squire and Herman van der Tak.[1] The aim has merely been to introduce the reader to shadow prices in an elementary way. But it should be clear that their estimation often requires study of the economy as a whole, going outside the expertise necessary to evaluate particular projects. It should also be clear that their estimation demands judgment as much as calculation.

For this latter reason, some skepticism is often expressed about their usefulness. Yet to dispense with them amounts to the assumption that none of the distortions that they reflect exists or, alternatively, that though they do exist they are not very relevant to the particular project under examination. Consequently, it is open to the proponents of systematic shadow pricing to argue that even very crude estimates of them will influence appraisals in the right direc-

---

1. See *Economic Analysis of Projects* (Baltimore: Johns Hopkins University Press, 1975), especially pp. 47–97. Also very useful is I. M. D. Little and J. A. Mirrlees, *Project Analysis and Planning for Developing Countries* (New York: Basic Books, 1974), a substantially revised version of their OECD *Manual for Industrial Project Analysis*.

tion. Otherwise these distortions will have to be allowed for in an ad hoc way in each separate appraisal, which may make for inconsistency. Thus it may, to take an example, be better to use a rough shadow price for the labor employed by a project then merely to footnote the facts that the wages paid will involve an increase in imports but overstate the loss of output elsewhere entailed by recruiting the labor. Whether or not this is correct, some attention ought to be paid to such complications.

CHAPTER 13

Investment Planning Models

During the past thirty years, the electric power industries of many high and low income countries have expanded at average rates of 7 percent a year to as much as 20 percent a year. This expansion has required investments of the order of $150 billion in the United States and $1.5 billion in a developing country the size of Colombia; it is expected that total investments will be larger in the next decade. The problems of determining optimum investment policies in the face of such rapid increases of demand, the high costs, the large number and diversity of alternative investment policies, and the numerical tedium of evaluating in depth even a single policy have motivated the development of mathematical models to assist the engineer in scanning and costing alternative policies. This chapter reviews these models and presents some extensions to the linear programming (LP) versions.

This chapter condenses a study prepared by Dennis Anderson for the World Bank in 1970, which is cited in the list of references at the end of the chapter. The present condensation appeared in slightly different form as "Models for Determining Least-cost Investments in Electricity Supply," *The Bell Journal of Economics and Management Science* 3 (Spring 1972). The discussion is for the most part derived from the work of others and from working with and talking to others in the field. Particular thanks are due to Narong Thananart of the World Bank for writing many programs to test and apply the various models discussed, and for correcting some mistakes in the formulations in the section discussing extensions to linear programming models. The following people have been most generous in communicating their ideas and experience: Frank Jenkin, Ivan Whitting, George Hext, Eric Parker, and Bill Billington, on work in Great Britain; MM. Stengel and Pouget of Electricité de France; Mr. Askerlund and his colleagues of the Statens Vattenfallsverk, Sweden; Herman van der Tak, Thomas Berrie, and Bernard Russell of the World Bank; John Rixie of USAID and his colleagues in the American Institute of Electrical and Electronics Engineers; Alan Manne, Stanford University; and Ralph Turvey. Paul MacAvoy, Massachusetts Institute of Technology, and an anonymous reviewer also provided very helpful comments on an earlier draft. All views, mistakes, and misinterpretations are, of course, those of the author.

The investment decision variables of the industry interact strongly at a point in time and over time. Interaction occurs for a number of reasons which are perhaps most easily explained through two examples. First, different energy sources have complementary functions in modern interconnected power systems. The main sources are single- and multipurpose hydro schemes of widely varying power and energy storage capacities;[1] fossil fuels, mainly fuel oil, coal, gas, and lignite; thermal and (eventually) fast neutron breeder reactors; and special-purpose peaking plants, mainly gas turbines and pumped storage. Gas turbines have low capital but high generation costs; fossil, higher capital but lower generation costs; nuclear, high capital and low generation costs; and hydro, high or low capital costs (depending on the site) and generation costs near zero, but with constraints on energy output that may stem from a multipurpose nature, water inflows, or both. Gas turbines are thus used for peak loads; fossil, for loads of longer duration; nuclear, for base (continuous) loads; and hydro, somewhere in between, depending on the energy constraint. Thus the optimum balance of plant in the system at any point in time will depend on the relative capital and generation costs of the alternative energy sources.

Second, the optimum balance will depend on both the inherited and the expected structure of the power system. For example, more nuclear and fewer fossil plants in future years means that the future system fuel savings of hydro schemes installed now will be less; a large nuclear power program in future years may thus shift the present balance toward fossil and away from hydro. Similarly, if the inherited structure is predominantly fossil, then the present emphasis will be on more nuclear or hydro or both to save on system fuel costs.

Because of these kinds of interaction among decision variables, models must be multidimensional and couched in terms of historical dynamics. The investment decisions to be taken at the present time depend upon the past and future evolution of investments and thus upon the past and future evolution of factor prices. We shall find that the models discussed below are designed to reflect this problem.

Although developed by engineers and operations researchers in the industry, and specifically concerned with investment decisions, these models are not without interest to economists. They have been applied occasionally in the cost–benefit studies of single- and multi-

---

1. In Turkey, for example, there are over 168 as yet untapped hydro sites, ranging in size from a 1-megawatt scheme to a proposed 4,000-megawatt multidam complex on the Euphrates River, capable of irrigating 700,000 hectares (see Chapter 8).

purpose hydro schemes.[2] A second and increasingly more common application is in the determination of the marginal cost structure of the industry for purposes of pricing policy. Bessière and Massé and Turvey in particular have demonstrated the practical value of linear and nonlinear programming (LP and non-LP) global models for this purpose, and the pricing models of Littlechild, Pressman, and Williamson, for example, can be viewed as approximations of the global models discussed in this chapter.[3]

2. See, for example, the study by A. Maass and others, eds., *Design of Water-Resource Systems* (Cambridge, Mass.: Harvard University Press, 1962); the World Bank study of the Indus Basin project published as H. P. Jacoby, "Analysis of Investments in Electric Power," mimeographed (Cambridge, Mass.: Harvard University Center for International Affairs, 1967), and P. Lieftinck and others, *Water and Power Resources of West Pakistan,* 3 vols. (Baltimore: Johns Hopkins Press, 1969); the simulation studies of M. M. Hufschmidt and M. B. Fiering, *Simulation Techniques for Design of Water Resource Systems* (Cambridge, Mass.: Harvard University Press, 1966); R. Turvey, "On Investment Choices in Electricity Generation," *Oxford Economic Papers* 15 (1965): 279–86; A. R. Prest and R. Turvey, "Cost-Benefit Analysis: A Survey," *Economic Journal* 75 (December 1965): 683–735; O. Eckstein, "A Survey of the Theory of Public Expenditure Criteria," paper delivered at the National Bureau of Economic Research Conference on Public Finances, 1961; and J. V. Krutilla and O. Eckstein, *Multiple Purpose River Development* (Baltimore: Johns Hopkins Press, 1958). More recently, researchers have been linking these models into wider studies of resource allocation in the energy sector and the economy—see C. I. K. Forster, "The Statistical Basis to National Fuel Policy" (London: Institute of Actuaries, 1969); C. I. K. Forster and I. J. Whitting, "An Integrated Mathematical Model of the Fuel Economy," *Statistical News* no. 3 (November 1968); G. Fernandez and A. S. Manne, "A Model for Planning Investments in Generating Facilities," mimeographed internal working paper (Stanford: Stanford University, 1969); G. Fernandez, A. S. Manne, and J. A. Valencia, "Multi-Level Planning for Electric Power Projects," mimeographed internal working paper (Stanford: Stanford University, 1970); and Alan S. Manne, "DINAMICO: A Dynamic Multi-Sector, Multi-Skill Model," in *Multi-level Planning: Case Studies in Mexico,* ed. Louis M. Goreux and Alan S. Manne (Amsterdam: North-Holland, 1973), pp. 107–51.

3. On the matter of LP models, see F. Bessière, "Methods of Choosing Equipment at Electricité de France: Development and Present Day Concept," *European Economic Review* 1 (Winter 1969): 199–211, and F. Bessière and P. Massé, "Long Term Programming of Electrical Investments," in *Marginal Cost Pricing in Practice,* ed. J. R. Nelson (Englewood Cliffs, N.J.: Prentice-Hall, 1964); regarding non-LP models, see R. Turvey, *Optimal Pricing and Investment in Electricity Supply* (London: George Allen and Unwin, 1968), and idem, ed. *Public Enterprise* (New York, Penguin, 1968). See also R. Turvey, "Note," *Economic Journal* 81 (June 1971): 371–75. The Littlechild, Pressman, and Williamson models appear in S. C. Littlechild, "Marginal Cost Pricing with Joint Costs," *Economic Journal* 80 (June 1970): 323–31; I. Pressman, "A Mathematical Formulation of the Peak-Load Pricing Problem," *The Bell Journal of Economics and Management Science* 1 (Autumn 1970): 304–26; and O. E. Williamson, "Peak-Load Pricing and Optimal Capacity under Indivisibility Constraints," *American Economic Review* 56 (September 1966): 810–27.

A third, but as yet unexplored, aspect of these models is their relation to the empirical studies of the type undertaken by Nerlove, Johnston, Galatin, and Dhrymes and Kurtz.[4] These workers have attempted to estimate economies of scale and technical progress in the industry using Cobb–Douglas and constant elasticity of substitution production function (CES) types of empirical relations between the factor inputs and an optimizing condition for a single time period. The cost structure and the relations among the factor inputs in the electricity supply industry, however, are defined precisely in the models of engineers without recourse to such empirical relations. Moreover, it is the daily occupation of planning engineers in the industry to search for optimum investment programs over many time periods. Taken into consideration are economies of scale attainable from large units, economies of scale attainable from interconnection, technical progress embodied in new equipment, substitution among factor inputs, replacement, the putty-clay nature of the investment decision, the putty-putty nature of the operating decision, the possibility of storage (hydro schemes, pumped storage), and as noted above, the past and expected evolution of the system. It would seem, therefore, that the models of engineers are not without significance for econometricians who wish to study the industry.[5]

This chapter begins by formulating the investment problem in cost minimization form. We then review the various approaches used to find optimum solutions. These are three approaches that we review under separate subheadings: marginal analysis, simulation models, and global models. We shall find that, while outwardly different in form—ranging from graphical devices and marginal analysis to dynamic, linear, and nonlinear programming—they differ only in algorithms; they are different methods of solving the same kind of problem. We shall also find that the approaches are often complementary. Global models can give only approximate answers in most practical situations because the details of the alternative programs, particularly of the individual projects in the programs, are too numerous to be handled in one computer run. Having obtained approximate solutions from the global models, marginal analysis using simulation models may be used to focus on the fine details of individual

4. See M. Nerlove, "Returns to Scale in Electricity Supply," in *Measurement in Economics: Studies in Mathematical Economics and Econometrics*, ed. C. F. Christ (Stanford: Stanford University Press, 1963); J. Johnston, *Statistical Cost Analysis* (New York: McGraw-Hill, 1960); M. Galatin, *Economies of Scale and Technical Change in Thermal Power Generation* (Amsterdam: North-Holland, 1968); and P. J. Dhrymes and M. Kurtz, "Technology and Scale in Electricity Generation," *Econometrica* 32 (July 1965): 287–315.
5. Turvey makes a similar point, but more strongly, in *Public Enterprise*, p. 8.

project selection and design. Finally we present three LP extensions to the global and simulation models reviewed; they cover (a) a fresh treatment of replacement, (b) the introduction of decision variables for hydro storage capacity and storage policy, and (c) regional decision variables, to give a fuller treatment of transmission.

Before proceeding, let us make clear a number of limitations of this chapter. First, it is assumed that the quantities demanded are exogenous and that the objective is always cost minimization. These assumptions could be relaxed if required so as to maximize the consumers' plus producers' surplus. The papers of Littlechild and Pressman would be good starting points in this respect. It is thought, however, that the most practical way to treat interactions of demand and supply when formulating an investment program is by iteration, taking demand as given (but hopefully related to some kind of rational pricing policy), searching for least-cost solutions, and then revising demand estimates on the basis of marginal costs and prices. In connection with formulating pricing policy, Turvey has also argued for an iterative approach.[6]

Second, use of one or more investment models is the first of several stages of the investment decision process. Engineering analysis of solutions follows and generally requires a revision of the solutions. The investment program finally selected must satisfy a number of engineering criteria regarding system stability, short-circuit performance, the control of watts, vars, and voltage, and the reserves and reliability of supply.[7] The search for an investment program that satisfies engineering and economic criteria is an iterative, multidisciplinary process.

Third, all the formulations presented are deterministic. Allowances are made for uncertainties in demand, plant availability, and flows of water to hydro schemes, but in the simple form of margins of spare capacity. This is frequent practice, although people are working with stochastic counterparts to the models presented, and their work is noted.

Fourth, there is no discussion of terminal conditions as analyzed by Hopkins[8] or of the optimum breakdown of the time period of the

6. See Littlechild, ''Marginal Cost Pricing''; Pressman, ''A Mathematical Formulation''; T. W. Berrie, ''The Economics of System Planning in Bulk Electricity Supply,'' *Electrical Review* 181 (September 15, 22, and 29, 1967); and R. Turvey, ''Marginal Cost,'' *Economic Journal* 79 (June 1969), p. 288.

7. See, for example, G. W. Stagg and A. H. El-Abiad, *Computer Methods in Power System Analysis* (New York: McGraw-Hill, 1968).

8. D. S. P. Hopkins, ''Sufficient Conditions for Optimality in Infinite Horizon Linear Economic Models,'' mimeographed Technical Report no. 69-3 (Stanford: Stanford University, 1969).

study into discrete periods. Fifth, there is no discussion of the dual variables from the LP models or of pricing policy. Thus, we neglect much important work of Bessière and Petcu, Turvey, Littlechild, Williamson, and many others.[9] Finally, we do not explore the connection between these models and those customarily used in econometric research (that is, of the type mentioned in footnote 4 to this chapter).

The Investment Problem in Cost Minimization Form

The principles of the following formulation were first enunciated in the early 1950s by Massé and Gibrat, who solved the investment problem using linear programming. A subsequent paper by Bessière and Massé and the book by Massé formulate the problem more generally.[10]

The search for an optimum (least-cost) investment program also entails, for each plant program considered, the search for an optimum operating schedule. Let the power capacity of any plant in the system be defined by X_{jv}, j denoting the type of plant (hydro, fossil, nuclear and so on) and v the vintage (year of commissioning). Also, let the power output of this plant at any instant t be $U_{jv}(t)$, $0 \le U_{jv}(t) \le X_{jv}$. The operating costs of this plant over the interval $t = 0$ to T are given by:

$$\int_{t=0}^{t=T} F_{jv}(t) \cdot U_{jv}(t) \cdot dt,$$

where $F_{jv}(t)$ are the discounted operating costs for each unit of energy output.

At any instant t the operator has before him $j = 1, \ldots, J$ types of plants of different vintages, comprising the initial plant composition of the system, $v = -V$ to 0, and the plant installed (at discrete

9. See F. Bessière and M. Petcu, "Analyse Marginales et Optimisation Structurelle des Investissements: Application au Secteur de L'Electricité," *RIRO*, no. 6 (1967): 61–81; Turvey, *Optimal Pricing and Investment;* idem, "Marginal Cost"; Littlechild, "Marginal Cost Pricing"; and Williamson, "Peak-Load Pricing."

10. See P. Massé and R. Gibrat, "Application of Linear Programming to Investments in the Electrical Power Industry," in *Marginal Cost Pricing in Practice,* for an English translation of their original paper, or *Management Science* 3 (January 1957): 149–66; Bessière and Massé, "Long Term Programming"; P. Massé, *Optimal Investment Decisions* (Englewood Cliffs, N.J.: Prentice-Hall, 1962); and Bessière, "Methods of Choosing Equipment," which outlines the development of methods used by EDF during the 1950s.

intervals) between 0 and t. To obtain the total system operating costs in the interval dt, we must summate over all vintages $v = -V$ to t and over all types of plant. The total future operating costs are then:

$$\int_{t=0}^{t=T} \sum_{v=-V}^{t} \sum_{j=1}^{J} F_{jv}(t) \cdot U_{jv}(t) \cdot dt.$$

The investor's objective is to minimize the sum of capital and operating costs over some future time period 0 to T:

$$\text{Minimize} \sum_{v=1}^{T} \sum_{j=1}^{J} C_{jv} \cdot X_{jv} + \int_{t=0}^{T} \sum_{v=-V}^{t} \sum_{j=1}^{J} F_{jv}(t) \cdot U_{jv}(t) \cdot dt,$$

$$(13.1)$$

where C_{jv} are the capital costs per unit of capacity of plant j, vintage v. All costs, of course, are expressed as social opportunity costs.

The discrete approximation to (13.1) is often a more convenient function to use:

$$\text{Minimize} \sum_{v=1}^{T} \sum_{j=1}^{J} C_{jv} \cdot X_{jv} + \sum_{t=1}^{T} \sum_{v=-V}^{t} \sum_{j=1}^{J} F_{jvt} \cdot U_{jvt} \cdot \theta_t, \quad (13.2)$$

where θ_t is the width of the time interval considered at time t.

The search for optimum capacities (optimum X_{jv}) and for optimum operating schedules (optimum U_{jvt}) is subject to a number of important conditions. First sufficient plant must be operating at all times to meet the instantaneous power demand, which we define by Q_t. Thus:

$$\sum_{j=1}^{J} \sum_{v=-V}^{t} U_{jvt} \geq Q_t, \qquad (t = 1, \ldots, T). \ (13.3)$$

Only at times of peak load will all of the plant be in operation (an allowance for plant outages is considered below). At other times the instantaneous power demand can be met with much of the plant not operating (that is, some of the U_{jvt} are zero); this plant, in general, will be that with the highest operating costs.

Second, no unit of plant can be operated above its peak available capacity:

$$0 \leq U_{jvt} \leq a_{jv} \cdot X_{jv}, \qquad \begin{aligned} &(j = 1, \ldots, J; \quad (13.4) \\ &v = -V, \ldots, t; \\ &t = 1, \ldots, T), \end{aligned}$$

251

where a_{jv} is the availability of plant j, vintage v (a_{jv} is usually about 0.9).[11] Note that X_{jv} for $v = -V$ to 0 are predefined constants and represent the capacities of the inherited capital stock.

Third, there may be constraints on the operation of a hydro plant. Seasonal shortages of water inflow or the requirements of irrigation and flood control will impose restrictions on the amount of electricity to be generated in, for instance, a given season. There still will be a choice, however, on the timing of the hydro operation within the season (in general, it will be operated at times of peak demand, when fossil energy is most expensive). The simplest form taken by the hydro constraints is the following. Let H_{vs} be the hydroelectric energy to be delivered in season s by the hydro scheme of vintage v. Then we must choose the decision variables for hydro operation, $U_{jv}(t)$ ($j = \text{hydro} = h$) such that, in minimizing total system operating costs, all available hydro energy will be utilized:

$$\int_{\text{season } s} U_{hv}(t) \cdot dt = H_{vs}. \tag{13.5}$$

(At a later stage in this chapter we shall be discussing methods of searching for optimum values of H_{vs}.)

Fourth, there are constraints to represent what the French writers call the "guarantee conditions." These are to guarantee supply, to an acceptable probability limit, in event of contingencies—water shortages in dry seasons, peak demand above mean expectations, or plant outage. These constraints take two forms, one to guarantee peak power supplies, and the other to guarantee energy supplies in critical periods. Let us take them in turn. Following Massé and Morlat,[12] suppose that e is the probability that the yearly peak demand, defined by $\hat{Q}_t$, will be met; that is, the probability that the aggregate available capacity is greater than $\hat{Q}_t$ equals e, as follows:

$$Pr \left(\sum_{j=1}^{J} \sum_{v=-V}^{t} a_{jv} \cdot X_{jv} - \hat{Q}_t \geq 0 \right) = e, (t = 1, \ldots, T). \tag{13.6'}$$

11. Data on a_{jv} for different countries are discussed in P. W. Cash and E. C. Scott, "Security of Supply in the Planning and Operation of European Power Systems," paper read to the Fourteenth Congress, International Union of Producers and Distributors of Electricity, Madrid, 1967.

12. See, respectively, P. Massé, "Electrical Investments," and G. Morlat, "On Instructions for the Optimal Management of Seasonal Reservoirs," both in *Marginal Cost Pricing in Practice.*

where a_{jv} and $\hat{Q}_t$ are stochastic variables. This is a "chance constraint" of the type discussed by Charnes and Cooper.[13]

When reviewing the practices adopted by European countries in planning system security, Cash and Scott found that the actual choice of e varies widely between countries.[14] They also found that, while the choice is sometimes backed up by statistical and economic calculation, it is generally determined by experience. This is partly because estimating the costs and benefits to the economy of a given level of security is exceedingly difficult and subject to large errors, and partly because the required level may rest on a number of non-economic factors—for example, the hostility of press and public opinion in the event of supply shortages (which, almost by definition, seem to occur when least desired). Finally, they found that most countries think of the guarantee condition in terms of a "margin of available capacity" over and above that required to meet the mean expected peak demand.

The guarantee condition (13.6′) is therefore frequently simplified in practice. Let m be the margin of spare available capacity required to meet demands above the mean expectation; then (13.6′) is expressed as

$$\sum_{j=1}^{J} \sum_{v=-V}^{t} a_{jv} \cdot X_{jv} \geq \hat{Q}_t(1 + m), \qquad (t = 1, \ldots, T), \quad (13.6)$$

where, once again, a_{jv} and $\hat{Q}_t$ are mean expected quantities.

It should be added that while condition (13.6) is much simpler than condition (13.6′), it by no means implies a loss of rigor in the planning process. On the contrary, calculating the probability distribution of available capacity in various regions of a modern interconnected system is itself a highly complex and specialized computation which may require the use of Monte Carlo techniques. For this reason it is perhaps best treated as a separate calculation, even though this may result in repetition and modification of the least-cost exercises. System planning, as we remarked in the introduction, is an iterative, multidisciplinary operation.

A similar pattern of discussion follows when we examine the problem of guaranteeing energy supplies in dry seasons on mixed

13. A. Charnes and W. Cooper, "Chance-Constrained Programming," *Management Science* 6 (October 1959): 73–79; idem, "Chance Constraints and Normal Deviates," *Journal of the American Statistical Association* 57 (March 1962): 134–48; and idem, "Deterministic Equivalents for Optimizing and Satisfying Under Chance Constraints," *Operations Research* 11 (January-February 1963): 18–39.

14. See Cash and Scott, "Security of Supply."

hydro-thermal systems. Let e now denote the probability that the potential energy available from both hydro and thermal plant will be greater than the energy demand in the critical period; and let $t = t', \ldots, t''$ represent the critical period. The potential energy output from a thermal plant is limited by its available capacity, $a_{jv} \cdot X_{jv}$. The potential energy output from a hydro plant is limited by constraints of type (13.5). The guarantee condition is therefore:

$$Pr \left\{ \sum_{t=t'}^{t''} \left(\sum_{v=-V}^{t} \sum_{j=1}^{J} a_{jv} \cdot X_{jv} + \sum_{v=-V}^{t} \sum_{j=1}^{J} U_{jvt} - Q_t \right) \theta_t \geq 0 \right\} = e,$$

$$(j \neq \text{hydro}) \qquad (j \neq \text{thermal}) \qquad (13.7')$$

where a_{jv}, U_{jvt}, and Q_t are stochastic.

Again it is possible to approximate the chance constraint (13.7'), postponing a more rigorous study of the reserves and reliability of supply for a separate stage of the planning process. Let β_{jv} (with $j = $ hydro) be the ratio of the energy output of hydro plant j, v, in the critical period of a dry year, to its mean expected output in this period of an average year. Then (13.7') simplifies to:

$$\sum_{t=t'}^{t''} \sum_{v=-V}^{t} \left(\sum_{j=1}^{J} a_{jv} \cdot X_{jv} \cdot \theta_t + \sum_{j=1}^{J} \beta_{jv} \cdot U_{jvt} \cdot \theta_t \right) \geq \sum_{t=t'}^{t''} Q_t \cdot \theta_t,$$

$$(j \neq \text{hydro}) \qquad (j \neq \text{thermal}) \qquad (13.7)$$

where a_{jv}, U_{jvt}, and Q_t are once again mean expected quantities. Note that for hydro schemes with highly uncertain water supplies, β_{jv} will be low, and if such schemes are included, then other thermal or hydro capacity will be required to satisfy this constraint. Thus, β_{jv} indirectly applies a cost penalty on schemes according to the variability of their supplies.

To complete the formulation of the investment problem, there generally will be a number of "local" constraints. A few examples are constraints to limit expenditures on capital or foreign exchange, regional development constraints (for example, a lower limit to the use of coal or hydro resources), and political and social constraints.

It will be evident that this formulation can be extended or contracted in many ways. Simulation models, for example, extend the formulation in one direction and contract it in another. Essentially the X's (that is, the investment plans) are predefined constants in a simulation model; this leaves more computer space (core storage) available to examine the U's (the dispatching schedules) in more detail. Another extension is to treat uncertainties in costs, water supplies, and demand forecasts through stochastic programming. Some formulations have also been adapted to optimize the operation of multipurpose, multidam hydro schemes. Replacement decisions have been included in the objective function. Efforts are being made to treat both supply and demand on a regional basis. Finally, some workers are embodying the formulation for the electricity sector into larger models of the energy sector and of the economy.[15] We shall discuss some of these and other extensions subsequently.

Marginal Analysis

Marginal analysis was first applied to investments in electricity supply by Electricité de France in the late 1940s. Since then it has been applied regularly in many other countries.[16] The analysis starts

15. Discussion of models that have some stochastic elements, either for demand or water supply variables, appears in F. Bessière, "Le modèle 'Investissements 85' d'Electricité de France," *Revue Française de l'Energie,* no. 182 (1966): 568ff.; idem, "Methods of Choosing Equipment"; Electricité de France, "L'étude à Long-Terme des Investissements a l'Aide d'un Programme Non'Lineaire: Le Modèle Investissements 85," note from the Department of General Economic Studies (Paris, 1965); Fernandez and Manne, "A Model for Planning Investments"; J. Lindqvist, "Operation of a Hydrothermal Electric System: A Multi-stage Decision Process," *IEEE Transactions* (April 1962); J. D. C. Little, "The Use of Storage Water in a Hydro-Electric System," *Journal of the Operations Research Society of America* 3 (May 1955): 187–97; and J. Gessford and S. Karlin, "Optimal Policy for Hydro-Electric Operations," in *Studies in the Mathematical Theory of Inventory and Production,* ed. K. J. Arrow, S. Karlin, and H. Scorf (Stanford: Stanford University Press, 1958). For adaptations to multipurpose, multidam hydro schemes, see Jacoby, "Analysis of Investments in Electric Power" and United Nations, Economic Commission for Europe, "Symposium on Problems of Multiple Purpose River Development Connected with Hydro-Electric Power Production," MAD/SYMP/EP (Brussels, August 1969). With regard to replacement decisions, see Massé, *Optimal Investment Decisions.* For regional treatments of supply and demand, see Electricité de France, "L'étude à Long-Terme des Investissements" and Fernandez, Manne, and Valenica, "Multi-Level Planning." Examples of formulations that incorporate the electricity sector into broader focused models appear in Forster and Whitting, "An Integrated Mathematical Model" and Manne, "DINAMICO: A Dynamic Multi-Sector, Multi-Skill Model."

16. See R. Giguet, "Les Programmes d'Equipment Electrique Considéres du Point de Vue de l'Economie Appliquée," mimeographed (n.p., Institute de Science Economique Appliquée, 1951); P. Massé, "Electrical Investments," in *Marginal Cost Pricing in Practice;* and Bessière, "Methods of Choosing Equipment," and the bibliography contained therein. For examples of applications in other countries see United Nations, Economic Commission for Europe, "Economic Methods and Criteria Used in the Electric Power Industry," ST/ECE/EP21 (Brussels, 1963) and H. G. van der Tak, *The Economic Choice between Hydro-Electric and Thermal Power Development,* Staff Occasional Paper no. 1 (Washington, D.C.: World Bank, 1966).

from an arbitrary but reasonable initial program—a "reference solution"—and then seeks to improve it (reduce costs) by marginal substitutions. The reference solution, and the solution obtained after a marginal substitution have been made, satisfy the same power and energy demands. Whenever the cost function is convex,[17] marginal analysis should ultimately lead to a uniquely optimum investment and operating program over time.

A common application of marginal analysis has been the comparison of fossil and hydro alternatives to meet a given demand for electricity. The hydro plant may require a higher investment (I) than fossil ($I_h > I_f$), but the total system operating costs in subsequent years are less. The total, discounted system operating costs at time t are:

$$(1 + r)^{-t} \sum_{j=1}^{J} \sum_{v=-V}^{t} F_{jvt} \cdot U_{jvt} \cdot \theta_t = (1 + r)^{-t} \cdot \phi_{th}$$

if the hydro project is adopted, and:

$$(1 + r)^{-t} \cdot \phi_{tf}$$

if the fossil project is adopted.

The present worth of the savings if hydro is substituted for fossil is then:

$$PW = (I_f - I_h) + \sum_{t=0}^{T} (1 + r)^{-t}(\phi_{tf} - \phi_{th}), \tag{13.8}$$

and depending on whether this value is positive or negative, the hydro is or is not preferable to the fossil investment. The value of PW (savings) calculated in (13.8) is sometimes known as the relative profitability of the hydro investment, since the calculation shows whether or not the hydro investment improves upon the reference solution.

Among the advantages of this calculation are its practical simplicity and the feature that it is easy to adjust the arithmetic for many local costs and benefits of a project. For example, different locations of hydro and fossil stations will lead to different transmission costs; maintenance costs for hydro stations are lower; the fossil station,

---

17. D. Phillips and others prove convexity for the mixed fossil and nuclear system of Great Britain in "A Mathematical Model for Determining Generating Plant Mix," paper read to the Third Power System Computation Conference, Rome (London: Queen Mary College Department of Electrical and Electronic Engineering, 1969). Their model is described later in the chapter under "Nonlinear programming."

with a lifetime of about thirty years, will be replaced before the hydro, the lifetime of which is about fifty years, so that the discounted replacement costs may have to be included; the hydro may have flood control benefits; and the fossil plant may induce more employment in local coal mines. Such local features can be included readily in the arithmetic. The calculation also can be readily formulated for comparisons between nuclear and fossil plants at base load; or between fossil, pumped storage, and gas turbines, at peak load.[18]

There are, however, two difficulties with marginal analysis. First, it is tedious to calculate operating and fuel costs over a twenty- or thirty-year period, when the demand fluctuates rapidly by the hour, when there may be four or more types of plant on the system, thirty or more vintages of plant, and when the expansion of the system introduces new vintages and types of plant while replacing others. The analysis is also an optimizing problem in itself, since each plant must be located on the system operating schedule so that total fuel and operating costs are minimized.[19] Second, the marginal substitutions to the investment plan may be many, requiring special routines to scan and cost the alternatives. It was to overcome the first difficulty that simulation models were developed, and to overcome the second that global models were developed.

Simulation Models

Three formulations of simulation models are (a) models that integrate the load duration curve directly, (b) models that use dynamic programming, and (c) models that use linear programming. Nonlinear programming could also be used, but the LP or non-LP simulation models are infrequently discussed in the literature.[20]

Direct integration of the load duration curve

Simulation models which integrate the load duration curve directly are particularly suitable for power systems having thermal

---

18. For formulations comparing fossil and hydro plants, see van der Tak, *The Economic Choice;* M. Boiteux, "Marginal Cost Pricing," in *Marginal Cost Pricing in Practice;* and Turvey, "On Investment Choices." Formulations comparing other choices appear in E. Openshaw-Taylor and G. A. Boal, *Power System Economics* (London: Edward Arnold, 1969), which also considers many other kinds of decisions—for example, on transmission and distribution equipment.

19. The system generating schedule is sometimes called the load dispatching schedule.

20. LP and non-LP models are used extensively for real-time scheduling. See the section on "Linear programming" below.

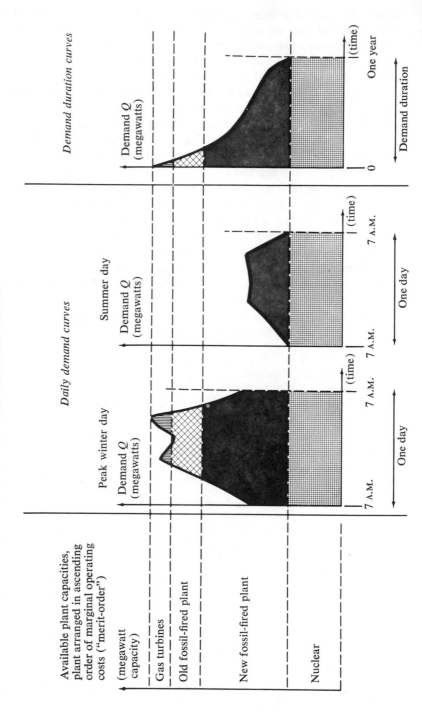

FIGURE 13.1. LOAD DISPATCHING ON AN ALL-THERMAL SYSTEM

plant only, although they have been adapted for mixed fossil and hydro systems by Jacoby.[21] We shall first consider the thermal power system and then look at Jacoby's model.

On an all-thermal system the cheapest way to meet the demand at any point in time is to run the stations with the lowest operating costs. The system operator tabulates the power stations in ascending order of marginal operating costs and loads and unloads the stations sequentially as the demand rises and falls (merit-order operation). This situation appears graphically in Figure 13.1. For clarity we aggregate the system into four representative power stations; in ascending order of marginal operating costs they are nuclear, new fossil, old fossil, and gas turbines. By projecting the plant capacities horizontally through the daily demand curves, we see the times when the different plants are started up, loaded, unloaded, and shut down on different days. By continuing the projection horizontally through the demand duration curve, we can find the total operating time of each plant for the period represented by the curve. By estimating the areas sliced out of the demand duration curve, we can estimate the energy delivered by each plant and thus the total system operating costs. These costs will be at a minimum under this arrangement because the plant with the highest operating costs (older vintage of fossil plant and gas turbines) will be operated the least.

This type of simulation model is used by the Central Electricity Generating Board in Great Britain for the estimation of generation savings associated with different investment programs; it is reported by Berrie and Whitting and by Jonas.[22] The simulation can be re-

21. The load duration curve is defined in Appendix A of this chapter. The Central Electricity Generating Board in Great Britain has pursued in meticulous detail simulation models that directly integrate the load duration curve—see, for example, P. J. Jonas, "A Computer Model to Determine Economic Performance Characteristics of British Generating Stations," paper read to the British Computer Conference, Brighton, 1966; T. W. Berrie and I. J. Whitting, "The Exploration of Alternative Plans for an Expanding Electricity Power System," in proceedings of the First Power System Computation Conference on Digital Computation for Electric Power Systems, London (London: Queen Mary College Department of Electrical and Electronic Engineering, 1963); and Berrie, "The Economics of System Planning," pp. 22 and 29. For adaptations to mixed hydro and fossil systems, see Jacoby, "Analysis of Investments in Electric Power"; also Lieftinck, Sadove, and Creyke, *Water and Power Resources of West Pakistan,* vol. 3.

22. See T. W. Berrie, "Further Experience with Simulation Models in System Planning," in proceedings of the Second Power System Computation Conference, Stockholm (London: Queen Mary College Department of Electrical and Electronic Engineering, 1966); Berrie and Whitting, "The Exploration of Alternative Plans"; and Jonas, "A Computer Model."

fined in many ways, of which we shall mention three. First, because of maintenance schedules, the table of available plant capacities will differ between seasons. The horizontal projections will only hold, say, for a season, and not for a year as indicated in the diagrams. Thus a different demand duration curve is required for each season. Second, the operating costs of each station should be adjusted for transmission losses; this introduces a small quadratic term into the operating cost of each station. Third, the transportation of the coal from several collieries to the power stations is an important element in operating costs. The model determines the operating costs of each power station as follows:

> Trial (marginal operating) costs are used to obtain an initial merit order. A loading simulation study is carried out to obtain trial fuel consumptions, which are then fed into the standard (linear programming) transportation calculation to determine the minimum-cost coal allocation and the corresponding station (marginal operating) costs. These are then substituted for the trial value to form a new merit order, this process being repeated until there is no significant change in the costs of generation, when generator loadings and fuel consumptions are consistent with minimum-cost fuel allocations.[23]

Monte Carlo studies using this model have also been undertaken to examine the effects on costs of uncertainties in data input, but the results remain unpublished.

We now look at Jacoby's adaptation of this kind of model for a mixed storage hydro-thermal system. We first consider the optimum position of a single storage hydro station on the power system load dispatching schedule (that is, the optimum position in the "merit order" table). If a system has several such stations, then the single one we consider is taken to represent the aggregate characteristics of all hydro stations.

Suppose that in any period t the hydro energy allotted for electric power generation is H_t and that the peak power capacity of the hydro is X_{ht}.[24] If the hydro is to maximize fuel savings it must discharge the full amount H_t. It must also be operated at times when the fuel costs on the system are most expensive; this happens at times of peak demand (during the period t) when the older and less efficient

23. Berrie, "Further Experience with Simulation Models."
24. Assuming as Jacoby does that H_t is given. Later we consider the problem of finding the optimum value of H_t when there is an option to store hydro energy for the period $t + 1$. See the sections on "Dynamic programming" and "Linear programming" immediately following below.

units of the thermal plant are operating. Consider a particular weekday (Figure 13.2). The hydro plant should begin operating at point A in the morning, generate full power output at B and through to C, and then reduce power to D during the night; however, it will not (in the optimum) be delivering full power every day. In the second example of Figure 13.2—for a weekend day—the hydro is still operated over the peak demand periods of the weekends, but, in view of the higher demands and fuel costs during the week, it is cheaper to store energy for delivery during weekdays.

In the optimum, the hydro stations will occupy the same place in the system dispatching schedule every day throughout the period. If they occupied a higher place at the weekends (that is, if they were operated at lower values of total system demand), less energy would be available for operation during the weekdays; the low efficiency thermal stations would then have to supply extra energy during the peak demand periods of the weekdays. If the hydro occupied a lower place at weekends, extra energy would be available for use during the week, when two things could happen: (a) the hydro would be unable to discharge the extra energy, because of insufficient capacity, and there would be a spillover, unless (b) it were to operate at a higher place in the dispatching schedule. If (a) were to happen there would simply be a waste of energy. If (b) were to happen, the more efficient thermal plant would be removed from base load operation during the week, and less efficient thermal plant would be operating in place of hydro during the weekends. To conclude: In the optimum the hydro station will occupy the same place in the table of merit order operation every day throughout the period t.

This conclusion enables us to use the load duration curve to determine the optimum position of the hydro station in the merit order table. The horizontal lines which represent the power capacity of the hydro (in Figure 13.2) must cut the load duration curve at those points (a) where the area cut out of the load duration curve exactly equals the energy to be supplied by the hydro in period t, and (b) where the gap between the lines represents the peak power capacity of the hydro. For two or more hydro plants, the technique is the same. Each plant must deliver all the energy allotted for period t, and it must occupy that place on the load dispatching schedule defined above.

The areas under the load duration curve can be calculated graphically or by numerical integration, and the hydro plant located by trial and error. The approach used by Jacoby is, however, much simpler: first to integrate the load duration curve directly and plot the integral (the energy demand) against power demand. This gives

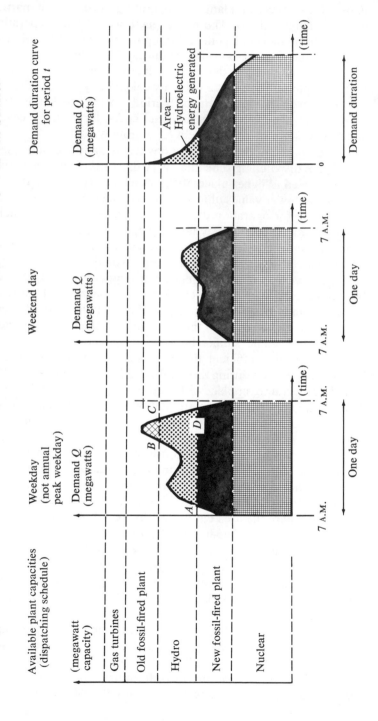

FIGURE 13.2. LOAD DISPATCHING ON A MIXED HYDRO-THERMAL SYSTEM HAVING ONE HYDRO STATION

us a curve known as the integrated load function shown in Figure 13.3. The energy delivered by each plant can be read directly off the abscissa. The energy delivered by nuclear plant, for example, is obtained by projecting a line vertically downward into the abscissa from point a. Similarly, projections downward from points (b,a), (c,b), (d,c), and (e,d) give the energy delivered by base load thermal, hydro, old thermal, and gas turbines, respectively.

These are the types of computation embodied in Jacoby's model, which allows estimation of operating costs in considerable detail. For example, the total system operating costs may be evaluated for each month of a twenty-year period; several hydro units and over 20 to 30 thermal units may be considered. The model was used extensively in the Indus Basin project in Pakistan, and El Chocon in Argentina.[25] The model can also be formulated to calculate the operating savings associated with transmission links, although this becomes very difficult if there are many regions of generation and demand.

An assumption of the Jacoby model is that H_t, the hydro energy allotted for electric power generation during each month, is known in advance. For large irrigation projects, where power is often a fringe benefit, this assumption is realistic. But it is less realistic in many hydroelectric schemes, when the problem is to determine an optimal water storage policy from period to period. If the next period's demands are high and water inflows low, how much water should be stored for the next period? This type of problem was solved by Massé, who in doing so apparently adumbrated the technique of dynamic programming as applied to this problem. Little formulated the problem explicitly in terms of dynamic programming (DP). Since then the method has been refined and developed by many workers, in particular the Swedish engineers, who use the type of calculations undertaken in Jacoby's model as a routine to compute the total system operating costs for a wide range of storage policies scanned by the DP algorithm.[26]

Dynamic programming

Dynamic programming or DP techniques have been used by many workers to determine the optimum operating schedules for long-

25. See Jacoby, "Analysis of Investments in Electric Power" and Lieftinck, Sadove, and Creyke, *Water and Power Resources of West Pakistan*.

26. See P. Massé, *Les Rèserves et Regulation de l'Avenir dans la Vie Economique*, vol. 1 (Paris: Hermourn, 1946); Little, "The Use of Storage Water"; and Lindqvist, "Operation of a Hydrothermal Electric System." Note that it is not clear whether calculations undertaken in Jacoby's model work with a load duration curve or an integrated load function.

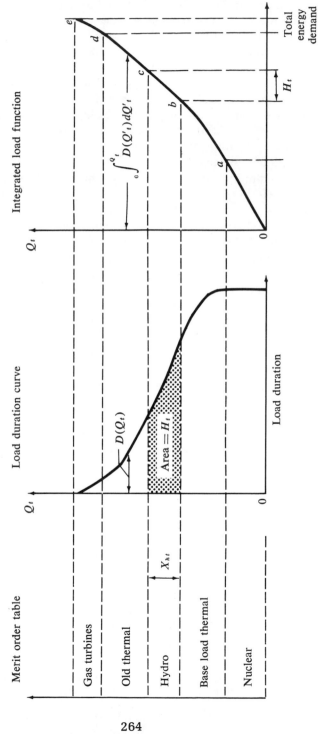

FIGURE 13.3. JACOBY'S METHOD FOR DERIVING THE INTEGRATED LOAD FUNCTION

Merit order table

Gas turbines

Old thermal

Hydro

Base load thermal

Nuclear

Load duration curve

Q_t

$D(Q_t)$

Area $= H_t$

X_{ht}

Load duration

0

Integrated load function

Q_t

$\int_0^{Q_t} D(Q'_t)\,dQ'_t$

e
d
c
b
a

H_t

Total energy demand

0

range storage reservoirs (fortnightly, monthly, seasonal reservoirs) on mixed hydro-thermal systems. Additionally, the method can be adapted for flood control and irrigation projects. The answers it gives can also be obtained by linear programming.[27] The question to be answered is the following: Given that demand and water supplies fluctuate periodically, how much water should be stored for the next period and how much should be used in the present period? The decision process is sequential, since the next period's decisions will always depend upon how much water should be stored for the period following that.

We formulate the problem assuming water supplies are known with certainty. This assumption can be relaxed readily if required.[28] Discrete time intervals are taken. The model below also assumes *one* long-range storage reservoir weighted to correspond to a whole system's reservoirs, one hydroelectric generator (also equivalent to that of the whole system), and a number of thermal stations (fossil or nuclear or both). This follows the practice of all previous writers. It is quite straightforward to extend the model and represent the system's hydro stations with two or more equivalent stations with different storage capacities and water inflow patterns, but this enlarges the dimensions of the problem considerably. Let S_t equal storage at the beginning of period t (in kilowatt-hours), H_t equal hydro energy (water) discharge during period t (in kilowatt-hours), and W_t equal water inflow during period t adjusted for losses and ex-

27. Lindqvist, "Operation of a Hydrothermal Electric System" presents the model that was developed for the Swedish State Power Board, which has been used extensively for the technical and economic long-term planning of system extensions. Lindqvist's work builds on Little, "The Use of Storage Water." See also T. C. Koopmans, "Water Storage Policy in a Simplified Hydro-Electric System," Cowles Foundation for Research in Economics paper no. 115 (New Haven: Yale University, 1958), and Gessford and Karlin, "Optimal Policy for Hydro-Electric Operations." The subject of the optimal management of seasonal reservoirs has a long history— for example, see Massé, *Les Réserves et Regulation,* vol. 1, and G. Morlat, "On Instructions for the Optimal Management of Seasonal Reservoirs," in *Marginal Cost Pricing in Practice.* For adaptations to flood control and irrigation, for example, see A. S. Manne, "Product-Mix Alternatives: Flood Control, Electric Power and Irrigation," Discussion Paper no. 95 (n.p., Cowles Foundation, 1960); Maass and others, *Design of Water-Resource Systems;* and I. Haissman, "Optimizing the Long-Range Operation of the California Aqueduct by Incremental Dynamic Programming," mimeographed (Berkeley: University of California Operations Research Center, 1968). Linear programming is taken up later in this chapter; see also A. S. Manne, "Linear Programming and Sequential Decisions," *Management Science* 6 (April 1960): 259–67.

28. All of the references in footnotes 26 and 27 save Koopmans work with stochastic models.

FIGURE 13.4. TOTAL SYSTEM OPERATING
COSTS AS A FUNCTION OF THE HYDRO
ENERGY USED IN PERIOD t

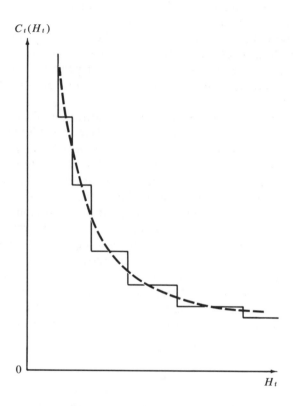

pressed in units of potential energy (in kilowatt-hours). The storage
at the end of period t is:

$$S_{t+1} = S_t + W_t - H_t. \tag{13.9}$$

Suppose we specify a value for H_t. Following the methods outlined above (for example in Jacoby's model), it is possible to determine the optimum system operating schedules and costs for this
period. As we increase H_t, the total system costs will decrease because less fuel is burned in the thermal plant. By computing total
system operating costs (denoted by C_t) for a range of H_t, we can obtain the kind of curve shown in Figure 13.4. The shape of this curve
(neglecting discontinuities) generally will be concave to the origin
because (a) an increase of H_t will always reduce the energy to be
delivered by fossil plant, (b) the marginal operating costs of the

thermal plant, because of merit-order operation, increase with the amount of thermal plant operated, and (c) the plants with the highest operating costs are generally the oldest and smallest.

The objective is to operate the hydro scheme so as to minimize the total system operating costs over some time period T. That is, we require:

$$\text{Min}_{H_1 \cdots H_T} \sum_{t=1}^{T} C_t(H_t), \tag{13.10}$$

subject to constraints (13.9).

This is in fact a standard deterministic inventory problem, which is often solved by the recursive methods of DP.[29] The principles of the method are as follows: Suppose we fix the amount of water to be stored at the beginning of period t (end of period $t - 1$) at some value of S_t; and suppose that for this value of S_t we know the values of H_1 to H_{t-1} that minimize total costs up to the beginning of t. We define these costs by ϕ_{t-1}, the minimum of which will depend on the value we have chosen for S_t:

$$\phi_{t-1}(S_t) = \text{Min}_{H_1 \cdots H_{t-1}} \left\{ \sum_{j=1}^{t-1} C_j(H_j) \right\}. \tag{13.11}$$

Now suppose that we know $\phi_{t-1}(S_t)$ for a range of values of S_t between zero and, say, $\hat{S}_t$. The next step we can take is to find $\phi_t(S_{t+1})$ for a whole range of S_{t+1} between zero and $\hat{S}_{t+1}$, as follows:

$$\phi_t(S_{t+1}) = \text{Min}_{0 \leq S_t \leq \hat{S}_t} \{C_t(H_t) + \phi_{t-1}(S_t)\}. \tag{13.12}$$

In view of constraints (13.9), the hydro flows H_t are implied by S_{t+1} and S_t so that:

$$\phi_t(S_{t+1}) = \text{Min}_{0 \leq S_t \leq \hat{S}_t} \{C_t(S_t - S_{t+1} + W_t) + \phi_{t-1}(S_t)\}. \tag{13.13}$$

This can be viewed as a forward recursive decision rule of DP. For each period t, the system operating costs are evaluated for a range of S_{t+1} and the range S_t considered in the previous period. For each S_{t+1}, the optimum value of S_t is found using equation

29. See, for example, G. Hadley, *Non-Linear and Dynamic Programming* (Reading, Mass.: Addison-Wesley, 1962), Chapters 10 and 11.

(13.13). Similarly, at $t + 1$ a range of S_{t+2} is taken, and for each S_{t+2} the optimum S_{t+1} is found. At the beginning, S_1 is known so that:

$$\phi_1(S_2) = \underset{0 \leq S_1 \leq \hat{S}_1}{\text{Min}} \{C_1(S_1 - S_2 + W_1)\}. \tag{13.14}$$

This equation gives us the starting point. The forward recursions are continued until the optimum decisions of interest are not influenced by extra recursions.

To solve the problem for the case when hydro supplies are treated stochastically, it is necessary to use backward recursive formulas. These formulas (but including the frequency distributions) are a mirror image of the formulas above.

DP simulation models have been applied to many problems. Lindqvist, writing in 1962, informs us that, in Sweden,

> the model has been utilized since the Spring of 1959 for several hundred calculations, e.g., for the calculation of utilization times for nuclear and thermal plants during drought years, for the optimum ratio between hydro-electric and thermal power as a function of interest rates, fuel costs and capital costs; furthermore, for the calculation of the economic consequences of errors in the long-range prediction of net consumption, and for possible secondary deliveries to neighbor countries in the future, and so on.[30]

Apparently, the model is still used for such purposes.

Linear programming

The investment problem as formulated earlier in this chapter is already in a linear programming or LP form. It is convenient to alter the notation slightly and let each period t be represented by a load duration curve broken down into $p = 1, \ldots , P$ blocks each of width θ_p (see Figure 13.5). The periods t may represent months, seasons, years, or any other time interval, according to the approximation desired. If there is to be seasonal or monthly storage hydro on the system, t will accordingly represent seasons or months. Since the capacity variables X_{jv} are predefined constants in the simulation model, the objective is to choose the operating decision variables U_{jtvp} such that the total system operating costs are at a minimum. Thus [see expression (13.2) above]:

---

30. See Lindqvist, "Operation of a Hydrothermal Electric System."

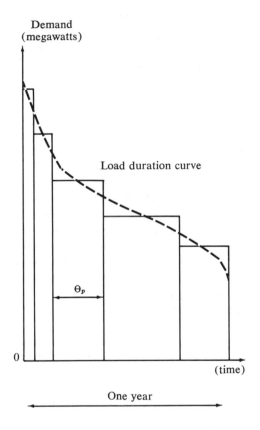

Figure 13.5. Block Representation of the Load Duration Curve

Minimize $\displaystyle\sum_{j=1}^{J} \sum_{t=1}^{T} \sum_{v=-V}^{t} \sum_{p=1}^{P} F_{jtvp} \cdot U_{jtvp} \cdot \theta_p.$ (13.15)

This objective is subject to the capacity constraints:

$$0 \leq U_{jtvp} \leq a_{jv} \cdot X_{jv}, \qquad\qquad\text{(all } j, t, v, p)\ (13.16)$$

and to the constraint that aggregate output must be sufficient to meet the demand at all times:

$$\sum_{v=-V}^{t} \sum_{j=1}^{J} U_{jvtp} \geq Q_{tp}, \qquad\qquad\text{(all } t, p).\ (13.17)$$

Note that the "guarantee conditions" have to be handled through a separate calculation, since X_{jv} is not an endogenous decision variable in the simulation model. In addition, there are the hydro-energy constraints. Let $j = h$ denote hydro, and let the decision variable S_{hvt} be the energy stored at the beginning of period t in the hydro station of vintage v. If $\hat{S}_{hvt}$ is the storage capacity of the reservoir, $0 \leq S_{hvt} \leq \hat{S}_{hvt}$. Also let W_{hvt} be the water inflow in period t, expressed in energy units and adjusted for losses due to seepage and evaporation. Then the water stored at the end of the period plus the water used for generation during the period must be less than or equal to the water stored at the beginning plus the inflow:

$$S_{hvm,t+1} + \sum_{p=1}^{P} U_{hvtp} \cdot \theta_p \leq S_{hvt} + W_{hvt}, \qquad \text{(all } h, v, t\text{)}, \quad (13.18)$$

and these constraints will be satisfied with equality if there is no spillage.

The above linear program can be solved using standard computer programs. It can be extended in various ways, as will be shown later in this chapter, to include multipurpose schemes, regional decision variables, and transmission losses. The objective function is also separable, so that nonlinearities in the cost coefficients can be treated by separable programming.

A difficulty with LP simulation models is the large number of constraints that must be satisfied in any realistic formulation of a problem. Constraints (13.16) in particular can become exceedingly numerous if the load duration curve is broken down into many periods, and the types and vintages of plant are many. But it is possible to overcome this difficulty. Since the capital structure is predefined and fixed, these constraints form an upper bound set and can be treated by bounded variable LP methods.[31] For predominantly thermal systems, the problem can be decomposed into several independent and much smaller linear programs (for example, one for each year) since the operating decisions for one year are, to a good approximation, independent of those of previous years. Although LP and non-LP simulation models for planning calculations have not been reported as frequently as the other models we have discussed, it is interesting to note that they are used extensively by engineers for "real-time" load dispatching calculations.[32]

31. See G. Hadley, *Linear Programming* (Reading, Mass.: Addison-Wesley, 1962).

32. Articles are frequently published on this topic by the Institute of Electronics and Electrical Engineers in the United States and by the Institute of Electrical Engi-

Global Models

One difficulty with marginal analysis is the large number of marginal changes to a basic plan that must be considered. If it were only necessary to consider investment decisions to be made at the present time, the number of marginal changes might not be too many—although this is not true if regional variables and transmission are included in the model. The situation, however, is otherwise: investment decisions over time must be considered, and this adds enormously to the dimensions of the problem. It is the function of global models to overcome this second difficulty with marginal analysis. Specifically, the models are designed to scan and cost a large number of present and future investment policies and to select the optimum. For each investment policy costed, they must simulate system operation and calculate optimum operating schedules and costs. Simulation models are therefore a special case of global models.

Simulation models are not, however, superseded by global models. To arrive at a uniquely optimum policy in one computer run is perhaps asking too much. A formulation of a global model necessarily entails approximation. But once approximate global solutions have been reached, they can be, and are, examined in more detail by marginal analysis using simulation models. In this way, as Bessière and Petcu have argued, global models and marginal analysis using simulation models are complementary techniques.[33]

The first global models to be developed were formulated as linear programs. In recent years, some workers have turned to non-LP formulations on the grounds that they are computationally more efficient. We shall consider linear programming, nonlinear programming, and then return to an LP reformulation of the global models that appears to be at least as computationally efficient as the non-LP formulations.

---

neers in Great Britain. See also four papers published in the proceedings of the Third Power System Computation Conference, Rome (London: Queen Mary College Department of Electrical and Electronic Engineering, 1969): B. J. Cordy and A. M. Sasson, "Non-Linear Programming Techniques for the Load-Flow, Minimum Loss, and Economic Dispatching Problems"; P. Ariatti, D. Grohmann, and D. Venturini, "A Method for Economic Load Dispatching in a Thermal Power System"; E. D. Farmer, K. W. James, and D. W. Wells, "Computer Scheduling of Generation in a Power Supply System"; and L. Tyren, "Short-Range Optimization of a Hydro-Thermal System by a Gradient Method Combined with Linear Programming." The well-known study by L. K. Kirchmayer, *Economic Operation of Power Systems* (New York: John Wiley, 1958), used Lagrange multipliers to solve the load dispatching problem.

33. See Bessière and Petcu, "Analyse Marginales."

Linear programming

The following formulation borrows in particular from Massé, Bessière, and Forster and Whitting.[34] It is very similar to the initial formulation in the section on "The Investment Problem in Cost Minimization Form," except that, as with the LP simulation model, we break down the load duration curve into $p = 1, \ldots, P$ discrete blocks. Adding the capital cost terms to the generation costs, the investor's objective is to choose the investments X_{jv} over $v = 1, \ldots, T$ and the associated operating decisions U_{jvtp} over $t = 1, \ldots, T$ and $p = 1, \ldots, P$, so as to minimize total discounted system costs:

$$\text{Minimize} \sum_{j=1}^{J} \sum_{v=1}^{T} C_{jv} X_{jv} \tag{13.19}$$

$$+ \sum_{j=1}^{J} \sum_{t=1}^{T} \sum_{v=-V}^{t} \sum_{p=1}^{P} F_{jtvp} \cdot U_{jtvp} \cdot \theta_p$$

subject to six constraints. The first constraint is that the plant in operation must be sufficient at all times to meet the instantaneous power demand:

$$\sum_{j=1}^{J} \sum_{v=-V}^{t} U_{jtvp} \geq Q_{tp}, \qquad\qquad (t = 1, \ldots, T; \tag{13.20}$$
$$p = 1, \ldots, P).$$

Second, the output of each plant must not be greater than the available capacity. In general, the available capacity is somewhat lower than actual capacity on account of planned outage (maintenance) and unplanned outage (faults). If the availability factor for plant X_{jv} in year t is a_{jvt}, this constraint is:

$$U_{jtvp} \leq a_{jvt} \cdot X_{jv}, \qquad\qquad (j = 1, \ldots, J; \tag{13.21}$$
$$v = -V, \ldots, t;$$
$$t = 1, \ldots, T;$$
$$p = 1, \ldots, P).$$

The third constraint is that there will be an upper limit to the hydro energy available in any period t. Let this limit for each vintage be H_{vt}. Then:

---

34. See Massé, *Optimal Investment Decisions;* Bessière and Massé, "Long Term Programming of Electrical Investments"; Forster, "The Statistical Basis"; and Forster and Whitting, "An Integrated Mathematical Model."

$$\sum_{p=1}^{P} U_{htvp} \cdot \theta_p \leq H_{vt}, \qquad (t = 1, \ldots, T; \quad (13.22)$$
$$v = V, \ldots, t;$$
$$j = h \text{ [hydro]}).$$

Fourth, equality constraints represent the initial capital stock. Let the plant initially on the system be denoted by $\hat{X}_{jv}, j = 1, \ldots, J$ and $v = -V, \ldots, 0$. Then:

$$X_{jv} = \hat{X}_{jv}, \qquad (j = 1, \ldots, J; \quad (13.23)$$
$$v = -V, \ldots, 0).$$

Fifth, to guarantee peak power supplies to an acceptable probability limit, the installed capacity must be sufficient to meet the mean expected demand with a margin of reserve capacity (m) to allow for demands above the mean expectations:

$$\sum_{j=1}^{J} \sum_{v=-V}^{t} X_{jv} \geq Q_{tp} \cdot (1 + m), \qquad (t = 1, \ldots, T; \quad (13.24)$$
$$p = 1).$$

Similarly, there may be a guarantee condition for energy supplies, requiring a constraint similar to (13.7). A proper study of this condition will generally require a seasonal model, which adds substantially (but not prohibitively) to the dimensions of the model. Note, however, that the effect of (13.7) is essentially to limit the ratio of hydro to thermal plant on the system. As a shortcut, therefore, but one evidently involving assumptions that may sometimes be rather approximate, an annual model still can be used but with a restriction on the ratio of hydro to thermal plant on the system. This ratio can be ascertained from separate reserve and reliability studies.

Finally, there are a number of "local" and other constraints. For example, the number of hydro sites may be limited, certain decisions may be political, and the future investment program may have been determined partly by previous studies. Constraints to represent shortages of capital and foreign exchange may also be introduced. All decision variables, of course, are nonnegative.

The constraint matrix has a very simple form. The coefficients are mainly zeros and ones, and fall into regular patterns. Matrix generator programs can be written to produce the constraint matrices. This cuts down on data and input preparation considerably. Since the constraint matrix is not very dense, computation can be very fast. Although this is the simplest form of the global model, much has been, and can be, accomplished with it, and the use of LP and its extensions by the electricity supply industry is common practice in many countries. Bessière informs us that LP formulations were first studied for Electricité de France in the mid-1950s by Massé and Gibrat, who published their results in 1957.[35]

The model described above can be extended in many directions to include, for example: (a) optimum replacement; (b) optimum locations of plant and directions of bulk energy transmission; (c) optimum storage capacities and storage policies for hydroelectric plant, including special constraints on the operation of multipurpose hydro schemes involving electricity generation; (d) integer variables to represent the large fixed-cost component of hydro and nuclear schemes and transmission equipment; and (e) nuclear fuel cycling.[36]

Examples of the first three extensions are presented in the following section. The simulation models corresponding to each of these extensions follow in a rather obvious way by predefining all the capacity variables and using the LP to search for optimum dispatching schedules only.

A difficulty with LP models of the type described above is the

35. Bessière, "Methods of Choosing Equipment," and Massé and Gibrat, "Application of Linear Programming." The paper by Massé and Gibrat was soon followed by Bessière and Massé, "Long Term Programming," which offers principles that appear to remain the same, whatever the country involved and whatever the date—compare, for example, Forster, "The Statistical Basis"; Forster and Whitting, "An Integrated Mathematical Model"; V. Nitu and others, "Models for the Study of Power Systems Development by Means of Digital Computers," in the proceedings of the Third Power Systems Computation Conference, Rome (London: Queen Mary College Department of Electrical and Electronic Engineering, 1969); United Nations, "Economic Methods and Criteria"; United Nations, "Symposium on the Application of O.R. Methods in the Solving of Economic Problems of Planning and Operation of Large Electric Systems and on the Use of Computers for that Purpose," Varna [Bulgaria], May 25–27, 1970; and three papers read to the International Atomic Energy Authority symposium, Vienna, 1970; J. Eibenschutz, "Planeacion de Centrales Nucleoelectricas," IAEA/SM139/1: W. Frankowski, "Economic Integration of Nuclear Power Stations in Electric Power Systems in the Light of Optimization Research," IAEA/SM139/10; and D. E. Deonigi, "A Computer Simulation for Evaluating Nuclear Power Stations in a National Electric Power Company," IAEA/SM139/40. Among the richest sources of information are the Power Systems Computation Conferences held in London in 1963, Stockholm in 1966, Rome in 1969, and Grenoble in 1972, the proceedings of which are published by the Department of Electrical and Electronic Engineering, Queen Mary College, University of London.

36. See, for (a), Massé, *Optimal Investment Decisions;* for (b), Fernandez, Manne, and Valencia, "Multi-Level Planning"; for (c), D. Gately, "Investment Planning for the Electric Power Industry: An Integer-Linear Programming Approach," research report 7035 (London: University of Western Ontario Department of Economics, 1970), and Fernandez, Manne, and Valencia, "Multi-Level Planning"; and for (d), Frankowski, "Economic Integration of Nuclear Power Stations."

large number of constraints encountered in any realistic formulation of a problem. The principal cause of this is constraint (13.21): We must ensure that the output of every plant on the system in every year of the study and on every interval of the load duration curve does not exceed its maximum available capacity. This is the same problem as was raised in connection with the LP simulation models; this time, however, the X's are not constants but decision variables, and the constraint cannot be handled by bounded variable LP methods. If there are, on the average, twenty plants on the system, and we break the load duration curve into ten discrete intervals and take a thirty-year period broken down into six five-year intervals, then we have about 1,200 constraints of this type and about 1,500 constraints in the problem. This is quite a large linear program, although standard computer programs are now available which can handle up to 10,000 constraints with integer variable facilities;[37] and the use of matrix generators and "report writers" make data preparation and output processing quick and simple.

Nonlinear programming

In the early 1960s computers could not handle anything like this number of constraints. Bessière and Albert and Larivaille report that 180 constraints and 200 unknowns approached the maximum that computers could handle in 1958; apparently the main reason why Electricité de France turned to nonlinear programming was to overcome this constraint problem. For the all-thermal system of Great Britain, Phillips and others also developed a non-LP model; it will be described here briefly in order to show how nonlinear programming overcomes the constraint problem to a large extent.[38]

The idea of the non-LP model is to prearrange all the plants that are or may be connected to the system in any year in "merit order" in the data input. That is, the operating sequence is decided in advance by inspecting the marginal operating costs before the computer run is commenced. By this device, all the operating variables and their associated capacity constraints can be satisfied implicitly and deleted from the formulation.

To reduce notation, we shall drop the subscript t until needed.

---

37. This is the capacity of the OPHELIE II LP System for the Control Data Corporation 6600 computer.

38. See Bessière, "Methods of Choosing Equipment"; M. Albert and P. Larivaille, "Utilisation de Modèles Globaux pour le Choix des Opérations des Programmes EDF," paper read to the IFORS–HELORS conference on Operational Research and Electric Energy, Athens, 1968; and Phillips and others, "A Mathematical Model."

FIGURE 13.6. LOAD DURATION CURVE
WITH NOTATION FOR A NONLINEAR
PROGRAMMING MODEL

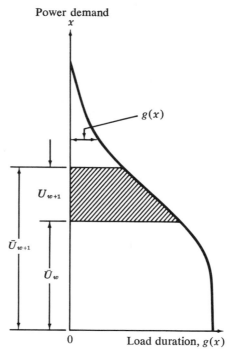

U_w = Output of plant w

$$\bar{U}_w = \sum_{w'=1}^{w} U_{w'}$$

Moreover, we shall represent plant type j, vintage v, by a single subscript, w, where $w = 1, 2, 3, \ldots , W$, and W is the total number of plants of all vintages in year t. We let X_w be the *available* power capacity of thermal plant w; U_w its power output at any instant; and F_w its operating cost. The ordinate on the demand duration curve (Figure 13.6) is denoted by x, where x is in units of power demand, and we denote the duration of demand x by $g(x)$. Now define the subscripts w such that their sequence locates the plant in merit order, as follows:

$$0 \le F_1 \le F_2 \le F_3 \cdots \le F_w \cdots \le F_W, \tag{13.25}$$

where F_w is the new notation for the operating costs of plant j, vintage v, in year t.

The cost of operating plant w in merit order is then given by:

$$\int_{\bar{U}_{w-1}}^{\bar{U}_w} F_w \cdot g(x)dx = F_w\{G(\bar{U}_w) - G(U_{w-1})\}, \tag{13.26}$$

where:

$$G(\bar{U}_w) = \int_0^{\bar{U}_w} g(x)dx, \text{ and } \bar{U}_w = \sum_{w'=1}^{w} U_{w'}.$$

Adding (13.26) over $w = 1$ to W gives the total operating cost (TOC):[39]

$$\text{TOC} = \sum_{w=1}^{W} (F_w - F_{w+1})G(\bar{U}_w),$$

which, after substitution for $\bar{U}_w$, becomes:

$$\text{TOC} = \sum_{w=1}^{W} (F_w - F_{w+1})G \left(\sum_{w'=1}^{w} \bar{U}_{w'} \right). \tag{13.27}$$

A reasonable simplifying assumption can be made to reduce the size of the problem further: that the available plant capacity X_w will be operated at full power in the interval w to $w + 1$, so that $U_w = X_w$ exactly.[40] Therefore:

$$\text{TOC} = \sum_{w=1}^{W} (F_w - F_{w+1})G \left(\sum_{w'=1}^{w} X_{w'} \right). \tag{13.28}$$

Reintroducing the subscripts j, v, and t into the formulation, we find that the investor's objective is:

$$\text{Minimize } \sum_{j=1}^{J} \sum_{v=1}^{T} C_{jv} \cdot X_{jv} \tag{13.29}$$

$$+ \sum_{t=1}^{T} \sum_{j=1}^{J} \sum_{v=-V}^{t} (F_{j,v,t} - F_{j,v+1,t})G_{jvt},$$

39. Note that $G(\bar{U}_0) = 0$, and we use the convention $F_{w+1} = 0$.
40. This assumption is not made by Phillips and others, "A Mathematical Model."

where:

$$G_{jvt} = G_t \left(\sum_{j=1}^{j} \sum_{u=-V}^{v} X_{iu} \right),$$

subject to:

$$\sum_{j=1}^{J} \sum_{v=-V}^{t} X_{jv} \geq \hat{Q}_t, \qquad\qquad (t = 1, \ldots, T), \quad (13.30)$$

where $\hat{Q}_t$ is the peak power demand in year t.

Thus it is possible to represent the operating cost explicitly in terms of the plant capacities of the system, plant operating costs, and the shape of the load duration curve. No special algorithm is needed to schedule the plant optimally. All variables U_{jtvp} satisfy the operating capacity constraints implicitly. Moreover, the demand constraints are satisfied implicitly except at times of peak demand. The formulation thus accomplishes an enormous reduction in the number of constraints to be satisfied—at the expense, however, of a complex, nonseparable, but convex objective function.

Apparently this model is now in constant use in Great Britain for the evaluation of investment plans. The nonlinear program of Electricité de France has also been in use for several years.[41]

The problem with turning to nonlinear programming is that we lose very considerable advantages of LP computer software, which include flexibility, very versatile management processing systems, input and output processors, and integer facilities. Also not to be underestimated is the fact that the LP formulations are simpler and can be rewritten readily to cover other problems such as replacement, bulk electrical energy transmission, hydro storage policy, and multipurpose projects.

The question arises: Can we retain an LP form and yet reduce the constraint problem? The answer is that we can. The non-LP model reduces the number of constraints, not because it is intrinsically more efficient than LP but because it includes a priori information about system operating characteristics which we exclude from LP models. It is because this information is excluded that we get so many constraints in the LP model. By including it, we can reduce the problem size to virtually the same numerical proportions as in non-LP forms.

---

41. See Bessière, "Le modèle 'Investissements 85' "; Albert and Larivaille, "Utilisation de Modèles Globaux"; and the references cited in Bessière, "Methods of Choosing Equipment."

Recovering an LP form

The way we include the additional information about system operating characteristics is as follows.[42] We know that as we move along the time axis of the load duration curve the output of any plant will not be increased. In fact, either it will remain the same or it will be reduced. Suppose that we define new operating decision variables, Z's, to replace the U's, which represented the output of each plant. These Z's (which we will call Z-substitutes) are defined to be the *decrease* in output of any plant as we move along the load duration curve. For any plant j,v:

$$Z_{jtvp} = U_{jtvp} - U_{jtv,p+1} \geq 0, \quad (p = 1, \ldots, P - 1) \quad (13.31)$$

with:

$$Z_{jtvP} = U_{jtvP} \geq 0. \tag{13.32}$$

As we move along the load duration curve (that is, as load decreases), the power output of plant j,v, is never increased;[43] it follows that the sum of power reductions from $p = 1$ to P is less than the available power capacity of plant j,v. Hence:

$$\sum_{p=1}^{P} Z_{jtvp} \leq a_{jvt} \cdot X_{jv}, \quad \text{(all } j, t, v). \quad (13.33)$$

This constraint and the nonnegativity constraints on Z_{jtvp} are necessary and sufficient conditions for constraints (13.21) to be satisfied. First, in view of (13.32), U_{jtvP} is nonnegative if Z_{jtvP} is nonnegative, and it follows from (13.31) that if Z_{jtvp} is nonnegative for all p, so must be U_{jtvp}. Second, in view of (13.33), no combination of the values of Z_{jtvp} can exceed $a_{jvt} \cdot X_{jv}$. From (13.31) and (13.32) we derive the relation that:

$$U_{jtvp} = \sum_{p'=p}^{P} Z_{jtvp'} \leq a_{jvt} \cdot X_{jv}. \tag{13.34}$$

---

42. I am grateful to Ivan Whitting of the National Gas Council in Great Britain for pointing out the device that follows. The idea apparently was suggested by E. M. L. Beale during a conversation; it does not appear to have been published before this chapter appeared in *The Bell Journal of Economics and Management Science*.

43. Unless seasonal variations in hydro flows and maintenance schedules are important, in which case it is necessary to use one load duration curve for each season, and the above statement holds once again for each load duration curve.

Hence U_{jtvp} cannot exceed $a_{jvt} \cdot X_{jv}$ if (13.31), (13.32), and (13.33) are satisfied.

Thus, we can replace the U's, which had to satisfy plant capacity constraints on every portion of the load duration curve, with new nonnegative variables, the Z-substitutes, which satisfy one constraint for the whole curve. Approximately, the number of capacity constraints is reduced by $1/P$. The 1,200 capacity constraints in the 1,500-constraint problem we mentioned earlier[44] are now reduced to about 120. Additionally, it has been our experience that, although the density of the constraint matrix is increased, computing times have been reduced by a factor of 2 or more (sometimes by a factor of 5).

This is a useful result for those who prefer to work with the simpler LP models. For those directly involved with investment planning in the industry, it means that computational problems are kept to a manageable size, without loss of generality and with many advantages in terms of computer software. If the cost coefficients are nonlinear (as happens for example with studies of hydro resources), the objective function is separable so that nonlinearities can be treated by interpolation and the LP form recovered. For those involved with economic research, it means that global models based on LP can provide a realistic view of the investment problem—at least from the supply side. If demand is introduced as an endogenous variable, however, we have to return to non-LP, particularly if peak and off-peak demands are considered interdependent, since the objective function is then no longer separable.

Three Extensions to Linear Programming Models

A contraction in the size of the problem, together with a rapid expansion in the size of linear programs that can be handled on computers, also enables us to expand the detail and content of both global and simulation models. Below we look at three extensions to the models: replacement, an approximate treatment of transmission, and investment and operating decisions in systems with hydro storage schemes.

Inclusion of replacement

Optimum replacement of a power station usually occurs when it is cheaper to expand and operate the power system without this

44. See page 275.

power station—because of rising operating and maintenance costs relative to those of new plants, or because sites for new power stations are short and old ones need to be scrapped to make room for new and larger ones.

An accurate treatment of replacement requires explicit separation of fixed annual operation and maintenance costs from other costs. Usually these costs are added to the annuitized charges on capital, while the variable maintenance costs are added to the other variable operating costs. Following Massé[45] we could define a new decision variable X_{jv}^* to represent the plant scrapped of type j, vintage v, and write the capital cost terms in the objective function as $C_{jv}(X_{jv} - X_{jv}^*)$, where C_{jv} equals the fixed annual costs plus annuitized charges on capital; however, this can lead to solutions which scrap a plant before capital costs have been accounted for by the annuities. Since the decision to scrap a new plant requires a new decision variable, we can associate this variable directly with fixed maintenance and operating costs.

We denote by M_{jvt} the discounted, fixed maintenance and operating costs of plant type j, vintage v, in year t. The problem is to decide how much of this plant should remain in service in year t. Let R_{jvt} be the amount of type j, vintage v, remaining in service in year t. The objective and the constraints follow much the same pattern as before. Using the same notation, the objective is to:

$$\text{Minimize} \left\{ \begin{array}{l} \displaystyle\sum_{j=1}^{J} \sum_{v=1}^{T} C_{jv} \cdot X_{jv} + \sum_{j=1}^{J} \sum_{t=1}^{T} \sum_{v=-V}^{t} M_{jtv} \cdot R_{jtv} \\[2em] + \displaystyle\sum_{j=1}^{J} \sum_{t=1}^{T} \sum_{v=-V}^{t} \sum_{p=1}^{P} F_{jtvp} \cdot U_{jtvp} \cdot \theta_p \end{array} \right. \qquad (13.35)$$

with the following constraints:

Total plant remaining greater than peak demand requirements (plus an allowance for reserves),

$$\sum_{j=1}^{J} \sum_{v=-V}^{t} R_{jtv} \geq Q_{tp} \cdot (1 + m)$$
$$(t = 1, \ldots, T; \quad (13.36)$$
$$p = 1),$$

Plant types j, v, remaining less than plant installed of type j, v,

$$R_{jtv} \leq X_{jv} (j = 1, \ldots, J;$$
$$t = 1, \ldots, T; \quad (13.37)$$
$$v = 1, \ldots, t),$$

Plant remaining of given type j, v, never increases,

$$R_{j,t+1,v} \leq R_{jtv} (j = 1, \ldots, J;$$
$$t = 1, \ldots, T; \quad (13.38)$$
$$v = 1, \ldots, t),$$

45. Massé, *Optimal Investment Decisions*, p. 187ff.

Total plant operating always
sufficient to meet demand,

$$\sum_{j=1}^{J} \sum_{v=-V}^{t} U_{jtvp} \geq Q_{tp}$$

$$(t = 1, \ldots, T; \qquad (13.39)$$
$$p = 1, \ldots, P),$$

A plant's output never exceeds
remaining available capacity,

$$U_{jvtp} \leq a_{jtv} R_{jtv} (j = 1, \ldots, J;$$
$$t = 1, \ldots, T;$$
$$v = 1, \ldots, t; \qquad (13.40)$$
$$p = 1, \ldots, P),$$

Restrictions on energy available
from each hydro plant,

$$\sum_{p=1}^{P} U_{htvp} \cdot \theta_p \leq H_{vt}$$

$$(t = 1, \ldots, T; \qquad (13.41)$$
$$v = -V, \ldots, t).$$

Finally, there are "local" and nonnegativity constraints, and initial conditions. Z-substitutes, of course, can be used in this formulation. Constraints (13.36) are the "guarantee conditions" for peak power; constraints to guarantee energy supplies can also be introduced in the ways previously discussed.

Approximate inclusion of transmission

Transmission systems reduce costs of supply in four ways. First, if regions are interconnected, in the event of generator failure in one region, it is possible to call upon the reserves of other regions; aggregate reserve capacity with interconnection is less than is required without interconnection. Second, if peak demands occur at different times in different regions, interconnection permits peak power capacity to be exported and imported, and the aggregate peak demand can be met with less capacity. Third, if the transmission system is designed to transmit energy in large quantities, the markets of regions rich in energy resources (fossil or hydro) can be expanded, and regions less rich can import the cheaper energy. Fourth, with interconnection, larger units can be installed embodying considerable economies of scale. These four aspects of the transmission system—the pooling of reserve capacity, the pooling of peak capacity, the opening of markets to regions rich in low-cost resources, and economies of scale—can make large savings compared to the costs of the transmission lines and transmission losses.

In the following formulas, regions of generation are denoted by integers $g = 1, \ldots, G$, and regions of demand by integers $d = 1, \ldots, D$. Y_{gdv} denotes the increment of transmission capacity (expressed in megawatts) connecting g, d, installed in year v; L_{gdv} is the discounted cost per megawatt installed of this increment. The power delivered to region d by station type j, vintage v, in period t, p, from region g is denoted by U_{jtvpgd}; and its total output is $\Sigma_d \, U_{jtvpgd}$. The capital and operating costs are as before, except that they must now be summed over all regions. A cost term is also required for the transmission capital costs.[46] The objective function is therefore:

$$\text{Minimize} \begin{cases} \displaystyle\sum_{g=1}^{G} \sum_{j=1}^{J} \sum_{v=1}^{T} C_{jvg} \cdot X_{jvg} \\ + \displaystyle\sum_{g=1}^{G} \sum_{d=1}^{D} \sum_{v=1}^{T} L_{gdv} \cdot Y_{gdv} \\ + \displaystyle\sum_{g=1}^{G} \sum_{d=1}^{D} \sum_{j=1}^{J} \sum_{t=1}^{T} \sum_{v=-V}^{t} \sum_{p=1}^{P} F_{jtvpgd} \cdot U_{jtvpgd} \cdot \theta_p. \end{cases} \qquad (13.42)$$

The first constraint to be satisfied is the peak power guarantee condition that the installed capacity must be greater than the peak load presented at the terminals of power stations by a margin m, to allow for demands above mean expectations.[47] We also introduce a "diversity factor" c, which is the ratio of the aggregate peak demand to the arithmetic sum of the regional peak demands. The capacity requirements are then:

$$\sum_{g=1}^{G} \sum_{j=1}^{J} \sum_{v=-V}^{t} X_{jvg} \geq (1 + m)c \sum_{g=1}^{G} \sum_{d=1}^{D} \sum_{j=1}^{J} \sum_{v=-V}^{t} U_{jtvpgd}, \qquad (13.43)$$

$$(t = 1, \ldots, T;$$
$$p = 1).$$

The diversity factor might have to be modified if the solutions suggest a different pattern of connections than the pattern used for computing the factor. In addition, transmission capacity must be sufficient to carry the peak load transfers:

$$\sum_{v=-V}^{t} Y_{gdv} \geq (1 + m) \sum_{j=1}^{J} \sum_{v=-V}^{t} U_{jtvpgd}, \qquad (13.44)$$

$$(t = 1, \ldots, T;$$
$$p = 1;$$
$$g = 1, \ldots, G;$$
$$d = 1, \ldots, D).$$

46. We do not treat replacement in this model, although it is quite possible to do so if required. Integer variables can also be introduced to represent the indivisibilities of transmission investments, but this is not done here.

47. Of course, there may also be a guarantee condition for energy supplies, which we do not list here.

Next, the output of plants must meet the demand and the transmission losses. If b_{gd} is the per-unit power attenuation between g, d, then the plant must be operated in each period p such that:[48]

$$\sum_{v=-V}^{t} \sum_{g=1}^{G} \sum_{j=1}^{J} U_{jtvpgd} (1 - b_{gd}) \geq Q_{dtp}, \qquad (13.45)$$

$$\begin{aligned} (t &= 1, \ldots, T; \\ p &= 1, \ldots, P; \\ d &= 1, \ldots, D). \end{aligned}$$

Next we have the constraints that no plant can be operated above its peak available capacity:

$$c \cdot \sum_{d=1}^{D} U_{jtvpgd} \leq a_{jtvg} \cdot X_{jvg}, \qquad (j = 1, \ldots, J; \quad (13.46)$$

$$\begin{aligned} v &= -V, \ldots, t; \\ t &= 1, \ldots, T; \\ p &= 1, \ldots, P; \\ g &= 1, \ldots, G). \end{aligned}$$

(Again, these constraints can be reduced by $1/P$ by the use of nonnegative Z-substitutes.) The hydro-energy constraint takes the same form as before:

$$c \cdot \sum_{d=1}^{D} \sum_{p=1}^{P} U_{htvpgd} \cdot \theta_p \leq H_{vtg}, \qquad (t = 1, \ldots, T; \quad (13.47)$$

$$\begin{aligned} v &= -V, \ldots, t; \\ g &= 1, \ldots, G). \end{aligned}$$

Finally, there are "local," budget, foreign exchange, and nonnegativity constraints; constraints to represent the initial conditions; and a constraint to guarantee energy supplies.

Inclusion of water storage capacity and operating policy variables

We now formulate the model to search for least-cost, evolving investment programs to satisfy an exogenous demand for electricity, a

---

48. The power attenuation will vary with the square of the load transfer between g, d. This would make constraint (13.45) quadratic. We can retain linearity only by taking b_{gd} as a weighted average value (in fact, a "mean-square" average).

planned delivery of water to irrigation, and a planned degree of flood control. The peak storage capacity and the amount stored in each season are treated as decision variables. The model can be couched easily in a regional context, as has been done elsewhere,[49] to allow for the strong regional dependence of hydro resources and the high economies of scale which they may yield if the interconnected system is large enough to absorb them. However, to reduce notation, this is not done below; the principles are in any case identical to the ones presented in the subsection just above.

Thermal schemes will now be denoted by subscript $j = 1, \ldots, J$ and hydro storage schemes by $h = 1, \ldots, H$. As before, maximum power capacities will be denoted by the decision variable X, the instantaneous outputs by U, and incremental capital and generation costs by C and F, respectively. Each year will be denoted by t and divided into $m = 1, \ldots, M$ periods, which can represent months, seasons, weeks, or any other appropriate time interval, according to the accuracy desired. The demands within each period m will be represented by a load duration curve divided into $p = 1, \ldots, P$ blocks. We have the following additions to notation for the hydro schemes: $\hat{S}_{hv}$ = decision variable representing the maximum storage capacity (expressed in energy units) of scheme h, v; K_{hv} = corresponding incremental capital cost of providing the storage capacity; S_{htvm} = decision variable representing the actual water in storage (expressed in energy units) of scheme h, v, at the beginning of m in year t; and W_{htvm} = water inflows to scheme h, v, during m of year t, expressed in energy units and corrected for losses due to evaporation and seepage.

The objective function is then:

$$
\text{Minimize} \left\{
\begin{aligned}
& \sum_{j=1}^{J} \sum_{v=1}^{T} C_{jv} \cdot X_{jv} + \sum_{h=1}^{H} \sum_{v=1}^{T} C_{hv} \cdot X_{hv} \\
& + \sum_{h=1}^{H} \sum_{v=1}^{T} K_{hv} \cdot \hat{S}_{hv} \\
& + \sum_{j=1}^{J} \sum_{t=1}^{T} \sum_{v=-V}^{t} \sum_{m=1}^{M} \sum_{p=1}^{P} F_{jtvmp} \cdot U_{jtvmp} \cdot \theta_p \\
& + \sum_{h=1}^{H} \sum_{t=1}^{T} \sum_{v=-V}^{t} \sum_{m=1}^{M} \sum_{p=1}^{P} F_{htvmp} \cdot U_{htvmp} \cdot \theta_p.
\end{aligned}
\right.
\tag{13.48}
$$

49. See D. Anderson, "Investment Analysis in Electricity Supply Using Computer Models," Economics Department Working Paper no. 91 (Washington, D.C.: World Bank, 1970).

Note that the last term is small for hydro schemes, and that there is no cost term associated with actual water in storage, S_{htvm}.

The following five constraints are exactly analogous to the ones presented above: (a) installed capacity must be greater than or equal to the annual peak demand plus a margin for reserves; (b) there must be sufficient energy reserves to meet energy demand in dry seasons; (c) the aggregate plant output must meet the instantaneous power demand at all times; (d) no plant can be operated above its peak available capacity—again (d) can be reduced by $1/P$ using Z-substitutes—and (e) "local" constraints, initial conditions, and so on.

There are additional constraints introduced by storage hydro. First, the water stored at the end of period m (beginning of $m + 1$) plus the water used for generation is less than or equal to the initial storage plus the inflow:

$$S_{htv,m+1} + \sum_{p=1}^{P} U_{htvmp} \cdot \theta_p \leq S_{htvm} + W_{htvm}, \tag{13.49}$$

for $m = 1, \ldots, M - 1$; and for $m = M$:

$$S_{h,t+1,v,1} + \sum_{p=1}^{P} U_{htvMp} \cdot \theta_p \leq S_{htvM} + W_{htvM}, \tag{13.50}$$

where (13.49) and (13.50) must be satisfied for all h, t, v, and m.

If a hydro scheme is multipurpose, involving irrigation and flood control, there will be further restrictions on the timing and the rate of energy output. Suppose the water requirements of irrigation in period m of year t are I_{htvm}. There will still be considerable flexibility in the pattern of discharge within the period m (for example, a choice between night and day discharges or between weekdays and weekends); but the aggregate amount of water discharged through turbines must at least be equal to the requirements of irrigation:[50]

$$\sum_{p=1}^{P} U_{htvmp} \cdot \theta_p \geq I_{htvm}, \qquad \text{(all } h, t, v, m). \tag{13.51}$$

Flood control, on the other hand, sets an upper limit to the rate of discharge in certain periods. Let D_{htvm} represent this limit in period

---

50. We also assume in this example that all the water, other than that lost by spillage and seepage, is discharged through turbines. If desired, the assumption may be relaxed.

m. Then the water discharged from the hydro, minus the quantity diverted to irrigation, must not exceed this limit:

$$\sum_{p=1}^{P} U_{htvmp} \cdot \theta_p \leq I_{htvm} + D_{htvm}, \qquad \text{(all } h, t, v, m\text{)}. \quad (13.52)$$

This completes the present formulation. The approach is very flexible and new features can be introduced readily. If hydro schemes are large, they can be expanded in stages instead of being introduced in one period, v. Variable head schemes, pumped storage schemes, and multidam cascade schemes can also be given a full analysis. Approximations can be introduced in the representation of the costs of electric power from thermal stations so as to allow room for more detail elsewhere—for example, in the representation of multidam schemes.[51]

Appendix A. A Note on the Load Duration Curve

The difficulty of calculating optimum operating schedules and costs is presented by the high variability of power demand, which varies throughout the day and throughout the year (compare Figures 13.7 and 13.8). The operating costs are the area under this curve weighted at each time interval θ_t by the fuel costs and the outputs of the plant in that interval. To simplify the calculation of operating costs it is usual to construct a curve known as the load duration curve.[52] This curve is constructed from the above demand curve by rearranging each load for each time interval θ_t to occur in descending order of magnitude (see Figure 13.9). Thus, the operating costs are the area under the load duration curve again weighted at each time interval by the operating costs per unit energy output and the output of each plant operating in that interval. The load duration curve makes integration of costs less difficult because it can be represented by simpler functions than the curves of Figures 13.7 and 13.8. It is a convenient form to check approximations to the patterns of demand shown in Figures 13.7 and 13.8; and we can also use Z-substitutions if we use the load duration curve.

---

51. See Hufschmidt and Fiering, *Simulation Techniques,* and Maass and others, *Design of Water-Resource Systems.*

52. See also Berrie, "The Economics of System Planning"; Openshaw-Taylor and Boal, *Power System Economics;* and L. K. Kirchmayer, *Economic Operation of Power Systems* (New York: John Wiley, 1958).

FIGURE 13.7. VARIABILITY OF POWER
DEMAND FOR A WINTER DAY

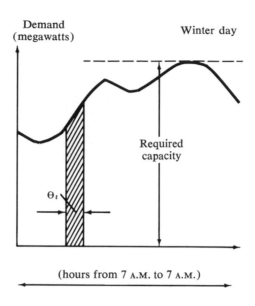

FIGURE 13.7. VARIABILITY OF POWER
DEMAND FOR A WINTER DAY

FIGURE 13.8. VARIABILITY OF POWER
DEMAND FOR A SUMMER DAY

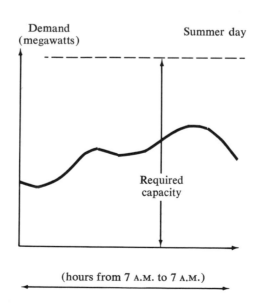

FIGURE 13.9. LOAD DURATION CURVE
FOR ONE YEAR'S DEMAND

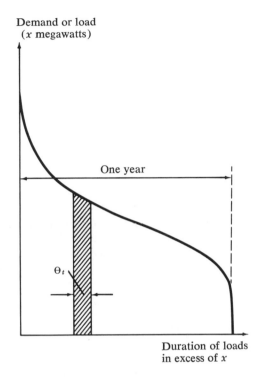

Use of the load duration curve for calculations of operating costs introduces one important assumption: *that the costs and availability of supply depend only upon the magnitude of the load and not on the time at which the load occurs*. This assumption is quite accurate for all-thermal systems (although plant availability, because of maintenance schedules, is seasonal), but it is only approximate for hydro schemes. To analyze hydro operation accurately it is often necessary to construct a separate load duration curve for each season and sometimes each month; if this is done, the assumptions of the load duration curve are tenable again.

Appendix B. Reference Reading

The following reference list includes most works cited in the chapter and other titles containing relevant material. In addition, new papers on long-range planning and scheduling are continually being published by the Institute of Electrical and Electronics Engineers in *Transactions,* and in the proceedings of both the biennial meetings of the Power Engineering Society and the Power Industry Computer Application Conferences.

Albert, M., and Larivaille, P. "Utilisation de Modèles Globaux pour le Choix des Opérations des Programmes EDF." Paper read to IFORS–HELORS Conference on Operational Research and Electrical Energy, Athens, 1968.

Anderson, D. "Investment Analysis in Electricity Supply Using Computer Models." Economics Department Working Paper no. 91. Washington, D.C.: World Bank, 1970.

Ariatti, P.; Grohmann, D.; and Venturini, D. "A Method for Economic Load Dispatching in a Thermal Power System." Paper read to the Third Power Systems Computation Conference, Rome. London: Queen Mary College Department of Electrical and Electronics Engineering, 1969.

Arvanitidis, N. V., and Rosing, J. "Optimal Operation of Multi-Reservoir Systems Using a Composite Representation." *IEEE Transactions, Power Apparatus and Systems* PAS-89 (February 1970).

Beglari, E., and Laughton, M. A. "The Combined Costs and Method for Optimal Economic Planning of an Electrical Power System." IEEE Power Engineering Society Meeting conference paper, n.p., 1974.

Bernard, P. J.; Dopazo, J. F.; and Stagg, G. W. "A Method for Economic Scheduling of a Combined Pumped Hydro and Steam Generating System." *IEEE Transactions, Power Apparatus and Systems* PAS-83 (1964).

Berrie, T. W. "The Economics of System Planning in Bulk Electricity Supply." *Electrical Review* 181 (September 15, 22, and 29, 1967). Reprinted in *Public Enterprise,* ed. R. Turvey. New York: Penguin, 1968.

————. "Further Experience with Simulation Models in System Planning." Paper read to the Second Power Systems Computation Conference, Stockholm, 1966. London: Queen Mary College Department of Economics, 1966.

Berrie, T. W., and Whitting, I. J. "The Exploration of Alternative Plans for an Expanding Electrical Power System." Paper read to the First Power Systems Computation Conference on Digital Computation for Electric Power Systems, London. London: Queen Mary College Department of Electrical and Electronic Engineering, 1963.

Bessière, F. "Methods of Choosing Equipment at Electricité de France: Development and Present Day Concept." *European Economic Review* 1 (Winter 1969): 199–211.

————. "Le modèle 'Investissements 85' d'Electricité de France." *Revue Française de l'Energie,* no. 182 (1966), p. 568.

Bessière, F., and Massé, P. "Long Term Programming of Electrical Investments." In *Marginal Cost Pricing in Practice,* ed. J. R. Nelson. Englewood Cliffs, N.J.: Prentice-Hall, 1964.

Bessière, F., and Petcu, M. "Analyse Marginales et Optimisation Structurelle des Investissements: Application au Secteur de L'Electricité." *RIRO,* no. 6 (1967): 61–81.

Bessière, F., and Sautter, E. "Optimization and Sub-Optimization: The Method of Extended Models in the Non-Linear Case." *Management Science* 15 (September 1968): 1–11.

Boiteux, M. "The Choice of Equipment for the Production of Electric Energy"; "Marginal Cost Pricing"; and "The 'Tarif Vert' of Electricité de France." In *Marginal Cost Pricing in Practice,* ed. J. R. Nelson. Englewood Cliffs, N.J.: Prentice-Hall, 1964.

Boiteux, M., and Stasi, P. "The Determination of Costs of Expansion of an Interconnected System." In *Marginal Cost Pricing in Practice,* ed. J. R. Nelson. Englewood Cliffs, N.J.: Prentice-Hall, 1964.

Booth, R. R. "Power Systems Simulation Model Based on Probability Analysis." *IEEE Transactions, Power Apparatus and Systems* PAS-91 (February 1972): 62–69.

Cash, P. W., and Scott, E. C. "Security of Supply in the Planning and Operation of European Power Systems." Paper read to the Fourteenth Congress of the International Union of Producers and Distributors of Electricity, Madrid, 1967.

Cazalet, E. G. "Decomposition of Complex Decision Problems with Applications to Electric Power System Planning." Menlo Park, Calif.: Stanford Research Institute, 1970.

Cory, B. J., and Sasson, A. M. "Non-Linear Programming Techniques for the Load-Flow, Minimum Loss, and Economic Dispatching Problems." Paper read to the Third Power Systems Computation Conference, Rome. London: Queen Mary College Department of Electrical and Electronic Engineering, 1969.

Davis, R. E., and Pronovost, R. "Two Stochastic Dynamic Programming Procedures for Long-Term Reservoir Management." Paper read to the IEEE Power Engineering Society Meeting Conference, n.p., 1972.

Deonigi, D. E. "A Computer Simulation for Evaluating Nuclear Power Stations in a National Electric Power Company." Paper read to the International Atomic Energy Authority symposium, Vienna, 1970 (IAEA/SM-139/40).

Dhrymes, P. J., and Kurtz, M. "Technology and Scale in Electricity Generation." *Econometrica* 32 (July 1965): 287–315.

Dillard, J. K., and Sells, H. K. "An Introduction to the Study of System Planning by Operational Gaming Models." *IEEE Transactions* 78 (1959), part III.

Eckstein, O. "A Survey of the Theory of Public Expenditure Criteria." n.p.: National Bureau of Economic Research Conference on Public Finances, 1961.

Eibenschutz, J. "Planeacion de Centrales Nucleoelectricas." Paper read to the International Atomic Energy Authority symposium, Vienna, 1970 (IAEA/SM/139/1).

Electricité de France. "L'étude a Long-Terme des Investissements a l'Aide d'un Programme Non-Lineaire: Le Modèle Investissements 85." Note from Department of General Economic Studies. Paris, 1965.

Farmer, E. D.; James, K. W.; and Wells, D. W. "Computer Scheduling of Generation in a Power Supply System." Paper read to the Third Power Systems Computation Conference, Rome. London: Queen Mary College Department of Electrical and Electronic Engineering, 1969.

Fernandez, G., and Manne, A. S. "A Model for Planning Investments in Generating Facilities." Mimeographed. Internal Working Paper. Stanford: Stanford University, 1969.

Fernandez, G.; Manne, A. S.; and Valencia, J. A. "Multi-Level Planning for Electric Power Projects." Mimeographed. Internal Working Paper. Stanford: Stanford University, 1970.

Forster, C. I. K. "The Statistical Basis to National Fuel Policy." London: Institute of Actuaries, 1969.

Forster, C. I. K., and Whitting, I. J. "An Integrated Mathematical Model of the Fuel Economy." *Statistical News,* no. 3 (November 1968).

Frankowski, W. "Economic Integration of Nuclear Power Stations in Electric Power Systems in the Light of Optimization Research." Paper read to the International Atomic Energy Authority symposium, Vienna, 1970 (IAEA/SM-139/10).

Galatin, M. *Economies of Scale and Technical Change in Thermal Power Generation.* Amsterdam: North-Holland, 1968.

Gately, D. "Investment Planning for the Electric Power Industry: An Integer-Linear Programming Approach." Research Report 7035. London: University of Western Ontario Department of Economics, 1970.

Gessford, J., and Karlin, S. "Optimal Policy for Hydro-Electric Operations." In *Studies in the Mathematical Theory of Inventory and Production,* ed. K. J. Arrow, S. Karlin, and H. Scorf. Stanford: Stanford University Press, 1958.

Giguet, R. "Les Programmes d'Equipment Electrique Considerés du Point de Vue de l'Economie Appliquée." n.p.: Institute de Science Economique Appliquée, 1951.

Goldsmith, K. "The Influence of Nuclear Generation on the Planning and Operation of Interconnected Power Systems." Paper read to the International Atomic Energy Authority symposium, Vienna, 1970 (IAEA/SM-139/15).

Hadley, G. *Linear Programming.* Reading, Mass.: Addison-Wesley, 1962.

———. *Non-Linear and Dynamic Programming.* Reading, Mass.: Addison-Wesley, 1964.

Haissman, I. "Optimising the Long-Range Operation of the California Aqueduct by Incremental Dynamic Programming." Mimeographed. Berkeley: University of California Operations Research Center, 1968.

Harberger, A., and Andreatta, N. "A Note on the Economic Principles of Electricity Pricing." In *Pricing and Fiscal Policies,* ed. P. N. Rosenstein-Rodan. Cambridge, Mass.: MIT Press, 1964.

Hoffman, A. G.; Homer, L. E.; Guberman, R. P.; Coulter, J. C.; and Vierra, R. H. "Hydro-Thermal Optimisation of the Pacific Gas and Electric System." Paper read to the IEEE Power Engineering Society Meeting, n.p., 1972.

Hopkins, D. S. P. "Sufficient Conditions for Optimality in Infinite Horizon Linear Economic Models." Mimeographed. Technical Report no. 69-3. Stanford: Stanford University, 1969.

Hufschmidt, M. M., and Fiering, M. B. *Simulation Techniques for Design of Water Resource Systems.* Cambridge, Mass.: Harvard University Press, 1966.

Jacoby, H. P. "Analysis of Investments in Electric Power." Mimeographed, economic development series. Cambridge, Mass.: Harvard University Center for International Affairs, 1967.

Johnston, J. *Statistical Cost Analysis,* New York: McGraw-Hill, 1960.

Jonas, P. J. "A Computer Model to Determine Economic Performance Characteristics of British Generating Stations." Paper read to the British Computer Conference, Brighton, 1966.

Kirchmayer, L. K. *Economic Operation of Power Systems.* New York: John Wiley, 1958.

Koopmans, T. C. "Water Storage Policy in a Simplified Hydro-Electric System." Cowles Foundation for Research in Economics paper no. 115. New Haven: Yale University, 1958.

Krutilla, J. V., and Eckstein, O. *Multiple Purpose River Development.* Baltimore: Johns Hopkins Press, 1958.

Larivaille, P. "Etude des Problemes Posés pour l'Insertion dans un Réseau Electrique d'un Réacteur Nucléaire d'une Puissance Importante par Rapport à Celle du Réseau." Paper read to the International Atomic Energy Authority symposium, Vienna, 1970 (IAEA/SM-139/22).

Lencz, L. "The Planning of the Power System Development with Mathematical Model for Two Points." Paper read to the Third Power Systems Computation Conference, Rome. London: Queen Mary College Department of Electrical and Electronic Engineering, 1969.

Lieftinck, P.; Sadove, A. R.; and Creyke, T. C. *Water and Power Resources of West Pakistan,* 3 vols. Baltimore: Johns Hopkins Press, 1969.

Lindqvist, J. "Operation of a Hydrothermal Electric System: A Multi-stage Decision Process." *IEEE Transactions* (April 1962).

Little, J. D. C. "The Use of Storage Water in a Hydro-Electric System."

Journal of the Operations Research Society of America 3 (May 1955): 187–97.

Littlechild, S. C. "Marginal Cost Pricing with Joint Costs." *Economic Journal* 80 (June 1970): 323–31.

Maass, A.; Hufschmidt, M. M.; Doreman, R.; Thomas, H. A.; Marglin, S. A.; and Fair, G. M., eds. *Design of Water-Resource Systems.* Cambridge, Mass.: Harvard University Press, 1962.

Manne, A. S. "DINAMICO: A Dynamic Multi-Sector, Multi-Skill Model." In *Multi-level Planning: Case Studies in Mexico,* ed. Louis M. Goreux and Alan S. Manne, pp. 107–51. Amsterdam: North-Holland, 1973.

———. "Linear Programming and Sequential Decisions." *Management Science* 6 (April 1960): 259–67.

———. "Product-Mix Alternatives: Flood Control, Electric Power and Irrigation." Cowles Foundation Discussion Paper no. 95 n.p., October 1960.

Massé, P. "Electrical Investments" and "Some Economic Effects of the 'Tarif Vert.'" In *Marginal Cost Pricing in Practice,* ed. J. R. Nelson. Englewood Cliffs, N.J.: Prentice-Hall, 1964.

———. *Optimal Investment Decisions.* Englewood Cliffs, N.J.: Prentice-Hall, 1962.

———. *Les Reserves et Régulation de l'Avenir dans la Vie Economique,* 2 vols. Paris: Hermourn, 1946.

Massé, P., and Gibrat, R. "Application of Linear Programming to Investments in the Electrical Power Industry." In *Marginal Cost Pricing in Practice,* ed. J. R. Nelson. Englewood Cliffs, N.J.: Prentice-Hall, 1964.

Miller, R. H., and Thompson, R. P. "Long-Range Scheduling of Power Production (Part III)." Paper read to the IEEE Power Engineering Society Conference, n.p., 1972.

Morlat, G. "On Instructions for the Optimal Management of Seasonal Reservoirs." In *Marginal Cost Pricing in Practice,* ed. J. R. Nelson. Englewood Cliffs, N.J.: Prentice-Hall, 1964.

Nerlove, M. "Returns to Scale in Electricity Supply." In *Measurement in Economics: Studies in Mathematical Economics and Econometrics,* ed. C. F. Christ. Stanford: Stanford University Press, 1963.

Nitu, V.; Bordeian, N.; Goldenberg, C.; and Monolescv, C. "Models for the Study of Power Systems Development by Means of Digital Computers." Paper read to the Third Power Systems Computation Conference, Rome, 1969. London: Queen Mary College Department of Electrical and Electronic Engineering, 1969.

Openshaw-Taylor, E., and Boal, G. A. *Power System Economics.* London: Edward Arnold, 1969.

Phillips, D.; Jenkin, F. P.; Pritchard, J. A. T.; and Rybicki, K. "A Mathematical Model for Determining Generating Plant Mix." Paper read to the Third Power Systems Computation Conference, Rome, 1969. London:

Queen Mary College Department of Electrical and Electronic Engineering, 1969.

Pressman, I. "A Mathematical Formulation of the Peak-Load Pricing Problem." *The Bell Journal of Economics and Management Science* 1 (Autumn 1970): 304–26.

Prest, A. R., and Turvey, R. "Cost-Benefit Analysis: A Survey." *Economic Journal* 75 (December 1965): 683–735. Reprinted in E. A. Robinson, ed., *Surveys of Economic Theory*, New York: St. Martin's, 1966.

Rabar, F. "Simulation of Investment Policy in the Energy Economy." Research Program in Industrial Economics Working Paper no. 16, Cleveland: Case Western Reserve University, 1970.

Roberts, J. T. "The IAEA's WASP Computer Code for Electricity System Expansion Planning." Appendix A in *Nuclear Power Planning Study Manual*. n.p.: International Atomic Energy Authority, 1974.

Rogers, S. "A Dynamic Model for Planning Capacity Expansions: An Application to Plant Reliability and Electric Power Systems." Stanford: Stanford University Department of Operations Research, 1970.

Stagg, G. W., and El-Abiad, A. H. *Computer Methods in Power System Analysis*. New York: McGraw-Hill, 1968.

Stanford Research Institute. "Decision Analysis of Nuclear Power Plants in Electrical System Expansion." Project 6469. Menlo Park, Calif., 1968.

Turvey, R. "Marginal Cost." *Economic Journal* 79 (June 1969): 282–300.

_____. "Note." *Economic Journal* 81 (June 1971): 371–75.

_____. "On Investment Choices in Electricity Generation." *Oxford Economic Papers* 15 (1965): 279–86.

_____. *Optimal Pricing and Investment in Electricity Supply*. London: George Allen and Unwin, 1968.

_____, ed. *Public Enterprise*. New York: Penguin, 1968.

Tyren, L. "Short-Range Optimisation of a Hydro-Thermal System by a Gradient Method Combined with Linear Programming." Paper read to the Third Power Systems Computation Conference, Rome, 1969. London: Queen Mary College Department of Electrical and Electronic Engineering, 1969.

United Nations, Economic Commission for Europe. "Economic Methods and Criteria Used in the Electric Power Industry." (ST/ECE/EP21) Brussels, 1963.

_____. "Symposium on the Application of O.R. Methods in the Solving of Economic Problems of Planning and Operation of Large Electric Systems and on the Use of Computers for that Purpose." Proceedings of a conference held at Varna, Bulgaria, May 25–27, 1970. Brussels [?], n.d.

_____. "Symposium on Problems of Multiple Purpose River Development Connected with Hydro-Electric Power Production." (MAD/SYMP/EP) Brussels, August 1969.

van der Tak, H. G. *The Economic Choice between Hydro-Electric and Thermal Power Developments.* Staff Occasional Paper no. 1. Washington, D.C.: World Bank, 1966.

Williamson, O. E. "Peak-Load Pricing and Optimal Capacity under Indivisibility Constraints." *American Economic Review* 56 (September 1966): 810–27.

CHAPTER 14

Optimal Electricity Pricing under Uncertainty

This chapter derives optimal pricing and investment rules for public enterprises where both the demand for output and available production capacity are subject to random disturbances. The analysis relates to thermal electricity generation, but much of it is relevant to other public enterprises producing nonstorable outputs.

Most of the literature on public enterprise pricing ignores these stochastic phenomena affecting demand and available capacity. The analysis of the deterministic case, which has now become standard, produces the rule that price should equal whichever is the higher of either marginal running costs or the price necessary to restrict demand to capacity. Such analysis also produces the investment rule that the present worths of the dual (shadow) values of different kinds of capacity should be equated with their marginal costs. According to this approach, if both rules are always followed, price will equal marginal running costs plus marginal capacity costs.[1]

In seeking equivalents of these results for the stochastic case, two papers offer relevant and useful discussion: one by Lhermitte and Caillé of Electricité de France, which was very stimulating though, to us, not entirely comprehensible, and another by Black, which includes one case analysis substantially identical to the first part of our analysis in this chapter, though couched in different terms. A paper by Brown and Johnson is limited because of their curious treatment of the expected social costs of supply shortfalls when deriving pricing and investment rules. A paper by Littlechild assumed that

---

1. For a statement of the analysis in general terms, see R. Turvey, *Economic Analysis and Public Enterprises* (London: George Allen and Unwin, 1971), pp. 91–93, and idem, "Recent Contributions to the Theory of Marginal Cost Pricing: A Reply," *Economic Journal* 81 (June 1971), p. 374.

price is not set until after demand is known and, thus, is not relevant to our problem.[2]

Consideration of uncertainty raises a number of new problems for pricing policy. The most significant one is that, for a wide class of random disturbances (but not for all), it is not possible to respond to the resultant random excess or shortage of capacity by adjusting prices. Equipment failures and demand fluctuations above or below mean expectations (particularly those induced by the weather) often occur far too rapidly for there to be any price response to the situation. Failure of a generating plant on Thursday cannot be followed by a higher price on Friday, and the price in January cannot be raised when it becomes apparent that January is colder than usual. Even though telecontrol makes the necessary metering technically possible, it would be expensive and, as Black remarks, there would be difficulties in informing consumers of the new price. It would also be scarcely possible to estimate its market clearing level.[3] Sudden and random price fluctuations would in any case impose considerable costs and irritation on consumers. Hence, responsive pricing that always restrains demand to capacity is not practicable, and some interruptions must be accepted unless capacity margins are huge. As huge capacity margins would involve a very large cost, some interruptions are thus desirable. Interruptions are rare or occur for very short durations, and the social cost in such circumstances (letting consumers resort to candles, batteries, emergency diesel-electric supplies, making do with lower voltages, or simply doing without) is judged to be less than the addition to costs for providing yet more reserve generating capacity.[4]

There is one partial exception to the generalization just made that

2. See P. Lhermitte and P. Caillé, "Marginal Cost Pricing in a Random Future," in *Essays on Public Utility Pricing and Regulation,* ed. H. M. Trebbing (East Lansing: Michigan State University Institute of Public Utilities, 1971); Jane Black, "Socially Optimal Pricing with Stochastic Demand," mimeographed (Exeter: University of Exeter, n.d.); G. Brown and M. B. Johnson, "Public Utility Pricing and Output under Risk," *American Economic Review* 59 (March 1969), as well as subsequent correspondence of Brown and Johnson with Turvey and Salkever in *American Economic Review* 60 (June 1970); and S. C. Littlechild, "A State Preference Approach to Public Utility Pricing and Output Under Risk," *The Bell Journal of Economics and Management Science* 3 (Spring 1972): 340–45.

3. See Black, "Socially Optimal Pricing."

4. For a review of the methods of several European countries for determining reserve capacity, see P. W. Cash and E. C. Scott, "Security and Supply in the Planning and Operation of European Power Systems," paper read to the congress of the International Union of Producers and Distributors of Electricity (UNIPEDE), Madrid, 1967. This paper is now a little out of date but, nevertheless, remains interesting and informative.

responsive pricing is not practicable. This exception involves inter-ruptible supplies, where certain consumers agree to be cut off some-times in the event of capacity shortages in return for a lower tariff. Such tariffs are applied to industrial consumers and, where telecon-trol is used, to space- and water-heating appliances in homes. These tariff arrangements are, of course, extremely useful devices; we ig-nore them in most of what follows, not in order to denigrate them but simply in order to concentrate on the main issue of the security of ordinary supply.

Once we leave the very short-run situation, price response to some foreseeable and longer lasting disturbances is possible. Three cases in point are: (a) when there are errors in the forecasts used as the bases for capacity expansion plans (five- to ten-year lead times); (b) when capacity reserves have been based on incorrect estimates of unplanned equipment outages (as has happened, rumor has it, with nuclear stations and large turbo-alternators); and (c) when there is slippage in construction schedules.[5] In such situations, some temporary corrective action in prices may be possible until capacity adjustments can be made.

The peak price of electricity, apart from such longer-term situa-tions, has to be fixed in advance and chosen so as to keep the proba-ble extent of interruptions to an acceptable level. A price too low will increase the probability and thus the expected social cost of interruptions; a price too high will unduly restrict demand and out-put at other times. At the same time, price can still perform the tra-ditional task of showing whether or not more investment is justified.

Off-peak interruptions are not considered below. Significant off-peak interruptions due to inadequate generating capacity should not occur, apart from inadequate spinning or "hot-standby" reserves, a problem we do not discuss. Off-peak maintenance can cause prob-lems of capacity shortages on occasions, but this really calls for a redefinition of the peak period to include such occasions.

In the following analysis of the optimal policy, the objective is to maximize the mean expected area under the demand curve minus the costs of capacity, the mean expected costs of output, and the mean expected social costs of interruptions. The decision variables are capacity, output, price, and (by implication) the probability of supply interruptions. Price is to be fixed in advance, though

---

5. A further case may be to adjust seasonal prices on predominantly storage hydro systems according to the extent of winter snowfall and other factors having foreseeable but lagged effects on water availability. The analysis in this chapter, how-ever, is confined to all-thermal systems.

response is possible over longer periods (for example, between peak periods of different years).

We begin with the simplest case we can construct. This case serves to explain the central ideas in general terms. In the section describing a multiperiod, multiplant case, we introduce some of the complications that are necessary in order to apply the analysis to electricity pricing in a thermal system. Then, in the last section, we discuss various further complications of the problem. Throughout the chapter, all problems of income distribution, externalities, and distortion in other prices are left aside. In addition, distribution costs and investment are not considered, though they are discussed elsewhere.[6]

Peak Period of a Single-Plant System

Suppose, to start, that electricity is generated by only one kind of plant at a constant running cost per kilowatt-hour of f, which may be thought of as a fuel cost. The installed capacity of the plant, which we are to determine, is denoted by X (assumed divisible), and the cost per kilowatt capacity, by C. Since capacity availability is stochastic, the amount that can be used sometimes falls short of X, the difference consisting of unplanned outages. We consider only a single period Θ hours long. We are to determine the kilowatt-hour price, P, which is to be fixed in advance for the whole of the period.

The consequence of uncertainty is that the kilowatt demand at price P is expected to exceed available capacity on occasions. We can say that whether or not this happens depends on the "state of the world." States, s, are defined with respect to both demand and capacity availability. The joint probability of any demand and capacity state is denoted by Π_s. There is a large technical literature on the calculation of such probabilities,[7] but here we do not need to go into the details of the calculation.

Whenever demand exceeds available capacity, operators follow a series of contingency plans, using their judgment to minimize the social cost of shedding load by choosing some combination of voltage reductions, frequency reductions, or power cuts for some customers. We shall treat each kilowatt-hour demanded but not supplied as involving a uniform social cost, a penalty, of b. For each

6. See R. Turvey, *Optimal Pricing and Investment in Electricity Supply* (London: George Allen and Unwin, 1968).

7. For example, see U. G. Knight, *Power Systems Engineering and Mathematics* (Oxford: Pergamon, 1972), Chapter 4.

customer this cost will *exceed* the maximum price he normally would be willing to pay for that electricity rather than do without it. This circumstance arises because the nuisance and cost of an unanticipated sudden power cut exceeds the nuisance and cost that would be involved in doing without that consumption if voluntarily planned ahead and initiated by the consumer. As power cuts affect so many different industrial, commercial, and domestic activities in complicated ways, estimating the nuisance value and costs of power cuts is extremely difficult. The reader will appreciate this fact if he tries to work out for himself how much he would pay to avoid a postulated unexpected power cut of a particular duration at a particular time. Manufacturing firms may be able to estimate the losses from power cuts, or these may be related to value added per kilowatt-hour consumed by industry. Actual numerical estimates are very rare, however, and it is better to think of b as a direct guesstimate by the electricity supplier of the social costs per kilowatt-hour of a typical supply interruption. Thus we shall measure the gross benefits of supply as the area under the demand curve up to the amount demanded *less b* times the kilowatt-hour demanded but not supplied.[8] The objective function is therefore:

$$\sum_s \Theta\Pi_s \int_0^{Q_s} P_s(Q'_s)dQ'_s \quad - \quad \sum_s \Theta\Pi_s V_s f$$

$$\begin{bmatrix} \text{expected area under} \\ \text{demand curve} \end{bmatrix} - \begin{bmatrix} \text{expected fuel} \\ \text{costs} \end{bmatrix}$$

$$- \quad CX \quad - \quad \sum_s \Theta\Pi_s e_s b,$$

$$- \begin{bmatrix} \text{capital} \\ \text{cost} \end{bmatrix} - \begin{bmatrix} \text{expected cost of} \\ \text{interruptions} \end{bmatrix}$$

8. Some economists have commented that they do not like this simple treatment of the expected cost of interruption, preferring to derive b from the demand curve and from assumptions about the incidence of power cuts among consumers with respect to their willingness to pay. We have argued, however, that the price a consumer will pay for planned consumption is different from the price he would pay to avoid a sudden unplanned reduction in supply. Hence, a theoretical treatment would involve elaborate sets of demand curves. Since even the crudest estimates of demand curves are difficult enough in practice, and since our simple analysis using b yields useful results, we have rejected such an approach. It is not an original approach, incidentally, since the concept has been used by several electricity utilities in Europe. See M. Boiteux, "Quality of Service in Generation and Transmission," report of a working group to the UNIPEDE congress, Madrid, 1967; also a subsequent report of the working group with the same title by P. Stasi and R. Janin read to the UNIPEDE congress, Cannes, 1970.

where Q_s = power demand in state s, V_s = power generated in state s, e_s = excess of demand over power generated in state s, and $P_s(Q_s')$ = inverse demand function for state s. These all have the dimension of kilowatts and are multiplied by Θ to get kilowatt-hours.

Our objective function is to be maximized subject to three sets of constraints for all states s. First, there is the relation, just mentioned, between power generated, excess demand, and demand:

$$V_s + e_s - Q_s = 0, \qquad \text{(dual variables } \mu_s\text{).}$$

We could of course use this to substitute for e_s in the objective function, but we have found it algebraically more convenient not to do this, instead, treating e_s, the amount not to be supplied, as though it were an independent, nonnegative decision variable.

Second, there is the requirement that the power generated cannot exceed available capacity. Let $A_s(X)$ be the random variable representing the available capacity:

$$A_s(X) - V_s \geq 0, \qquad \text{(dual variables } K_s\text{).}$$

Finally, the prices are the same in all states of the world and equal to the chosen price P:

$$P_s(Q_s) - P = 0, \qquad \text{(dual variables } \lambda_s\text{).}$$

Multiplying the left-hand side of each constraint by its dual variable and adding them all to the objective function gives the Lagrangian that can now be differentiated with respect to Q_s, V_s, e_s, X, and P, in turn, to yield the first-order conditions. We shall set them out and use them to derive three results that will be given an intuitive meaning in the discussion. In the first condition P is substituted for $P_s(Q_s)$ according to the third set of constraints.

$$\Theta \Pi_s P - \mu_s + \lambda_s \frac{\partial P_s}{\partial Q_s} = 0, \qquad (Q_s > 0); \text{ (A)}$$

$$- \Theta \Pi_s f + \mu_s - K_s = 0, \qquad (V_s > 0); \text{ (B)}$$

$$- \Theta \Pi_s b + \mu_s \leq 0, \qquad (e_s \geq 0). \text{ (C)}$$

(C) means that $\mu_s = \Theta \Pi_s b$ when $e_s > 0$, that is, when demand at P exceeds available capacity, in which case, K_s, the dual of the constraint on capacity, will be positive, too. The equalities in (A) and (B) only hold when demand and generation, Q_s and V_s, are positive, but we assume this to be the case for all s. Similarly we can assume capacity is positive and write as an equality the condition:

$$-C + \sum_s K_s \cdot \frac{\partial A_s}{\partial X} = 0, \qquad\qquad (X > 0). \ (D)$$

Last:

$$\sum_s \lambda_s = 0, \qquad\qquad (P > 0). \ (E)$$

Without pausing to interpret these conditions, we now use them to derive some further expressions which can be interpreted. To do this, we shall denote by ω the subset of states of the world for which demand exceeds available capacity, $e_s > 0$. In these states, the duals of the capacity constraints, the K_s, are necessarily positive. We do not know in advance which of the states are within ω; this emerges from the optimization. The number of states will increase, of course, as the "penalty price" b for failure to supply decreases, and as the cost of an extra kilowatt of capacity increases, that is, as C increases. But, as the present analysis merely describes some characteristics of the optimum, we can proceed as if we know which s are so included.

To obtain the optimal price, P, add (A) and (B), multiply through by $\partial Q_s/dP_s$ and sum over s (which gets rid of the λ_s). Substitute $\partial Q_s/dP$ for $\partial Q_s/dP_s$, substitute for K_s according to (B) and (C), rearrange, and cancel out Θ:[9]

$$P = \frac{\displaystyle\sum_{s \notin \omega} \Pi_s \cdot \frac{\partial Q_s}{\partial P} \cdot f + \sum_{s \in \omega} \Pi_s \cdot \frac{\partial Q_s}{\partial P} \cdot b}{\displaystyle\sum_s \Pi_s \cdot \frac{\partial Q_s}{\partial P}}. \qquad (14.1)$$

If, for the minute, we assume that all $\partial Q_s/\partial P$ are the same, then they cancel out and disappear from the expression, giving P as: $[f \cdot$ (probability of meeting demand)$] + [b \cdot$ (probability of not meeting it)$]$ which is a probability-weighted average of the marginal cost of meeting demand and the marginal social cost of failing to meet it. This is intuitively acceptable as the stochastic equivalent of the deterministic pricing rule cited at the beginning of this chapter. (Note

9. This solution is similar to that posed for the well-known "newsboy problem" of operations research.

that if the probability of not meeting demand approaches zero, it is because b is commensurately larger, so that price does not tend to f as the probability of meeting demand tends to unity.)

To understand how the $\partial Q_s/\partial P$ complication affects the answer, suppose these slopes (of demand with respect to price) to be greater (absolutely) in states of the world where available capacity is inadequate and there are power cuts $s\epsilon\omega$ than in states where all the demand can be met, $s\notin\omega$. A rise in P then would do more to reduce power cuts for $s\epsilon\omega$ than before, giving a net benefit of:

$$\sum_{s\notin\omega} \frac{\partial Q_s}{\partial P} \cdot (b - P).$$

But it would do no more than before to reduce the volume of generation when there are no cuts, giving a loss of net benefit of:

$$\sum_{s\epsilon\omega} \frac{\partial Q_s}{\partial P} \cdot (P - f).$$

Conversely, if demand were more responsive to price in states of the world where demand is less than available capacity, the optimal price would be nearer to f, falling further below b. Which way around the relation may be in practice difficult to decide. Availability and demand responsiveness are presumably related, while demand and demand responsiveness are no doubt connected in some way.

Having obtained the optimal pricing rule, (14.1), we now go on to derive the optimal investment rule. Substituting for K_s in (D) according to (B) and (C) for $s\epsilon\omega$ gives:

$$C = \sum_{s\epsilon\omega} \Pi_s\Theta(b - f) \frac{\partial A_s}{\partial X}. \tag{14.2}$$

The term inside the summation is the net expected benefits from a unit increase of capacity in state s, times the probability of that state, Π_s. Each kilowatt-hour of power cut avoided means that a penalty of b is escaped but that a marginal fuel cost of f is incurred; of the marginal capacity increase, $\partial A_s/\partial X$, is available. Thus investment rule (14.2) simply says that the marginal cost of capacity equals its expected marginal net benefit. This is the stochastic equivalent of the deterministic investment rule cited at the beginning of this chapter.

The combination of the optimal pricing rule (14.1) and the optimal investment rule (14.2), both of which involve the penalty price b and marginal fuel cost f, implies some relation between the optimal price, P, and incremental capacity cost, C. We now proceed to derive this relation. But first it is very important to understand its significance in a world of change where plans and expectations seldom coincide. New generating capacity coming into operation in, say, the years 1973–78 was decided upon during the 1968–73 period. But prices charged from 1973 onward were decided, say, toward the end of 1972. These prices will reflect, therefore, the knowledge and expectations of 1972, which may well be very different from what was previously known and expected and what comprised a basis for determining the shape of the system during 1973. Such divergences are assumed not to exist in the relation to which we now turn. It supposes that forecasts of demand and estimates of costs and plant availability are correct, that construction schedules proceed as planned, and, therefore, that no "corrective" action through prices is necessary. Since expectations of decisionmakers rarely turn out to be so correct, this assumption that they do turn out right must be stressed.

If all the $\partial Q_s / \partial P$ are assumed to be equal, (14.1) can be expressed as:

$$P = f + \sum_{s \in \omega} \Pi_s \, (b - f).$$

Substituting into this expression for $(b - f)$ derivable from (14.2) gives:

$$P = f + \frac{C}{\Theta} \cdot \cfrac{1}{\cfrac{\displaystyle\sum_{s \in \omega} \Pi_s \frac{\partial A_s}{\partial X}}{\displaystyle\sum_{s \in \omega} \Pi_s}} \tag{14.3'}$$

Let us define a_ω as the expected availability of an extra (marginal) unit of capacity during ω, that is, as the denominator of the last part of (14.3'). Typically a_ω is about 90 percent for most thermal plant, though nuclear plant and plant using large turboalternator units are said to have availabilities somewhat lower than this. Expression (14.3') becomes:

$$P = f + \frac{C}{\Theta} \cdot \frac{1}{a_\omega}. \tag{14.3}$$

Thus, when expectations are correct and when all $\partial Q_s/\partial P$ are equal, price equals the marginal fuel costs, f, plus the cost of providing a marginal unit of *available* capacity. (The capacity cost is expressed on a kilowatt-hour basis by dividing by the duration of the period.) This is a similar result to the deterministic case, except that marginal capacity costs are scaled-up because some marginal capacity is not available.

The pricing rule (14.3) shows P independent of b while (14.1) makes P increase with b. There is, however, no contradiction. An increase in the penalty price b, according to (14.2), would justify an increase in capacity, and this would reduce the probability of power cuts. That is to say, it would lower $\Sigma_{s\epsilon\omega}\Pi_s$. So long as the costs of extra available capacity are constant, the rise in b and the fall in $\Sigma_{s\epsilon\omega}\Pi_s$ would exactly offset each other. This means, however, that the rise in b would be just offset by the decline in its weighting in (14.1), leaving P unaltered.

But if b changes when it is too late to alter capacity in response, so that (14.2) and (14.3) are not met, (14.1) still holds, so the optimal price will change, too. Once the time for altering capacity decisions has passed, any change in expectations of demand or available capacity as well as in the penalty price attached to failure of supply will alter the optimal price. Capacity will not be what it would have been if the new circumstances had been foreseen when plans were made. The equation (14.3), to repeat, only holds as long as the expectations relevant to (14.1) and (14.2) continue to coincide.

Now consider the case where $\partial Q_s/\partial P$ are not equal. It is possible that the random disturbances of demand will be heteroskedastic, as in Figure 14.1. We do not know if this is the case, except to note that the industry generally finds that it must scale up its reserve margins to allow for weather, forecasting, and other demand uncertainties in direct proportion to the level of demand.[10] Let:

$$Q_s = (1 + \beta_s)Q$$

and:

$$\frac{\partial Q_s}{\partial P} = (1 + \beta_s)\frac{\partial Q}{\partial P},$$

where Q is the mean expected demand, β_s is a random variable of constant variance, and $\beta_s Q$ is the size of the random disturbance. Substituting for $\partial Q_s/\partial P$ and using (14.1) and (14.2) gives:

10. See Cash and Scott, "Security and Supply," and also Chapter 4 of this book.

FIGURE 14.1. PRICE-DEMAND RELATION IN HETERO-
SKEDASTIC CASE

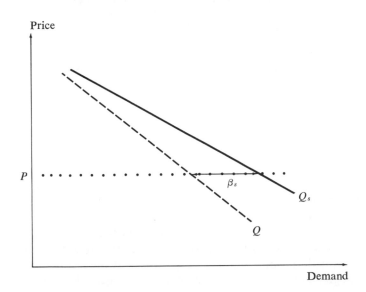

$$P = f + \frac{C}{\Theta} \cdot \frac{m_\omega}{a_\omega}, \qquad (14.3'')$$

where $m_\omega = \Sigma_{s\epsilon\omega}\Pi_s(1 + \beta_s)/\Sigma_{s\epsilon\omega}\Pi_s$ and is the ratio of mean expected demand during power cuts to mean expected demand.[11] The ratio m_ω may be 10 percent to 20 percent or more depending on climate and other uncertainties affecting demand. It is a little bit more than the percentage allowance the industry may make for demand uncertainty when estimating reserve margins, since these margins, of course, are related to the maximum demand that is to be met.

Roughly speaking, then, if expectations which were held when investment decisions were made are still held when prices are fixed, and if demand is heteroskedastic:

11. This result is not dissimilar to the marginal costs derived from typical investment models used in the industry that are of the form: Min $(C'X + F'V)$, where C and F are vectors of costs, and X and V are vectors of capacity and output, respectively. Subject to $V \geq Q$, Q being the vector of demand; $V \leq AX$, where A is a matrix of peak and off-peak availabilities for the various plant; and the "security conditions," $i'AX \geq \hat{Q}M$, where M (scalar) is the reserve margin allowed for uncertainties in peak demand, Q (scalar). The primes denote transpose, and i' is a vector of zeros and ones defined such that $i'A$ is a vector of peak-period availabilities. Such models are reviewed in Chapter 13.

Price per kilowatt-hour equals marginal fuel costs plus the marginal cost of capacity expressed per kilowatt-hour grossed up by (a) the ratio of mean expected demand during power cuts to mean expected demand, and (b) the reciprocal of mean expected availability of the marginal unit of capacity during power cuts.

This grossing up is of the order of 15 to 30 percent for primarily thermal systems.

Multiperiod, Multiplant Case

A single-period model has not got us very far, in view of the importance of daily, weekly, and seasonal variations in the demand for electricity. Such variations in the load involve variations in marginal fuel cost in thermal electricity supply systems where different vintages and types of generating plant can have very different cost structures. Hence, we want to extend the model to cover a whole year which is made up of a number of periods between which demand varies significantly. We use t to denote such a period, so that: $\Theta_t =$ length of period t; $\Pi_{st} =$ probability of state of the world s in period t; $Q_{st} =$ demand in state of the world s in period t; and $e_{st} =$ excess demand in state of the world s in period t. We continue to confine ourselves to generation costs and capacity, without discussing the distribution components of a price structure for electricity.

In principle, the inverse demand function ought to give P_{st} as a function of quantity demanded in all periods. (For example, night demand is *not* independent of day demand, and winter morning demand is *not* independent of autumn morning demand. The total gross expected benefit of supply over a whole year, therefore, is a line integral over all demand curves for all s and all t. Such complications are rehearsed for a deterministic case by Pressman.[12] However, we have not taken this approach here, since, to be frank, the algebra became too cumbersome. Instead, we have tried to manage by representing total gross expected benefit as B and assuming that its partial derivative with respect to the quantity demanded in a state of the world s in period t is the price then ruling. We treat demand in each period as independent of price in other periods so that in each period consumers will take electricity, in the absence of any supply interruption, up to the point where its marginal benefit to them is

12. See I. Pressman, "A Mathematical Formulation of the Peak Load Problem," *The Bell Journal of Economics and Management Science* 11 (Autumn 1970): 304–26.

equal to its marginal cost to them, that is, its price per kilowatt-hour at the time.

Let us assume that two kilowatt-hour prices are possible, a high one, P_h, and low one, P_l, and that a kilowatt price is precluded (a point to which we revert at the end). The first price is to rule in all states of the world in the subset of periods $t\epsilon h$ and the latter price in $t\epsilon l$. The division of the whole set of periods into these two subsets of high price and low price periods could be the subject of more algebra. In practice, however, the two periods can be chosen fairly easily by looking at swings in the load curve in recent years and planned outage schedules for maintenance, and by using common sense. In any case, all the elasticities and crosselasticities are as unmeasurable in this context as in any other. We therefore take the choice of high and low price periods as given.

Finally, we introduce several plant types, p. Thus $p = n$ is nuclear, $p = o$ is oil-fired, and $p = g$ is gas turbine. Their annuitized capacity costs per kilowatt stand in the relation $C^n > C^o > C^g$, while for fuel costs, they stand in the opposite order, $f^n < f^o < f^g$.

The objective function to be maximized is:

$$B - \sum_s \sum_t \sum_p \Theta_t \Pi_{st} V_{st}^p f^p - \sum_p C^p X^p - \sum_s \sum_t \Theta_t \Pi_{st} e_{st} b.$$

The first term, B, has been explained already. V_{st}^p in the second term is the power generated by plant type p in state s, period t. Multiplying by the length of the period, Θ_t, turns this into kilowatt-hours, and multiplying this by fuel cost per kilowatt-hour, f^p, gives the running cost for that type of plant in state s, period t, as $\Theta_t \cdot V_{st}^p \cdot f^p$. Multiplying by probability and summing over all states s, all periods t, and all three plant types p then gives total expected system running costs, the second term. The next term is total (annuitized) capital cost, and the last is the penalty price, b, times mean expected kilowatt-hours demanded but not supplied: the social cost of power cuts.

The constraints are similar to those in the simpler model. First are the constraints on output:

$$\sum_p V_{st}^p + e_{st} - Q_{st} = 0, \qquad \text{(dual variables } \mu_{st}).$$

Second, there are the constraints on capacity:

$$A_{st}^p(X^p) - V_{st}^p \geq 0, \qquad \text{(dual variables } K_{st}^p).$$

Finally, the constraints on price are:

$$P_{st} = \frac{\partial B}{\partial Q_{st}} = P_h \text{ for } t\epsilon h,$$

(dual variables λ_{st}).

$$P_{st} = \frac{\partial B}{\partial Q_{st}} = P_l \text{ for } t\epsilon l$$

These enable us to write out the Kuhn–Tucker conditions rather as before. Since Q_{st}, demand, is always positive, the first is written as an equality. In the next three, the paired conditions mean that the first part is an equality if the second part is an inequality:

$$\Theta_t \Pi_{st} P_{st} - \mu_{st} + \lambda_{st} \cdot \frac{\partial P_{st}}{\partial Q_{st}} = 0, \qquad (Q_{st} > 0); \quad \text{(A')}$$

$$-\Theta_t \Pi_{st} f^p + \mu_{st} - K_{st} \qquad \leq 0, \qquad (V_{st}^p \geq 0); \quad \text{(B')}$$

$$-\Theta_t \Pi_{st} b + \mu_{st} \qquad \leq 0, \qquad (e_{st} \geq 0); \quad \text{(C')}$$

$$-C^p \qquad + \sum_s \sum_t K_{st} \frac{\partial A^p}{\partial X^p} \leq 0, \qquad (X^p \geq 0); \quad \text{(D')}$$

$$\sum_s \sum_{t\epsilon h} \lambda_{st} \text{ and } \sum_s \sum_{t\epsilon l} \lambda_{st} = 0. \qquad \text{(E')}$$

Let us take the typical case that all three plant types are built, so X^n, X^o, and X^g are all positive. Then we can divide the set of all s and all t into eight subsets $h', \ldots, l''''$ classified according to the two column headings and four row stubs in the tableau below. In each of the four rows the tableau shows the production conditions, the corresponding value of the dual of the output constraint μ_{st}, and our notation for the eight subsets of s and t:

Production conditions	Value of μ_{st}	Subsets of s and t	
All $K_{st}^p > 0; e_{st} > 0$	$\Theta_t \Pi_{st} b$	h'	l'
$K_{st}^n, K_{st}^o > 0; K_{st}^g = 0$	$\Theta_t \Pi_{st} f^g$	h''	l''
$K_{st}^n > 0; K_{st}^o, K_{st}^g = 0; V_{st}^g = 0$	$\Theta_t \Pi_{st} f^o$	h'''	l'''
All $K_{st}^p = 0; V_{st}^g, V_{st}^o = 0$	$\Theta_t \Pi_{st} f^n$	h''''	l''''

Consider the second row of the tableau. Nuclear and oil-fired generation equal available capacity, so that K_{st}^n and K_{st}^o are positive, but this is not so for gas turbines, so that $K_{st}^g = 0$. Hence, from (B'), $\mu_{st} = \Theta_t \cdot \Pi_{st} \cdot f^g$. States of the world in high price periods when this happens are denoted by h'', and in low price periods by l''.

Let us assume that all $\partial P_{st}/\partial Q_{st}$ are equal for $t\epsilon h$, so that when (A') is summed over all s and $t\epsilon h$ the λ_{st} term disappears on account of (E'). We perform this summation of (A') for $h', h'', h''',$ and h'''' using the values of μ_{st} shown in the tableau and substituting P_h for P_{st}. The result is an expression for the optimal high price:

$$P_h = \frac{\sum_{h'} \Theta_t \Pi_{st} b + \sum_{h''} \Theta_t \Pi_{st} f^g + \sum_{h'''} \Theta_t \Pi_{st} f^o + \sum_{h''''} \Theta_t \Pi_{st} f^n}{\sum_s \sum_{teh} \Theta_t \Pi_{st}}. \quad (14.4)$$

This is simply a time- and probability-weighted average of marginal costs: $b, f^g, f^o,$ and f^n. $\sum_s \Pi_{st}$ in the denominator sums to unity, so the denominator reduces to $\sum_{teh} \Theta_t$, that is, the total number of hours in the high price periods. It is evident that a completely similar expression holds for the low price, P_l.

Differences in $\partial P_{st}/\partial Q_{st}$ play the same role as differences in $\partial P_s/\partial Q_s$ in the simpler case treated earlier. If demand is more responsive to price during times of shortage (that is, during h' and l') than at other times, the optimum price is above that indicated by (14.4). We shall discuss this situation a little more, shortly.

It is sensible to divide the whole set of periods which constitute the year in such a way that the chances of power cuts during the low price period are negligibly small. In other words, it would be silly to charge the low price at times when demand could exceed available capacity. Thus l' can be treated in practice as an empty subset so that h' is the only subset of s and t when available gas turbine capacity is fully used (and K_{st}^g and e_{st} are positive). It follows, from (B') and (C') that:

$$\sum_s \sum_t K_{st}^g = \sum_{h'} K_{st}^g = \sum_{h'} \Theta_t \Pi_{st} (b - f^g).$$

Using this and (D') gives the marginal investment condition for gas turbine capacity as:

$$C^g = \sum_{h'} \Theta_t \cdot \Pi_{st} (b - f^g) \cdot \frac{\partial A_{st}^g}{\partial X^g}. \quad (14.5)$$

Parallel to (14.2) in the simple case, this says that, if optimized, the marginal annual capacity cost of gas turbines must equal the benefit per extra kilowatt-hour generated, times the mean expected annual hours of use, times the proportion of each marginal kilowatt of capacity that is available.

Investment conditions for an oil-fired and a nuclear plant can also be derived. They are more complicated, however, as they involve a term for fuel savings. The subject is discussed by Turvey in deterministic terms but will not be pursued here.[13]

In the context of this chapter, it is the investment condition for gas turbines that is most interesting; since they take less time to install, changes in expectations are less of a problem. Furthermore, the absence of any fuel-savings term in the optimal investment condition for gas turbines means that straight annuitization of capital costs is legitimate. For base-load plant this is not the case, and a multiyear system analysis is essential.

Combining (14.4) and (14.5) gives a pricing rule parallel to (14.3):

$$P_h = \frac{\sum_{h',h''} \Theta_t \Pi_{st} f^g + \sum_{h'''} \Theta_t \Pi_{st} f^o + \sum_{h''''} \Theta_t \Pi_{st} f^n}{\sum_s \sum_{t \epsilon h} \Theta_t \Pi_{st}}$$

$$+ \frac{\dfrac{C^g}{\sum_{t \epsilon h} \Theta_t}}{\dfrac{\sum_{h'} \Theta_t \Pi_{st} \cdot \dfrac{\partial A_{st}^g}{\partial X^g}}{\sum_{h'} \Theta_t \Pi_{st}}} \cdot \quad (14.6)$$

The first term is simply the time- and probability-weighted average of marginal fuel costs during the high price period. The second is marginal capacity cost of gas turbines spread over the number of hours in the high price periods and grossed up to allow for expected availability of this marginal gas turbine capacity in h'. We can denote the latter quantity by $a_{h'}^g$; it is the denominator of the second term in (14.6).

Suppose that the number of periods in $t \epsilon h$ is chosen so as to include only those periods when, in pretty well all possible states of the world, gas turbines will be running; h''' and h'''' are then empty subsets and (14.6) reduces to:

$$P_h \simeq f^g + \frac{C^g}{\sum_{t \epsilon h} \Theta_t} \cdot \frac{1}{a_{h'}^g}. \qquad (14.7)$$

This means that price per kilowatt-hour in "potential peak periods" should approximately equal the marginal fuel cost of gas

13. See Turvey, *Optimal Pricing*, Chapter 2.

turbines plus their marginal capacity cost per kilowatt of available capacity spread out over the number of potential peak hours. The price for all other hours, P_l, will then equal the time- and probability-weighted average of marginal system fuel costs in all those other hours. (If there were to be more than one price outside potential peak periods, each of these other prices would equal a similar average for the periods to which it related.)

The result expressed in (14.7) assumes that the expectations held when the pricing rule (14.6) is applied are the same as those held when the investment rule (14.5) was applied to determine gas turbine capacity. Thus, if decisions are made in 1974 about gas turbines which are to come into operation in 1976, (14.7) expresses the "potential peak hours" price per kilowatt-hour that will be appropriate in 1976 if no changes in costs or demand expectations occur during the intervening years. This is a difficult condition, but, nonetheless, if there is to be a kilowatt-hour potential peak price, (14.7) may be more useful than the "short-run" pricing rule (14.4). There are two reasons for this. One is that limited information and rough and ready decisionmaking in practice may make (14.7) easier to apply. The second is that it may be desirable to fix tariffs for a few years in advance and to avoid altering them frequently (apart from adjustments to allow for inflation).

This second point is related to the rather confused issue of whether tariffs should reflect short-run or long-run marginal costs. The ideal answer, presumably, is that tariffs should be announced now, in the light of present expectations, for each of the next ten or so years so that customers have the information that will enable them, in their turn, to take optimal short-, medium- and long-term decisions. But, in practice, what is wanted is a tariff structure that will endure for a longer period and only be modified to reflect major changes in cost levels. Thus, the aim is rather to frame a tariff which will be right on average over a succession of years and which must contain some sort of compromise between long-run and short-run considerations; (14.7) is clearly useful in this context, together with the equivalent of (14.4) for the low price, p_l (or for more than one low price).

Indeed, investments in gas turbines, which have short lead times, are a typical short-run response to a situation of capacity shortages and can be thought of as a way of stabilizing prices. Such investments are a cheaper way of meeting peak demand at an acceptable probability than price increases; it also happens that their economic characteristic of low capital and high running costs makes them attractive for peak-load service, and this fact, combined with the desirable technical characteristic of fast startup during emergency, often makes it desirable to include them in long-run plans. Hence, it will often be found that (14.7) is not irrelevant to computations of short-run or long-run marginal costs.

Finally, we may wish to consider the case where demand disturbances (like capacity disturbances) are heteroskedastic:

$$Q_{st} = (1 + \beta_{st})Q_t,$$

and:

$$\frac{\partial Q_{st}}{\partial P} = (1 + \beta_{st}) \frac{\partial Q_t}{\partial P_h},$$

where Q_t is the mean expected value of Q_{st}, β_{st} is a random variable of constant variance, and the size of the disturbance is assumed to increase directly with Q_t, and is $Q_t \cdot \beta_{st}$. (Our analysis so far in this section has assumed all $\partial P_{st}/\partial Q_{st}$ to be equal, that is, a homoskedastic disturbance of the form $Q_{st} = Q_t + \zeta_{st}$, where ζ_{st} is a random variable of constant variance.) Using the above expressions for $\partial Q_{st}/\partial P_h$, we find that (14.7) becomes:

$$P_h \simeq f^g + \frac{C^g}{\sum_{t \in h} \Theta_t} \cdot \frac{m_{h'}}{a_{h'}{}^g}, \tag{14.8}$$

where $m_{h'}$ is the mean expected demand during power cuts divided by mean expected demand (exactly as in the simple case). Some people may regard expression (14.8) as being more realistic than (14.7).

Note that expected marginal running costs are unaffected by assumptions as to the nature of the disturbance terms; thus, the off-peak rule derived above (that is, expression (14.4) for $t \epsilon l$) is unaffected.

Further Complications

Our analysis has related only to generation on all thermal systems. In Chapter 15 we look briefly at hydro-thermal systems. We do not inquire here into the problems of outages on transmission and distribution networks, nor do we discuss problems related to holding spinning and "hot-standby" reserves on the system. All these matters are highly relevant to the topic we are discussing; we bypass them merely to keep this chapter at a tolerable length. We shall, however, conclude with a few miscellaneous remarks on: analysis with several investment periods, planned outages (maintenance), two-part tariffs, and interruptible tariffs.

It is certainly possible to incorporate the above analysis in the context of multiyear investment models of the type reviewed and discussed in Chapter 13. (Note that the stochastic models can be formulated in the LP form.) How much the stochastic equivalents of these models would add to our analysis is not obvious. Where gas turbines are the main peak-load plant, our conclusions are unaffected for the reason given earlier—straight annuitization of capital costs is legitimate. Where the peak-load plant consists of old vintages of thermal plant, or pumped storage, the answer may be more complicated. Certainly the actual design of an investment program—and to that extent the computation of mean expected marginal costs—must rest on a dynamic analysis.

Planned outages for maintenance may extend to as much as six weeks for some plants. Such scheduled work withdraws plant from availability in quite a different way from the stochastic fluctuations that alone have been brought into the analysis above. (It does, however, itself contain a stochastic element in that the amount of work required may not be known fully until it has started, since problems may be spotted during the process.)

The cost of planned maintenance work will be minimized if it is spread evenly over the year, apart from holidays. But this will subtract from the amount of capacity available at times of potential peak, necessitating a larger total capacity and adding to capital costs. Even if there were no technical system security constraints on the planning of maintenance, an even spread will therefore be avoided; there is a trade-off between maintenance costs and capacity costs. The selection of the optimal schedule of planned maintenance is thus a complex matter. Developing a maintenance schedule has to be a separate exercise from long-term system planning, on the one hand, and short-term operational planning (for which it forms part of the background), on the other. Consequently, no purpose would be served by adding a simplified representation of the maintenance schedule to the model formulated above. But if planned maintenance is treated as exogenously determined, it impinges upon our analysis in three ways. The first is that the annual expected maintenance costs of different types of capacity enter into marginal capacity costs alongside their capital component. The C term, therefore, must have these costs added in. The second consequence is that since available capacity varies systematically through time as planned maintenance is carried out, the times when the gap between expected load and expected availability is low—times when there is a risk of power cuts—may not be confined to the time when the load is greatest. In a system with a winter peak, for example, large outages for maintenance in spring and autumn may mean that the risk of power cuts is as large on weekdays then as in the winter. Our analysis still applies to such a case, provided that "potential peak hours" is understood to cover all these days and not just the winter days when the load is greatest in absolute terms. What matters is the gap between expected demand $\Sigma_s \Pi_{st} \cdot Q_{st}$ and total expected available capacity $\Sigma_s \Sigma_p \Pi_{st} \cdot A_{st}^p(X^p)$, where availability, A_{st}^p, now reflects planned as well as unplanned outages. P_h should apply to all periods when this gap is small enough for the probability of supply interruptions to be worth bothering about.

The third consequence of the planned maintenance pattern is its influence upon the cost structure in other periods. Marginal cost may change (even when the load is constant) as some plants are taken out for maintenance and others are brought back. This can be particularly important in small systems, on account of the indivisibility of plant, a phenomenon that we have ignored in our algebra. In addition to this, maintenance costs have variable components, in that they increase with the frequency of plant startups and shutdowns, and running times.

Next we wish to make the point that, in taking a system of kilowatt-hour prices in our analysis, we do not mean to assert that a kilowatt charge is never preferable to a higher kilowatt-hour price during potential peak periods. Even if, on account of diversity, there are problems in a charge for kilowatts, it may be preferable because metering is easier or because it is better for reflecting transmission and distribution costs. Fundamentally, the choice between a kilowatt charge and a peak kilowatt-hour price rests on the incentives they present to consumers; this is a matter that cannot be illuminated by the model discussed above.

Finally, we turn to interruptible tariffs, a device applicable in practice only to a small number of large consumers. In terms of the tariff structure that we have assumed, an interruptible tariff would involve a lower P_h equal to a time- and probability-weighted average of marginal fuel costs over states and periods when total demand is less than available capacity. In system planning, the amount of interruptible load would have to be considered in calculating the probability of interruptions in supply to all other consumers.

CHAPTER 15

Cost Structure in Hydro and Hydro-Thermal Systems

Hydroelectric systems where water is stored present a more complicated picture than do thermal systems because the choice between using water now or storing it for use in a later period introduces an interdependence of costs in different periods. Furthermore, there are many different types of mixed hydro-thermal systems. The balance between hydro and thermal capacity and the pattern of operation also depends on a large number of factors, including relative costs, the potential for water storage, and the seasonal and daily fluctuations in load and water flow.

This complexity and variation necessitate simplification and preclude generality. In order to gain insight into cost structure, we find that we have to conduct our analysis in terms of simple and three particular cases.

We have chosen to make four main simplifications: First, we deal with a stationary rather than a growing generating system. This means that the analysis relates to a single year, so that the system costs that are to be minimized are one year's operating costs plus annuitized capital costs. Second, we argue in terms of a single reservoir and hydro plant. There are, in fact, procedures for treating a set of reservoirs and hydro plants in terms of a single "equivalent," this simplification being one often adopted by engineers for some problems.[1] Third, we shall confine ourselves to a deterministic anal-

---

1. See, for example, J. Lindqvist, "Operation of a Hydrothermal Electric System: A Multi-stage Decision Process," *IEEE Transactions* (April 1962); N. V. Arvanitidis and J. Rosing, "Composite Representation of a Multireservoir Hydro-Electric Power System" and "Optimal Operation of Multireservoir Systems Using Composite Representation," both *IEEE Transactions, Power Apparatus and Systems* PAS-89 (February 1970); and R. R. Booth, "Power System Simulation Model Based on Probability Analysis," *IEEE Transactions* (February 1972).

FIGURE 15.1. WATER INFLOWS AND OUTFLOWS OF AN
ALL-HYDRO SYSTEM

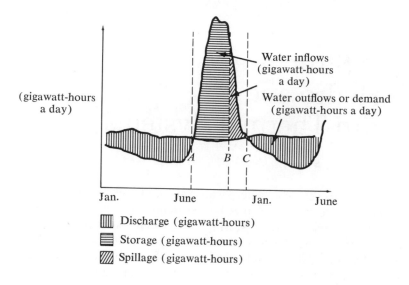

FIGURE 15.1. WATER INFLOWS AND OUTFLOWS OF AN
ALL-HYDRO SYSTEM

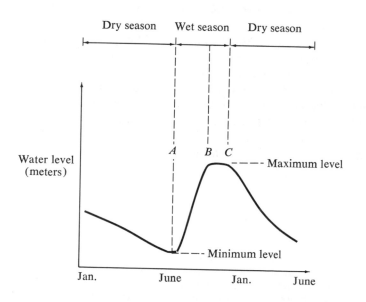

FIGURE 15.2. RESERVOIR LEVEL OF AN
ALL-HYDRO SYSTEM

ysis to start with, leaving out all formal analysis of uncertainty until the final section. Fourth, for mixed hydro-thermal systems, we shall consider the case where there is only one type of thermal plant.

The three particular cases chosen are a pure hydro system and two mixed systems where thermal energy is used to augment hydro energy: In the first case, the pure hydro system has a single wet season and a single dry season where water has to be put into storage in the wet season to help meet requirements in the dry season. In the first mixed system, thermal plant is necessary because sufficient water cannot be stored in the wet season to enable hydro generation to provide all the energy required in the dry season. This case arises when wet season flows are too limited, when there are physical limitations on reservoir capacity, or when further capacity could be built but would cost more than thermal supplementation. In the other case of a mixed system, thermal plant is necessary because even in the wet season insufficient water is available to meet energy requirements.

The growth of the load and development of hydro resources can move a system from the one to the other of these sets of circumstances, so the latter is more common in high income countries. In the next three sections of this chapter we examine these cases one by one, starting each section with an intuitive analysis and then deriving the results algebraically. The first case naturally is the simplest and serves as an introduction to the other two.

A Hydro System

It is convenient to treat the demands on a hydro system for power and energy separately, putting the analysis together afterward. We first consider the energy demands, assuming that there is spare turbine capacity all year around.

The river flow into the system may typically fluctuate as in Figure 15.1, where inflows are measured in kilowatt-hours of potential energy a day. Storage, shown in Figure 15.2, begins at A, the end of the dry season and the beginning of the wet season, and increases until the reservoirs are full at B. Spilling or sluicing of the water, or both, then begins and continues as long as energy demands are below the energy inflows. It is not until energy demands exceed inflows that discharge begins (point C) and reservoir levels fall.

For many countries, where hydro energy is provided at a few points on one or two large rivers, the spilling and sluicing period, B to C, can be quite long, since the energy inflows far exceed wet season energy demands plus what needs to be stored. Extra output in the whole of the wet season, A to C, can be provided simply by passing more water through the turbines (if, as we assume for the moment, there is sufficient turbine capacity). The marginal costs of output in the wet season are therefore zero.

For countries where hydro energy is or can be provided by many rivers, or at several points on one or two large rivers, or both, storage capacities can be matched more closely to the river flows. In such a case the spilling and sluicing period, B to C, will be quite short. In fact, there may be no spilling or sluicing at all in dry years. Nevertheless, the marginal costs of providing energy are still zero in the wet season, provided forecasts and planning are accurate, since the plans must insure that there is sufficient access to this hydro energy. Energy demands in the wet season could be met, after all, by a run-of-river plant with zero running costs; it is only when there is unused hydro energy, either in the form of spilling or sluicing at existing schemes, or in the form of the river flows of untapped sites, that the marginal cost of energy in the wet season is zero. Note that a more general definition of this season is that it is the time of year when energy inflows exceed demands.

It is when energy inflows are less than energy demands—that is, during the "dry season"—that marginal costs arise. Extra energy demands then cannot be met without the provision of extra storage capacity, so the marginal costs of energy at any point in time of the dry season are the marginal costs of providing storage capacity. In the short run, when capacity is given, if energy demand in the dry season threatens to exceed energy in storage plus energy available from dry season river flows, then the price required is one that will keep energy demands down to this amount. If the growth of energy demand in the dry season is such that this rationing price exceeds the marginal cost of extra storage, then more storage capacity is worthwhile. Thus with correct forecasting and optimal investment, the optimal rationing price will equal the marginal cost of extra storage.

We can now bring the demand for power capacity into the picture. In off-peak hours, marginal costs are as just described. In the hours when power demands approach the capacity of the system, the marginal costs of providing extra capacity are to be added to the marginal cost of providing energy. Suppose, for example, that the marginal cost of energy in the dry season is R a kilowatt-hour, and the capacity cost per kilowatt-hour of peak demand is $C^h/\Theta_{t'}$, where $\Theta_{t'}$ is the duration of the peak. We then have the following marginal cost structure:

	Peak	Off-peak
Dry season	$\dfrac{C^h}{\Theta_{t'}} + R$, or 0	R
Wet season	$\dfrac{C^h}{\Theta_t}$, or 0	0

More generally, marginal cost in any period will be: (a) Zero when water is spilling or otherwise unused and demand is less than generating capacity; (b) marginal annuitized generating capacity cost when demand equals generating capacity but water is spilling or otherwise unused; (c) marginal annuitized effective storage cost during those discharge periods when demand is less than generating capacity;[2] or (d) the sum of (c) and (d) when both constraints (capacity and energy) are effective simultaneously.

Cases when water is never spilled (except due to random fluctuations in demand and water supplies) occur when hydro resources are fully used or are not competitive with thermal energy. Marginal costs of supply are then no longer zero, even at off-peak during the wet season, signifying the need to ration hydro energy by price and to provide the extra output from thermal plant, a case we consider in the next section.

The above results can be derived more compactly from a simple model of the system, which has the additional advantage that we can better represent the constraint on capacity expansion planning. Let X^h, then, be the system's aggregate available hydro power capacity (measured in kilowatts) and $\hat{S}$ be its peak storage capacity (measured in kilowatt-hours). If C^h is the annuitized capital cost per kilowatt of available hydro power capacity, and R is the annuitized capital cost per kilowatt-hour of reservoir storage capacity, the total costs to be minimized are:

$$C^h X + R\hat{S} \tag{15.1}$$

This minimization is subject to fixed constraints (discussed more fully in Chapter 8) that provide equations (15.2) through (15.6). The first of these is the capacity constraint that output of the hydro plant in period t, U_t^h, can never exceed the available capacity, X^h:

$$U_t^h - X^h \leq 0; \qquad \text{(dual variables } K_t\text{).} \tag{15.2}$$

Available capacity is actual capacity multiplied by an availability allowance for planned and forced outages; this allowance is gener-

---

2. Often these discharge periods are referred to as the critical period.

ally better than 0.9 for hydro systems. Correspondingly, C^h is the cost per kilowatt of available capacity and, thus, is somewhat higher than the cost per actual kilowatt.

The second constraint relates to water flows and storage: that the amount used during a period plus that in store at its end cannot exceed the inflow during the period (corrected for evaporation and seepage) plus the water in store at the beginning of the period. These are all expressed in kilowatt-hours. The water constraint is:

$$S_t \quad + \quad U_t^h \Theta_t \quad - \quad w_t W \quad - \quad S_{t-1} \quad \leq \quad 0,$$

$$\begin{bmatrix} \text{Water in} \\ \text{store at} \\ \text{end of} \\ \text{period} \end{bmatrix} + \begin{bmatrix} \text{Power output} \\ \text{during period} \\ \text{times length} \\ \text{of period} \end{bmatrix} - \begin{bmatrix} \text{Water} \\ \text{inflow} \\ \text{during} \\ \text{period} \end{bmatrix} - \begin{bmatrix} \text{Water in} \\ \text{store at} \\ \text{beginning} \\ \text{of period} \end{bmatrix}$$

$$\text{(dual variables } E_t\text{).} \quad (15.3)$$

S_t is the amount in store at the end of t; U_t^h is the kilowatt output of the hydro plant, so is multiplied by the length of the period Θ_t to get output in kilowatt-hours. W is annual water inflow corrected for losses, and w_t is the fraction of W occurring during t. (This information will prove useful for discussion of the stochastic case, since, though W varies from year to year, the time pattern within each year is roughly similar.)

Third and fourth, there are constraints relating to the highest and lowest possible amounts of storage and to these we attach the respective dual variables H_t and L_t. The first of these thus states that the amount of water stored S_t can never exceed capacity $\hat{S}$:

$$S_t - \hat{S} \leq 0 \qquad \qquad \text{(dual variables } H_t\text{).} \quad (15.4)$$

Similarly, the reservoir can never contain less than some minimal amount of water, q:

$$q - S_t \leq 0 \qquad \qquad \text{(dual variables } L_t\text{).} \quad (15.5)$$

Both of these last two constraints leave out possible complications in order to keep the analysis simple. For instance, we could have made the minimum required level of storage a large amount, expressed as a fraction of capacity, in order to represent a policy of carrying over some energy from one year to another because of the risk that the coming year might be a particularly dry one.

The fifth constraint requires hydro power output, U_t^h, to meet power demanded, Q_t. Since the duals of this constraint are marginal costs, we symbolize them with M_t:

$$Q_t - U_t^h \leq 0 \qquad\qquad \text{(dual variables } M_t\text{)}. \quad (15.6)$$

Finally, just as we have allowed a margin for stochastic plant availability in our deterministic formulation by having a fixed (implicit) relation between available and total capacity, so we need to allow a margin for stochastic demand variability. We can express this implicitly, too, by interpreting X^h as actual capacity less not only an allowance for nonavailability but also less an allowance for the risk of peak demand exceeding its expected value. Thus, if a hydro plant margin of 20 percent is required to allow for uncertain availability and uncertain peak demand together, X^h is $1/1.2$ of actual capacity and C^h is 1.2 times the cost of a kilowatt of new capacity.

The Kuhn–Tucker conditions for minimization subject to these constraints can be written out as follows:

$$C^h - \sum_t K_t = 0, \qquad\qquad \text{(A)}$$

$$E_t - E_{t+1} + H_t - L_t = 0, \qquad\qquad \text{(B)}$$

$$R - \sum_t H_t = 0, \qquad\qquad \text{(C)}$$

$$K_t + \Theta_t E_t - M_t = 0. \qquad\qquad \text{(D)}$$

We have written these as equalities because X^h, S_t, $\hat{S}$ and all U_t^h—that is, generating capacity, actual storage, storage capacity, and output in all periods of the year—are all positive.

What we are interested in is M_t, marginal cost per kilowatt, or M_t/Θ_t, marginal cost per kilowatt-hour. Consider first the case when the generating capacity constraint (15.2) is never effective, so that K_t is zero. Then, from (D) above, M_t equals $\Theta_t E_t$.

When (B) is an equality, E_t will remain constant from one period to another, except that it will go up by H_t when the upper storage constraint is binding and down by L_t when the lower constraint becomes binding. Since we are dealing with a recurring cycle, this means that E_t has only two values. One, the higher one, lasts from the last period when the reservoir is full until the period when it becomes empty, that is, during discharge periods. The lower value lasts all the rest of the time, or during both filling and spilling periods.

During spilling periods the water constraint (15.3) is not binding, so that E_t is zero. Hence, the lower value of E_t is zero. Since $\Theta_t E_t = M_t$ (when K_t is zero), we have thus shown that marginal cost (in the absence of any shortage of generating capacity) is zero not only when water is being spilled but also during the whole preceding sequence of filling-up periods. Extra generation during any of these periods would involve less filling-up then and more later. But this, in turn, only involves less spilling later, and so is costless.

The storage constraint (15.4) may be binding for several successive periods, during each of which water is spilled. But H_t will be positive only for the last of these periods, since extra reservoir capacity is only useful if it provides more water for discharge. Hence, if period f is the next period, that is, the first drawdown period, (B) tells us that:

$$E_f = H_{f-1},\tag{15.7}$$

since $E_{f-1} = 0$ and $L_f = 0$. As H_t is positive only in $f - 1$, (C) thus becomes:

$$R = H_{f-1},\tag{15.8}$$

so:

$$E_f = R,\tag{15.9}$$

and:

$$\frac{M_f}{\Theta_f} = R, \text{ when } K_f = 0.\tag{15.10}$$

During all the drawdown periods the marginal cost of a kilowatt-hour is thus R, the annuitized cost of an extra kilowatt-hour of storage capacity.

We now bring in generating capacity costs, supposing that the capacity constraint (15.2) is binding and, hence, that K_t is positive in periods $t'\epsilon t$. Then (A) and (D) give:

$$C^h = K_{t'},\tag{15.11}$$

$$M_{t'} = \Theta_{t'}E_{t'} + K_{t'},\tag{15.12}$$

so marginal cost per kilowatt-hour is:

$$\frac{M_{t'}}{\Theta_{t'}} = E_{t'} + \frac{C^h}{\Theta_{t'}},\tag{15.13}$$

which equals $R + C^h/\Theta_{t'}$ if the peak period occurs in the dry season and $C^h/\Theta_{t'}$ if the peak period occurs in the wet season.

If there are several peak periods, that is, several periods when $U_t^h = X^h$, then C^h is a joint cost and cannot be allocated among the various peak periods. If this were a benefit-minus-cost maximizing model instead of a cost minimizing model, there would be, of course, a unique demand-determined allocation of the joint cost.

Thermal Supplementation in the Dry Season

In the wet season, hydro energy inflows exceed energy demands, and the marginal costs of energy are still zero. When the daily peak demands approach the system's power capacity, total marginal costs rise accordingly to reflect the marginal costs of providing capacity.

In the dry season, an increment of energy demand can be met only by more output from the thermal plant. If there is spare capacity on the thermal plant, the marginal cost will clearly be the marginal costs of fuel. But this situation is unlikely unless there is overinvestment in thermal capacity, since in the dry season thermal plant will be on base load operation, as illustrated in Figure 15.3

FIGURE 15.3. HYDRO-THERMAL SYSTEM OPERATIONS WITH THERMAL BACKUP FOR DRY SEASON

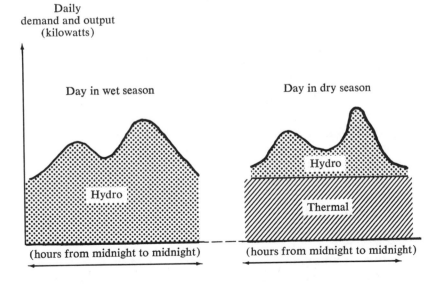

FIGURE 15.4. HYDRO-THERMAL SYSTEM OPERATIONS WITH THER-
MAL BACKUP FOR DRY SEASON AND PEAKS IN WET SEASON

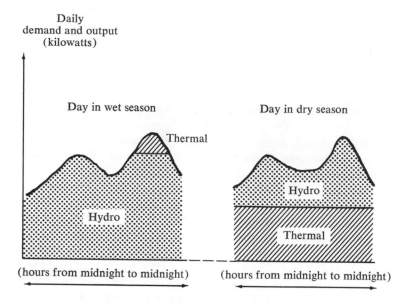

Thus, an increment of energy demand requires extra thermal capacity. The cheapest way to obtain the extra thermal energy, given
that this extra thermal capacity is needed, will be to keep the extra
thermal capacity down to a minimum and to use it fully by spreading
the extra thermal output over all the hours of the dry season. Thus,
the following elements appear in the marginal cost per kilowatt-hour:
(a) marginal fuel costs, and (b) marginal capacity costs of thermal
plant divided by the number of hours in the dry season. But since
extra thermal capacity means that commensurately less hydro power
capacity is needed (we have a given peak demand), we subtract from
(a) and (b) the following: (c) marginal capacity costs of hydro plant
divided by the number of hours in the dry season. This substitution
of thermal for hydro capacity may have the effect of requiring some
thermal production to help meet peak demand in the wet season, depending on the shape of the daily demand curves, as shown in Figure
15.4. In this case, the subtraction of (c) from (b) will be partially
offset by the fuel cost now incurred at peak in the wet season. Peak
kilowatt-hours in the wet season now will have a marginal cost of
fuel, and only off-peak wet season kilowatt-hours will have a zero
marginal cost.

Turning from energy to capacity, extra peak demand will be met
most cheaply by extra hydro capacity, in the kind of system we are

discussing, so its marginal capacity cost will determine the marginal cost of kilowatts. It is worth noting, however, that one of the complications that we have omitted, and that occasionally could give a different answer, is that the effective capacity of hydro plant can vary according to water conditions. Our assumption that water is measured in kilowatt-hours effectively rules out variations in water-head.[3] Such complications can be very important in practice.

Again it is instructive to derive our results from a simple model. To our previous model we add the costs of thermal generation, with the following notation: X^f and C^f are the power capacity and annuitized capacity costs, respectively, of thermal plant; U_t^f is the power output of the thermal plant in period t; and F is fuel costs per kilowatt-hour (which we assume not to vary with output). Our model is now:

$$\text{Minimize} \quad \underbrace{C^h X^h}_{\begin{bmatrix} \text{Cost of} \\ \text{hydro} \\ \text{capacity} \end{bmatrix}} + \underbrace{C^f X^f}_{\begin{bmatrix} \text{Cost of} \\ \text{thermal} \\ \text{capacity} \end{bmatrix}} + \underbrace{R\hat{S}}_{\begin{bmatrix} \text{Cost of} \\ \text{storage} \end{bmatrix}}$$

$$+ \underbrace{\sum_t F U_t^f \theta_t,}_{\begin{bmatrix} \text{Fuel costs} \end{bmatrix}} \quad (15.14)$$

subject to capacity constraints on plant output:

$$U_t^h - X^h \leq 0 \qquad \text{(dual variables } K_t^h\text{)}, \quad (15.15)$$

$$U_t^f - X^f \leq 0 \qquad \text{(dual variables } K_t^f\text{)}, \quad (15.16)$$

Second, to the water flow and storage constraints (15.3), (15.4), and (15.5), restated here for convenience. The water constraint is $S_t + U_t^h \cdot \theta_t - w_t W - S_{t-1} \leq 0$ (dual variables E_t); the storage constraints are $S_t - S \leq 0$ (dual variables H_t), and $q - S_t \leq 0$ (dual variables L_t). Third, to the constraints that output must meet demand:

$$Q_t - U_t^h - U_t^f \leq 0 \qquad \text{(dual variables } M_t\text{)}, \quad (15.17)$$

---

3. To relax this assumption, (15.3) and (15.17) would be written in terms of water quantities and use a conversion factor, which is a function of the waterhead, to obtain U_t^h from the rate of discharge. Intuitively, marginal cost is the cost of providing available hydro kilowatt capacity that is needed to cater for low waterhead conditions.

and, finally, to a constraint on the maximum level of storage capacity that can be constructed:

$$\hat{S} - S \text{ max} \leq 0 \qquad \text{(dual variable } \lambda\text{). (15.18)}$$

The Kuhn–Tucker conditions can now be set out as follows:

$$C^h - \sum_t K_t^h = 0, \qquad (\text{A}')$$

$$C^f - \sum_t K_t^f = 0, \qquad (\text{B}')$$

$$E_t - E_{t+1} + H_t - L_t = 0, \qquad (\text{C}')$$

$$R - \sum_t H_t + \lambda = 0, \qquad (\text{D}')$$

$$K_t^h + \Theta_t E_t - M_t = 0, \qquad (\text{E}')$$

$$\Theta_t F + K_t^f - M_t = 0; \; U_t^f \geq 0. \qquad (\text{F}')$$

In (F′), the left-hand expression equals zero only when U_t^f, thermal generation, is positive. The other five conditions have been written as equalities because the relevant decision variables—X^h (hydro capacity) and X^f (thermal capacity), S_t (actual storage) and $\hat{S}$ (storage capacity), and U_t^h (hydro generation)—are always positive.

As before, we can interpret generating capacities as being net of the reserve percentages that allow for the risks of plant outages and of demand being higher than expected.

In the wet season, as in the pure hydro case, we suppose that water is spilled some of the time so that the marginal cost of energy is zero for the whole of the season. If the peak demand period occurs in the wet season, then, for the period in question, the peak marginal cost is C^h/Θ_t. This cost, too, is no different from the pure hydro case.

The contrast with the pure hydro case arises in the dry season when the thermal plant is continuously on base load. We denote the periods constituting the dry season by $d\epsilon t$. During the dry season, that is, from the first period when the reservoir is less than full until the period when it reaches its minimum level, (C′) shows the E_d will be constant. Hence, according to (E′), M_d/Θ_d will be the same in all d except for the peak period, when K_d^h/Θ_d becomes positive. Since F is given, (F′) shows this to imply that K_d^f/Θ_d will also be the same in all d except for the peak period. From (E'), in the peak period d', $M_{d'}/\Theta_{d'}$ and $K_{d'}{}^f/\Theta_d$ both rise from these uniform levels by $K_d{}^h/\Theta_{d'}$, and this, from (A'), equals $C^h/\Theta_{d'}$.

Consider first all the nonpeak periods of the dry season, $d \neq d'$ where d' is the peak period, and denote the common value of K_d^f/Θ_d in these nonpeak periods by K. Then (B') can be transformed as follows:

$$C^f = \sum_d K_d^f = \sum_d \Theta_d \cdot \frac{K_d^f}{\Theta_d} \tag{15.19}$$

$$= K \sum_{d \neq d'} \Theta_d + \Theta_{d'} \left(K + \frac{C^h}{\Theta_d} \right)$$

$$= K \sum_d \Theta_d + C^h.$$

Hence:

$$K = \frac{C^f - C^h}{\sum_d \Theta_d}, \tag{15.20}$$

and substituting in (F') gives marginal cost per kilowatt-hour in a nonpeak period as:

$$\frac{M_d}{\Theta_d} = F + \frac{C^f - C^h}{\sum_d \Theta_d}. \tag{15.21}$$

In the peak period, as we have just seen, marginal cost per kilowatt-hour is higher by $C^h/\Theta_{d'}$:

$$\frac{M_{d'}}{\Theta_d} = F + \frac{C^f - C^h}{\sum_d \Theta_d} + \frac{C^h}{\Theta_{d'}}. \tag{15.22}$$

Equation (15.21) is, of course, the result described earlier. To interpret equation (15.22) we rearrange it as:

$$\begin{array}{c}\text{Peak marginal}\\ \text{kilowatt-hour}\\ \text{cost}\end{array} = C^h \left(\frac{1}{\Theta_{d'}} - \frac{1}{\sum_d \Theta_d} \right) + C^f \left(\frac{1}{\sum_d \Theta_d} \right) + F. \tag{15.23}$$

One extra kilowatt-hour spread evenly over the $\Theta_{d'}$ hours of the peak period requires extra capacity of $1/\Theta_{d'}$ kilowatts, net of the plant margin; $1/\Sigma_d \Theta_d$ of the extra capacity will have to be thermal, so that, over the dry period as a whole, 1 kilowatt-hour can be added to the base load met by the thermal plant. The fuel cost of this will be F.

Thermal Energy in Both Seasons

In the wet season, hydro generally will be on base load, with thermal providing the peaking capacity (and, in larger systems, a portion of base load capacity, too). In the dry season, the situation is reversed, with thermal on base load service and hydro providing peaking capacity. These operations are illustrated in Figure 15.5. In the dry season, thermal plant may also be operated for short duration at the peaks, if hydro capacity is insufficient (see Figure 15.6).

An increase of demand in the wet season will require extra output from the thermal plant if the hydro is operating at capacity. Marginal costs are then equal to marginal costs of fuel, plus, if demand is at the peak, the marginal costs of providing capacity.

At time of low demand in the wet season, thermal plant may not

FIGURE 15.5. HYDRO-THERMAL SYSTEM OPERATIONS WITH THERMAL BACKUP FOR WET AND DRY SEASONS

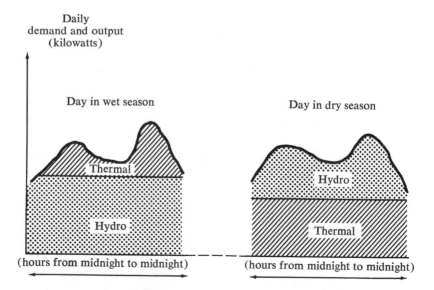

330

FIGURE 15.6. HYDRO-THERMAL SYSTEM OPERATIONS WITH THER-
MAL BACKUP FOR WET SEASON AND DRY SEASON WITH THER-
MAL PEAKING

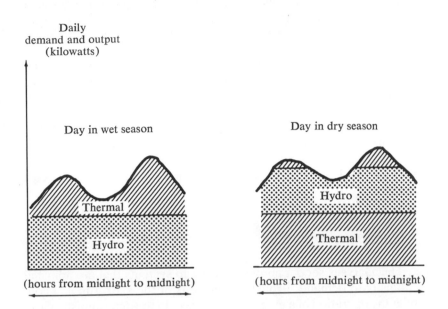

be operating at all, and the hydro plant may be operating at below
capacity. Extra demand could thus be met by hydro. However, in
the case we are now considering, available hydro energy is
restricted even in the wet season, so hydro output will have to be reduced at a later time and thermal energy eventually will be required
to restore storage to the desired level. Hence the above rule, that
marginal energy costs equal marginal fuel costs, still applies.

The results determined above also apply to the dry season, where
thermal energy is needed at and near peak as well as for the base
load (see Figure 15.6). Extra output eventually must come from the
thermal plant, and so marginal costs equal marginal fuel costs plus,
at peak demand times, marginal capacity costs. If, throughout the
dry season, the thermal plant is working at full capacity (as in figure
15.5), extra thermal capacity will be needed to meet extra demands
whenever they occur.

These results can be obtained from the model. Away from the
peak period, expression (F′) gives:

$$\frac{M_t}{\Theta_t} = F + \frac{K_t^f}{\Theta_t}, \qquad \text{(for } U_t^f > 0\text{), (15.24)}$$

331

so that, whenever the thermal plant is operating at less than capacity, the marginal cost of energy is F.

Even if there are periods when thermal plant is not operating, the marginal cost of energy would still be F, since equation (E') shows that it would equal E_t and equation (C'), in turn, shows that E_t would remain constant from period to period within both dry and wet seasons.

With the system operating as shown in Figure 15.5, during the dry season an extra kilowatt-hour requires an increase of thermal capacity of $1/\Sigma_d\Theta_d$ kilowatts and, in addition, extra hydro capacity during the peak period.

With the system operating as shown in Figure 15.6, extra thermal capacity is required only when there is an increase in the peak period of demand, at which time marginal cost of a peak kilowatt-hour is equal to $(F + C^f/\Theta_{d'})$. At all other times, marginal cost equals F.

Uncertainty

The analyses set out above all relate to systems that are adjusted optimally to demand. If, instead, we look at the short run and consider the operation of a given system, then, in the deterministic case, there are only three levels of marginal costs: zero, at times when water is being spilled or sluiced; the rationing price, at times either when all capacity is utilized fully or when only thermal capacity is utilized fully but all the water in store is needed to meet later demand; and F, at all other times.

Although our formulation so far has been deterministic, we have required that generating capacity exceeds maximum demand in order to allow a margin for plant unavailability and for demand in excess of the predicted level. We also mentioned the possibility of making the minimum required amount of storage reflect the need to allow for variations in water availability and (we now add) for energy requirements exceeding the predicted level. Thus if all of these allowances are brought into the picture, the analysis can be interpreted as relating to average expectations.

In principle, such an approach is rather crude. A formally correct approach would minimize costs subject to constraints on the probabilities of capacity shortage and energy shortage; alternatively, it would minimize costs including the penalty cost of supply failure. This is what we do in Chapter 14, although there we are analyzing the maximization of benefits minus costs. But, for several reasons, we shall not attempt to set out such an analysis in relation to cost-minimizing investment in a wholly or partly hydro system. Uncertainty is only one of many complications which have been omitted so far in this chapter. When interpreted in terms of average expectation, the analysis set out above does give an intuitive understanding of cost structure when capacity is adapted optimally to demand. In any case, a short-run analysis is more developed and, in principle, more relevant to optimal pricing.

Leaving aside investment in new capacity, we concentrate on the operation of a given system and discuss the stochastic equivalent of the marginal costs described in the last section. We shall include in costs not only fuel costs but also the "penalty value" of kilowatt-hours not supplied because of capacity shortage or energy shortage. This notion is discussed further in Chapter 14. Here it suffices to say that we take a value of b per kilowatt-hour not supplied as a measure of the social cost of the failure to meet requirements.

The introduction of uncertainty relating both to demand and to plant and water availability requires us to think in terms of a set of possible states of the world defined with respect to these three variables. Such states are denoted s, and the probability of state s in period t is denoted Π_{st}. The size of power cut in kilowatts in state s in period t is e_{st}. Hence, the objective function to be minimized is:

$$\sum_t \sum_s \Pi_{st} F U_{st}^f \Theta_t + \sum_t \sum_s \Pi_{st} b e_{st} \Theta_t, \qquad (15.25)$$

[expected fuel cost] + [expected penalty cost]

and the constraints include water flow constraints for all states of the world for all t:

$$S_{st} + U_{st}^h \Theta_t - w_{st} W - S_{st-1} \leq 0. \qquad (15.26)$$

This formulation involves a complication which prevents us from analyzing expected marginal cost $\sum_s \Pi_{st} M_{st}$ in Kuhn–Tucker terms. The complication arises in the above water flow constraints. Each of them must hold for a given amount of water carried over in storage from the preceding period, S_{t-1}. This, in turn, depends not only upon what state of the world actually occurred in $t - 1$ but also upon the whole preceding sequence of states of the world and generation decisions.

Such complicated temporal interdependence involves a recursive formulation and the introduction of "water value" as a means of linking optimization in successive periods. The point is that what is optimal in period t is affected by S_{t-1} but not by the whole history of how it happened to be just that much. The only link between period t and subsequent periods is how much water is left over at the end of t, S_{st}. If the future usefulness of this water can be reflected in a storage value function $V_t (S_{st})$, then optimization in period t can be formulated as minimizing expected period t costs less the expected value of the water left over for period $t + 1$, as determined by this function. This gives us a single-period optimization, so the t subscript can be dropped (except for the water initially in storage), and the function to be minimized can be written as:

$$\sum_s \Pi_s FU_s^f \Theta + \sum_s \Pi_s be_s \Theta - \sum_s \Pi_s V (S_s). \qquad (15.27)$$

If α_s is the proportion of capacity available in state of the world s, the capacity constraints are:

$$U_s^h - \alpha_s^h X^h \leq 0 \qquad \text{(dual variables } K_s^h), \quad (15.28)$$

$$U_s^f - \alpha_s^f X^f \leq 0 \qquad \text{(dual variables } K_s^f). \quad (15.29)$$

The water flow constraint is:

$$S_s + U_s^h \Theta - w_s \cdot W - S_{st-1} \leq 0 \qquad \text{(dual variables } E_s), \quad (15.30)$$

and the upper and lower storage constraints are:

$$S_s - \hat{S} \leq 0 \qquad \text{(dual variables } H_s), \quad (15.31)$$

$$q - S_s \leq 0 \qquad \text{(dual variables } L_s). \quad (15.32)$$

The demand constraint is:

$$Q_s - U_s^h - U_s^f - e_s = 0 \qquad \text{(dual variables } M_s). \quad (15.33)$$

This is an equality, e_s being the shortfall.

Since the last term in the objective function is the expected value of the water left over for the next period, its derivative, $\Sigma_s \Pi_s \cdot \partial V/\partial S_s$, on the one hand, is the marginal value of water available at the beginning of the next period. On the other hand, $\Sigma_s \Pi_s \cdot E_s$ is the expected marginal value of water available at the beginning of this period. So if we start with a given $V(S_s)$ for this period, by minimizing the objective function for all possible values of water available at the beginning of the period, S_{t-1}, we can calculate the water value function for $t - 1$.

If this recursive procedure is applied to work back toward the present from a date sufficiently remote, the initial assumed water value function can be chosen arbitrarily. Thus, one way of calculating costs for, say, the next twelve months is to start with an arbitrary water value function for December, work back to January and then go back to December and cycle through the year again. After a few iterations, the water value function for each period of the year will cease to vary much and the computation can be stopped.[4]

We can now consider the properties of such a recursively calculated solution by setting out the Kuhn–Tucker conditions.

$$-\Pi_s \frac{\partial V}{\partial S_s} + E_s + H_s - L_s = 0; \tag{15.34}$$

$$\Pi_s F\Theta + K_s^f - M_s \geq 0 \qquad (U_s^f \geq 0); \tag{15.35}$$

$$K_s^h + E_s\Theta - M_s \geq 0 \qquad (U_s^h \geq 0); \tag{15.36}$$

$$\Pi_s b\Theta - M_s \geq 0 \qquad (e^s \geq 0). \tag{15.37}$$

It is apparent that expected marginal cost per kilowatt-hour will be a weighted average of F, E_s, and b : F for s where $0 < U_s^f < \alpha_s^f \cdot X^f$, E_s for s where $0 < U_s^h < \alpha_s^h \cdot X^h$, b for s where $U_s^f = \alpha_s^f \cdot X^f$, and $(U_s^h = \alpha_s^h \cdot X^h$ or $S = q)$. These derive from expressions (15.35), (15.36), and (15.37) and signify that marginal cost is F when the thermal plant is running but can produce more, E_s/Π_s when the hydro plant is running but could produce more, and b when there is a power cut. As shown in (15.36), E_s/Π_s will exceed $\partial V/\partial S_s$ if the reservoir ends up empty and will fall short of it if the reservoir ends up full. In other words, extra water in this period is worth less than extra water next period if there is plenty, and more if it is all used up, as we would expect. When neither is likely and when hydro generation is less than available capacity, we thus have:

$$\frac{M_s}{\Theta} = E_s = \Pi_s \cdot \frac{\partial V}{\partial S_s}, \tag{15.38}$$

4. There is a link here between our model and the stochastic dynamic programming models used by engineers to compute optimum operating schedules. See, for example, Lindqvist, "Operation of a Hydrothermal Electric System."

$$\frac{M_s}{\Pi_s \cdot \Theta} = \frac{\partial V}{\partial S_s},$$
(15.39)

that is, marginal cost in state s equals the marginal value of water in the next period.

The reason why water values are calculated in practice, as in Sweden, for example, is to provide rules for the system operators to follow. The amount of water in the reservoir when read off against the value function gives the marginal value of water. Within the constraints, thermal generation is then scheduled to equate its marginal fuel cost with this marginal value, and the rest of the load is met by hydro generation.

Models including water value calculations are also used for system planning purposes to simulate alternative proposed expansion plans. Both for operating and planning purposes these models are a great deal more complicated than has been suggested above. However, our only purpose here has been to show the *nature* of marginal generation cost.

CHAPTER 16

Tariff Structures with Simple Metering

There is a great deal of confusion in the terminology of tariffs, particularly when translating from one language to another. To keep concepts clear, this chapter will classify tariffs according to the kind of metering used; this classification has the advantage of being related to metering costs.

Confusion that is more than merely terminological has been caused by engineers using imprecise economic concepts in discussions of tariff principles. Many such discussions are just as misleading as would be discussions of purely engineering problems by economists. This chapter, however, is avowedly an economic analysis of an economic problem. The discussion assumes that tariffs will be fixed by a systems analysis which has provided estimates of marginal costs. It also assumes that the irrelevance of accounting cost allocation to decisionmaking is recognized.

Given, it is thus assumed, a complete understanding of the structure of marginal costs, we shall consider some tariffs for each of two metering systems: kilowatt-hours only, and kilowatt-hours and each consumer's own maximum kilowatts. In each case, we suppose that the utility aims to induce consumers to behave as similarly as possible to the way they would behave if they faced and understood a really complicated tariff that reflected the structure of marginal costs in detail. Such a tariff, if practicable, would enable consumers at any time to pay or save the amount for a kilowatt-hour that it would cost society as a whole to provide or avoid that kilowatt-hour, namely: (the marginal cost of supplying 1 kilowatt-hour) · (the probability that one extra kilowatt-hour can be supplied) + (a penalty price for the failure to supply 1 kilowatt-hour) · (the probability that 1 extra kilowatt-hour cannot be supplied). Alternatively, we can say that such a tariff equals the marginal cost of a kilowatt-hour except when a higher price is necessary to keep the risk of failure within acceptable limits, that is, during "potential peak" hours. While the analysis thus concentrates on optimal resource allocation, it is clear that, in practice, income distribution considerations or a need to raise more revenue or both can also affect the choice of tariff. We therefore add a few words about these issues.

Kilowatt-hour Metering Only

Several kinds of kilowatt-hour tariff are found in practice. These tariffs range from simple, single kilowatt-hour rates, to declining block rates, to more complicated forms based on nonelectrical quantities such as house or office size. This section discusses these alternatives in turn.

A simple, single kilowatt-hour tariff

If, for instance, the tariff is to consist simply of a price per kilowatt-hour of P, if we ignore customer costs, and if there are no income distribution or revenue considerations, then P should equal a weighted average of marginal costs. What is not immediately obvious is what weights to use.

Suppose that the year is made up of periods $1, \ldots, n$, that marginal cost per kilowatt-hour in each is given as $m_1, \ldots, m_n$, and that the kilowatt-hour consumption in each period of a group of consumers is $Q_1, \ldots, Q_n$. A change in P to $P - \Delta P$ would raise consumption. The value to the group of consumers of this change would be:

$$\frac{P + (P - \Delta P)}{2} \cdot (\Delta Q_1 + \cdots + \Delta Q_n),$$

while the change in costs would be:

$$\Delta Q_1 \cdot m_1 + \cdots + \Delta Q_n \cdot m_n.$$

P will be optimal when a small change in it does not alter benefits more than costs. So we equate the above two expressions for ΔP infinitely small:

$$P \cdot \left(\frac{\partial Q_1}{\partial P} + \cdots + \frac{\partial Q_n}{\partial P} \right) = m_1 \cdot \frac{\partial Q_1}{\partial P} + \cdots + m_n \cdot \frac{\partial Q_n}{\partial P}.$$

The weights applied to $m_1, \ldots, m_n$ to get optimal P are thus the effects on kilowatt-hour consumption in the various periods of a change in P. Note that those are not the same as the partial derivatives that would show how consumption in each period would change if price were altered in that period alone. The effect on, say, summer daytime consumption of a decrease in a single uniform kilowatt-hour price is what matters here, not that of a decrease confined to summer daytime kilowatt-hours, and these are unlikely to coincide.

One reason why the $\partial Q / \partial P$ may vary between periods is that the lengths of the periods differ. If period 7 is winter weekday evenings and period 8 is winter Sunday evenings, $\partial Q_7 / \partial P$ will probably exceed $\partial Q_8 / \partial P$, simply because Q_7 exceeds Q_8. But leaving this aside for a minute, the question is whether consumption would respond to a price reduction more at some times than at others. One can imagine circumstances when this question could be answered, for example: a group of very small domestic consumers with lighting and radios who could expand their use of electricity for other purposes with a different time pattern; or an extremely electricity-intensive process where a night shift is not worked. But even for a relatively homogeneous group of consumers, it usually is difficult to produce convincing answers of this sort. So it seems sensible, in practice, to weight the marginal costs $m_1, \ldots, m_n$ in the different periods by their respective consumptions:

$$P = \frac{m_1 \cdot Q_1 + \cdots + m_n \cdot Q_n}{Q_1 + \cdots + Q_n}.$$

This amounts to saying that if seven times as many kilowatt-hours are consumed at breakfast time as in the small hours, a reduction in P will stimulate breakfast-time consumption seven times as much as small-hour consumption. Thus price coincides with the optimum only if the elasticity of demand is the same for all time periods. Not only does such coincidence require an unverifiable condition but even the $Q_1, \ldots, Q_n$ may be unknown for the group of consumers in question. Load curve measurements at substations supplying such consumers may help. Otherwise, the analysis may resort to the even simpler device of weighting $m_1, \ldots, m_n$ by the lengths of the periods $1, \ldots, n$. If breakfast time and the small hours last for two and four hours, respectively, this coincides with the optimum only if $\partial Q / \partial P$ at breakfast time is half of what it is in the small hours.

The conclusion from all of this is that to establish a single, simple, correct kilowatt-hour tariff demands either a great deal of research, for example by experimental tariffs, or a great deal of inspired guessing.

A simple, block kilowatt-hour tariff

If the tariff is to consist of a price of P_a a kilowatt-hour up to X_a kilowatt-hours a month (or a quarter, or a year), followed by P_b a kilowatt-hour for kilowatt-hours above X_a up to X_b a billing period, and so on, then, with the same other assumptions as before, the ideal P_a will be the average of $m_1, \ldots, m_n$ weighted by the $\partial Q/\partial P$ of consumers whose consumption is less than X_a, the ideal P_b will be the average weighted by the $\partial Q/\partial P$ of those, for example, with $X_a <$ consumption $< X_b$.

As before, even to guess the $\partial Q/\partial P$ may be impossible. Yet a simple, block kilowatt-hour tariff with $P_a, P_b, \ldots$, and so on, is only superior on resource allocation grounds to a simple, single kilowatt-hour tariff with one P if there is some reason to believe that the ideal:

$$\frac{m_1 \cdot \dfrac{\partial Q_1}{\partial P} + \cdots + m_n \cdot \dfrac{\partial Q_n}{\partial P}}{\dfrac{\partial Q_1}{\partial P} + \cdots + \dfrac{\partial Q_n}{\partial P}},$$

is systematically different between blocks. In other words, to have $P_b < P_a$, instead of just one P, requires that a consumption increase that is caused by a price reduction and that occurs among consumers taking more than X_a will be relatively less concentrated on high-cost periods than that occurring among consumers taking less than X_a. Thus it is as difficult to show that $P_a, P_b, \ldots$, and so on, is better than just P as to show what ought to be the relative magnitudes of $P_a, P_b, \ldots$, and so on, if the block tariff were adopted.

It is tempting, once again, to use the $Q_1, \ldots, Q_n$ as weights by way of proxy for the $\partial P/\partial Q$. But now this device is more difficult to justify than the use of a single kilowatt-hour price, for two reasons. First, more load research is required to determine the time pattern of consumption for different groups. Second, differences in $Q_1, \ldots, Q_n$ between such groups may well be unrelated to differences in their $\partial Q_1/\partial P, \ldots, \partial Q_n/\partial P$.

This second point can be illuminated by supposing, for the moment, that the only reason why some consumers use more electricity than others is that they are richer and so own more electrical appliances. These extra appliances may well involve the richer, larger consumers in a time pattern of consumption different from that of the poorer consumers. Thus, Q_7 may be both absolutely and relatively larger for the large consumers. But this does not necessarily mean that $\partial Q_7/\partial P$ also will be larger for the rich. To say that Q_7 goes up a great deal when a man becomes richer does not tell us whether his $\partial Q_7/\partial P$ has gone up relatively.

An example

Any example that is simple enough to be obvious probably will be too simple to be realistic. Nonetheless, to illustrate the above discussion, suppose that: most small consumers use electricity only for lighting, most larger consumers also use it for cooking, and that marginal cost for lighting is 2 cents and for cooking is 1 cent.

To set a single P it is necessary to know how much a cut in price would stimulate lighting and how much it would stimulate cooking. If we do not know the answer but are prepared to guess that the demand *elasticities* are equal, then estimates of total lighting kilowatt-hours and total cooking kilowatt-hours can stand as proxies. If we think that cooking demand is more elastic, we take a figure a little nearer to 1 cent.

Thus, let the subscripts l and c stand for the lighting period and the cooking period, respectively. We then have:

$$\frac{2 \cdot \dfrac{\partial Q_l}{\partial P} + 1 \cdot \dfrac{\partial Q_c}{\partial P}}{\dfrac{\partial Q_l}{\partial P} + \dfrac{\partial Q_c}{\partial P}} = \frac{2 \cdot Q_l + 1 \cdot Q_c}{Q_l + Q_c},$$

if:

$$\frac{\dfrac{\partial Q_l}{\partial P}}{Q_l} = \frac{\dfrac{\partial Q}{\partial P}}{Q_c}.$$

If both of these are divided by P, we get the two elasticities. So, conversely, if it is believed that these elasticities are not equal, but the amount that they differ is unknown, a direct guess at $\partial Q_l/\partial P$ may be more useful than measurement of Q_l and Q_c.

If the problem is to set a first-block price P_a and a second-block price P_b in a simple two-block kilowatt-hour tariff, we now need to find a dividing line between the blocks: below it, increases in consumption caused by price reduction are mainly in lighting, so P_a should be nearly 2 cents; above it, increases in consumption caused by price reduction include cooking to a significant extent, so P_b should be nearer to 1 cent than to 2 cents. Such a division may not be possible, however. The relative magnitude of $\partial Q_l/\partial P$ and $\partial Q_c/\partial P$ simply may not vary systematically with total consumption, so that a two-block tariff may be quite inappropriate. This may be so, even if the difference between larger and smaller consumers is that the larger ones have a wider range of uses. A higher income effect on some kinds of appliance use and ownership than on other kinds does not necessarily signify anything about response to changes in the unit price of a kilowatt-hour.

Customer costs

If we bring in customer costs (that is, costs independent of the amount and timing of consumption such as billing) of F per customer per billing period, there are two possibilities: adding a fixed charge of F per billing period—that is a month, quarter, or year—or charging a first-block price for X_a of P_a such that $(P_a - P_b) \cdot X_a = F$. If X_a can be chosen so that practically all consumers use more than X_a, these are equivalent. If not, the first will reflect costs better.

More complicated kilowatt-hour tariffs

Still assuming that only ordinary kilowatt-hour meters are employed, we next bring in the complication that a consumer's bill can be made a function of some nonelectrical magnitude as well. For domestic consumers, the most important possibilities are the size or value of dwellings. Another possibility is the ownership or rating of certain electrical appliances, for example, the possession of a cooker or the rating of electric motors. Such facts are difficult to ascertain and to check, but, having noted this very important point, let us continue to concentrate on the cost-reflection aspect.

Suppose that one of these nonmetered magnitudes, which we call M, is highly correlated with consumption during the period of potential peak. This is a strong assumption, and verifying it may require a lot of load research. However, we take the case where this assumption is definitely known to be true. In this case, it is clear that the differences in the billing of different consumers can be made to reflect the differences in the total costs of supplying them in either of two ways (or some combination of them): (a) a fixed charge per billing period that equals F plus some function of M, together with a single kilowatt-hour charge, P, the latter reflecting a weighted average of marginal costs in periods outside the potential peak; or (b) two or more block kilowatt-hour prices, P_a, P_b—where the size of each block for any consumer is a function of his M. Such a tariff will reflect costs in the sense that the total bill of any consumer will equal approximately the saving in costs that would result from ceasing to supply him.

But the decision about whether or not to consume may be much less important—except for the smallest consumers—than the decision about how much to consume. Under these tariffs, the marginal cost of a kilowatt-hour to a consumer will be, respectively: (a) the single kilowatt-hour charge P, or (b) the kilowatt-hour price of the block he is on, say P_b. Yet P or P_b, respectively, will be less than the cost of providing an increment in consumption. M is fixed for each consumer taken separately, even though differences in M between consumers do roughly reflect cost differences. Thus, even if an M can be found, measured, and incorporated in a tariff so that tariff differences among consumers reflect cost differences among consumers, the tariff will make the marginal tariff cost to each consumer too low for that part of his consumption that is related to M. The apparent gain in the ability of a tariff to reflect costs is an illusion—unless the M of each consumer varies with his own consumption. In the case of electrical appliance ownership, this condition may be fulfilled partially, but where M is related to dwelling size or value it is not.

Distributional considerations

For a variety of reasons that do not need to be spelled out, it may be desired to charge certain consumers more than costs (in order to raise revenue) or less than costs (perhaps because the consumers are poor). In the second case, that of making electricity cheap, we need to distinguish two motives: (a) encouraging consumption, and (b) keeping down the size of the consumer's bill.

The first of these is a matter of resource allocation, while the second is a matter of income distribution. In practice, any reduction in a tariff from the level at which it reflects costs will have both effects, but different ways of reducing the tariff will affect different groups. Thus, a reduction in a fixed charge per billing period will encourage consumption only in the case of potential consumers, hitherto unconnected; a reduction in a kilowatt-hour charge will encourage consumption by existing consumers, too.

Consider, for example, the effect in Figure 16.1 of changing from the dashed tariff line to the dotted tariff line (a two-block tariff). Consumers taking more than OR will pay more than before, consumers taking less than OR will pay less. Consumers taking more than OS face the same marginal cost as before (the new P_b equals the old P); consumers taking less than OS face higher marginal cost (the new P_a exceeds the old P). Consumption by the former group will not be discouraged directly, whereas consumption by the latter group will be. But now potential small consumers will be encouraged to become consumers.

It is thus clear that redistribution and resource allocation are

FIGURE 16.1. ELECTRICITY BILLS ON TWO-PART
AND TWO-BLOCK TARIFFS

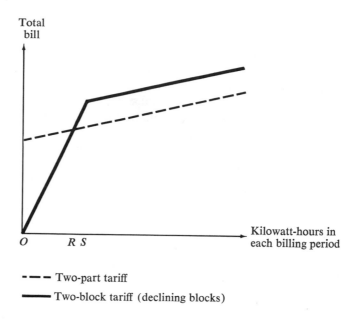

—‑— Two-part tariff

——— Two-block tariff (declining blocks)

intertwined. No general discussion of all conceivable cases is possible, so consider two, one that is theoretical and one that is important in practice.

The theoretical case is provided by Martin Feldstein,[1] who supposes that if resource allocation alone mattered, the optimal tariff would be a fixed charge of F and a kilowatt-hour price of P. He then supposes that people with higher incomes are less deserving than, and consume more electricity than, people with lower incomes. Assuming that the income distribution is given, that the rich deserve relatively less than the poor, and that the income and price elasticities of demand for electricity are known and quantified (which they hardly ever are), Feldstein then derives an optimal fixed charge of less than F and an optimal kilowatt-hour charge of more than P. His qualitative conclusions are that the kilowatt-hour price should exceed P by more: (a) the greater is the inequality of income, (b) the

1. M. Feldstein, "Equity and Efficiency in Public Sector Pricing: The Optimal Two-Part Tariff," *Quarterly Journal of Economics* 86 (May 1972).

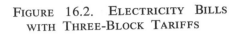

FIGURE 16.2. ELECTRICITY BILLS
WITH THREE-BLOCK TARIFFS

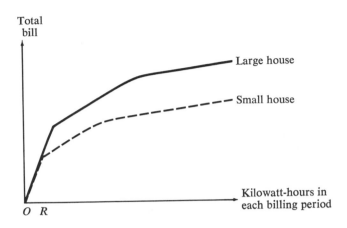

higher is the income-elasticity of demand, (c) the lower is the price-elasticity (which is assumed to be the same at all levels), and (d) the less deserving are the rich relative to the poor. This theory, however, is not easy to apply in practice, if only because the relevant elasticities are difficult to estimate.

The practical case is a block tariff where the size of each block increases with the tax value of the consumer's dwelling. As mentioned above, this could conceivably reflect cost differences, albeit in an irrelevant way. Here, however, we examine examples where the aim is simply the distributional one of making those occupying expensive dwellings pay more for their electricity than those occupying cheap ones. This aim, of course, really relates to income or wealth, but tax values are used because they are more easily obtained.

Consider the two three-block tariffs in Figure 16.2. For any combination in excess of OR, the owner of a big house pays more than the owner of a small one. This is the intended consequence. But there is the further consequence that differences in the marginal tariff costs of electricity between owners of big houses and owners of small houses may not be related to anything at all. One wonders whether the complication is worthwhile, particularly if a large number of tax-value brackets is used. Under these circumstances, tariff adjustments over a series of years can reflect a series of political compromises, allowing the degrees of cost reflection in the tariff to decline progressively.

Kilowatt and Kilowatt-hour Metering

This section begins with a simple case and then introduces complications regarding demand diversity, the utilization factor, and uncertainty about the timing of peak hours.

The simplest case

The simplest case imaginable is one in which a single price of K a kilowatt of maximum demand and a single price of P a kilowatt-hour are to be charged and in which there is no diversity or uncertainty so that all consumers record their individual maximum demands simultaneously at a time known in advance. Under these highly improbable circumstances, it might seem obvious that: (a) K should equal marginal capacity costs, C; and (b) P should equal an average of marginal running costs $m_1, \ldots, m_n$, weighted by the respective $\partial Q/\partial P$.

Obvious or not, it is wrong in principle. A change in K may effect off-peak consumption as well as peak demand. For example, such a change may cause a shift away from the peak, or it may induce a fall in the installed capacity of some electrical appliances and processes. Thus, the value to consumers of the rise in consumption resulting from a fall in K will involve the two terms:

$$\left(P + \frac{K + (K - \Delta K)}{2}\right) \cdot \Delta Q_1 + P \cdot (\Delta Q_2 + \cdots + \Delta Q_n)$$

where 1 is the one-hour peak period. With $m_1, \ldots, m_n$ now representing running costs, the changes in costs will be:

$$(m_1 + C) \cdot \Delta Q_1 + m_2 \cdot \Delta Q_2 + \ldots + m_n \cdot \Delta Q_n.$$

K will be optimal when a small change in it does not alter benefits more than costs. So we equate the above two expressions for K infinitely small:

$$(P + K) \cdot \frac{\partial Q_1}{\partial K} + P \cdot \frac{\partial Q_2}{\partial K} + \cdots + P \cdot \frac{\partial Q_n}{\partial K}$$

$$= (m_1 + C) \cdot \frac{\partial Q_1}{\partial K} + m_2 \cdot \frac{\partial Q_2}{\partial K} + \cdots + m_n \cdot \frac{\partial Q_n}{\partial K},$$

which gives:

$$K = C + \frac{(m_1 - P) \cdot \frac{\partial Q_1}{\partial K} + \cdots + (m_n - P) \cdot \frac{\partial Q_n}{\partial K}}{\frac{\partial Q_1}{\partial K}}.$$

If all the m are the same, then P should equal m and K should equal C. The problem arises in the realistic case when all the m are not equal. If P is determined as before as an average of $m_1, \ldots, m_n$ weighted by the $\partial Q/\partial P$, then K will equal C only if each $\partial Q/\partial K$ equals the corresponding $\partial Q/\partial P$. But this is not likely. First, $\partial Q_f/\partial K$ is the effect on consumption in period f of a rise in the price a kilowatt of maximum demand, that is, the price charged in the peak period. Second, $\partial Q_f/\partial P$ is the effect of a rise in the price a kilowatt-hour charged in all periods. Hence it is not optimal to determine P as before and to set K equal to C.

Since a change in K will affect the level and time pattern of those uses of electricity that enter into consumption during the peak period, this change will consequently affect some off-peak consumption, too. To the extent that P differs from the marginal costs of this off-peak consumption, some allowance for this should ideally be made in setting K. Intuitively, this is the right principle to follow.

In practice, the chances of plausibly guessing the $\partial Q/\partial K$ are even lower than those of estimating the $\partial Q/\partial P$, so that setting K in relation to peak-period marginal cost C and weighting the other marginal costs by the time pattern of consumption $Q_2, \ldots, Q_n$ is the best that can be done. The above bit of theory has been included to show that this apparently correct procedure is not really correct. Hence, minor departures from it cannot be criticized on a priori grounds.

Coincidence or diversity

We now bring in the important fact that individual maximum demands do not coincide, so that for a group of consumers:

$$\frac{\text{Group maximum kilowatts}}{\text{Sum of individual maximum kilowatts}}$$
$$= \text{Coincidence factor} = \frac{1}{\text{Diversity factor}}.$$

If the coincidence factor is, say, 0.8, this apparently suggests that a kilowatt charge of $0.8C$ will be appropriate where C is the marginal cost with respect to group maximum kilowatts. Once again, however, we discover that this simple solution is what is possible and

347

convenient but not what is correct in purest principle. Following reasoning similar to that used earlier, the optimal condition is a matter of the ratio between the effect of a change in K on group maximum kilowatts and its effect on the sum of the individual maximum demands. Thus suppose that this ratio is unity, all m are equal, and $P = m$ (so avoiding the complication discussed above under "The simplest case"). Then we should want to set $K = C$. If, however, this ratio between the two effects were 0.7, we should want to see $K = 0.7C$. The point is that what matters is the reaction of consumers to a *change* in K, not their behavior at a given *level* of K. Yet it is only the latter that can be measured.

Hours of utilization or load factor

For any period—here we take a year—we can define the load factor (or utilization factor), for individual consumers or for a group:

$$\text{Load factor} = \frac{\text{Average kilowatts over the year}}{\text{Maximum kilowatts during the year}}$$

$$= \frac{\text{kilowatt-hours during the year}}{8{,}760 \cdot \text{maximum kilowatts during the year}}$$

$$\begin{matrix}\text{Utilization} \\ \text{factor}\end{matrix} = \frac{\text{kilowatt-hours during the year}}{\text{Maximum kilowatts during the year}}$$

The load factor is usually expressed as a percentage, while the utilization factor is measured in hours a year.

Statistical studies show that some relations exist for particular types of consumer between coincidence or diversity, on the one hand, and the hours of utilization or load factor, on the other. These can be expressed in many ways but all involve relations among: kilowatts at time of group maximum kilowatts, individual maximum kilowatts, and kilowatt-hours. Taking a year as the period, the one absolutely certain relation is that when annual kilowatt-hours = $8{,}760 \cdot$ maximum kilowatts during the year, it is necessarily true that individual maximum kilowatts = kilowatts at the time of group maximum, that is, when load factor = 100 percent, coincidence factor = 1. At the other extreme, when annual kilowatt-hours are very small in relation to individual maximum kilowatts, the chances are considerable that kilowatts at the time of group maximum will be low in relation to the latter. This would not be the case if lighting were the only load, for individual maximum kilowatts would then coincide fairly well, but seems plausible when the use of electricity is diversified.

Rough statistical studies have been made showing that if con-

FIGURE 16.3. EMPIRICAL RELATION
BETWEEN COINCIDENCE FACTOR
AND HOURS OF USE/LOAD FACTOR

FIGURE 16.3. EMPIRICAL RELATION
BETWEEN COINCIDENCE FACTOR
AND HOURS OF USE/LOAD FACTOR

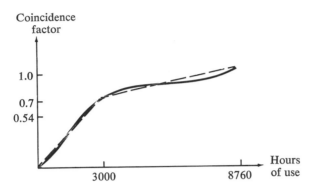

sumers are divided into groups according to hours of utilization, or load factor, and if one point is plotted for each group, the points fall on a line shaped somewhat as in Figure 16.3. The statistical procedures are rarely made explicit and are probably dubious. However, let us accept that the curve does mean something, and that it can be approximated by two linear sections, as the dashed lines show, with a point of inflection at 3,000 hours of utilization and a coincidence factor of 0.7. The details naturally vary between studies and these figures have been chosen purely for illustrative purposes.

The point of this relation is that, if it holds, contribution to peak can be inferred from measured individual maximum kilowatts and annual kilowatt-hours, that is, with only simple metering of kilowatts and kilowatt-hours. Hence, the temptation is to construct a tariff that, though it only involves this simple metering, embodies the relation so that the bill paid by the individual consumer in some way reflects his contribution to the peak.

Let us take the simplest possible case, where C is marginal cost a kilowatt of system peak and m is marginal cost a kilowatt-hour at all hours of the year. If a consumer takes $3,000J$ kilowatt-hours a year and has an individual maximum kilowatt demand of J, the cost of supplying him is:

$$J \cdot (3,000m + 0.7C),$$

that is, a cost per kilowatt-hour of:

$$\frac{0.7C + 3,000m}{3,000} = \frac{0.7C}{3,000} + m.$$

349

This same cost applies to all consumers who take up to 3,000 kilowatt-hours a kilowatt of their individual maximum kilowatts.

Now consider consumers taking between 3,000 and 8,760 kilowatt-hours a kilowatt of individual maximum demand. Each extra kilowatt-hour costs m and is associated with an increase of:

$$\frac{0.3C}{8,760 - 3,000}$$

in cost a kilowatt of their individual maximum kilowatts.

It follows from all this that a kilowatt-related block kilowatt-hour tariff will make the bill of any consumer to whom Figure 16.3 relates equal to the total cost of his supply, given the simple structure that we have assumed if: the first block up to 3,000 kilowatt-hours a kilowatt of individual maximum is priced at $(0.7C/3,000) + m$, and the second block is priced at $(0.3C/5.760) + m$. If H = kilowatt-hours taken and D = an individual's maximum demand, the total bill of a consumer will thus be:

$$\left[m + \frac{0.7C}{3,000} \right] \cdot H, \qquad\qquad \text{for } H < 3,000D$$

and:

$$\left. \begin{array}{l} \left[\left(m + \dfrac{0.7C}{3,000} \right) \cdot 3,000D \right. \\[2ex] \left. + \left(m + \dfrac{0.3C}{5.760} \right) \cdot (H - 3,000D) \right] \\[2ex] = \left[H \cdot \left(m + \dfrac{0.3C}{5,760} \right) + D \cdot (0.544C) \right]. \end{array} \right\} \quad \text{for } H \geq 3,000D$$

Comparison shows that the differences in marginal costs to the consumers of a kilowatt-hour, that is, in the derivatives of the bill with respect to H, is:

$$\frac{0.7C}{3,000} - \frac{0.3C}{5,760} = 0.00018C.$$

It is only this much higher for consumers with $H < 3,000D$ than for consumers with $H \geq 3,000D$, a negligible difference. But the marginal cost to the consumer of his individual maximum demand is: zero for the first group, and $0.544C$ for the second, which is very far from reflecting the cost structure!

The marginal cost of a kilowatt is zero when $H < 3,000D$ because there is no kilowatt charge. It is positive when $H \geq 3,000D$ because a 1-kilowatt increase in D means that 3,000 more kilowatt-hours will be charged at the first-block rate and 3,000 less at the second-block rate.

The conclusion is that though this tariff reflects cost differences between groups of consumers on the assumption that the relation in the diagram holds, it fails to convey a proper message to the individual consumer about the cost consequences of changes in his individual behavior.

Other attempts to embody in a tariff the cost relation among consumers that emerges from Figure 16.3 can have equally curious results. Thus, consider the idea that, for consumers with $H > 3,000D$, total cost and, hence, the bill can be represented as:

$$0.54C \cdot D + \left(m + \frac{0.3C}{5,760} \right) \cdot H,$$

0.54 being the intercept of the upper dashed line with the vertical axis in Figure 16.3. Since the kilowatt charge of $0.54C$ is too high for consumers with $H < 3,000D$, it may be deemed necessary to reduce their kilowatt charge proportionately to the amount by which their H/D falls short of 3,000. Such a tariff was actually proposed on one occasion. In terms of the numerical example, it would involve a reduction of:

$$\frac{0.7}{3,000} \cdot \left(\frac{H}{D} - 3,000 \right),$$

in the kilowatt charge so that it becomes:

$$0.54C \cdot \left[1 - \frac{0.7}{3,000} \left(\frac{H}{D} - 3,000 \right) \right].$$

This would give a consumer with $H < 3,000D$ a total bill of:

$$0.54C \cdot \frac{2,499.3}{3,000} (H - 3,000D) + \left(m + \frac{0.3C}{5,760} \right) \cdot H,$$

making the marginal cost to the consumer fantastically high for H (since an increase in H would raise his kilowatt charge) and negative for D (since an increase in D would lower the kilowatt charge)!

We have thus shown with the aid of two simple examples that, even if a reliable statistical relation can be shown to exist between coincidence or diversity and hours of utilization or the load factor, their use to construct tariffs can produce silly results. The aim of a tariff is as much to tell consumers the cost to them of a change in their H and D as to describe cost differences between consumers. The latter, alone, would be all that mattered if consumers who changed their kilowatts at the time of group maximum kilowatts, individual maximum kilowatts, and kilowatt-hours, always changed all three in such a way as to remain "on" the curve.

Potential peak versus actual peak

The last section argued as though the ideal kilowatt charge should be related to a consumer's kilowatts at the time of the system peak and considered, with rather negative results, how to allow for diversity. Thus, it examined a problem often discussed in electricity supply and showed a major defect in the way that problem is usually approached. We now turn to an additional and intellectually distinct defect in the traditional approach, namely, a failure to take a forward-looking approach to tariffmaking. The aim in connection with the peak, as we said at the beginning, is to reduce to an acceptable level the chances that demand may exceed capacity. This is forward looking in the sense that it is a matter of influencing the behavior of customers, not of measuring retrospectively the contribution of customers to the last actual peak.

Once we start to think about future peaks rather than past ones, we have to allow explicitly for uncertainty. Instead of talking about the hour in the past when a system peak occurred, we have to consider all the hours in the future when one *could* occur. Indeed, in many cases even this is not enough. We are concerned with the hours when the probability of failure to meet demand is nonnegligible—that is, in thermal systems, all hours when demand may be high relative to available capacity, or in predominantly hydro systems, all hours during the critical period when more water in the reservoirs would reduce the risk of failure. We call these the "potential peak" hours. They can range in number from 200 to 2,000, according to the type of system and the characteristics of the system load.

An ideal tariff would charge a price per kilowatt-hour that exceeded marginal operating cost in potential peak hours by an amount that would be higher in any such hour (a) the greater the probability of failure in that hour, and (b) the higher the notional penalty price attached to failure to supply a kilowatt-hour at that time. Consequently, the way to judge among alternative simple tariffs (on grounds of resource allocation) is according to how well their incentives to consumers approximate those that an ideal tariff would provide. The criterion is *not* how well the simple tariff is related to actual contribution to an actual peak; it is how much greater an incentive it gives to consumers to economize in electricity usage during potential peak hours than during other hours.

As far as simple single or block kilowatt-hour tariffs are concerned, all the argument earlier in this chapter still holds. The $m_1, \ldots, m_n$ simply equal: (Marginal cost of 1 extra kilowatt-hour supplied) $\cdot$ (probability of supply) + (penalty price of 1 extra kilowatt-hour not supplied) $\cdot$ (1 − probability of supply), and the weights should ideally be the $\partial Q_l/\partial P, \ldots, \partial Q_n/\partial P$, not the $Q_l, \ldots, Q_n$.

With a kilowatt meter in addition to a kilowatt-hour meter, local distribution costs that are partly related to kilowatts can be reflected better in the tariff. But leaving these and customer costs aside, as in most of this chapter, the problem is whether reducing P or P_a, $P_b \ldots$ (the block prices) and introducing a kilowatt charge, or relating P or P_a, $P_b \ldots$ to kilowatts, or some mixture thereof, provides a better set of incentives.

No amount of cross-section statistics will resolve this problem. How consumers would respond to a change in tariff has nothing to do with how they do differ when they all have the same tariff.

Conclusions

One theme that, hitherto, has not been sufficiently appreciated emerges clearly from our discussion. This theme is that consumer reactions are more relevant to choosing a simple tariff of the kind discussed here than to choosing more complicated ones with time-of-day and seasonal elements. What we have called the "ideal" tariff—that is, one as complicated as the cost structure—could, if it were costless to operate, be recommended for a particular consumer without any analysis of his reactions whatsoever! We need to know about consumer reactions only when we are considering, for example, charging the same price for Q with different m, or charging individual maximum kilowatts at one price for consumers who record them at different times. Thus, take the simplest case when a single price has to lie somewhere between two marginal costs, m_1 and m_2. Push the price toward m_1 and resource allocation is improved in period 1 and worsened in period 2. If the first reaction is strong and the second small, the increase may be desirable.

The second general point to emerge is that designing tariffs to reflect cost differences between consumers is a very poor way of getting those tariffs to reflect cost changes resulting from changes in a consumer's behavior.

This need to know more about consumer reactions and to take less notice of cost differences between consumers in designing tariffs mean that many actual tariffs of the types considered in this chapter cannot be defended easily on resource allocation grounds. In a state of ignorance it is probably best to go for simplicity and uniformity. When only kilowatt-hour metering is justified, seasonal variations in a single kilowatt-hour price are more worth thinking about than are block structures. When more complex metering is justified in systems where the number of potential peak hours is large, the use of a time-of-day tariff with two kilowatt-hour rates is worth considering instead of a charge for kilowatts with one kilowatt-hour rate. But cost characteristics, consumer acceptance of change, consumer behavior, and metering possibilities vary so much from system to system that such positive recommendations are difficult to make in general terms. That explains why this chapter has had more to say about how *not* to design simple tariffs. The aim has been constructive, nevertheless.

CHAPTER 17

A Note on Optimal Pricing and Indivisibilities

If we ignore complications relating to income distribution, externalities, and pricing distortions elsewhere, and if we ignore stochastic variations in demand and in the availability of production capacity, the rules for optimal resource allocation are simple. There is the pricing rule that price should equal whichever is the higher of marginal operating costs or the price necessary to restrict demand to capacity. There is also the investment rule that the present worth of the dual (shadow) value of capacity should be equated with its marginal capacity cost.

If these rules are applied to a one-product enterprise where demand is growing through time and where capacity can only be increased in large lumps, each sufficient to cover several years' growth in output, the development through time will show a pattern of the sort displayed in Figure 17.1.

Even if we ignore the difficulty of knowing enough about the price elasticity of demand to set prices in this way, it is apparent that, for one reason or another, such fluctuations may be unacceptable. We are led, therefore, to redefine the problem and ask what is the optimal rule for setting price if it is constrained from fluctuating in this way. The problem now is to find the pricing rule that will maximize the present worth of willingness-to-pay for the product less the present worth of all costs, subject to the constraint that a uniform price must be charged during a considerable period of time.

More specifically, suppose that a uniform price, p, has to be chosen to rule from now, $t = 1$, to some time in the future, $t = F$, well after the next lump of capacity becomes necessary. This new capacity will have to be brought into operation (that is, commissioned) sooner, the lower is p, since a low price will stimulate demand.

If Q_t is the volume of consumption in period t, the present worth

FIGURE 17.1. CHANGES IN OPTIMUM
PRICES OVER TIME WHEN INVEST-
MENTS ARE DISCONTINUOUS

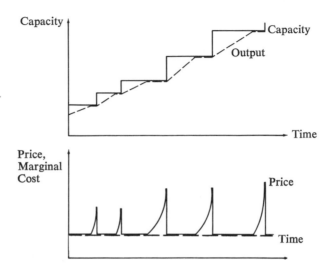

of the value in the changes in consumption brought about by a small
change in p will be:

$$\sum_{t=1}^{t=F} p \cdot \frac{\partial Q_t}{\partial p} \cdot \frac{1}{(1 + r)^t} \cdot \delta p, \tag{17.1}$$

where r is the relevant rate of interest for discounting future benefits
and costs.

We simplify the analysis of costs by ignoring operating costs and
concentrating on the capital costs of new capacity. For a higher level
of demand brought about by a lower price, the extra cost will consist
either of having built the last addition to capacity larger *or* of building the next one sooner. The first of these would be relevant, however, only if price were being fixed further back in time under conditions of perfect foresight. Hence, in practice, the relevant cost of
providing for a higher or lower level of demand consists of bringing
forward or postponing the next addition to capacity. If this is
planned for commissioning in $t = T$, then the effect upon the present
worth of its cost will be approximately:

$$\frac{\partial Q_T}{\partial p} \cdot \frac{\partial T}{\partial Q_T} \cdot \frac{rC}{(1 + r)^T} \cdot \delta p. \tag{17.2}$$

356

The product of the first two terms gives the rate of change of commissioning date T with respect to p. The third term gives the rate of change of the present worth of capital cost C with respect to the commissioning date.

The optimal commissioning date and price are determined jointly by setting $(17.1) = (17.2)$, since, if the marginal gain and cost from altering them were unequal, p and T should be changed:

$$\sum_{t=1}^{t=F} p \cdot \frac{\partial Q_t}{\partial p} \cdot \frac{1}{(1+r)^t} = \frac{\partial Q_T}{\partial p} \cdot \frac{\partial T}{\partial Q_T} \cdot \frac{rC}{(1+r)^T}. \tag{17.3}$$

This gives:

$$p = \frac{rC}{\dfrac{\partial Q_T}{\partial T}} \cdot \frac{\dfrac{\partial Q_T}{\partial p} \cdot \dfrac{1}{(1+r)^T}}{\displaystyle\sum_{t=1}^{t=F} \dfrac{\partial Q_t}{\partial p} \cdot \dfrac{1}{(1+r)^t}}. \tag{17.4}$$

The first term on the right-hand side is marginal cost at T. Postponing or bringing forward commissioning saves or costs interest per unit time period by an amount equal to r times C. Dividing by the time-rate of growth of consumption gives marginal cost per unit of consumption. (Note that marginal costs do not necessarily decline as the rate of growth of consumption increases, since the increments of investment, and thus the values of C, also rise with the rate of growth of demand.)

We can now regard p as a weighted average of marginal cost over the whole interval from $t = 1$ to $t = F$. The weights are the discounted slopes of the demand curves and marginal cost is zero at all times except T. This result is thus an example of the proposition that when a tariff has to be simpler than the cost structure that it is to reflect, it should be a weighted average of the relevant marginal costs. The appropriate weights are proportional to the effects of a divergence between price and marginal cost upon the objective function.

If it is supposed, as it has to be in the absence of information, that all the $\partial Q_t/\partial p$ are the same, then (17.4) can be written:

$$\sum_{t=1}^{t=F} p \cdot \frac{1}{(1+r)^t} = \frac{1}{(1+r)^T} \cdot \frac{rC}{\dfrac{\partial Q_T}{\partial T}}. \tag{17.5}$$

This means that optimal price is such as to make the present worth of the revenue from a unit increase in consumption from $t = 1$ to

$t = F$ equal the present worth of the marginal cost of catering for it. Constrained optimal pricing with indivisibilities thus turns out to be pricing at a weighted average of marginal costs.

For many practical purposes, it is possible to simplify (17.5) and use average incremental costs as a basis for pricing policy. Let T now denote the average period between investments. Price revisions might usefully be considered every T years so as to reflect changes in the costs of expansion. Then, if we denote the average incremental cost of the next investment by K, and let ΔQ_T be the increment of demand which it is to meet and L be the economic lifetime of the investment:

$$C = \frac{K \cdot \Delta Q_T}{[1 - (1 + r)^{-L}]},$$

where the denominator reflects depreciation (which we have neglected so far). Hence:

$$rC = A \cdot K \cdot \Delta Q_T,$$

where A is the annuity rate. Substituting this into (17.5) and rearranging gives:

$$p = \frac{A \cdot K \cdot \Delta Q_T}{\dfrac{\partial Q_T}{\partial T}} \cdot \frac{r}{(1 + r)^T - 1}. \tag{17.6}$$

In many instances, $\partial Q_T / \partial T \approx \Delta Q_T / T$ and $(1 + r)^T$ is close enough to $(1 + rT)$ so that (17.6) becomes:

$$p \approx A \cdot K, \tag{17.7}$$

that is, the annuitized value of average incremental cost.

While (17.7) is rough and ready, it should be remembered that many factors bear on pricing policy besides indivisibilities. Very often, the average incremental cost formula will be more than good enough; however, where indivisibilities are exceptionally important, the more precise formulae of (17.5) or (17.6) might be used.

Index